Integrating Business Management Processes

Integrating Business Management Processes

Processes

Volume 3: Harmonising Quality, Food Safety and Environmental Processes

Dr. Titus De Silva, PhD

Consultant, Pharmacy Practice, Quality Management, Food Safety

BSc (Chemistry), BSc (Pharmacy) Hons. Post-graduate Dipl (Computer Sci), MBA, PhD, CChem, FRSC, MRPharms, MPS

Routledge
Taylor & Francis Group

A PRODUCTIVITY PRESS BOOK

First published 2021
by Routledge
52 Vanderbilt Avenue, New York, NY 10017

and by Routledge
2 Park Square, Milton Park, Abingdon, Oxon, OX14 4RN

Routledge is an imprint of the Taylor & Francis Group, an informa business

© 2021 Taylor & Francis

Library of Congress Cataloging-in-Publication Data
Names: De Silva, Titus, author.
Title: Integrating business management processes. Volume 3. : harmonising
quality, food safety and environmental processes / Titus De Silva.
Description: New York, NY : Routledge, 2020. | Includes bibliographical
references and index.
Identifiers: LCCN 2020011551 (print) | LCCN 2020011552 (ebook) |
ISBN 9780367487867 (hardback) | ISBN 9780367485474 (paperback) |
ISBN 9781003042846 (ebook)
Subjects: LCSH: Industrial management. | Environmental management.
Classification: LCC HD31.2 .D42 2020 (print) | LCC HD31.2 (ebook) |
DDC 658—dc23
LC record available at https://lccn.loc.gov/2020011551
LC ebook record available at https://lccn.loc.gov/2020011552

ISBN: 978-0-367-48786-7 (hbk)
ISBN: 978-0-367-48547-4 (pbk)
ISBN: 978-1-003-04284-6 (ebk)

Typeset in Garamond
by codeMantra

This book is dedicated to my dear wife, Anoma De Silva, a librarian and an archivist, for sharing her life with me for the last 50 years with great affection and love.

Contents

SECTION 1 MANAGEMENT PROCEDURES

SECTION II CORE PROCEDURES

SECTION III   SUPPORT PROCEDURES

SECTION IV ASSURANCE PROCEDURES

List of Figures

List of Tables

List of Flowcharts

List of Forms

Disclaimer

While the author has used reasonable efforts to include accurate and up-to-date information for the content in the publication, he does not represent, warrant or promise (whether express or implied) that any information is or remains accurate, complete and up to date, or fit or suitable for any purpose. Any reliance a reader places on the information in this publication is at their own risk (including their use of the forms and procedures), and this publication is not intended as a substitute for ISO standards, including ISO 9001, ISO 22000 and ISO 14001. Reprinted material is quoted with permission, and sources are indicated. The authors and publishers apologise to copyright holders if permission to publish in this form has not been obtained. If any copyright material has not been acknowledged, please write and let us know so we may rectify in any future reprints.

These three books on *Integrating Business Management Processes* are designed to provide practical guidance and do not constitute technical, financial or legal advice or any other type of advice and should not be relied on for any purposes. It is not intended to guarantee certification of the integrated management system.

The procedures in this book are based on the author's personal experience of developing, implementing and auditing management systems in pharmaceutical, cosmetic and food industries in an executive quality assurance role during a period of over 25 years as well as on contributions from numerous resources. The author does not claim them to be original and/or have been developed specifically for this publication. In particular, the author acknowledges the valuable contribution from the resources listed in the bibliography.

Foreword

The usual definition of a business management system is that it is a set of policies, processes and procedures used by an organisation to ensure that it can fulfil the tasks required to achieve its objectives, covering all the key aspects of the organisation's operations. But this definition doesn't really do justice to the importance and complexity of an effective business management system. It should be, but often isn't, an integrated and dynamic system which links the organisation's key activities and provides guidance and motivation for staff at all levels. Not a set of stand-alone, isolated procedures and objectives but something which drives the organisation to continuous improvement and ultimately, business success.

The integration of different activities into a cohesive and inter-linked system is key to this. Various books and articles have been written analysing different approaches in an attempt to provide guidance on how to derive effective integrated management systems, often based on satisfying the requirements of ISO standards. But this book takes the approach a step further, on the premise that it is more logical to integrate management processes, rather than management systems, and to focus on customer satisfaction and not just ISO standards.

It is aimed principally at manufacturing and consulting organisations where quality, food safety and environmental management are key and also covers the full gamut of management processes, which are integral to most businesses.

Based on his own wide-ranging experience, Dr. De Silva presents a series of three volumes on *Integrating Business Management Processes*, which sets out a rational and detailed approach to the development of a fully integrated business management system using process-based principles. Volume 1 gives a comprehensive coverage of the key management and core, processes and also makes a case for the inclusion of good manufacturing, quality and food safety practices, which are often dealt with separately. Volume 2 sets out support and assurance processes in a business environment. This is followed by Volume 3, which describes the integration of quality, food safety and environmental processes, complete with procedures and flowcharts, based on Dr. De Silva's own personal journey in developing successful integrated business management systems.

It is an account and an approach which I thoroughly recommend. The series of these three volumes is a valuable resource for any organisation, large, small or medium in the development, implementation, maintenance and improvement of an integrated management system.

Dr. David C Taylor
BSc Pharmacy (Hons), PhD Former Director of Product Development, Analytical Development and Project Management, AstraZeneca.
December 2019

Review of Integrating Business Management Processes, Volumes 1, 2 and 3

Dr. De Silva has written an excellent series of three books on Integrating *Business Management Processes* that provides a structure to manage four key elements of a modern business:

- Quality and food safety.
- Respect for the environment.
- Respect for employee well-being.
- Good business.

Dr. De Silva demonstrates that these principles need not be at odds with each other. Rather, when applied with understanding and care, they work harmoniously for the good of the business, its employees, customers and community.

The process of integration adopts a novel approach, focusing on processes encountered in day-to-day business operations without the need for formalised third-party accreditations.

To write this series encompassing quality, food safety and environmental activities requires a comprehensive knowledge of these disciplines. Dr. De Silva's wide experience in developing management systems and auditing provides the essential competency to put together complex processes in a simple format.

I worked extensively with Titus to set up formalised quality and business management systems so this work is no surprise. An added bonus is the historical and philosophical context Titus provides to frame our modern position.

These books, with their series of examples and procedures, show how organisations can benefit from satisfying customer requirements and the requirements of ISO standards to gain entry into lucrative markets.

The series is detailed enough to be comprehensive as a complete guide to systems development or the reader may be selective in addressing specific issues that they may be encountering. Volumes One and Two provide a broad knowledge base on management, core, support and assurance processes encountered in the business environment. In Volume Three, quality, food safety and environmental procedures are merged to form an integrated management system.

The aim of the series is to enable readers, at very little cost, to set up an effective and efficient integrated quality, food safety and environmental management system for themselves. The three books complement each other, and this series on *Integrating Business Management Processes* is a complete business management system capable of being adapted to suit a business without the need of a specialist to do it for them.

All three volumes are practical workbooks necessary for any organisation, small, medium or large, to develop, implement, maintain and improve an integrated quality, food safety and an environmental business management system. They are highly recommended.

Nick Rowe
Supply Chain Manager and Logistics Consultant
Marisco Wines, New Zealand
December 2019

Preface

The three books on *Integrating Business Management Processes* cover quality, food safety and environmental processes encountered in a business environment. Volume 2 describes ten support processes and three assurance processes required to assure quality, food safety and good environmental practices. Volume 1 includes five chapters on management processes and ten chapters on core business processes. Good Manufacturing Practices (GMPs) and Hazard Analysis and Critical Control Point (HACCP) are key chapters in Volume 1. Volume 3 is about building an integrated management system (IMS) by merging quality, food safety and environmental processes.

Management systems form an integral part of any business. Business organisations have to satisfy not only the customers they serve but also statutory and regulatory requirements, industry standards and their own internal requirements, while keeping the environment clean. To meet these needs, organisations have developed a multitude of stand-alone management systems. Most organisations that design integrated management systems resort to satisfying the clauses of relevant ISO standards. These standards *per se* are not management systems but are tools that can be used to evaluate the effectiveness of management systems. Organisations that design management systems merely to satisfy the clauses of ISO standards lose sight of the ultimate aim of implementing these systems. Books on IMSs that focus on procedures that are only relevant to ISO standards tend to ignore programmes such as marketing and finance, which are integral parts of any business organisation. Employees do not take ownership of such systems, which is an important consideration for the success of the programme. A management system should be designed to cover all business activities to satisfy its stakeholders, and certification should only be used to evaluate its effectiveness and promote continual improvement.

These three volumes on *Integrating Business Management Processes* include many disciplines encountered in the business environment. Numerous case studies are included in the chapters. The integration approach used in Volume 3 is unique: (a) most books on integration deal with the integration of quality, environmental and occupational safety and hygiene standards with management systems or ISO standards. A rational approach is to integrate management processes rather than management systems or ISO standards; (b) quality, food safety and environmental processes are integrated, a rare combination not found in books on integrated management systems. It is a rational approach, because food safety is closely linked to quality, GMPs and environmental issues; (c) business processes are described in sufficient detail in Volumes 1 and 2 to provide a comprehensive understanding; (d) business processes have been classified into management, core, support and assurance procedures and are described using the process-based approach. Procedures associated with these processes in Volume 3 can easily be tailored to suit the needs of the organisation; (e) the procedures are supplemented with numerous forms, tables and flowcharts and (f) procedures specific to quality, food safety and the environment are also described.

Food safety is an integral part of quality and GMPs. Therefore, these three books take the lead in integrating closely-related, but different, business processes. The management skills necessary for developing and implementing management systems are well described in my previous book, *Essential Management Skills for Pharmacy and Business Managers* (CRC Press, 2013).

In my corporate role as the Head of Quality Assurance in the largest winery in New Zealand (Montana Wines Limited), the experience of developing and implementing management systems, auditing them and exposure to several industry sectors (such as pharmaceutical, cosmetic, food and beverage and retail pharmacy) provided me with the depth of knowledge and expertise required to write this series.

The books focus on business processes and not on ISO standards, and as such it is not intended as a substitute for these standards. Those who intend to use this book for developing or integrating management systems should thoroughly understand the processes described in Volumes 1 and 2. Then, the necessary management, core, support and assurance processes required to satisfy the needs of the organisation and its customers should be identified. The final phase is to adopt the procedures presented in Volume 3 of the series to suit individual needs. *The Way Forward* in Volume 3 takes you through this process. The primary aim should be to satisfy the needs of stakeholders rather than the clauses of ISO standards. When the system has been implemented and found to meet expectations, the organisation can work towards certification, consulting the relevant ISO standards.

The journey is arduous. Staff development and team work are essential ingredients for success. It is a dynamic process, and continual improvement takes place when employees take ownership of the system.

The Way Forward

The backbone of any organisation is its management system. It must reflect the needs of the organisation and the requirements of its customers. Compliance with legal requirements and ethical environmental practices contributes towards the sustainability of the management system. Whatever the stage of maturity of the management system, these three books on *Integrating Business Management Processes* provide useful guidance to design, implement, maintain and improve its effectiveness.

In my corporate quality assurance role in the largest winery in New Zealand, I was responsible for designing and implementing quality, food safety and environmental management systems throughout the organisation. Those organisations who embark on this journey must understand the key check points for success:

- My first task was to train all operators to accept responsibility for their operations by transforming an inspector-based quality control system to a quality assurance-based system. This transformation gave them the dignity that they deserved.
- It was necessary for all staff at all levels to have a clear understanding of the mission, objectives and operations for which they were responsible.
- The operations were classified into management, core, support and assurance processes.
- Existing documents and records were incorporated into procedures in the new management system.
- Supporting activities such as information technology, human resources and laboratory procedures were built around these procedures.

Commitment, dedication and management involvement were components for success. During the design and implementation phase, certification was not considered as the aim. When the system reached maturity, our organisation became the first winery in Australasia to gain ISO 9001 certification of our quality management system. This book captures the essence of my journey.

The series of books on *Integrating Business Management Processes* is intended to provide you with practical "how to" method for integrating your quality, food safety and environmental management processes. When you need the information, you will find a chapter in Volume 1 or 2 to help. Thus, it is a practical book for real managers aimed at helping you manage your business more effectively in the real world of competitive business. These books identify the operations with multiple management systems, merge them and end up with one integrated management system. The focus has been on operations rather than on clauses of ISO standards. This blending or integration is essential for streamlining the processes while improving profits and gaining competitive advantage.

The integration process involves the development of a close relationship among quality, food safety and environmental professionals. It is vital that these professionals work together as a team to accomplish the same goal and the integration of their respective management systems.

To obtain the maximum benefit from this series, it is recommended that you adopt a stepwise approach:

- Create a policy manual using the company mission, vision and objectives with relevant chapters in Volumes 1 and 2 and the Procedure BMS 000 in this volume as a guide. This is documentation level 1. (Responsibility: QA, Environmental and Food Safety Managers).
- Design the process map incorporating quality, environmental and food safety elements of the organisation and include sales, marketing, design, manufacturing, finance and warehouse functions. Use Figures MP 005-1 and MP 006-1 in this volume for guidance (Responsibility: QA, Environmental and Food Safety Managers).
- Form cross-functional teams (Responsibility: QA Manager).
- Identify the necessary processes using the information presented in the Procedure MP 006 and Forms 014, 015, 016 and 017 in Volume 3 and relevant chapters in Volumes 1 and 2 as guides (Responsibility: QA, Environmental and Food Safety Managers).
- Classify the processes and identify processes common to quality, food safety and environmental programmes. Use Procedure MP 006 and Forms 014, 015, 016 and

017 for guidance (Responsibility: QA, Environmental and Food Safety Managers).

■ Identify processes specific to quality, food safety and environmental management systems. Use Procedure MP 006 and Forms 014, 015, 016 and 017 in this book and chapters in Volumes 1 and 2 for guidance. It is useful to study Chapter one in this book (*Integrated Management Systems*) to understand the structure of integrated management systems (Responsibility: QA, Environmental and Food Safety Managers).

■ Develop procedures using the sample procedures described in this book for guidance. This is level 2 documentation (Responsibility: QA, Environmental and Food Safety Managers with support from Supervisors and floor staff).

■ Implement and measure the effectiveness using the metrics described under each procedure (Responsibility: QA Manager).

■ Documentation level 3 refers to work instructions. Most organisations do have many work instructions. Form cross-functional teams (include Line Supervisors) to formalise the style and incorporate them into the IQFSE Management System (Responsibility: QA Manager).

■ Prepare the necessary forms, flowcharts and tables. This is level 4 documentation (Responsibility: QA Manager).

■ Modify and enhance the programme as necessary (continual improvement – Procedure AP 006) (Responsibility: QA Manager).

■ Conduct a gap analysis (Responsibility: QA, Environmental and Food Safety Managers).

■ Determine whether your programme is ready for certification on the basis of performance measures and internal audits (Responsibility: QA Manager).

The information presented in this book can be applied to any organisation, no matter its size – small, medium or large. It can also form the basis for assessing the organisation's management system to ensure that it has the ability to provide satisfactory goods and/or services while keeping the environment unpolluted.

Acknowledgements

During the five-year period of developing these three books on *Integrating Business Management Processes*, many individuals devoted their time and effort to make this project a success. Over the years, I have come to know many colleagues in management who shared their knowledge with me. I wish to thank Dr. David Taylor, in the UK, former Director of Product Development, Analytical Development and Project Management, AstraZeneca, for writing the foreword in this book in spite of his busy schedule. I am grateful to Mr. Nick Rowe, Logistics Consultant in New Zealand, for reviewing the chapters on new product development and warehouse management and writing a valuable review. I appreciate his comments and recommendations, which were incorporated in the chapters. I acknowledge with thanks the contribution made by Mr. Chanaka De Silva, a Chartered Accountant in New Zealand for reviewing the chapter on financial management and making worthy recommendations. I acknowledge with thanks the unwavering encouragement and enormous support given to me by son, Dr. Samitha De Silva, in the UK, a Partner at C'M'S', the seventh largest law firm globally. Special thanks go to my son, Pradeepa De Silva, Head of Global Marketing Programs at Facebook based in Singapore, who supported me in numerous ways, including the review of the chapters on marketing and sales management. My wife, Anoma De Silva, a Librarian and an Archivist, presented me with many recommendations and challenges for which I am very grateful. These enabled me to achieve my objective of completing the manuscript on time. I wish to thank Helen McDonald in New Zealand for excellent proofreading. I also thank the organisations I worked for in senior management roles in New Zealand (Hoechst NZ Limited, Penfolds and Montana Wines Limited), Japan (National Institute of Hygienic Sciences), the UK (Eli Lilly Research, Boots and Lloyds Pharmacy Limited), Kuwait (Ministry of Health) and Sri Lanka (Ministry of Health). Finally, I acknowledge with thanks the professionalism of the editorial team of Taylor & Francis.

Acknowledgements

Review

At a personal level, I have found that, with advancing years, I need the support of organised systems to ensure that I complete the tasks that I need to do, rather than those that are unnecessary or unhelpful. Having undertaken research and development as an employee in the pharmaceutical industry, as an academic member of multi-task industrial project teams and a governmental regulatory authority, I am well aware of the benefits of organisational systems to achieve successful outcomes. I was therefore fascinated to see the extensive aspects of such systems as provided by Dr De Silva in the three volumes on "Integrating Business Management Processes". He has considered the wider, fundamental aspects of the range of systems and their organisation in a manner which supports the delivery of a successful product or project.

While examples are provided for particular industries, the principles provided in the 29 chapters can be applied to many systems. Thus, the content of each chapter may not be relevant to every management system or situation, but Dr De Silva has emphasised that, where relevant, integration of relevant chapters is beneficial. He has evidenced this from the development stage of these systems, through to their implementation and control. The dynamic nature of these systems is clearly demonstrated, as is the likelihood that they will change as new knowledge, materials, and processing and test methods emerge and the operational performance of these management processes is observed.

The lists of references at the end of each chapter provide the source of the information used to present the text and indicate that each chapter could probably be expanded into a book. This work, however, offers succinct and comprehensive information regarding the important issues involved for each system. The figures, flowcharts, forms, procedures and tables provide a valuable contribution to the understanding of this work on organisational systems.

Dr J.M. Newton
Emeritus Professor of the School of Pharmacy of London University, Honorary Professor in the Department of Mechanical Engineering at University College, London, Member of CPS (Chemistry, Pharmacy and Standards), a subcommittee of the CSM (Committee on the Safety of Medicines: 1978–1995), and Member of the Medicines Commission: 1978–2000).
March 2020

Author

Titus De Silva, PhD, is a Consultant in management skills development, pharmacy practice, quality management and food safety and has been an Advisor to the newly established National Medicines Regulatory Authority in Sri Lanka.

Dr. De Silva gained his pharmacy degree (with Honours) from the University of Manchester in the UK. In addition, he has a BSc degree in Chemistry, a Post-Graduate Diploma in Computer Science (NZ) and an MBA and PhD in Management Science (USA). He is a Chartered Chemist (CChem) and a Fellow of the Royal Society of Chemistry, UK (FRSC), a member of the Royal Pharmaceutical Society of Great Britain (MRPharmS) and a member of the Pharmaceutical Society of New Zealand (MPS).

For over 30 years, he held senior management positions in New Zealand, the UK and Sri Lanka. He has worked in the UK, New Zealand, Japan and Kuwait in many sectors including manufacturing, research, cosmetics, beverage and hospital and community pharmacy. Before immigrating to New Zealand, he was the Head of the National Drugs Quality Control Laboratory in Sri Lanka. During his time in Sri Lanka, he was a Visiting Lecturer and Examiner at the Faculty of Medicine of the University of Colombo, School of Pharmacy. While in Kuwait, he served as a Specialist in drug analysis and quality control in the Ministry of Health. In Japan, he was attached to the National Institute of Hygienic Science in Tokyo, where he worked with experts in pharmaceutical science. Other organisations he has worked for include the Southland Hospital Board (New Zealand), Hoechst Pharmaceuticals (New Zealand), Pernod-Ricard (New Zealand), Eli Lily Research (UK), Ballinger's Pharmacy (New Zealand), Boots Chemists (UK) and Lloyds Pharmacy (UK).

Pernod-Ricard (previously Montana Wines Limited) owned the largest winery in New Zealand, with wineries in four regions. In his role as Corporate Quality Assurance Manager, he was responsible for developing and implementing management systems to comply with international standards. In this role, he coached and trained staff for management positions. He gained competency as a Lead Auditor and was a registered auditor in quality management and occupational safety and hygiene. He worked closely with suppliers, auditing their management systems and providing encouragement and support. His auditing experience enabled him to gain broad knowledge of many disciplines encountered in the business environment.

Dr. De Silva's expertise has been sought by many professional organisations. He has presented numerous papers at international seminars and published a number of papers and articles on quality management, food safety, pharmacy practice and topics of general interest in management journals and magazines. He was the Co-author of the chapter, "Hazard Analysis and Critical Control Point" in the book *Handbook of Food Preservation* published by Marcel Dekker, New York (1st Edition) (1999). In the second edition of the book, published by CRC Press, Boca Raton, Florida in July 2007, he was the Author of the revised "Hazard Analysis and Critical Control Point (HACCP)" chapter and the "Good Manufacturing Practices" chapter. His book, *Handbook of Good Pharmacy Practice* was published in 2011 in Sri Lanka. In 2013, his book *Essential Management Skills for Pharmacy and Business Managers* was published by CRC Press.

Dr. De Silva was a member of the Review Board of the Joint Accreditation System of Australia and New Zealand (JAS-ANZ) and its Technical Advisory Council. JAS-ANZ is the sole body responsible for accrediting certifying bodies in Australia and New Zealand. He was enlisted as a Consultant to the United Nations Industrial Development Organization (UNIDO).

In 2004, the New Zealand government conferred the Queen's Service Medal (QSM) for his services to the New Zealand community.

Author

Chapter 1

Integrating Management Systems

1.1 Introduction

Businesses operate on management systems. Most common management systems in the business environment are quality, environment, occupational health and safety and food safety. The performance of these management systems has been evaluated using ISO standards. Operating individual management systems in isolation duplicates the effort and uses valuable resources. Therefore, in order to manage these systems efficiently and effectively, organisations have employed various techniques to integrate several management systems into one common programme. Several publications on integrated management systems (IMSs) have emerged providing guidance on the techniques and the tools to be employed in the integration process. Most publications on IMS deal with the integration of the various clauses of ISO standards, but these standards by themselves are not management systems. They are tools to be used in evaluating the performance of management systems, like an electrician using an instrument to measure the strength of the current. The approach used in this book is the integration of quality, environmental and food safety management processes to create an integration management system that meets the requirements of the relevant ISO standards.

1.2 Reasons for Integration

The survival of a business organisation depends on its ability to meet the numerous challenges posed due to the ever-changing business environment. Some of these challenges are:

- Increased competition
- High customer and community expectations as a result of enhanced awareness of food safety, health, environmental and quality assurance issues

- Return on investment
- Need to comply with regulatory requirements
- Executive liable risk.

Standards and regulations applicable to health, the environment, safety, quality and food safety programmes share some common elements. Significant improvements can occur in many areas of the business such as waste production, non–value-added activities, rationalisation of end products and documentation when these common elements are integrated into a common programme.

Traditionally, these programmes have been operating in isolation as separate and specialised facets of management. Therefore, decisions and actions are taken in isolation, often leading to information overload and conflicting instructions. Organisations that have implemented the total quality management (TQM) programme realise that there are some commonalities and differences between this programme and the environmental management system (EMS). For example, while both systems encourage continuous improvement, the "zero defects" concept in TQM cannot be applied to the EMS because zero impact is not a reality (OpenLearn, 2017).

Governments and legislative action tend towards self-regulation and accountability. Violations result in the increased cost of incidents and heavy penalties. Employees expect a safe, healthy and pollution-free work environment. Businesses demand adherence to health and safety and/or environments as a condition for doing business. Therefore, a change in focus from monitoring and control to systems identification, management and improvement is needed in all aspects of the organisation. Significant are those aspects that have the ability to cause undesirable effects on safety, health, the environment and quality and food safety. An integrated approach can effectively manage multiple requirements (Standards Australia, 2003).

1.3 Benefits of IMSs

IMSs offer numerous benefits, both external and internal, to the organisation (Stamou, 2003; Cekanova, 2015).

1.3.1 Internal Benefits to the Organisation

a. **Organisational benefits**
   - Alignment of policies, objectives, processes and resources in three functional areas into one, improving management and cross-functional communication (a single system is easier to implement, maintain and improve)
   - Elimination of duplication of work and rationalisation of resources
   - Improved efficiency by harmonising organisational structures with similar elements and enhancing information flow across organisational boundaries
   - Better structured processes and clearer roles and responsibilities.
b. **Financial benefits**
   - Reduction in external certification costs
   - Reduction in cost savings by having to manage a single management system and adding to the profit margin.
c. **Human resource (HR) benefits**
   - Improved motivation, awareness and competencies among employees
   - Availability of joint training sessions and better communication at all levels of management.

1.3.2 External Benefits to the Organisation

a. **Commercial**
   - Better competitive advantage, improved market position, ability to gain new customers while satisfying existing ones
   - Enhanced corporate image as a result of a single certified management system.
b. **External communication benefits**
   - Improved relationship with all stakeholders
   - Unified approach to identify the needs of customers.
c. **Quality, environmental and food safety benefits**
   - Improved customer satisfaction achieved through better quality, and better environmental and food safety performance arising from an integrated and standardised management system
   - Ability to continually meet customers, stakeholders and regulatory requirements
   - Unified approach to identify and address business, environmental and food safety risks
   - Improved environmental performance.

1.4 Drivers of Organisations Adopting IMS

Every organisation driven by their policies strives to satisfy five stakeholders (Quality Austria, 2012):

1. Employees: Their demands refer to work content, motivation and health and safety in the workplace.
2. Customers: Customer requirements refer to the quality and safety of products and services offered by the organisation.
3. Owners and investors: They demand satisfactory return on their investments, value enhancement and reasonable risk management.
4. Suppliers and partners: They require reliability and dealings to be conducted in an ethical manner.
5. Community and regulatory authorities: They require organisations to demonstrate responsibility to the society, environmental protection and compliance with codes of practice and regulatory requirements. In order to satisfy these diverse needs, organisations have to consider the integration of management systems in terms of three dimensions:

1.4.1 Top-Down Integration

Top-down integration requires the mission and strategic plan to be reflected in business processes. An effective management system serves the interests of the organisation and drives it to success. Best possible integration adds value in the value creation process. Management's role in the integration is to clearly formulate policies and design a framework for action. Thus, an IMS provides a consistent leadership framework that enables the managers and other employees to understand the different requirements and deliver the expectations.

1.4.2 Integration of Topics and Requirements

In designing an IMS, several elements come into play. Quality, the environment, occupational safety and hygiene, risk management, food safety, regulatory requirements and industry sector requirements are given priority. These requirements from standards and industry sector requirements are clearly reflected in various stakeholders' demands. Traditionally, these requirements are considered in isolation and appear in separate management systems. In the challenging and competitive environment, factors such as speed of delivery, flexibility, operational performance and agility are demanded by the customers. These needs can only be met by: (a) understanding the interactions among the processes; (b) integrating the different requirements; (c) avoiding duplication of documents and (d) keeping them simple.

1.4.3 Integration of Day-to-Day Processes

In this dimension, the leadership role becomes important. By focusing on day-to-day operations, economic benefits can be realised. In this dimension, clarity of one's daily work, use of synergies and a unified approach to scarce resources are fundamental components of an IMS.

1.5 Approaches to Integration

An IMS can be viewed as making transverse connections among the different management systems where these have some commonalities such as policy, planning and documentation, evaluation. A synergy among an IMS can be formed with different levels of integration.

1.5.1 Two Levels of Integration

Hines (2002) proposed two levels of integration: alignment and integration.

Alignment: Here similarities among the different management systems are structured together in one system. There are separate procedures for each area, but they are placed in one manual and this approach reduces the administration and audit costs.

Integration: All relevant procedures and instructions are fully integrated. The basis of this approach is TQM, which focuses on employees, customers and continuous improvement.

1.5.2 Three Levels of Integration

Jorgensen et al. (2006) recommended three levels of integration: (a) integration as correspondence; (b) integration as coordination and (c) integration as a strategic and inherent approach.

1.5.2.1 Integration as Correspondence

This level of integration refers to increased compatibility with cross-references between parallel system elements. The following initiatives by the ISO have contributed to improved compatibility among different standards: (a) a high-level (HL) structure common to most ISO standards; (b) processes focusing on continual improvement; (c) improved coherence with ISO 9001 standards and clarification of connections to the EMAS II – Regulation No. 761/2001 of the EU and (d) the availability of a common standard for an auditing quality and an EMS. The main elements in this level are compatibility, cross-references and the internal coordination of management system elements. The benefits of this approach are: (a) less documentation and records; (b) less administrative and paperwork; (c) cost savings by optimising time and resources and (d) simplification of internal and external audits.

1.5.2.2 Integration as Coordination

This level of integration refers to a generic management system focusing on processes of coordination. Coordination provides a solution to problems related to managing tasks and projects across different functional units and departments. This approach is based on the integration of requirements of different management systems into the generic processes such as policy, planning, implementation, checking, corrective action and a management review of the IMS according to the PDCA (Plan, Do, Check and Act) cycle. Potential benefits include a focus on interactions, coordinated and balanced objectives and targets and a clear definition of the roles and responsibilities in one place of the management system.

1.5.2.3 Integration as a Strategic and Inherent Approach

This level of integration resolves problems related to realising real continuous improvements such as improved competitive advantages and contributing to sustainable development. It involves the promotion of a culture of learning and continuous improvement of performance as well as stakeholders' involvement related to external and internal changes.

1.5.2.3.1 Integration as Organisational Embeddedness and Shareholder Relationships

In order to bring about continuous improvement of performance, competitive advantage and achieve sustainable development, IMS has to be embedded by institutionalising the IMS throughout the organisation and interaction with a broader range of stakeholders by management commitment, employee motivation and changes in routines and traditions. Competitive advantage can be gained by focusing on customers in the quality system and food safety system and on products in the EMS at the same time. This will create synergy among quality, environment and food safety while focusing on continuous improvement and product design. The focus will shift from traditional production processes to the entire supply chain.

For this level of integration, organisations must satisfy three pre-conditions (Patience, 2008):

1. Shared understanding of internal and external challenges involving organisational culture, learning and the active participation of employees.

2. Creation of a learning organisation and a culture of responsibility. The learning process should ensure a better design and redesign of systems in order to ensure continuous adaptation to new challenges.
3. Interaction with stakeholders achieved through cooperation, dialogue and transparency. This will improve the quality, environment, health, safety and social responsibility aspects in the entire product life cycle.

1.6 Models of Integration

Since the introduction of multiple management standards, organisations worldwide have been integrating their management systems to enhance efficiency and effectiveness. The most common IMS involves the integration of quality, environmental and occupational health and safety management systems to meet the requirements of individual standards. All the models follow the PDCA cycle. The following models offer the basis for designing IMSs that are appropriate for different organisations:

1. European Foundation for Quality Management (EFQM) model.
2. Integration model based on ISO standards.

1.6.1 EFQM Model

The EFQM excellence model is a non-prescriptive model applicable to any organisation and its advantages are (EFQM, 2012) as follows:

■ It can be applied to organisations of any size or maturity belonging to any sector
■ It offers a common language enabling sharing of knowledge and experience, both within and outside the organisation

■ The model ensures that the management practices used by the organisation form a coherent system subjected to continual improvement and deliver strategy-oriented results.

The model encompasses nine criteria which includes five enablers and four results. Enablers define what the company does and how they are done. The organisation's achievements are included under results (Figure 1.1).

1.6.1.1 Enablers

1. Leadership: Leaders influence people, shape the future of the organisation and get things done. They inspire trust among the staff by acting as role models for its ethics and values and ensure success in the organisation by anticipating and reacting in a timely manner.
2. Strategy: Excellent organisations implement their mission and vision by focusing on a strategy that is shareholder-focused.
3. People: An excellent organisation considers its people to be the most important resource and creates a culture that promotes the achievement of organisational and personal goals. It is committed to developing people and being fair and equal. It cares for the people, communicates with them and rewards and recognises their achievements. Therefore, people are motivated, develop commitment and apply their knowledge to the advancement of the organisation's goals.
4. Partnerships and resources: In order to support the strategy, policies and operations of the organisation, excellent organisations effectively manage their relationships with partners, suppliers and internal resources. These relationships ensure effective management of the impact on society and the environment.

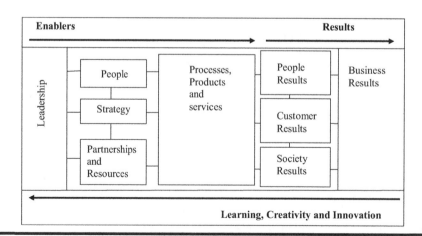

Figure 1.1 EFQM excellence model of integration. (*Source*: Reproduced with permission from EFQM, 2012. Copyright © EFQM.)

5. Processes, products and services: Through proper design, management and improvement of products and services, excellent organisations are able to increase value to all stakeholders.

1.6.1.2 Results

Excellent organisations achieve their strategic goals by:

- Developing effective key performance indicators (KPIs)
- Establishing clear targets
- Analysing the performance of specific areas of the organisation and identifying the experience, needs and expectations of stakeholders
- Analysing the trends and the impact on the performance
- Having confidence in the future
- Reviewing targets by analysing competitors' data.

Excellent organisations achieve and maintain outstanding results that meet and exceed the expectations of customers, people, the community and other stakeholders.

1.6.2 Integration Based on ISO Standards

Because of the dissimilarity of ISO 9001:2008 and ISO 14001:2004, two models were proposed by Ahsen and Funck (2001). However, most ISO standards now share a common HL structure consisting of ten elements (Tangen & Warris, 2012; Jensen, 2016):

- Clause 1 – Scope
- Clause 2 – Normative references
- Clause 3 – Terms and definitions
- Clause 4 – Context of the organisation
- Clause 5 – Leadership
- Clause 6 – Planning
- Clause 7 – Support
- Clause 8 – Operation
- Clause 9 – Performance evaluation
- Clause 10 – Improvement.

The HL structure shares some common definitions and identical texts. A generic model based on this HL structure (Ahsen and Funck, 2001) for an IMS is presented in Figure 1.2a and b.

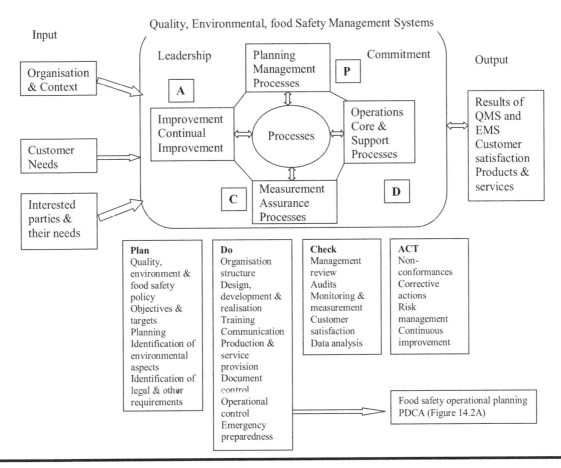

Figure 1.2 (a) Integration according to ISO standards.

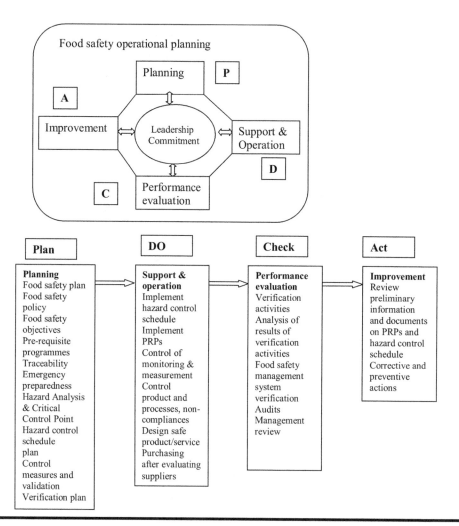

Figure 1.2 (b) Food safety operational planning PDCA.

1.6.3 Process-Based Model

Badreddine et al. (2009) have proposed a process-based model to integrate quality, security and environment (QSE) management systems using process cartography. This model captures the whole processes of the company and their interactions (Figure 1.3). The main features of this model are as follows:

■ It identifies the inputs and outputs of each process, providing an understanding of the generic process and an examination of synergies and trade-offs
■ It employs the alignment of policies, objectives and targets
■ It identifies the sources of hazards and potential causes of risks, enabling managers to make appropriate decisions, control processes and define requirements such as HRs, technical and financial.

The model follows the PDCA cycle.

Plan phase: During this phase, the current situation is assessed to derive objectives and identify requirements, methods, tools, responsibilities and resources for each process. The six steps involved in this phase are shown in Figure 1.3. The last step considers several performance indicators such as customer satisfaction, audits, controls and KPIs of processes, and these enable the organisation to take into account diversified objectives.

Do phase: The global QSE management plan and the global monitoring plan generated from the plan serve as an input to this phase. During the "Do" phase, selected treatments are implemented.

Check and act phase: In this phase all the selected performance indicators are measured in order to assess the effectiveness of selected treatments and the extent of realisation of objectives. The three steps in this phase are: (a) collate the indicators of each objective; (b) review the management plan in order to satisfy unrealised objectives and (c) revise objectives which have not been achieved in order to contribute to sustainable development.

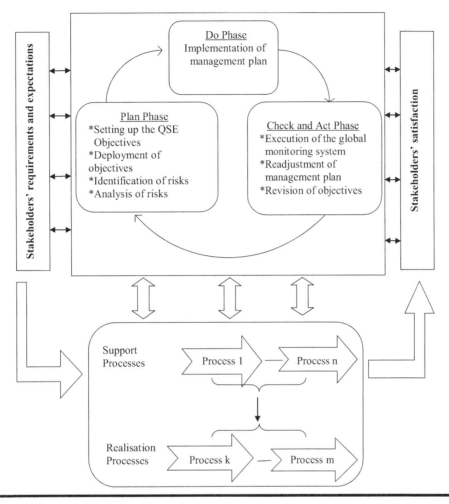

Figure 1.3   Model based on process-based approach. (*Source*: Reproduced with permission from Badreddine et al., 2009. Copyright © International Association of Engineers (IAENG).)

1.6.4 Process-Based Model with Focus on Critical Aspects

A management system is a tool to develop and achieve the organisation's policy and objectives in certain areas. The aim of the policy is to improve the environment outside the organisation (ISO 14001), occupational safety and hygiene within the organisation (OSHAS18001) and to deliver customer expectations by enhancing the quality of its products (ISO 9001). In order to achieve this policy, the organisation should successfully manage the critical aspects of its activities, processes, products and services. The following examples show the relationship between activities/products, critical aspects (focal points) and potential impact (risk) applied to quality, environment and occupational safety and health systems.

Example 1 – *Activity: Vehicle maintenance*
Environmental aspect: Spillage of used oil
Environmental impact: Potential soil–water contamination

Example 2 – *Activity: Receiving glass bottles*
Quality characteristic: Inclusions in the wall
Impact on quality: Potential for breakage

Example 3 – *Activity: Manufacturing hall operations*
Occupational health and safety aspect: Noise exceeding permitted levels
Health impact: Loss of hearing.

In this model (Hortensius et al., 2004), which is based on the ISO 72 guide, all core, support and management operations essential to improve and manage the business are presented according to the PDCA cycle. Thus, the product realisation steps needed to satisfy stakeholders' requirements are represented in a sequence. Integration of management support processes can be achieved by designing integrated processes for the development of policies, objectives and programmes; building training and the awareness of requirements among employees and carrying out auditing and a management review. At the operational level, each process is assessed to identify any QSE aspects and determine whether they can be controlled in one integrated process or have separate processes.

1.6.5 IMS Model Based on Total Quality Approach

In this model proposed by Wilkinson and Dale (2001), quality, environment and health and safety management resources, processes and procedures interact through the structure and culture to conduct planning, controlling, implementing, measuring, improving and auditing operations and transform inputs into outputs. The outputs are compared with the goals, which have been established through company policies and stakeholders' needs. If the performance falls short of expectations, then objectives are revised. This model has been recommended to small- and medium-sized enterprises wishing to integrate quality, environment and occupational health and safety management systems. A simplified form of the model is shown in Figure 1.4.

1.6.6 Optimal IMS of Quality and Safety for Food Enterprises

This model (Figure 1.5) is based on the integration of the following systems:

a. QMS
b. Food safety management system (FSMS) based on Hazard Analysis and Critical Control Point (HACCP),

Good Manufacturing Practices (GMP) and Good Handling Practices (GHP) and a sensor control system to ensure the stability and safety food
c. EMS
d. Occupational safety and health system
e. Energy management system
f. Principles of social responsibility of business.

The foundation of the IMS is the ISO 9001 standard. The model takes into account the general requirements included in the standards for the management system such as policy, planning and implementation and production, productivity assessment, improvement and a management review. Identification of the needs of the organisation in each management system and the expected benefits from integration are important decisions in the development of the IMS (Surkov et al., 2015).

1.7 Classification of Business Processes

Business processes have been classified in many ways, and the three models commonly cited are: (1) Porter's model; (2) business process management model and (3) the Sturgeon and Gereffi model. Table 1.1 shows a description of the three models.

1. Porter's model: In 1985, Michael Porter applied the term "value chain" to activities that are performed to design, manufacture, market, deliver and support the product of the organisation. He classified processes into primary processes and support processes. Primary processes are key processes needed to deliver customer requirements, while support processes support the value creation in the value chain (Kannegiesser, 2008).

2. Business process management model: This model classifies business processes into three categories: primary processes, support processes and management processes. Primary processes are end-to-end cross-functional processes that directly deliver value to customers. They can move across cross-functional boundaries such as departments, enterprises and functional organisations. Support processes manage resources required by primary processes, but do not add value to customers. Management processes are designed to measure, monitor and control business processes (Antonucci & Bariff, 2009).

3. The Sturgeon and Gereffi model has different sets of core and support processes. Their proposed model adapted from the Bureau of Labour Statistics Mass Layoff Survey Programme includes six key processes identified as core processes and three support processes (Sturgeon & Gereffi, 2008).

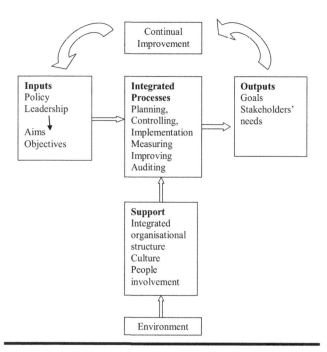

Figure 1.4   Model based on total quality approach.

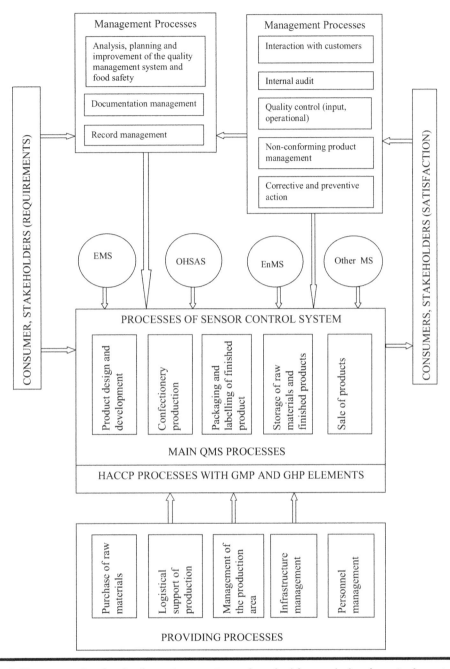

Figure 1.5   IMS model incorporating food safety. (*Source:* Reproduced with permission from Surkov et al., 2015. Copyright *Foods and Raw Materials*.)

In the Porter's model, product development has been classified as a support process, whereas in the model proposed by Sturgeon and Gereffi, it is a core business process. Similarly, procurement is a support activity in the Porter's model, while procurement and logistics are classified under core processes in the Sturgeon and Gereffi model. Another differentiation is that after a sale is a support activity in the Sturgeon and Gereffi, whereas in the business process management model, it is a core process.

1.8 Proposed Model for Integrating Quality, Environment and FSMSs

With the proliferation of ISO management standards, organisations have been looking for ways and means of reducing certification and auditing costs and streamlining their management systems. The literature offers numerous models for integrating management systems, particularly quality, environmental and occupational health and safety management

Table 1.1 Classification of Business Processes

Porter's Model	BPM Model	Sturgeon and Gereffi Model
Primary activities • Inbound logistics • Operations • Outbound logistics • Marketing and sales • Service in the core value chain creating value directly	Primary processes • Activities involved in the physical creation of product or service • Marketing • Delivery • After sales support	Core processes • Strategic management • Product development • Marketing, sales and account management • Intermediate input and material production • Procurement and purchasing • Operations • Transport logistics and distribution
Support activities • Procurement • Technical development • HR management • Firm infrastructure	Support processes • Planning • Finance • Procurement • Engineering • Manufacturing • Information technology	Support processes • Corporate governance • HRs • Technology and process development • Firm infrastructure, buildings and information technology • Customer and after sales
	Management processes • Activities involved with measuring, monitoring and controlling business activities	

systems. These models adopt a bottom-up approach commencing with the ISO standards requirements. However, there are two major issues with this approach: (a) the main aim of the IMS appears to be the desire to comply with ISO standards; and (b) ISO standards are not management systems. They specify minimum requirements for management systems and are valuable tools to measure their effectiveness. Satisfying the needs and expectations of customers while making a profit for the organisation should be the primary aim of any business organisation. Any other aim will only dilute the effectiveness of the management system. Certification to a particular standard should only be a "side effect" of the outcome.

The model proposed in this book commences with the identification of customers' requirements and addressing these for a combined quality, environment and FSMS. In the final stage, a gap analysis is performed to satisfy the requirements of the ISO 9001, ISO 14001 and ISO 22001 standards (De Silva, 2004). The point of commencement may vary depending on the development of the organisation (Figure 1.6).

1.8.1 Development of the Proposed IMS

Chandra (2013) has adopted a 10-step approach for implementing an integrated quality, environment and occupational safety management system in an organisation. These 10 steps can be implemented in four major stages.

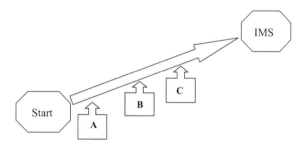

A No documented management system
B Stand-alone quality, environment or food safety management systems
C Single management system (quality, environment or food safety)

Figure 1.6 Progress of management systems.

1.8.1.1 Stage 1: Review

a. Describe the organisation

The first step is to describe the organisation in terms of its purpose, mission, vision, products and services offered and other preliminary information that sets the background.

b. Identify the needs of customers

Organisations exist to satisfy the demands of customers, and therefore, their needs and expectations must be clearly understood.

1.8.1.2 Stage 2: Identification, Classification and Documenting Processes

Identify the core, support, assurance and management processes.

The key processes that are required to meet customers' expectations are the core processes. Support processes are those needed to achieve the output of key processes. KPIs are assurance processes. Management processes provide leadership through the mission, vision, objectives, goals and strategic planning.

a. **Identify core processes**

Starting with customers' needs, immediately preceding activities are identified to establish core processes (Table 1.2).

b. **Identify support processes**

Support processes are processes derived from core processes, and they define the support needed to achieve the outcome of core processes (Table 1.3).

c. **Identify assurance processes**

Assurance processes measure and control the verification activities. The generic assurance processes

Table 1.2　Identification of Core Processes

Customers' Needs	Preceding Activity	Core Processes
Goods	Customer receives goods Deliver goods to the customer Receive order Process order Pick order Store goods Produce goods Purchase components	Storage and distribution (integrity) Selling (reliability) Orders fulfilment (reliability) Warehousing (reliability) Warehousing (reliability) Production, design (transformation) Purchasing (assembly)

Table 1.3　Identification of Support Processes

Core Process	Activities that Support the Core Process	Support Processes
Storage and distribution	HRs, information technology, management systems	HRs Information technology Management of Quality, Environment and Food Safety Systems
Sales	Marketing, accounting, HRs, customer services, management systems	Marketing Financial management HRs Customer services Management of uality, Environment and Food Safety Systems
Order fulfilment	Accounting (financial management), HRs, information technology, customer services, management systems	Financial management HRs Information technology Customer services Management of Quality, Environment and Food Safety Systems
Production, design	HRs, information technology, marketing, accounting, management systems	HRs Information technology Marketing Financial management Management of Quality, Environment and Food Safety Systems
Purchasing	HRs, information technology, marketing, accounting, management systems	HRs Information technology Marketing Financial management Management of Quality, Environment and Food Safety Systems

are shown in Table 1.4. The results of these activities contribute towards continual improvement.

d. **Identify sub-processes**

Each core process and sub-process includes several sub-processes, and they are identified in terms of entry and exit criteria as shown in Table 1.5.

e. **Classify management, core, support and assurance processes according to the PDCA cycle**

Figure 1.7 presents a view of the PDCA cycle applied to the processes identified in Step 3.

f. **Identify quality, environment and food safety requirements associated with each process**

Table 1.6 shows quality, environment and food safety requirements applied to some processes.

Table 1.4 Assurance Processes

Control Measures	Verification Activities
In-process controls Efficiency reports Production figures Sales Price Timeliness of delivery Feedback Accuracy of payment Evaluation of training	Audits, non-conformance work reviews, corrective and preventive actions, equipment calibration, monitoring and data analysis, management reviews Sales performance, audits Audits Supplier performance Customer services Financial audits Performance reviews

Table 1.5 Identification of Sub-processes

Process	Entry Criteria	Exit Criteria	Activities
Purchasing	Select suppliers	Receive goods	Evaluate suppliers, generate specifications, purchasing data, the process, verification of purchased product
Production	Plan production	Send finished goods to the warehouse	Production planning, process control, manage resources, validate processes, control specifications, control identification and traceability of products, review non-conforming product
Design	Design requirements	Design output	All design activities
Storage and distribution	Receive finished goods	Deliver goods to customer	Store goods, assemble orders, package and deliver, stock management, manage non-conforming goods
Order fulfilment	Take order	Generate pick list	Determine customer requirements, customer communication, order process
Information technology	Request for information services support	Completeness of service	Control of documents, backup, knowledge management, help desk, software and hardware management
Sales and marketing	Request for sales marketing information and support	Provision of information and support to customers	Product development, promotions, sales visits, customer communication
HRs	Request for HR support	Provision of HR services	Training, recruitment, induction, dismissal, promotion, performance review leave, internal communication
Financial management	Receipt of invoices, orders and request for financial support	Payments and financial reports	Payroll, accounts payable, accounts receivable, taxes, GST, budget preparation, reports
Management of Quality, Environment and Food Safety Systems	Goals and objectives	Systems and procedures to meet objectives and goals	Planning and management, provision of resources, continual improvement

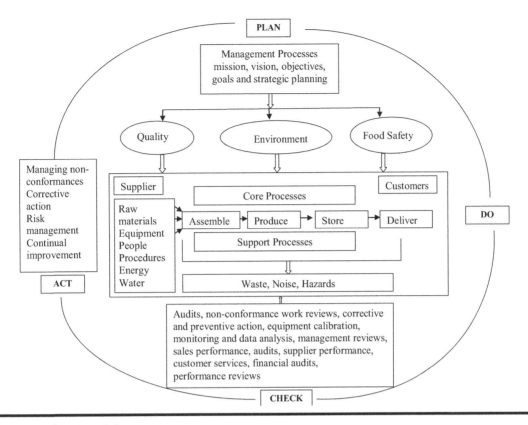

Figure 1.7   Proposed IMS model.

Table 1.6   Quality, Food Safety and Environmental Requirements Associated with Some Processes

Process	Quality Requirements	Environment Requirements	Food Safety Requirements
Planning (P)	Achieve product quality, customer satisfaction and continuous improvement	Planning to reduce undesirable impact on the environment, customer satisfaction and continuous improvement	Planning to control food safety hazards, customer satisfaction and continuous improvement
Approval of suppliers (D)	Ability to meet quality, cost and delivery requirements	Ability to meet environmental requirements, necessary processes, environmental permits, cost and delivery requirements	Ability to meet food safety requirements, cost and delivery requirements
Customer satisfaction (C)	Customer views and perception of the organisation, its processes and goods and services	Customer views and perception of the organisation on environmental issues, evaluate compliance with legal requirements and voluntary obligations	Customer views and perception of the organisation, its processes and its goods and services, particularly with regard to food safety
Managing non-conformances (A)	Detail structure of how to deal with non-conformity	Detail structure of how to deal with non-conformity	Detail structure of how to deal with non-conformity and disposal of unsafe product

g. **Develop procedures using the information gained in Step 5**

These procedures form the framework for the IMS. A business activity model can now be constructed (Figure 1.8). This model is based on the quality, environment and food safety requirements of the organisation and is not related to the ISO standards and reflects the business activities of the organisation that the employees are familiar with.

Integration of quality, environment and food safety

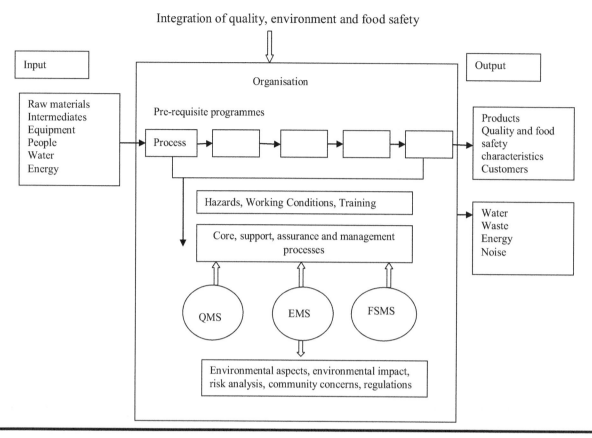

Figure 1.8   Business activity model.

1.8.1.3 Stage 3: Integration

a. **Perform a gap analysis**

In order to comply with ISO 9001, ISO 14001 and ISO 22000 standards, this model has to be evaluated against their requirements. This process enables the organisations to identify: (a) common elements; (b) integrable elements; (c) parallel elements and (d) separate elements (Rößler & Schlieter, 2015) in the three standards. The IMS model is structured on the basis of this classification.

  i. Common elements: In this category, all three standards share common elements. For example, the HL structure is identical in all three standards. Structural similarity, content similarity/identity and absence of functional specificity are characteristics of identical elements.

 ii. Integrable elements: Integrable elements include common elements and functional-specific requirements. The characteristics of integrable elements are: (a) structural similarity; (b) differences in content; (c) whole-part relationship between management aspects (d) and function-specific extensions of common elements. For example, the purchasing procedure is identical in all three standards.

But quality, environment and food safety have functional-specific requirements. The focus of the QMS is the quality of the product or service. The EMS requires the supplier to have an environmentally friendly environment and deliver environmentally friendly material, whereas the focus of the food safety system is the safety of the products for human consumption.

iii. Parallel elements: The elements in parallel/semi-integrable requirements are similar in structure, differ in content and cannot be reasonably combined. For example, the requirement for a management representative and their role is common in all three standards. However, a total combination is not meaningful because of the strong diversity of specialisation requirements.

 iv. Separate elements: In this category are elements unique to each standard, and these cannot be combined. These elements and function-specific procedures apply specifically to the management system. For example, the identification of environmental aspects is unique to the EMS and has to be treated as a separate procedure. Similarly, HACCP is a food safety system requirement.

1.8.1.4 Stage 4: Monitoring the Effectiveness

a. **Change management**

A significant and genuine effort is required by top management to overcome the obstacles. The following are some of the methods of getting the support of staff to make changes (Ritz-Carlton, 2015):

1. Solicit buy-in prior to implementation of the change.
2. Communicate consistently.
3. Demonstrate commitment and lead by example.
4. Reinforce and remind.
5. Establish accountability.
6. Encourage feedback.
7. Monitor and celebrate success.

b. **Monitor and celebrate success**

Any management system model is a dynamic system. It has to be regularly monitored through management reviews and audits to promote continual improvement and sustainability of the business

1.9 Barriers to Overcome

The adoption of an IMS requires effort and commitment from top management. There are external and internal barriers to overcome (Rößler & Schlieter, 2015):

1.9.1 Internal Barriers

a. Resources: Lack of financial resources, management/staff knowledge, skills and training, employee participation and motivation and inability to allocate time for development and implementation can hinder the progress of the IMS.

b. Attitudes and perceptions: An initial response to any change is resistance, particularly when the change is perceived as revolutionary. Lack of awareness of the benefits of integration, bureaucracy and a focus on short-term orientation are some of the internal barriers.

c. Implementation: Cultural differences between interacting functions, complexity and differences between different management systems and the need for extra effort for implementation can hinder the development of the IMS.

1.9.2 External Barriers

a. Support and guidance: A project of this nature needs support schemes and industry-specific information tools and examples. Consultants may also be necessary for guidance. Poor quality information, conflicting guidance and lack of promotion of the IMS are also external barriers.

b. Economics of implementation: Inadequate drivers and benefits, uncertainty about the benefits of IMS in the marketplace and different stakeholders' demands are some of the economic barriers.

c. Cost of certification and verification: A high cost is involved in certification and verification activities. Inevitably, there is duplication of effort between certifiers, verifiers and internal auditors.

Top management support, training and involvement of the staff at every step are key ingredients of the success of the IMS. An IMS based on sound principles is a boon to the organisation and it satisfies the customers, as well as the organisation, and motivates the staff to perform at their best.

References

Ahsen, A.V. and Funck, D. (2001). Integrated management systems – Opportunities and risks for corporate environmental protection. *Corporate Environmental Strategy*, 8 (2), 165–176.

Antonucci, Y.L. and Bariff, M. (2009). *Business Process Management Common Body of Knowledge (BPM CBok)*, Version 2.0 (2nd ed.). South Carolina: Createspace.

Badreddine, A., Romdhane, T.B. and Amor, N.B. (2009). A new process based approach for implementing an integrated management system: Quality, security and environment. *Proceedings of the International Multi Conference of Engineers and Computer Scientists*, Vol. II, IMECS, March 18–20, 2009. Hong Kong.

Cekanova, K. (2015). Integrated management system – Scope, possibilities and methodology. Slovak University of Technology in Bratislava. *Research Paper 10.1515/rput-2015-0016*, 23 (36), 135–140.

Chandra, P.V. (2013). Implementation of integrated management systems in a manufacturing organisation with effectiveness for sustainable and continuous improvement. *International Journal of Engineering Science and Innovative Technology*, 2 (4), 214–220.

De Silva, T. (2004). *Designing a quality management system for a manufacturing organisation in New Zealand using process mapping supported by knowledge management*. (Unpublished doctoral thesis). California Coast University, California, USA.

EFQM. (2012). An overview of the EFQM Excellence model. Retrieved January 10, 2019 from https://www.bqf.org.uk/wp-content/uploads/2018/06/EFQM-Excellence-Model_abridged.pdf.

Hines, F. (2002). Integrated management systems – inclusivity of approach or dilution of problems? *Poster presentation at 10th International Conference of the Greening of Industry Network*. Sweden.

Hortensius, D., Bergenhenegouwen, L., Gouwens, R. and De Jong, A. (2004). Towards a generic model for integrating management systems. *ISO Management Systems*, 3 (6), 21–28.

Jensen, F. (2016). Integrated management system: Combining other standards with ISO 9001.

Jorgensen, T.M., Remmen, T.H. and Mellado, M.D. (2006). Integrated management systems: Three different levels of integration. *Journal of Cleaner Production*, 14 (8), 713–722.

Kannegiesser, M. (2008). *Value Chain Management in the Chemical Industry: Global Value Chain Planning and Commodities*. Germany: Physica-Verlag.

OpenLearn. (2017). *Integrated safety, health and environmental management: An introduction: Section 4.2: Why integrate management systems*. Retrieved January 10, 2019 from http://www.open.edu/openlearn/science-maths-technology/computing-and-ict/systems-computer/integrated-safety-health-and-environmental-management-introduction/content-section-4.2.

Patience, M.M.A. (2008). *Integrated management systems: A qualitative study of the levels of integration of three Danish companies*. (Master of Science Thesis in Engineering in Environmental Management). Aalborg University, Denmark. Retrieved June 30, 2017 from http://projekter.aau.dk/projekter/files/14167463/10th_semester_thesis.doc.

Quality Austria. (2012). *Succeed with Quality. Document No: RE_00_70e, Position IMS* (2nd ed.). Austria: Quality Austria.

Ritz-Carlton. (2015). *Seven ways to engage employees in change management*. Retrieved March 18, 2018 from http://ritzcarltonleadershipcenter.com/2015/08/change-management/.

Rößler, R. and Schlieter, H. (2015). Towards model-based integration of management systems. In O. Thomas. and F. Teuteberg, (Eds.), *Proceedings of the 12th International Conference on Wirtschaftsinformatik*, March 4–6, 2015, pp. 31–45. Germany: Osnabrück.

Stamou, T. (2003). Integrated management systems in small medium-sized enterprises: Theory and practice. (Master of Science Thesis), University of East Anglia, UK. Retrieved June 26, 2018 from https://www.uea.ac.uk/documents/541248/10797368/Stamou+Fanis.pdf/21065476-1976-4f59-b573-a002baf0337f.

Standards Australia. (2003). *Guidance on Integrating the Requirements of Quality, Environment and Health and Safety Management Systems*. Australia: Standards Australia.

Sturgeon, T.J. and Gereffi, G. (2008). *The challenges of global value chains: Why integrative trade requires new thinking and new data*. Prepared for Industry Canada. Retrieved March 10, 2018 from http://citeseerx.ist.psu.edu/viewdoc/download?doi=10.1.1.364.8489&rep=rep1&type=pdf.

Surkov, I.V., Kantere, V.M., Motovilov, K.Ya. and Ranzyaeva, T.V. (2015). The development of an integrated management system to ensure the quality, stability and food safety. *Foods and Raw Materials*, 3 (1), 111–119.

Tangen, S. and Warris, A.M. (2012). Management makeover: New format for future ISO management system standards. *International Organisation for Standardisation (ISO)*. Retrieved July 03, 2017 from https://www.iso.org/news/2012/07/Ref1621.html.

Wilkinson, G. and Dale, B.G. (2001). Integrated management systems: Model based on a total quality approach. *Managing Services Quality*, 11 (5), 318–330.

MANAGEMENT PROCEDURES 1

BMS 000 Business Management System

ABC Company Limited	Business Management System	Reference BMS 000 Page 1 of 8	
	Introduction to Procedures Manual	Date Released dd/mm/yyyy	Date Reviewed dd/mm/yyyy
Policy Manual	Approved:	Issue No: 01 Prepared by:	Revision No: 00

Process Owner		QA Manager
	Process Headings	**Process Details**
1.0	Purpose	To describe the integration and the management system to our stakeholders.
2.0	Mission and vision MP 000	Our mission and vision are described in our procedures manual.
3.0	Context MP 001	1. ABCCL has identified external and internal factors arising from legal, political, economic, social and technological issues that may impact on our strategic direction and our organisational context. 2. ABCCL has identified, analysed, monitored and reviewed the factors that may affect our ability to satisfy our stakeholders and may have an adverse influence on the stability and integrity of our processes and our management system. 3. ABCCL also has identified and analysed issues that have the potential to be affected by our products and services.
4.0	Needs of internal and external stakeholders MP 002	ABCCL has identified interested parties that are relevant to our Integrated Quality, Food Safety and Environmental (IQFSE) management system, determined their needs and assessed the impact or potential impact on our products, services and the management system.
5.0	Scope MP 004	1. ABCCL has described the scope of the IQFSE management system to implement our objectives and policies relevant to external and internal issues, needs of interested parties and our products and services. 2. The scope can be assessed through our webpage.
6.0	IQFSE management system MP 005	ABCCL has developed and maintained an integrated management system comprising quality, food safety and environmental activities related to our products and services. It includes the field of application of the IQFSE management system, documented procedures created for the management system and references to those procedures and a description of process interactions.
7.0	IQFSE management system processes MP 006	ABBCL has adopted the process approach and determined the processes required to achieve intended outputs. Four process groups are defined and by managing their inputs, activities, controls, outputs and interfaces, ABCCL ensures that system effectiveness is maintained.

ABC Company Limited	Business Management System	Reference BMS 000 Page 2 of 8	
	Introduction to Procedures Manual	Date Released dd/mm/yyyy	Date Reviewed dd/mm/yyyy
Policy Manual	Approved:	Issue No: 01 Prepared by:	Revision No: 00

	Process Headings	Process Details
8.0	Management commitment MP 010	Management commitment is demonstrated through the continual communication of quality, food safety and environmental requirements; implementing and supporting objectives, policies and plans; providing necessary resources and participating in improvement activities.
9.0	Legal requirements MP 003	ABCCL has identified and maintained legal, regulatory and other related requirements applicable to quality, food safety and environmental activities and the procedure provides identification and access to these requirements.
10.0	Objectives and policies MP 008, MP 009	1. ABBCL has developed policy statements for quality, food safety and environmental activities as a commitment to continually improve these activities across our operations. Policies form the focal point for the IQFSE management system with a series of supporting procedures to enable the fulfilment of the policy commitments. 2. Objectives which are consistent with policy statements are established at relevant levels and functions within the operations of ABCCL.
11.0	Risk management MP 007	ABCCL has identified and assessed hazards, risks and opportunities associated with our operations and implemented necessary control measures.
12.0	Roles and responsibilities MP 011	Roles and responsibilities are defined in job description and in individual procedures. The organisation structure shows the levels of responsibilities.
13.0	Planning processes MP 012, MP 013, MP 014, MP 015, MP 007, CP 013, CP 023, MP 018, CP 036, CP 037, CP 027, MP 020, MP 019	IQFSE management system defines several planning processes to meet statutory and regulatory requirements, customer requirements and the requirements of the IQFSE management: • Operational planning • Strategic planning • Production planning • Risk management planning • Design and development planning • Business continuity planning • Emergency planning • Sales and marketing planning • Hazard Analysis and Critical Control Point (HACCP) planning • Change management planning.

ABC Company Limited	Business Management System		Reference BMS 000 Page 3 of 8	
	Introduction to Procedures Manual		Date Released dd/mm/yyyy	Date Reviewed dd/mm/yyyy
Policy Manual	Approved:		Issue No: 01 Prepared by:	Revision No: 00

	Process Headings	Process Details
14.0	Customer-related processes MP 016, CP 016, CP 011, SP 047, SP 046	1. ABCCL has established the following customer-related processes: Customer focus Customer requirements Customer property Customer complaints Customer satisfaction. 2. ABCCL strives to identify current and future customer needs to meet and exceed their expectations and maintain by setting and reviewing objectives related to customer satisfaction at management review meetings. 3. These requirements are understood, converted to internal requirements and communicated to relevant functions of ABCCL. Customer complaints and customer feedback are continually monitored and measured to identify opportunities for improvement.
15.0	Resources SP 009, SP 010, SP 011–SP 020, SP 021–SP 031	Resources at ABCCL include human resources and specialised skills, infrastructure, technology, equipment, work environment and financial. Our procedures define the resource requirements for the implementation, management, control and continual improvement of the IQFSE management system, the maintenance of a safe work environment and the activities necessary to improve customer satisfaction.
16.0	Purchasing and external provision CP 001–CP 007, SP 045	ABCCL selects suppliers and contractors on their ability to meet our requirements, delivered on time and at the right price. All suppliers and contractors are subject to approval of suppliers and offer of contract procedures. The extent of control depends on the impact of the supplied product or process has on our products and services. All suppliers and contractors have been made aware of quality, food safety and environmental and regulatory requirements; delivery and price. A list of approved suppliers is maintained and reviewed annually.

ABC Company Limited	Business Management System		Reference BMS 000 Page 4 of 8	
	Introduction to Procedures Manual		Date Released dd/mm/yyyy	Date Reviewed dd/mm/yyyy
Policy Manual	Approved:		Issue No: 01 Prepared by:	Revision No: 00

	Process Headings	Process Details
17.0	Production CP 009, CP 012, MP 021	ABBCL has established, implemented and maintained documented plans and procedures that describe the processes and controls necessary for the provision of products and services. Procedures define the identification of requirements for products and services, criteria for acceptance, resource requirements and control measures.
18.0	Design and development CP 013, CP 020	ABCCL has established, implemented and maintained procedures to control and verify design activities to ensure that specified requirements are met. These procedures include design planning, design input/output, design verification and design changes and the completion of the design plan report.
19.0	Handling and storage CP 015, CP 041	Materials and products delivered to the site internally or externally are received, processed, stored and despatched in an appropriate and established safe and recognised manner to ensure no significant damage, deterioration or harm occurs that could result in reduction in material quality, safety and/or any potential statutory or environmental consequences.
20.0	Order processing CP 017, CP 018, CP 019, CP 021, CP 022	1. ABCCL reviews all enquiries, orders and contracts from customers to ensure that requirements can be met in full and issues resolved. Requirements not specified by the customer but required for product or service implementation and fulfilment of compliance obligations are also included in this process. 2. Determination of output product/service requirement includes any statutory and regulatory requirements applicable to the activity, post-delivery activities and any additional requirements considered necessary by ABCCL.
21.0	Emergency planning MP 017, MP 018, CP 023, CP 029	ABCCL has established and maintained a procedure to identify potential emergency situations and respond to accidents, incidents and emergency situations and for preventing and mitigating the likely occurrence of such events. They are reviewed and revised when necessary and in particular after the occurrence of such an event. Response plans include business continuity plans and food recall plans.

ABC Company Limited	Business Management System	Reference BMS 000 Page 5 of 8	
	Introduction to Procedures Manual	Date Released dd/mm/yyyy	Date Reviewed dd/mm/yyyy
Policy Manual	Approved:	Issue No: 01 Prepared by:	Revision No: 00

	Process Headings	Process Details
22.0	HACCP programme CP 024–CP 028	To ensure food safety, ABCCL has established and maintained an HACCP programme to ensure that food items are received, produced, stored and delivered under controlled conditions. The programme includes hazard assessment, HACCP plan, identification of Critical Control Points (CCPs), pre-requisite programmes and establishing a control schedule.
23.0	Environmental programme CP 030–CP 035	IQFSE management system incorporates environmental requirements in activities that have an impact on the environment from receiving raw materials to final despatch to customers. This is achieved by conducting an Initial Environmental Review (IER), identification and assessment of significant environmental aspects and managing environmental impacts.
24.0	Communication CP 040, SP 005, SP 006, SP 007, SP 029, SP 048	ABCCL has established and maintained a procedure for internal communication between various levels and functions and procedure for external communication for receiving, documenting and responding to relevant communications from external interested parties.
25.0	Document management SP 001, SP 002, SP 025–SP 028, SP 031, AP 001ç	A documented information system is maintained to provide evidence of conformity to IQFSE management system, customer and regulatory requirements. For electronic documents, a computer back-up system is maintained to provide appropriate document and data protection. All control documents are identified, approved, reviewed, updated and controlled in accordance with the document control procedure and record control procedure.
26.0	Maintenance management SP 003, SP 004	A maintenance management programme is in place to ensure that all essential machinery and equipment are reliable and maintained. A calibration schedule is maintained to ensure that they are calibrated at specified intervals.

ABC Company Limited	Business Management System		Reference BMS 000 Page 6 of 8	
	Introduction to Procedures Manual		Date Released dd/mm/yyyy	Date Reviewed dd/mm/yyyy
Policy Manual	Approved:		Issue No: 01 Prepared by:	Revision No: 00

	Process Headings	Process Details
27.0	Financial management SP 036–SP 044	ABCCL has established and maintained procedures for managing ABCCL's financial resources. They include budgeting, accounts payable and receivable; internal controls; payment of wages and salaries; management of financial accounts; preparation of management accounts and credit card management.
28.0	Sales and marketing CP 036–CP 040, SP 032, SP 035	Sales and marketing programmes are in place to enhance communication between ABCCL and its customers. Sales programme identifies customer requirements and provides support to customers. Marketing programme includes brand management, advertising and promotion, market forecast and market research.
29.0	Technology management SP 021–SP 031	An effective programme has been established and maintained to provide technological support in terms of communication media, managing software and hardware, security, managing electronic documents through storage, access, back-up and recovery and necessary support to users.
30.0	Verification activities CP 008, CP 010, CP 014, SP 039, AP 011	1. ABCCL has established and maintained procedures for the verification of products and material according to documented procedures prior to use (inwards goods inspection), during production (in-control tests) and prior to delivery (release of finished goods) to achieve conformance verification to quality, food safety and environmental requirements. 2. Controlled conditions include the availability and use of specifications and work instructions, monitoring at various stages of production, use of standard working methods and identification of acceptance criteria.
31.0	Performance evaluation AP 002, AP 003, AP 004	1. ABCCL applies suitable methods to identify the aspects of the IQFSE management system and its processes to be measured and analysed. All monitoring, measuring and evaluating items are analysed to determine the effectiveness of processes and compliance to requirements. 2. Services are only delivered after all compliance requirements have been completed.

ABC Company Limited	Business Management System	Reference BMS 000 Page 7 of 8	
	Introduction to Procedures Manual	Date Released dd/mm/yyyy	Date Reviewed dd/mm/yyyy
Policy Manual	Approved:	Issue No: 01 Prepared by:	Revision No: 00

	Process Headings	Process Details
32.0	Validation AP 009, AP 010	ABCCL has a programme to validate processes to ensure that planned results can be achieved. Validation is also applied during design and development phases.
33.0	Identification and traceability AP 007	1. ABCCL maintains procedures for identifying products and material from receipt to all stages of production, storage and delivery. Where traceability is a specified requirement, ABCCL has established and maintained procedures for unique identification of products and material. 2. Status of products and material is identified using appropriate labels.
34.0	Management review AP 005	1. Management reviews are conducted at specified intervals to ensure continuing adequacy, effectiveness and suitability of the IQFSE management system. The review includes opportunities for improvement and the need for changes to the management system. 2. Series of inputs are considered when conducting the management review. Actions to be taken include the improvement of the effectiveness of the management system, improvement of product related to customer requirements, address opportunities and risks and provide necessary resources.
35.0	Continual improvement AP 006, SP 048	The effectiveness of the IQFSE management system is continually improved through the use of communication, management review, internal audits, analysis of results of verification activities, validation of control measures and combination of control measures, corrective actions and updating the management system.
36.0	Internal audits AP 012	ABBCL conducts internal audits at specified intervals to verify the use and effectiveness of the management system. The audit programme is scheduled and distributed considering the status and importance of the processes to be audited as well as previous audit results.

ABC Company Limited	Business Management System	Reference BMS 000 Page 8 of 8	
	Introduction to Procedures Manual	Date Released dd/mm/yyyy	Date Reviewed dd/mm/yyyy
Policy Manual	Approved:	Issue No: 01 Prepared by:	Revision No: 00

	Process Headings	Process Details
37.0	Non-conformance and corrective actions AP 008, AP 013	1. ABCCL has established and maintained procedures to manage non-conforming products, processes and services to promote continual improvement of the IQFSE management system. 2. Corrective actions are implemented to address non-conformities and related causes. 3. Preventive actions are implemented proactively to address events that have the potential to cause injury, environmental harm and non-conformance.
38.0	Knowledge management SP 008	ABCCL has established and maintained a procedure for acquisition, coding, storing, distributing and assessing relevant knowledge for managing IQFSE management system and its processes.

MP 000 Our Company

ABC Company Limited	Procedures Manual		Reference MP 000 Page 1 of 2	
	Our Company		Date Released dd/mm/yyyy	Date Reviewed dd/mm/yyyy
Management Process	Approved:		Issue No: 01 Prepared by:	Revision No: 00

1.0 Purpose

This document describes our company.

2.0 About Our Company

Our organisation is specialising in producing premium wines to the local and international export markets. We have a 60% share of the local market. We export our products to the UK, Japan, the USA, Canada and several other Asian countries. We have a workforce of about 120 permanent employees. We source grapes from local growers on a renewable contract. In addition, we provide laboratory services and winemaking technology to other organisations. Our viticulturists visit our grape growers and ensure that their operations are conducted under controlled conditions, and comply with all regulatory requirements and our own requirements. During the picking and crushing season, we employ temporary staff who have provided their services for many years. We have many functional departments, which conduct their business activities through our policies, procedures and work instructions, which have been documented in our Integrated Quality, Food Safety and Environmental (IQFSE) management system.

The outputs of the IQFSE management system are as follows:

- Demonstrates our ability to consistently provide products and services that meet customers' expectations and statutory and regulatory requirements
- Enhances customer satisfaction through the effective application and implementation of IQFSE management system procedures and processes for the assurance of conformity to customer needs, statutory and regulatory requirements and relevant ISO standards
- Enhances environmental performance and protects the environment
- Fulfilment of quality, food safety and environmental objectives.

ABC Company Limited	Procedures Manual	Reference MP 000 Page 2 of 2	
	Our Company	Date Released dd/mm/yyyy	Date Reviewed dd/mm/yyyy
Management Process	Approved:	Issue No: 01 Prepared by:	Revision No: 00

3.0 Mission Statement

ABCCL has been producing and selling premium wines to the local and export market for over 22 years. We are dedicated to producing premium wines to satisfy all market segments by working with our grape growers to improve the quality of our grapes, adopting modern wine technology, enhancing the image of our products while focusing on social values of the community and minimising our environmental impact.

4.0 Vision

To supply the global market with the best quality market at any given price point.

MP 001 Internal and External Issues

ABC Company Limited	Procedures Manual	Reference MP 001 Page 1 of 4	
	Internal and External Issues	Date Released dd/mm/yyyy	Date Reviewed dd/mm/yyyy
Management Process	Approved:	Issue No: 01 Prepared by:	Revision No: 00

Process Owner		Management Team
	Process Headings	**Process Details**
1.0	Purpose	To describe the internal and external issues affecting the performance of our organisation.
2.0	Scope	Applies to all products and services offered by our organisation.
3.0	Input	External political, economic, societal and technology factors, strengths, weaknesses of ABCCL, opportunities for improvement and growth and threats imposed by internal and external environment.
4.0	Output	External issues which are applicable to the purpose of our organisation Internal issues which are applicable to the purpose of our organisation Environmental conditions that are affected by ABCCL's operations.
5.0	Competencies	Knowledge of external environment, internal issues, management system standards, ability to use PEST (political, economic, social, technological) and SWOT (strengths, weaknesses, opportunities and threats) tools.
6.0	Responsibilities	The Management Team is responsible for defining and monitoring the context of our organisation.
7.0	Associated documents	Vision and mission of the organisation SWOT analysis (Form 005) PEST analysis (Form 004) Internal and external issues (Form 002).
8.0	Resources	Tools for identifying the needs such as SWOT and PEST.
9.0	Measures and controls	Reviews of context Management review.
10.0	Definitions	**Context:** "Combination of internal and external issues that can have on effect on an organisation's approach to developing and achieving its objectives".[a] **External context:** External stakeholders, the operating environment and external factors that influence the selection and achievement of objectives. **Internal context:** Interested parties, approach to governance, relationship with contractors and the organisation's capabilities, culture and standards.

ABC Company Limited	Procedures Manual	Reference MP 001 Page 2 of 4	
	Internal and External Issues	Date Released dd/mm/yyyy	Date Reviewed dd/mm/yyyy
Management Process	Approved:	Issue No: 01 Prepared by:	Revision No: 00

	Process Headings	Process Details
11.0	System description	Context is the operating environment of the organisation. To establish the context, we define the external and internal factors that the organisation must consider when we manage risks. Internal and external contexts are defined in Form 001.
11.1	Identifying internal and external issues	Management Team conducts brainstorming sessions to gather relevant information. The team seeks input from the staff about internal and external issues that affect the performance of their activities.
11.2	Sources of information	These sources may be used to determine internal issues: • Internal audit results and management review records • Analysis of the cost of quality data • Analysis of technology and trend information • Competitive analysis • Results of customer surveys, complaints and audits • Actual versus intended internal values and culture • Performance of the organisation • Best practices of the organisation and the industry • Employee satisfaction surveys • SWOT analysis. These sources may be used to determine external issues: • Economic environment and trends • International trade conditions and agreements • Competitive products and service • Issues related to outsourcing • Technology trends • Availability of raw materials and their prices • Statutory and regulatory changes • Benchmarks both within and outside the industry • PEST analysis.

ABC Company Limited	Procedures Manual	Reference MP 001 Page 3 of 4	
	Internal and External Issues	Date Released dd/mm/yyyy	Date Reviewed dd/mm/yyyy
Management Process	Approved:	Issue No: 01 Prepared by:	Revision No: 00

	Process Headings	**Process Details**
11.3	Environmental issues	Management Team shall consider the environmental issues when identifying internal and external issues: • Air quality, both local and global impact • Water quality and soil contamination • Land use • Existing contamination and remedial issues • Depletion of natural resources • Impact on the local ecology and biodiversity • Wider community concerns.
11.4	PEST analysis	PEST analysis is carried out by the Management Team. PEST factors identify the external factors that influence ABCCL's operations. ABCCL cannot control these factors but shall seek to adapt to them. An example of a PEST analysis is shown in Form 004.
11.5	SWOT analysis	A SWOT analysis is an analytical tool used to evaluate an organisation's strengths, weaknesses, opportunities and threats. Identifying these factors helps organisations make decisions that align with their goals (Form 005).
11.6	Monitoring and reviewing of internal and external issues	The Management Team shall monitor and review internal and external issues at least annually at the management review meeting. Changes to the external environment, products, processes, services, equipment and regulations may require more frequent reviews (Form 003).
11.7	External and internal issues evaluation	External and internal issues are evaluated annually by our Management Team, and the information forms the basis for our strategic plan. Issues may reflect direct concerns (such as the quality of products or services offered by us) or indirect concerns (such as the display of our products in the market). Issues may be internal or external and are derived from the SWOT and PEST analyses.

ABC Company Limited	Procedures Manual	Reference MP 001 Page 4 of 4	
	Internal and External Issues	Date Released dd/mm/yyyy	Date Reviewed dd/mm/yyyy
Management Process	Approved:	Issue No: 01 Prepared by:	Revision No: 00

	Process Headings	Process Details
		At the time of assessment, these issues are reviewed and, if necessary, others are also considered. The significance of their impact is determined by a risk analysis. The strategic direction is defined by the mission, vision, strategic objective, goals and targets.
11.8	Strategic direction	List of internal and external issues Results of PEST and SWOT analyses.
12.0	Records	None.
13.0	Changes made	None.

[a] ISO 9000:2015 (en). *Quality Management System: Fundamentals and Vocabulary.* Retrieved June 2, 2016 from https://www.iso.org/obp/ui/#iso:std:iso:9000:ed-4:v1:en.

MP 002 Interested Parties

ABC Company Limited	Procedures Manual	Reference MP 002 Page 1 of 2	
	Interested Parties	Date Released dd/mm/yyyy	Date Reviewed dd/mm/yyyy
Management Process	Approved:	Issue No: 01 Prepared by:	Revision No: 00

Process Owner	Management Team	
	Process Headings	**Process Details**
1.0	Purpose	To identify and determine the needs of external and internal interested parties.
2.0	Scope	This procedure applies to both internal and external stakeholders.
3.0	Input	Information on internal and external stakeholders that the company deals with.
4.0	Output	List of external stakeholders and their needs, list of internal stakeholders and their needs and compliance obligations.
5.0	Competency requirements	Knowledge of external and internal environments, brainstorming skills and compliance obligations.
6.0	Responsibility	Defined in Flowchart MP 002.1.
7.0	Associated documents	Internal interested parties (Form 007) External interested parties (Form 006) Impact of needs (Form 008).
8.0	Resources	None.
9.0	Measures and controls	Management review Integrated Quality, Food Safety and Environmental (IQFSE) management system performance.
10.0	Definitions	**Interested party:** A person or an organisation that can affect, be affected by or be perceived to be affected by, a decision or an activity within the organisation. **Compliance obligations:** All relevant legal requirements, all relevant requirements imposed by higher authorities (e.g. corporate requirements) and all relevant requirements that we decide to comply with whether by contract (e.g. contractors) or voluntarily (e.g. environmental commitment).
11.0	System description	Flowchart MP 002.1 shows the process of identifying and assessing the needs of interested parties Form 007 shows some examples of internal interest groups Form 006 shows some examples of external interest groups Form 008 shows the impact of these needs on business activities.

ABC Company Limited	Procedures Manual	Reference MP 002 Page 2 of 2	
	Interested Parties	Date Released dd/mm/yyyy	Date Reviewed dd/mm/yyyy
Management Process	Approved:	Issue No: 01 Prepared by:	Revision No: 00

	Process Headings	Process Details
11.1	Issues of concern	1. A party such as the labour union leadership may be identified as an interested party, but the company is not obliged to develop policies and documents related to them. Issues may reflect direct concerns such as the quality of products or services or indirect concerns. Such concerns may impact on the interested party or may be issues derived from the party that impact on the company. 2. When identifying internal concerns consider issues such as technological issues and employee concerns. When external concerns are identified, consider competition, social issues, culture, labour relations, statutory and regulatory requirements, supply chain, economic issues, etc.
11.2	Risk analysis	These issues are subject to risk analysis.
11.3	Monitoring and reviewing of internal and external interested parties	The Management Team shall monitor and review internal and external issues at least annually at the management review meeting. Changes to the external environment, products, processes, services, equipment and regulations may require more frequent reviews.
11.4	Strategic direction	Our strategic direction is defined by the following: • The purpose of our organisation • Our mission • Our vision • Strategic plan, its implementation and its performance. Internal and external issues, as well as the needs of interested parties, are considered in the strategic planning process.
12.0	Records	List of interested parties Needs of interested parties.
13.0	Changes made	None.

ABC Company Limited	Procedures Manual	Flowchart MP 002.1 Page 1 of 1	
	Interested Parties	Date Released dd/mm/yyyy	Date Reviewed dd/mm/yyyy
Link MP 002	Approved:	Issue No: 01 Prepared by:	Revision No: 00

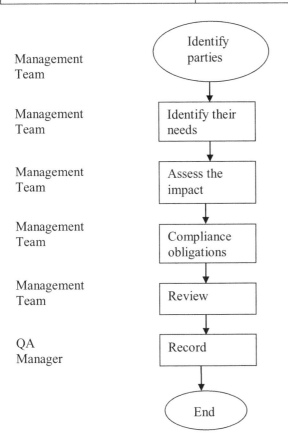

Management Team — Identify parties — Management Team identifies internal and external stakeholders through a brainstorming session. Members identify stakeholders that they deal with in their business activities

Management Team — Identify their needs

Management Team — Assess the impact — Assess how these needs impact on products, services and business activities

Management Team — Compliance obligations — Determine which are compliance obligations

Management Team — Review — Review at least annually or when changes to products, services, business activities, external and internal environment occur.

QA Manager — Record — List of internal and external issues
List of interested parties

End

MP 003 Statutory and Regulatory Requirements

ABC Company Limited	Procedures Manual	Reference MP 003 Page 1 of 5	
	Statutory and Regulatory Requirements	Date Released dd/mm/yyyy	Date Reviewed dd/mm/yyyy
Management Process	Approved:	Issue No: 01 Prepared by:	Revision No: 00

Process Owner	Legal Team Consisting of the Plant Manager, QA Manager, Food Safety Manager and Environment Manager	
	Process Headings	**Process Details**
1.0	Purpose	To identify and update statutory and regulatory requirements applicable to ABCCL's operations and to maintain access to these requirements.
2.0	Scope	This procedure applies to all ABCCL's operations, contract requirements, business codes of practice, benchmarks, guidance notes and other practice reports generated by government agencies and professional bodies. They include both mandatory and voluntary requirements.
3.0	Input	Applicable statutory and regulatory requirements, voluntary codes of practice, organisation and industry standards; contractual obligations; principles of good governance and community and ethical standards.
4.0	Output	Register of legal and other requirements, awareness and understanding of legal and other requirements relevant to the functions, compliance with legal requirements and other requirements, better community relations, better management of the environment and reports, memos or other methods used to convey the information to the staff.
5.0	Competency requirements	Knowledge of company's environmental aspects of activities, understanding the requirements of the Integrated Quality, Food Safety and Environmental (IQFSE) management system, knowledge of the relevant ISO standards, legislation, codes of practice, benchmarks, processes and products within his or her area and database maintenance.
6.0	Responsibility	Defined in Flowchart MP 003.1. Additional responsibilities are: Plant Manager shall: • Pay subscriptions • Obtain required licences and permits for operation. QA Manager shall: • Communicate the requirements to the staff. Department Managers shall: • Inform the Management Team of any changes relevant to their functions or departments to ensure that up-to-date copies of relevant legal and other requirements relevant to their functions can be obtained and accessed.

ABC Company Limited	Procedures Manual		Reference MP 003 Page 2 of 5	
	Statutory and Regulatory Requirements		Date Released dd/mm/yyyy	Date Reviewed dd/mm/yyyy
Management Process	Approved:		Issue No: 01 Prepared by:	Revision No: 00

	Process Headings	Process Details
7.0	Associated documents	Items for identifying legal requirements (Form 009) Determining the relevance of legislation (Form 010) Compliance plan (Form 011) Compliance evaluation form (Form 012).
8.0	Resources	Database.
9.0	Measures/controls	Number of obsolete legal and other requirements in use Awareness and understanding of the requirements Number of legal non-compliant issues.
10.0	Definitions	**Statutory requirements:** Laws passed by the state and/or central government. **Regulatory requirements:** Rules issued by a regulatory body appointed by the state or central government.
11.0	System description	Flowchart MP 003.1 shows the procedure for determining legal and other requirements.
11.1	Inventory	The Legal Team shall compile a list of activities, substances, products and services that demonstrate a significant environmental aspect or fall under local, regional and national legislation.
11.2	Application of legislation	1. Form 009 shows the information required for identifying the relevant legislation. The Legal Team shall determine the relevance by examining whether there are special provisions such as limitations on working hours and processes above a certain size or output. The organisation's special circumstances shall then be matched to the regulatory requirements to determine specific requirements attached to permits, licences contracts and consents (Form 010). 2. The Plant Manager shall appoint an external consultant if sufficient knowledge does not exist in the organisation and find the personnel, resources and expertise required for the project.

ABC Company Limited	Procedures Manual	Reference MP 003 Page 3 of 5	
	Statutory and Regulatory Requirements	Date Released dd/mm/yyyy	Date Reviewed dd/mm/yyyy
Management Process	Approved:	Issue No: 01 Prepared by:	Revision No: 00

	Process Headings	Process Details
11.3	Acquire	Plant Manager shall acquire the relevant legislation from original sources. QA Manager shall maintain a register of the legislation (Form 013).
11.4	Legal requirements database	1. QA Manager shall enter a database of legal requirements. The documents may be classified as follows: • Air emission control • Codes of practice • Professional guidelines • Technical circulars and memos • Noise control • Waste management • Water pollution • Food safety regulations • Others. At a minimum, the database shall consist of the these fields: • Title • Description • Date of acquisition • Regulator • Main requirements • Applicable to • Applicable area • Effective date and renewal date • Licences/permits • Distribution list.
11.5	Communication and access	Access shall be granted to users according to the document control procedure (SP 001). The users shall be directed first to the overview in Form 013 and those who need detailed information shall be directed to the database. The Legal Team shall ensure that the information is understood by the relevant staff.
11.6	Review of legal requirements	To maintain up-to-date regulations, the Legal Team shall track the regulatory requirements applicable to the organisation's operations and review the register every 6 months, or when relevant information becomes available, or when these changes occur: • Modification of product design and development • New processes or changes to existing processes • New technology • Changes to point sources of emissions and discharges • Changes in inventory levels of regulatory substances • Modifications to drainage patterns and introduction of new drainage systems • Significant reduction or expansion of capacity • Extension of the plant or relocation • Temporary construction projects, installations, etc.

ABC Company Limited	Procedures Manual	Reference MP 003 Page 4 of 5	
	Statutory and Regulatory Requirements	Date Released dd/mm/yyyy	Date Reviewed dd/mm/yyyy
Management Process	Approved:	Issue No: 01 Prepared by:	Revision No: 00

	Process Headings	Process Details
11.7	Update	Some employees may need hard copies of the legislation relevant to their activities. The QA Manager shall ensure that the most up-to-date copies of the requirements are made available to relevant employees. QA Manager shall control the hard copies of documents (e.g. regulations, code of practices, technical memoranda) according to the document control procedure.
11.8	Ensure compliance	The Plant Manager shall provide both the technical and non-technical resources needed to ensure compliance by assessing the impact of requirements on operations, technical provisions, organisational requirements, defining critical limits for food operations, further studies, necessary notifications, obligatory monitoring and monitoring reporting.
11.9	Evaluation of compliance	1. A legal compliance audit shall be conducted once every 6 months. It shall include: (a) permits, licences and consents; (b) notifications, publications by government authorities and responses; (c) compliance to other requirements and (d) updating of legal and other requirements. 2. A legal compliance audit shall be conducted by a qualified in-house person or a third party. Qualified personnel/third party shall hold a minimum of 2 years of relevant experience or equivalent combination of training and formal education in legal compliance. The Legal Team shall prepare an evaluation checklist (Form 012) that includes the requirement and evaluation frequency and the method of evaluation. Additional legal requirements may be identified when the list of legal requirements is reviewed by the compliance auditor. 3. Compliance audits may be conducted less frequently when repeated compliance has been observed. 4. Each requirement shall be rated as follows: 1. Fully compliant. 2. Not relevant. 3. Not fulfilled. In such instances, the Plant Manager shall take immediate action to ensure compliance. This may be in the form of a directive or through corrective action.

ABC Company Limited	**Procedures Manual**		**Reference MP 003** Page 5 of 5	
	Statutory and Regulatory Requirements		Date Released dd/mm/yyyy	Date Reviewed dd/mm/yyyy
Management Process	Approved:		Issue No: 01 Prepared by:	Revision No: 00

	Process Headings	Process Details
11.10	Actions to address non-compliances	All non-compliances, however trivial, shall be brought to the attention of the Managing Director who shall consult the Legal Team for advice and directions.
11.11	Legal risk	1. These documents shall be used for the assessment of legal risk: Form 020 Risk identification Form 024 Risk descriptors for legal non-compliance Form 022-1 Risk matrix to rank the significance of the legal non-compliance risk Form 025 Risk evaluation 2. Human Resource (HR) Manager shall organise necessary training to enable the staff to comply with the relevant legislation. 3. Plant Manager shall supervise and ensure the implementation of the action plan.
12.0	Records	Legal requirements Legal documents database Legal register.
13.0	Changes made	None.

ABC Company Limited	Procedures Manual	Flowchart MP 003.1 Page 1 of 2	
	Legal and Other Requirements	Date Released dd/mm/yyyy	Date Reviewed dd/mm/yyyy
Link MP 003	Approved:	Issue No: 01 Prepared by:	Revision No: 00

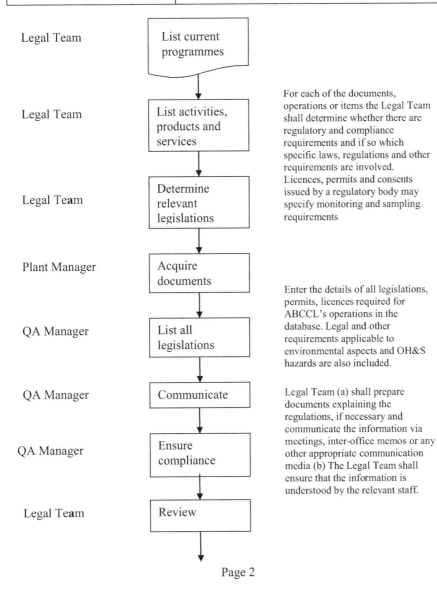

Legal Team	List current programmes	
Legal Team	List activities, products and services	For each of the documents, operations or items the Legal Team shall determine whether there are regulatory and compliance requirements and if so which specific laws, regulations and other requirements are involved. Licences, permits and consents issued by a regulatory body may specify monitoring and sampling requirements
Legal Team	Determine relevant legislations	
Plant Manager	Acquire documents	
QA Manager	List all legislations	Enter the details of all legislations, permits, licences required for ABCCL's operations in the database. Legal and other requirements applicable to environmental aspects and OH&S hazards are also included.
QA Manager	Communicate	Legal Team (a) shall prepare documents explaining the regulations, if necessary and communicate the information via meetings, inter-office memos or any other appropriate communication media (b) The Legal Team shall ensure that the information is understood by the relevant staff.
QA Manager	Ensure compliance	
Legal Team	Review	

Page 2

ABC Company Limited	Procedures Manual	Flowchart MP 003.1 Page 2 of 2	
	Legal and Other Requirements	Date Released dd/mm/yyyy	Date Reviewed dd/mm/yyyy
Link MP 003	Approved:	Issue No: 01 Prepared by:	Revision No: 00

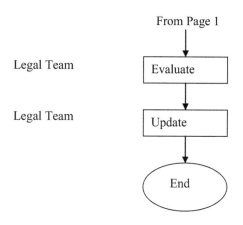

Legal Team — Evaluate

Legal Team — Update

End

From Page 1

Form 012 includes the requirements, evaluation frequency and the method of evaluation. Results are considered in continual improvement projects

MP 004 Scope

ABC Company Limited	Procedures Manual		Reference MP 004 Page 1 of 2	
	Scope		Date Released dd/mm/yyyy	Date Reviewed dd/mm/yyyy
Management Process	Approved:		Issue No: 01 Prepared by:	Revision No: 00

Process Owner		Plant Manager
	Process Headings	**Process Details**
1.0	Purpose	To define the scope of ABCCL's Integrated Quality, Food Safety and Environmental (IQFSE) management system.
2.0	Scope	Applies to the ABCCL's IQFSE management system.
3.0	Input	Internal and external context Views of interested parties Our products and services.
4.0	Output	Scope statement.
5.0	Competency requirements	Knowledge of items specified in Section 3.0.
6.0	Responsibility	Management Team shall: • Derive the scope statement. Plant Manager shall: • Approve the scope statement.
7.0	Associated documents	Internal and external context Views of interested parties Our products and services.
8.0	Resources	None.
9.0	Measures/controls	Alignment of the scope statement with the requirements of the organisation.
10.0	System description	

ABC Company Limited	Procedures Manual	Reference MP 004 Page 2 of 2	
	Scope	Date Released dd/mm/yyyy	Date Reviewed dd/mm/yyyy
Management Process	Approved:	Issue No: 01 Prepared by:	Revision No: 00

	Process Headings	Process Details
10.1	Considerations	1. This scope statement has been designed by the senior management taking into consideration ABCCL's product and service requirements, internal and external issues, needs of interested parties, compliance obligations and physical and functional boundaries.
		2. ABCCL's senior management has specified requirements for the IQFSE management system to demonstrate its: (a) ability to consistently deliver products and services that meet customer and applicable regulatory requirements; (b) aim to enhance customer satisfaction through effective application of the IQFSE management system's policies and procedures including processes for outsourcing, continual improvement of the system and for the assurance of compliance to customer and applicable regulatory requirements and (c) commitment to reduce the negative impact of our activities on the environment and consider information on significant environmental aspects, which are in control of ABCCL's operations or that ABCCL can be expected to have an influence on.
		3. The IQFSE management system has been developed to meet the requirements of the relevant ISO standards including those to ensure the safety of our food products.
		4. On rare occasions, our Engineering Team designs tools for wine processing, and therefore, design processes are included in the IQFSE management system.
		5. The scope statement is made available to the public and interested parties through our web page.
10.2	Scope statement	*ABCCL has been producing a wide range of premium wines at its facility in … for over 22 years to the local and international market. Grapes are purchased from contract growers with whom ABCCL has close relationships. All product requirements and specifications are derived from customers, regulatory requirements and industry codes of practice.*
11.0	Records	Scope statement.
12.0	Changes made	None.

MP 005 Planning IQFSE Management System

ABC Company Limited	Procedures Manual	Reference MP 005 Page 1 of 4	
	Planning IQFSE Management System	Date Released dd/mm/yyyy	Date Reviewed dd/mm/yyyy
Management Process	Approved:	Issue No: 01 Prepared by:	Revision No: 00

Process Owner		QA Manager
	Process Headings	**Process Details**
1.0	Purpose	To describe the procedure for planning for quality, food safety and environmental impact.
2.0	Scope	This procedure shall apply to products and services offered and managed by ABCCL.
3.0	Input	External and internal issues, needs and expectations of interested parties, product and system process performance, IQFSE processes, lessons learnt from previous experience, opportunities for improvement, significant environmental aspects, legal and other requirements and risks and opportunities.
4.0	Output	Responsibilities and authorities to implement the plans, identification of skills and knowledge needed, improvement methods, resource requirements, key performance indicators, documentation requirements and the IQFSE management system manual.
5.0	Competency requirements	Knowledge of ABCCL's operations, ISO standards, risk management techniques, environmental aspects identification and the Hazard Analysis and Critical Control Point (HACCP) programme.
6.0	Responsibility	The responsibilities are defined in Flowchart MP 005.1.
7.0	Associated documents	IQFSE management system and process interactions (Figure MP 005.1) ISO 14001:2015, ISO 9001:2015 and ISO 22000:2005 standards Environmental aspects identification procedure (CP 031) Risk management procedure (MP 007) Objectives procedure (MP 008).
8.0	Resources	None.
9.0	Measures/controls	Customer satisfaction Environmental performance Product complaints/recalls Internal audits Management reviews.
10.0	System description	Planning flowchart is shown in Flowchart MP 005.1.

ABC Company Limited	Procedures Manual	Reference MP 005 Page 2 of 4	
	Planning IQFSE Management System	Date Released dd/mm/yyyy	Date Reviewed dd/mm/yyyy
Management Process	Approved:	Issue No: 01 Prepared by:	Revision No: 00

	Process Headings	**Process Details**
10.1	IQFSE management system planning	a. Quality, food safety and environmental impact objectives shall be communicated to staff at all levels (MP 008) at team meetings and briefings; and b. Planning shall include: • What will be done • What resources will be required • Who will be responsible • When it will be completed. ABCCL has established an integrated management system manual which includes the procedures needed to deliver customer expectations, meet quality, food safety and environmental objectives and maintain environmental performance.
10.1.1	Step 1: Preliminary activities	1. Identify products and services appropriate to ABCCL. 2. Identify product and service requirements applicable to customers (CP 042). 3. Identify customer requirements (CP 016), internal and external issues (MP 001) and needs of interested parties (MP 002). 4. Identify applicable legal and regulatory requirements (MP 003). 5. Identify and evaluate environmental aspects (CP 031).
10.1.2	Step 2: Establish policy, objectives and targets	MP 009.
10.1.3	Step 3: Determine the process measures	Determine the processes necessary to achieve the objectives (MP 006) including inputs, outputs, competency requirements, resources needed and control measures, system description and records necessary for the activity. Documented procedures, work instructions and specifications provide support to the staff for the operation and monitoring of these processes.
10.1.4	Step 4: Conduct a risk analysis	Conduct a risk analysis and integrate actions into the processes (MP 007).
10.1.5	Step 5: Define the responsibilities and performance measures	Define the responsibilities and performance measures and resources needed to carry out the tasks. Identify criteria for effective performance and control.
10.1.6	Step 6: Documentation	Document the processes.

ABC Company Limited	Procedures Manual		Reference MP 005 Page 3 of 4	
	Planning IQFSE Management System		Date Released dd/mm/yyyy	Date Reviewed dd/mm/yyyy
Management Process	Approved:		Issue No: 01 Prepared by:	Revision No: 00

	Process Headings	Process Details
10.1.7	Step 7: Training	Assess training requirements and conduct training sessions (SP 014).
10.1.8	Step 8: Implementation	Implement the IQFSE management system.
10.1.9	Step 9: Review	Review performance through management reviews and audits.
10.2	Controls during planning	1. The integrity of the IQFSE management system is maintained through the change management procedure (MP 020). 2. Improvement opportunities are identified and considered through lessons learnt and other sources of information.
10.3	Planning for meeting customer requirements	Where appropriate, ABCCL shall consider these activities to meet customer requirements: • Identification: Identification of customer requirements (CP 016, MP 016) • Resources: Identification and acquisition of: (a) necessary resources and controls for monitoring, measurement, analysis, processes, production equipment (SP 009); and (b) inspection and test equipment, tools and skills necessary to achieve quality, food safety and environmental requirements (AP 003, AP 002) • Ensuring the fulfilment of the customer design, installation, inspection and test procedures and applicable documentation (CP 013) • Measurement and control: Identification and acquisition of any new measurement requirement in sufficient time to be made available (AP 003), identification of suitable control points and implementation of control measures to assure compliance to specified requirements (CP 012, CP 025), updating testing and inspection methods and techniques (AP 003) and clarification of all inspection criteria for the product before commencing production (CP 012).
10.4	Planning for food safety hazard identification and risk assessment methods	1. Establish food safety objectives. 2. Procedures are established and maintained for ongoing identification of food safety hazards, assessment of associated risk and implementation of necessary control measures (CP 025, 026, CP 027). 3. Identify food safety hazards at each step of food processing (e.g. purchasing, receiving raw materials) (CP 025, CP 026, CP 027). 4. Identify preventive measures and controls. 5. Provide skills for those whose activities affect food safety. 6. Establish monitoring required to ensure both the effectiveness and timeliness of food safety controls. 7. Establish corrective actions (AP 013).

ABC Company Limited	Procedures Manual	Reference MP 005 Page 4 of 4	
	Planning IQFSE Management System	Date Released dd/mm/yyyy	Date Reviewed dd/mm/yyyy
Management Process	Approved:	Issue No: 01 Prepared by:	Revision No: 00

	Process Headings	Process Details
10.5	Planning for environmental management	1. Establish environment policy (MP 009). 2. Establish environmental objectives and targets (MP 008). 3. Conduct a preliminary environmental review (CP 030). 4. Determine environmental aspects and impacts (CP 031). 5. Establish environmental management programme.
10.6	Contingency planning	Contingency planning includes the identification of contingencies (MP 017) and business continuity planning (CP 023).
10.7	Continual improvement	Continual improvement activities are carried out as described under AP 006.
10.8	Planning review	ABCCL Management Team shall review the plans at management review meetings or whenever input requirements change significantly.
10.9	Effectiveness of the IQFSE management system	Effectiveness of the IQFSE management system is maintained through management reviews, internal audits, customer complaints, corrective actions and other measures and controls described in individual procedures.
11.0	Records	IQFSE management system manual and associated documents.
12.0	Changes made	None.

ABC Company Limited	Procedures Manual		Flowchart MP 005.1 Page 1 of 1	
	Planning for Quality, Food Safety, Environmental Management		Date Released dd/mm/yyyy	Date Reviewed dd/mm/yyyy
Link MP 005/MP 006	Approved:		Issue No: 01 Prepared by:	Revision No: 00

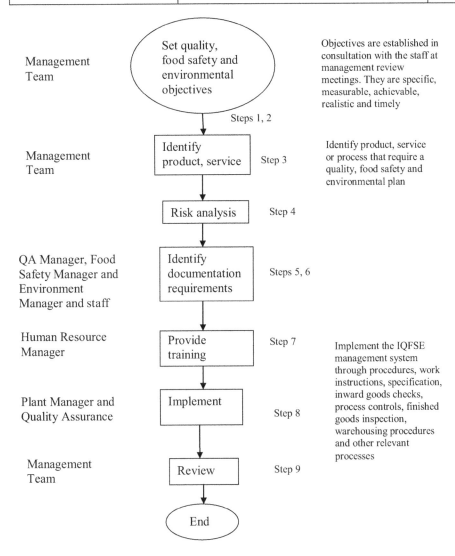

Management Team — Set quality, food safety and environmental objectives — Steps 1, 2 — Objectives are established in consultation with the staff at management review meetings. They are specific, measurable, achievable, realistic and timely

Management Team — Identify product, service — Step 3 — Identify product, service or process that require a quality, food safety and environmental plan

Risk analysis — Step 4

QA Manager, Food Safety Manager and Environment Manager and staff — Identify documentation requirements — Steps 5, 6

Human Resource Manager — Provide training — Step 7 — Implement the IQFSE management system through procedures, work instructions, specification, inward goods checks, process controls, finished goods inspection, warehousing procedures and other relevant processes

Plant Manager and Quality Assurance — Implement — Step 8

Management Team — Review — Step 9

End

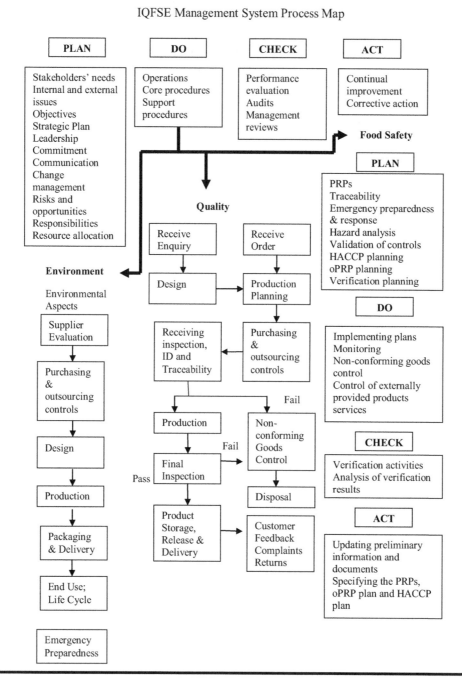

Figure MP 005.1   IQFSE management processes interactions.

MP 006 IQFSE Management System and Its Processes

ABC Company Limited	Procedures Manual	Reference MP 006 Page 1 of 4	
	IQFSE Management System and Its Processes	Date Released dd/mm/yyyy	Date Reviewed dd/mm/yyyy
Management Process	Approved:	Issue No: 01 Prepared by:	Revision No: 00

Process Owner		QA Manager
	Process Headings	**Process Details**
1.0	Purpose	To describe the development and implementation of the Integrated Quality, Food Safety and Environmental (IQFSE) management system and its processes using the process approach.
2.0	Scope	IQFSE management system applies to processes, activities and employees within the company.
3.0	Input	Needs and expectation of interested parties, internal and external issues, ABCCL's operational requirements, environmental aspects and impacts, legislative requirements, lessons learnt, risks and opportunities, company's products and services and food safety hazards.
4.0	Output	A manual describing the IQFSE management system.
5.0	Competency requirements	Knowledge of ISO 9001, ISO 14001 and ISO 22000 standards; ABCCL's operations; business plan; the organisation structure; legislative requirements; strategic plan and objectives and goals.
6.0	Responsibility	QA Manager, Environment Manager and Food Safety Manager shall: • Identify IQFSE management system requirements and the processes required • Prepare the necessary documents. QA Manager shall: • Establish the IQFSE management system • Communicate the requirements to staff.
7.0	Associated documents	Needs and expectations of interested parties (MP 002) Risks and opportunities (MP 007) Environmental aspects and impacts (CP 031) Legal requirements (MP 003) Strategic planning (MP 014).
8.0	Resources	None.
9.0	Measures/controls	Procedures needed to carry out the operations system review.
10.0	Definitions	**Procedure:** A series of actions done in a certain way or order. **Process:** A series of actions that produce something or lead to a particular result.
11.0	System description	Flowchart is shown in MP 005.1.

ABC Company Limited	Procedures Manual	Reference MP 006 Page 2 of 4	
	IQFSE Management System and Its Processes	Date Released dd/mm/yyyy	Date Reviewed dd/mm/yyyy
Management Process	Approved:	Issue No: 01 Prepared by:	Revision No: 00

	Process Headings	Process Details
11.1	Contents of the IQFSE management system	a. Management processes [**PLAN**]: Provide leadership through the mission, vision, objectives, goals and strategic planning; b. Core processes common to quality, environment and food safety requirements [**DO**]: Key processes that are required to meet customers' expectations; c. Core processes specific to quality, environment and food safety requirements [**DO**]: Key processes that are required to meet specific quality, food safety and environmental expectations; d. Support processes [**DO**]: Those needed to achieve the output of key processes; e. Assurance processes [**CHECK**]: Processes that define performance indicators and f. Improvement processes [**ACT**]: Continual improvement processes. Figure MP 006.1 shows an overview of the IQFSE management system. Core, support and assurance processes are shown in Forms 014, 015 and 016.
11.2	Identification of processes	With the information in the input panel key, processes are identified by the Management Team using one or more of these methods: • Brainstorming: Team discusses all the operations of the business and then decides which are the most important • Interviewing stakeholders: Talking to people affected by, or having an impact on, the processes • External consultant: Assigning a consultant to identify the processes • Adopt the generic model[a] to customise it to the organisation.
11.3	Identification of sub-processes	Each core process and support process includes several sub-processes and they are identified in terms of entry and exit criteria as shown in Form 017. Form 018 shows quality, environment and food safety requirements applied to some processes.

ABC Company Limited	Procedures Manual		Reference MP 006 Page 3 of 4	
	IQFSE Management System and Its Processes		Date Released dd/mm/yyyy	Date Reviewed dd/mm/yyyy
Management Process	Approved:		Issue No: 01 Prepared by:	Revision No: 00

	Process Headings	Process Details

11.4	Developing processes	1. Process approach: Using the process approach, individual procedures are developed. A procedure is formatted as shown in Form 019.
		Each process defines:
		  a. Inputs and outputs: Inputs are those required for performing the activities, and outputs are products that result from processes and services that are performed;
		  b. Criteria and methods: Measures and controls defined in each process identify how the effectiveness of the processes is evaluated. System description includes flowcharts, and forms and figures show the method of performing the activity;
		  c. Required resources are specified in each process and include raw materials, ingredients, supplies, specifications and utilities;
		  d. Responsibilities for carrying out the operations are specified in each procedure and flowchart, if applicable;
		  e. Risks and opportunities associated with processes are determined according to the risk management procedure (MP 007);
		  f. Activities are evaluated through in-process controls and final product inspection procedures; and
		  g. Continual improvement activities are conducted according to the procedure AP 006 and include projects such as cost reduction, efficiency improvements, environmental performance and new product development activities.

11.5	Nomenclature of processes	AP – assurance processes CP – core processes SP – support processes MP – management processes.
11.6	Outsourced processes	Outsourced processes are those assigned to an external agency. They are controlled via contract negotiation, plant visits, inspection at premises and audits. QA Manager is responsible for ensuring that IQFSE management system's requirements are adhered to via any of the methods described here.

ABC Company Limited	Procedures Manual	Reference MP 006 Page 4 of 4	
	IQFSE Management System and Its Processes	Date Released dd/mm/yyyy	Date Reviewed dd/mm/yyyy
Management Process	Approved:	Issue No: 01 Prepared by:	Revision No: 00

	Process Headings	**Process Details**
11.7	Process interactions	IQFSE management system process interactions are shown in Figure MP 005.1. Plan, check and ACT phases of the cycle share common processes. In the DO phase, activities are different and process interactions of the food safety system have two Plan, Do, Check and Act (PDCA) cycles: a higher-level cycle and a Hazard Analysis and Critical Control Point (HACCP) cycle.
11.8	Levels of documentation	IQFSE management system has four levels of documentation. L1 Policy manual (BMS 000) L2 Procedures (management, core, support and assurance) L3 Work instructions L4 Forms, flowcharts, tables.
11.9	Managing change	Changes are managed through the change control procedure (MP 020) and document control procedure (SP 001).
11.10	Implementation	The implementation of the IQFSE management system is carried out through training and development programmes, internal audits, management reviews and regular reviews of the system.
12.0	Records	List of management, core, support and assurance processes.
13.0	Changes made	None.

[a] Dumas, M., Laq Rosa M., Mendlimg, J. and Reijers, H.A. (2017). *Fundamentals of Business Process Management* (2nd ed.). Germany: Springer.

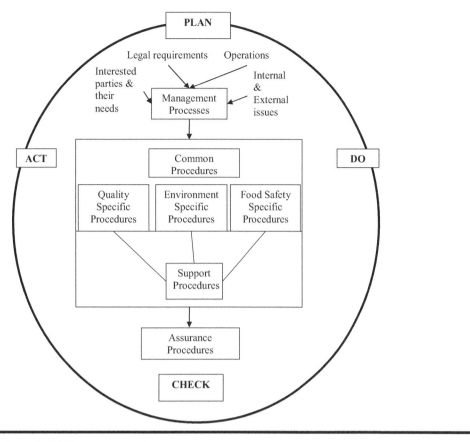

Figure MP 006.1   Overview of IQFSE management system.

MP 007 Risk Management

ABC Company Limited	Procedures Manual	Reference MP 007 Page 1 of 6	
	Risk Management	Date Released dd/mm/yyyy	Date Reviewed dd/mm/yyyy
Management Process	Approved:	Issue No: 01 Prepared by:	Revision No: 00

Process Owner	Chief Risk Officer
Process Headings	**Process Details**
1.0 Purpose	To describe the procedure for business risk management activities at ABCCL.
2.0 Scope	This procedure shall apply to the identification, analysis and management of risks that are associated with products, operational activities and the business environment.
3.0 Input	Internal and external issues, needs of interest parties; results of strengths, weaknesses, opportunities and threats (SWOT) and political, economic, social and technological (PEST) analyses; products, processes and operations; information on changes; legal requirements; environmental aspects and risk management tasks from management review meetings.
4.0 Output	Action plan to treat identified risks, process control decisions, data to evaluate effectiveness of processes, suggestions for changes and improvement and initiation of breakthrough projects.
5.0 Competency requirements	Knowledge of risk management techniques and ABCCL's operations.
6.0 Responsibility	Defined in Flowchart MP 007.1.
7.0 Associated documents	Risk identification form (Form 020) Risk register (Form 021) Risk matrix (Forms 022/022-1) Risk descriptors (Form 023) Risk descriptors legal (Form 024) Risk management guides Risk evaluation example (Form 025) Opportunity register (Form 026) Action plan (Form 027).
8.0 Resources	Budget allocation.

ABC Company Limited	Procedures Manual	Reference MP 007 Page 2 of 6	
	Risk Management	Date Released dd/mm/yyyy	Date Reviewed dd/mm/yyyy
Management Process	Approved:	Issue No: 01 Prepared by:	Revision No: 00

	Process Headings	Process Details
9.0	Measures/controls	Review of risk assessment Internal audits and management reviews.
10.0	Definitions	**Risk management:** Process of systematically identifying and evaluating any threats to ABCCL, establishing priorities for action and making decisions about which risk control measures need to be implemented. **Risk-based thinking.** This is an approach to identify and manage risks and opportunities associated with management processes that influence the manufacture and delivery of products and services to the customers. **Hazard:** Something that can cause harm. **Risk:** Potential threat that can impact on business activities. **Likelihood:** The probability of occurrence. Consequence: Outcome of an event: A loss, injury, disadvantage or gain. A single risk may have several outcomes. **Risk control:** Manner of treating risks – avoidance, mitigation, transfer. **Risk assessment:** Process of evaluating and comparing the level of risk against predetermined acceptable levels of risk. **Risk owner:** The person responsible for managing the risk and who is usually the person responsible for strategy, activity or function that relates to the risk. **Residual risk:** Risk remaining after treatment.
11.0	System description	
11.1	Negative risk management process	General process for risk management is shown in Flowchart MP 007.1.
11.1.1	Risk management plan (RMP): PLAN	RMP shall include the purpose, scope, organisation, roles and responsibilities, risk identification methods, risk assessment methods, risk treatment, assessment of residual risk, review and the action plan. i. **Risk identification [DO]:** Use Form 020 – Risk identification. Business unit managers identify risks in their own units. Risks include operational risk, project task-specific risk, dynamic risk, risk and opportunities affecting products, services and customer satisfaction and fire risk. Any of the following techniques or in combination may be used to identify risks: • Brainstorming • Tests and verifications • Pause and learn sessions • Previous analysis of risks

ABC Company Limited	Procedures Manual	Reference MP 007 Page 3 of 6	
	Risk Management	Date Released dd/mm/yyyy	Date Reviewed dd/mm/yyyy
Management Process	Approved:	Issue No: 01 Prepared by:	Revision No: 00

Process Headings	Process Details
	• Historical data • Lessons learnt • Checklists • Informal notifications • Failure mode and effects analysis (FMEA) • Fault tree analysis (FTA). **ii. Risk assessment [DO]:** Use Form 022 – Risk matrix, Form 023 – Risk descriptors, Form 025 – Process risk evaluation. **iii. Risk treatment [DO]:** Decide on course of action and implement. High risk: Eliminate risk before commencing work. Medium risk: Reduce or transfer risk. Low risk: Monitor and manage. Risk Management Team (RMT) shall ensure that actions taken to mitigate or eliminate threats are proportional to the significance of the impact. Treatment includes: 1. Elimination of risk at source. 2. Minimise the risk at source by, e.g. engineering measures, redesign, substitution and remove person from the risk protection measures. 3. Minimise risk by redesigning suitable system of work. 4. Creating awareness, instruction, training and supervision. 5. Personal protection equipment. When risk cannot be eliminated introduce control measures into operation to reduce the risk to a sufficient level to prevent harm.
11.2 Management of opportunities	i. The Risk Management Committee shall also identify opportunities which could improve the financial position and the market position. Examples of such opportunities are: (a) increase exports to take advantage of tax incentives for export; (b) introduce new technology; (c) gain access to new markets; (d) expand the customer base; (e) develop new products to meet market demands and (f) streamline the processes to improve the efficiency and productivity. ii. Opportunities are identified as part of the context of the organisation exercise. Top management shall discuss and analyse the opportunities at management review meetings. iii. To identify the opportunities to be pursued, the opportunity register (Form 026) may be used. It is similar to the risk register but classifies positive opportunities by the likelihood of success and potential benefits.

ABC Company Limited	Procedures Manual	Reference MP 007 Page 4 of 6	
	Risk Management	Date Released dd/mm/yyyy	Date Reviewed dd/mm/yyyy
Management Process	Approved:	Issue No: 01 Prepared by:	Revision No: 00

	Process Headings	Process Details
11.2.1	Process for managing opportunities	The process of managing opportunities is:

Process Details (11.2.1 — Process for managing opportunities):

The process of managing opportunities is:

a. Identify the opportunity;

b. Determine the process to which it is applicable;

c. Assign a rating based on the possibility of success (1–5) and previous occurrence (1–5). [1 = lowest and 5 = highest.] Final rating is the higher of the two.

d. Assign a benefit score base on:
- Potential for new business
- Potential for expansion of current business Potential to improve the ability to meet regulatory requirements
- Potential improvement of management systems
- Potential improvement of company image and reputation
- Estimated cost of implementation.

Each element is assigned a score between 1 (lowest benefit) and 5 (highest benefit). Final rating is the highest of the six scores.

Opportunity factor = probability score × benefit score.

Risk Management Committee shall establish an opportunity score threshold. Opportunities with factors greater than the threshold value are either targeted for action or rejected. Opportunity factors lower than the threshold values are rejected.

i. Treatment of opportunities

The opportunities are treated as follows:
- Pursue the opportunity
- Collect further data for review
- Accept the opportunity under controlled conditions
- Reject the opportunity because of lower benefit or higher risk
- Actions taken to mitigate or eliminate threats are proportional to the significance of the impact.

ii. Record and communicate

a. Communication and training: Internal communication in relation to environmental aspects and impacts is carried out through induction training, awareness briefings, and/or quarterly company meeting of the management team chaired by the Chief Risk Officer. It may be included as a part of management review meetings; and

b. Integrate into the Integrated Quality, Food Safety and Environmental (IQFSE) management system: Identified risks and action plans are considered in the development of the strategic plan and serve as inputs to objectives and targets.

ABC Company Limited	Procedures Manual	Reference MP 007 Page 5 of 6	
	Risk Management	Date Released dd/mm/yyyy	Date Reviewed dd/mm/yyyy
Management Process	Approved:	Issue No: 01 Prepared by:	Revision No: 00

	Process Headings	Process Details
11.3	Monitor and review: CHECK	a. Monitor and review to ensure effectiveness through audits, management reviews and strategic planning process. Assess residual risk using the same methodology and assessment scales taking into account the influence of controls and mitigation methods; and b. Evaluate the effectiveness of the action plan: Monitor and measure using safety audits, spot checks, Supervisor checks, etc. Monitor the effectiveness of control measures through continual review of internal audits; management reviews and feedback from employees; clients and regulatory authorities; non-conformance reports and near miss experiences and incidents, accidents and dangerous occurrences.
11.4	ACT	a. Evaluate improvements and desired outcome (every 12 months minimum): Review risk assessment, control measures and update where necessary the following: (i) monitoring feedback; (ii) operation, work practice, equipment and specification changes; (iii) regulatory changes; (iv) learning new and/or previously unforeseen risk and (v) actions following safety alerts, briefings and employee reports. Maintain an audit trail of risk assessment/changes following actions taken in response to accidents, incidents, near misses and identification of new and/or previously unforeseen hazards and risks. b. Request by external organisations shall be directed to the Managing Director who is authorised to release an uncontrolled copy of the document.

ABC Company Limited	Procedures Manual	Reference MP 007 Page 6 of 6	
	Risk Management	Date Released dd/mm/yyyy	Date Reviewed dd/mm/yyyy
Management Process	Approved:	Issue No: 01 Prepared by:	Revision No: 00

	Process Headings	Process Details
11.5	Integration into the IQFSE management system	Identified risks and action plans are integrated into the relevant processes and serve as inputs to the strategic planning process and objectives and targets. These are taken into consideration when designing products and processes.
12.0	Records	Risk and opportunities documentation: Use Form 021 – Risk register, Form 026 – Opportunity register and Form 027 – Action plan.
13.0	Changes made	None.

ABC Company Limited	Procedures Manual	Flowchart MP 007.1 Page 1 of 1	
	Risk Management	Date Released dd/mm/yyyy	Date Reviewed dd/mm/yyyy
Link MP 007	Approved:	Issue No: 01 Prepared by:	Revision No: 00

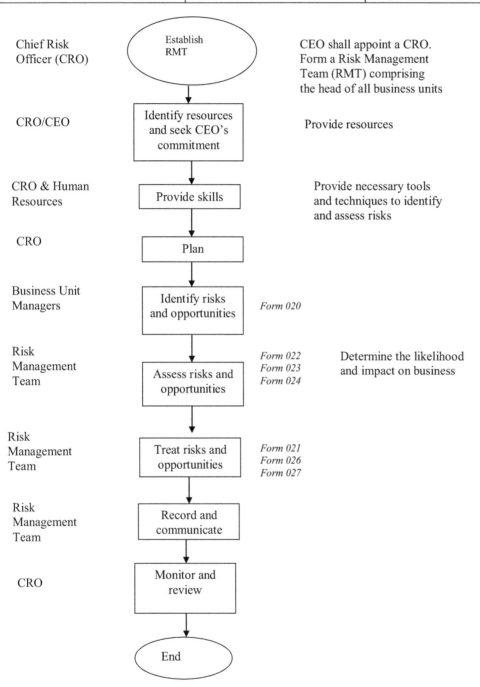

Chief Risk Officer (CRO) — Establish RMT — CEO shall appoint a CRO. Form a Risk Management Team (RMT) comprising the head of all business units

CRO/CEO — Identify resources and seek CEO's commitment — Provide resources

CRO & Human Resources — Provide skills — Provide necessary tools and techniques to identify and assess risks

CRO — Plan

Business Unit Managers — Identify risks and opportunities — *Form 020*

Risk Management Team — Assess risks and opportunities — *Form 022 Form 023 Form 024* — Determine the likelihood and impact on business

Risk Management Team — Treat risks and opportunities — *Form 021 Form 026 Form 027*

Risk Management Team — Record and communicate

CRO — Monitor and review

End

MP 008 Objectives

ABC Company Limited	Procedures Manual	Reference MP 008 Page 1 of 3	
	Objectives	Date Released dd/mm/yyyy	Date Reviewed dd/mm/yyyy
Management Process	Approved:	Issue No: 01 Prepared by:	Revision No: 00

Process Owner		Plant Manager
	Process Headings	**Process Details**
1.0	Purpose	To describe the process for establishing quality, food safety and environmental management system objectives and planning to achieve them.
2.0	Scope	The procedure applies to quality, food safety and environmental management system.
3.0	Input	Operational requirements, risk assessment, views of interested parties, business requirements, benchmarks standards/data, Integrated Quality, Food Safety and Environmental (IQFSE) policy, internal and external issues, significant environmental aspects, legal/other requirements, financial requirements and technological options.
4.0	Output	Set of objectives and targets and action plan.
5.0	Competency requirements	Knowledge of ABCCL's operations and skills in establishing goals and targets. All members should have conceptual knowledge of ISO 9001, ISO 14001 and ISO 22000 standards and on the eight management principles.
6.0	Responsibility	Defined in Flowchart MP 008.1.
7.0	Associated documents	Policy statements and mission statement Internal and external issues (Form 002) Quality, food safety and environmental management systems Risk management procedure (MP 007) Compliance obligations (MP 003) Identification of environmental aspects and impacts (CP 031) Analysis and evaluation (AP 004) Management plan (Form 028).
8.0	Resources	Financial resources as defined by objectives.
9.0	Measures/controls	Effectiveness of the management plan Internal audits Management review.
10.0	Definitions	**Risk-based thinking:** This is an approach to identify and manage risks and opportunities associated with management processes that influence the manufacture and delivery of products and services to the customers. **Objective:** Overall goal based on IQFSE policy that the organisation expects to achieve which is quantified, if practicable. **Target:** Detailed performance requirement associated with each objective, which is quantified, if practicable, and needs to be set and met in order to achieve the objective.

ABC Company Limited	Procedures Manual	Reference MP 008 Page 2 of 3	
	Objectives	Date Released dd/mm/yyyy	Date Reviewed dd/mm/yyyy
Management Process	Approved:	Issue No: 01 Prepared by:	Revision No: 00

	Process Headings	Process Details
11.0	System description	Flowchart MP 008.1 shows the process for setting objectives.
11.1	Setting criteria	a. The Management Team shall comprise members from all departments; and b. The Management Team shall set criteria for establishing objectives: All or any of inputs shall be considered when establishing objectives. During the development of objectives/goals, the Management Team shall ensure that they are SMART (Specific, Measurable, Achievable, Realistic and Time-bound).
11.2	Establish objectives	a. Feasibility, availability of resources, availability of technological options and government and industry sector guidelines are important considerations; b. Objectives shall be aligned with the integrated quality, food safety and environment policy; c. Applicable significant requirements which have not been incorporated in the integrated quality, food safety and environment policy shall be included in setting objectives and d. Objectives shall be related to products and services that we propose to offer.
11.3	Resource requirements	Management Team shall discuss with the Managing Director and obtain approval whether financial resources are required.
11.4	Management plan to achieve objective	(a) Management Team shall conduct a risk assessment based on selected objectives; and (b) Management Team shall develop a management plan (Form 028) which shall include the following information: • General information • Responsibilities for achieving them • Current performance, if applicable • Targets • Timeframe • Activities involved • Training needs. • Other information.

ABC Company Limited	Procedures Manual	Reference MP 008 Page 3 of 3	
	Objectives	Date Released dd/mm/yyyy	Date Reviewed dd/mm/yyyy
Management Process	Approved:	Issue No: 01 Prepared by:	Revision No: 00

	Process Headings	Process Details
11.5	Monitoring the progress	a. Responsible managers shall monitor the progress at intervals stated in the management plan; b. They are responsible for collecting the data to be presented at the management review meetings. QA Manager shall collate the performance data and present at management review meetings. The Management Team shall analyse the results and draw conclusion and c. If targets have not been achieved, the Management Team shall discuss the reason for not achieving and take necessary action which may include extending the timeframe, amending performance indicators and altering the objective.
11.6	Review of objectives	1. The Management Team shall review the objectives at least annually, or when new regulations come into force, or when new products or new changes in operations are introduced. 2. Objectives shall be revised whenever there is a change in strategy, the environment and customer requirements.
11.7	Integration into the IQFSE management system	In setting the strategic plan, the Management Team to consider the objectives and targets. They are linked to the IQFSE management system through performance measures in each process.
11.8	Communication of objectives	Objectives shall be communicated to all staff according to the relevance at team meetings.
12.0	Records	List of objectives (Form 029) Management plan to achieve objectives (Form 028).
13.0	Changes made	None.

ABC Company Limited	Procedures Manual	Flowchart MP 008.1 Page 1 of 1	
	Setting Objectives	Date Released dd/mm/yyyy	Date Reviewed dd/mm/yyyy
Link MP 008	Approved:	Issue No: 01 Prepared by:	Revision No: 00

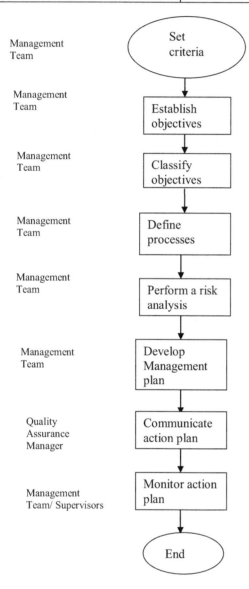

Management Team — Set criteria

Management Team — Establish objectives

Objectives may be set at various levels of the organisation: top management, departments, functional groups, processes, project teams etc. The individual members of the team shall frame objectives for their respective departments. The management team meeting shall finalise the objectives. Form 029

Management Team — Classify objectives

Classify into policy, performance, product related and management

Examples
Product: reduction of defects, scrap and rework, improvement of delivery time.
Process: Improvement of productivity through the elimination or reduction of process variability, waste in inputs, outputs, conversion processes and relate use of resources.
Customers: Reduction of product returns, customer complaints, improvement of customer satisfaction rating, delivery time.
Suppliers: Financial value of returns, supplier performance.
Resources: Availability, capability, utilisation, maintenance, personnel competency, absenteeism, production rates.
QMS: Customer satisfaction feedback, audit results, results of opportunities.

Management Team — Define processes

Management Team — Perform a risk analysis

Management Team — Develop Management plan

Quality Assurance Manager — Communicate action plan

Objectives shall be communicated to all the staff at regular team briefings and shall ensure that they are aware of the expectations.

Management Team/ Supervisors — Monitor action plan

End

MP 009 Integrated Quality, Food Safety and Environment Policy

ABC Company Limited	Procedures Manual		Reference MP 009 Page 1 of 3	
	Integrated Quality, Food Safety and Environment Policy		Date Released dd/mm/yyyy	Date Reviewed dd/mm/yyyy
Management Process	Approved:		Issue No: 01 Prepared by:	Revision No: 00

Process Owner		CEO
	Process Headings	**Process Details**
1.0	Purpose	To describe our policy statement.
2.0	Scope	This policy applies to our organisation and the products and services delivered by us.
3.0	Input	The purpose of the organisation, environment and strategy; directions to determine the objectives; requirements of the Integrated Quality, Food Safety and Environmental (IQFSE) management system and commitment to continually improve the system.
4.0	Output	Policy statement.
5.0	Competency requirements	Knowledge of our products and services, IQFSE management system and customer requirements.
6.0	Responsibility	The Senior Executive Team shall: • Define the quality, food safety and environment policy.
7.0	Associated documents	Activities of the organisation Customer requirements Regulatory requirements.
8.0	Resources	None.
9.0	Measures/controls	Alignment of company activities with the policy.
10.0	System description	
10.1	Formulation of ABCCL's IQFSE policy	The CEO and the Management Team shall formulate the IQFSE policy taking into consideration the mission, vision, customer requirements, needs of interested parties and relevant ISO standards and regulatory requirements.

ABC Company Limited	Procedures Manual		Reference MP 009 Page 2 of 3	
	Integrated Quality, Food Safety and Environment Policy		Date Released dd/mm/yyyy	Date Reviewed dd/mm/yyyy
Management Process	Approved:		Issue No: 01 Prepared by:	Revision No: 00

	Process Headings	Process Details
10.2	IQFSE policy statement	• *Our core business is the production and marketing of premium wines. Our dedicated team of winemakers and the marketing staff recognise consumer preferences and strive to satisfy them at competitive cost. This is achieved by establishing measurable objectives and by the use of effective quality, food safety and environmental procedures and quality improvement practices and environmentally friendly management practices, in a manner which meets all regulations, industry standards, best practices and strictest standards of hygiene and food safety and other relevant requirements* • *We will promote environmental quality by minimising waste and emissions, reusing and recycling, reducing the use of natural resources and encouraging pollution prevention efforts in the organisation. We are environmentally responsible to the community in which we operate and ensure that our operations do not endanger health, safety or the environment* • *The Director, management and the staff demonstrate commitment by being responsible for quality, food safety and environmentally friendly practices through our IQFSE management system seeking improvement through regular review with suppliers and sub-contractors who are encouraged to cooperate* • *We will develop staff competencies, creativity, empowerment and accountability through effective management programmes and adopt new technologies to deliver consumer demands at competitive prices* • *This policy will form the basis to derive quality, environment and food safety objectives and support the IQFSE management system.*
10.3	Commitment of our Management Team	The QA Manager, Food Safety Manager and Environment Manager are responsible for implementing the IQFSE policy. Managers will undertake supervision to ensure that all food operators comply with all requirements. The team will provide the necessary resources to implement the policy and provide the leadership to implement it.
10.4	Review of the IQFSE policy	The policy will be reviewed at least annually or in response to the changing requirements of our stakeholders and regulations applicable to our operations. The policy will be reviewed by the Management Team.

ABC Company Limited	Procedures Manual		Reference MP 009 Page 3 of 3	
	Integrated Quality, Food Safety and Environment Policy		Date Released dd/mm/yyyy	Date Reviewed dd/mm/yyyy
Management Process	Approved:		Issue No: 01 Prepared by:	Revision No: 00

	Process Headings	Process Details
10.5	Communication of the IQFSE policy	The IQFSE policy will be communicated to all the staff at induction and regular team briefings and will ensure that they are aware of the expectations.
10.6	Availability of the IQFSE policy	The policy will be made available to the public and our customers through our website.
11.0	Records	Policy statement.
12.0	Changes made	None.

MP 010 Our Commitment

ABC Company Limited	Procedures Manual		Reference MP 010 Page 1 of 3	
	Our Commitment	Date Released dd/mm/yyyy		Date Reviewed dd/mm/yyyy
Management Process	Approved:	Issue No: 01 Prepared by:		Revision No: 00

Process Owner		Management Team
	Process Headings	**Process Details**
1.0	Purpose	To describe how the top management demonstrate the leadership and commitment to the Integrated Quality, Food Safety and Environmental (IQFSE) management system.
2.0	Scope	This procedure applies to the top management who have direct influence and control over the IQFSE management system.
3.0	Input	Mission, vision, policies, objectives and targets; strategic planning; regulatory and customer requirements and the IQFSE management system.
4.0	Output	Motivated staff, availability of necessary resources, continual improvement, better financial performance and customer satisfaction.
5.0	Competency requirements	Understanding the IQFSE management system, leadership skills and ability to motivate employees.
6.0	Responsibility	Top management shall be: • Clearly responsible for demonstrating and maintaining commitment to the IQFSE management system. Management shall be: • Responsible for maintaining the system, and identifying and implementing continual improvement of the system.
7.0	Associated documents	IQFSE management system Strategic plan Objectives and targets Risks and opportunities.
8.0	Resources	None.
9.0	Measures/controls	Participation in management review meetings and continual improvement projects Employee satisfaction surveys Resource allocations.
10.0	System description	
10.1	Accountability for the IQFSE management system	Top management demonstrate accountability to the IQFSE management system by periodical review of the system through management review meetings, review of quality, food safety and environment objectives and provision of necessary resources.

ABC Company Limited	Procedures Manual	Reference MP 010 Page 2 of 3	
	Our Commitment	Date Released dd/mm/yyyy	Date Reviewed dd/mm/yyyy
Management Process	Approved:	Issue No: 01 Prepared by:	Revision No: 00

	Process Headings	Process Details
10.2	Establishing IQFSE objectives	The CEO and the top management are involved in formulating the objectives, goals and targets and defining the strategic direction (MP 009, MP 008, MP 014). Policies and objectives are compatible with the context of the organisation (MP 001, MP 002).
10.3	IQFSE management system	Our IQFSE management system comprises policies, procedures and work instruction documents for staff producing goods under controlled conditions to our customers. This IQFSE management system provides guidance for meeting customer expectations and the requirements of the three management systems – ISO 9001:2005, ISO 14001:20015 and ISO 22001: 2017.
10.4	Promoting the process approach	Procedures have been developed to manage all parts of the process including risk-based thinking. Procedures include all parts of the process, i.e. process owner, inputs, outputs, resources, monitoring requirements and other requirements.
10.5	Availability of resources	Resource needs are identified and the CEO ensures that adequate resources are provided to conduct business operations (SP 009, SP 011, SP 021). Management ensures that resources are used in a proactive manner and as efficiently as possible through monitoring activities.
10.6	Communication of IQFSE management system requirements	Managers communicate the importance of effective quality, food safety and environmental management and the need to conform to the requirements of the IQFSE management system through news bulletins, staff meetings and briefings (SP 005, SP 006).
10.7	Ensuring the expected outcome	1. Each process defines performance measures, and they are assessed against the expected outcome through internal audits, corrective actions, customer feedback and financial measures at management review meetings (AP 005). 2. Customer feedback is measured and the results are reviewed at management review meetings (SP 046, SP 047, AP 005).

ABC Company Limited	Procedures Manual	Reference MP 010 Page 3 of 3	
	Our Commitment	Date Released dd/mm/yyyy	Date Reviewed dd/mm/yyyy
Management Process	Approved:	Issue No: 01 Prepared by:	Revision No: 00

	Process Headings	Process Details
10.8	Involvement of staff	1. Management encourages the involvement of staff in various activities such as continual improvement projects, document changes, problem-solving activities and addressing risks and opportunities. 2. Through training and development activities, the Management Team creates an awareness of IQFSE management system requirements by promoting involvement in IQFSE activities (SP 014). 3. Through training and development activities, the Management Team creates an awareness of the importance of complying with all applicable statutory and other legal requirements (MP 003).
10.9	Provision of support	The top management supports the Management Team in achieving their goals by providing the necessary resources. CEO holds both formal and informal meetings with the Management Team to provide any assistance.
11.0	Records	Records associated with procedures.
12.0	Changes made	None.

MP 011 Roles, Responsibilities and Authorities

ABC Company Limited	Procedures Manual	Reference MP 011 Page 1 of 3	
	Roles, Responsibilities and Authorities	Date Released dd/mm/yyyy	Date Reviewed dd/mm/yyyy
Management Process	Approved:	Issue No: 01 Prepared by:	Revision No: 00

Process Owner	Managing Director
Process Headings	**Process Details**

	Process Headings	Process Details
1.0	Purpose	To describe the roles and responsibilities of ABCCL's staff.
2.0	Scope	This procedure applies to all levels of staff.
3.0	Input	ABCCL's operations, skill requirements and human resource (HR) requirements.
4.0	Output	Job descriptions, skill charts and organisation chart.
5.0	Competency requirements	HR skills.
6.0	Responsibility	HR Manager shall:

HR Manager shall:
- Evaluate HR requirements
- Review (at least annually) HR requirements
- In consultation with Department Managers, assess technical and other skills necessary for the effective operation of ABCCL's activities.

Department Managers shall:
- Prepare job descriptions
- Define roles and responsibilities for each position under his or her administration
- Specify job requirements and necessary skills for new positions.

Food Safety Team Leader (FSTL) shall:
- Appoint the Food Safety Team (FST)
- Initiate document action on food safety issues
- In coordination with the QA Manager, establish, implement, maintain and update food safety requirements of the IQFSE management system
- Provide leadership to the FST
- Provide the necessary training.

Supervisors shall:
- Clarify roles and responsibilities of employees under his or her administration
- Organise any training necessary to accomplish assigned tasks
- Explain the reporting structure and the organisation chart
- Obtain feedback from employees.

ABC Company Limited	Procedures Manual	Reference MP 011 Page 2 of 3	
	Roles, Responsibilities and Authorities	Date Released dd/mm/yyyy	Date Reviewed dd/mm/yyyy
Management Process	Approved:	Issue No: 01 Prepared by:	Revision No: 00

	Process Headings	Process Details
7.0	Associated documents	Job descriptions Organisation chart (Figure MP 011.1) Skill charts High-level responsibilities and authorities (Form 030) Specific responsibilities and authorities (Form 031).
8.0	Resources	None.
9.0	Measures/controls	Availability of job descriptions Extent of understanding of roles and responsibilities.
10.0	Definitions	**Responsibility:** The duty, obligation and accountability for the performance of assigned duties, tasks and activities. **Authority:** The power or the right to control, command, instruct, make decisions, allocate resources, delegate and ensure compliance to relevant standards, company policies and procedures. **Role:** Expected behaviour associated with a particular position, function or status within an organisation.
11.0	System description	
11.1	Top management	The top management includes the CEO, Managing Director, Financial Manager, HR Manager, Marketing Manager, Sales Manager, Plant Manager, QA Manager, Chief Risk Officer and Health and Safety Officer. QA Manager reports to the Managing Director and oversees environment and food safety activities through the Food Safety Manager and the Environment Manager.
11.2	Roles and responsibilities	Roles, responsibilities and authorities are defined in individual job descriptions. High-level responsibilities and authorities are shown in Form 030. Department Managers shall ensure that they are clearly understood at induction and at performance reviews. Thus, all employees become aware of their responsibilities as well as their position in the organisation chart. Job descriptions are reviewed at least annually at performance review time or when the activities specified in the job description change.

ABC Company Limited	Procedures Manual		Reference MP 011 Page 3 of 3	
	Roles, Responsibilities and Authorities		Date Released dd/mm/yyyy	Date Reviewed dd/mm/yyyy
Management Process	Approved:		Issue No: 01 Prepared by:	Revision No: 00

	Process Headings	**Process Details**
11.3	Positions for special projects	The Managing Director may appoint a person or a team for a specific project. These positions carry responsibilities and authorities in addition to the current ones.
11.4	Specific responsibilities and authorities	Form 031 shows some specific responsibilities and authorities.
11.5	FST	Food Safety Manager shall function as the FSTL. He or she shall appoint the FST consisting of staff who have completed an accredited food safety programme.
12.0	Records	Organisation chart (Figure MP 011.1) Job descriptions.
13.0	Changes made	None.

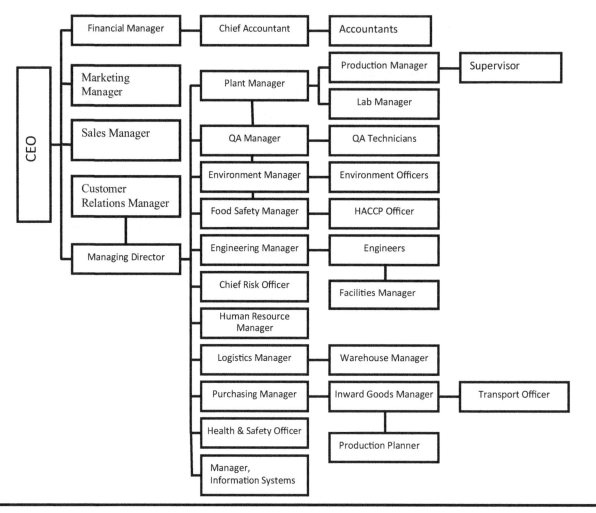

Figure MP 011.1   Organisation chart.

MP 012 IQFSE Management System Planning Processes

ABC Company Limited	Procedures Manual		Reference MP 012 Page 1 of 1	
	IQFSE Management System Planning Processes	Date Released dd/mm/yyyy	Date Reviewed dd/mm/yyyy	
Management Process	Approved:	Issue No: 01 Prepared by:	Revision No: 00	

Process Owner		Described under Individual Procedures
	Process Headings	**Process Details**
1.0	Purpose	This document describes the planning processes of the Integrated Quality, Food Safety and Environmental (IQFSE) management system.
2.0	Scope	This procedure applies to planning activities associated with the IQFSE management system.
3.0	Input	Described under individual procedures.
4.0	Output	Described under individual procedures.
5.0	Competency requirements	Described under individual procedures.
6.0	Responsibility	See Flowchart MP 005.1.
7.0	Associated documents	Described under individual procedures.
8.0	Resources	Described under individual procedures.
9.0	Measures/controls	Described under individual procedures.
10.0	Definitions	Described under individual procedures.
11.0	System description	See Flowchart MP 012.1 Process interactions are described under Figure MP 005.1
12.0	Records	Described under individual procedures.
13.0	Changes made	Described under individual procedures.

ABC Company Limited	Procedures Manual		Flowchart MP 012.1 Page 1 of 1	
	IQFSE Management System Planning Processes		Date Released dd/mm/yyyy	Date Reviewed dd/mm/yyyy
Link MP 012	Approved:		Issue No: 01 Prepared by:	Revision No: 00

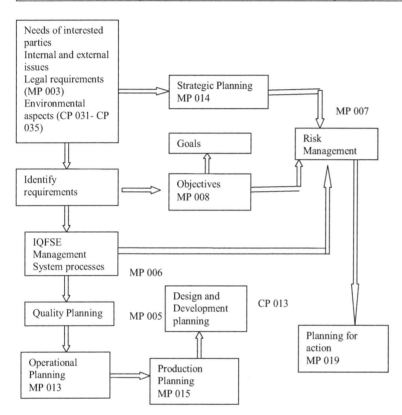

MP 013 Operational Planning and Control

ABC Company Limited	Procedures Manual	Reference MP 013 Page 1 of 4	
	Operational Planning and Control	Date Released dd/mm/yyyy	Date Reviewed dd/mm/yyyy
Management Process	Approved:	Issue No: 01 Prepared by:	Revision No: 00

Process Owner	**Department Managers**
Process Headings	**Process Details**
1.0 Purpose	To describe the procedure for planning and controlling ABCCL's operations. This procedure is a subset of MP 005 Planning of Integrated Quality, Food Safety and Environmental (IQFSE) management system and MP 006 IQFSE management system and processes.
2.0 Scope	This procedure is applicable to all significant procedures and activities included in the IQFSE management system.
3.0 Input	Product/service details: Customer requirements, significant risks and opportunities, legal requirements, external provision and Hazard Analysis and Critical Control Point (HACCP) plan.
4.0 Output	Applicable procedures and controls, quality plan, resource requirements, test data, design output and monitoring requirements.
5.0 Competency requirements	Knowledge of processes and control mechanisms.
6.0 Responsibility	Defined in Flowchart MP 013.1. Additional responsibilities are: Management Team shall:

Management Team shall:
- Identify critical operations and develop documented procedures to ensure compliance to ABCCL's requirements and legal requirements.

QA Manager shall:
- Provide the necessary training to the staff
- Present performance data at management review meetings.

Department Managers shall:
- Communicate the requirements at team briefings
- Monitor performance of activities
- Provide the information to the QA Manager.

Plant Manager shall:
- Provide the necessary resources for the operation
- Communicate with external providers in order to address environmental questions and issues that may arise.

ABC Company Limited	Procedures Manual	Reference MP 013 Page 2 of 4	
	Operational Planning and Control	Date Released dd/mm/yyyy	Date Reviewed dd/mm/yyyy
Management Process	Approved:	Issue No: 01 Prepared by:	Revision No: 00

	Process Headings	Process Details
7.0	Associated documents	MP 005 Planning of IQFSE management system
		CP 016 Customer requirements MP 003 Legal requirements SP 045 External provision CP 013 Design and development procedure.
8.0	Resources	Financial resources.
9.0	Measures/controls	Compliance to specified requirements in specification sheets Inspection reports Internal audits.
10.0	Definitions	**Operational control:** Controls necessary to ensure that operations are performed as specified under controlled conditions. They may be in the form of standard operating procedures (SOPs) or operational procedures. **Quality plan:** A document or a set of documents that together specify quality, food safety and environmental standards, practices, resources, specifications and the sequence of activities relevant to a product, service or contract.
11.0	System description	Flowchart MP 013.1 shows the operational planning procedure.
11.1	Product and process requirements	IQFSE management system planning (MP 005), IQFSE management system and its processes (MP 006), customer requirements (CP 016) and legal requirements (MP 003). They are implemented through individual procedures that specify the process owner; input, output and competency requirements; roles and responsibilities; measures and controls; resources needed and work instructions. A design process is also included in the IQFSE management system.
11.2	General criteria for controls	Controls are exercised through these activities: (a) Verification: Identification by visual or test methods, document and record control and by other methods as appropriate to the relevant procedure. When it is not possible to verify on receipt, the item is verified at the supplier's premises (AP 011), identification and traceability (AP 007) and inward goods inspection (CP 008). The design process includes verification and validation activities (AP 009);

ABC Company Limited	Procedures Manual	Reference MP 013 Page 3 of 4	
	Operational Planning and Control	Date Released dd/mm/yyyy	Date Reviewed dd/mm/yyyy
Management Process	Approved:	Issue No: 01 Prepared by:	Revision No: 00

Process Headings	Process Details
	(b) Control of processes: To ensure that activities are carried out as specified in individual procedures under controlled conditions, in-process controls have been introduced. QA Team monitors the records generated in the plant;
	(c) Release of finished goods: Finished goods are released on successful completion of the release of the finished goods procedure (CP 014). Storage and delivery are controlled through the storing of goods procedure CP 015);
	(d) Non-conforming items are treated according to the handing non-conformities procedure (AP 008) and the corrective and preventive action procedure (AP 013).
11.3 Criteria for specific controls	Specific controls are introduced and are implemented to ensure that food products are safe for consumption and to control activities that may have an adverse impact on the environment.
11.3.1 Food safety	In addition to the controls specified under Section 11.2, a hazard analysis plan (CP 027) has been implemented, Critical Control Points (CCPs) have been identified and specific controls have been implemented (CP 026) and monitored to assure food safety. Pre-requisite programmes (PRPs) are a part of control mechanisms (CP 028). ABCCL shall monitor, e.g. sanitation, pest management, environment cleanliness and waste disposal as required by the PRPs.
11.3.2 Environmental impact	1. Environmental impact of the activities is assessed according to procedure CP 031. Actions to address significant environmental aspects include elimination, substitution, engineering controls, administrative controls and the use of personal protective equipment. 2. QA Manager shall consider the following when controls are introduced: Emissions to air; waste management; packaging waste; suppliers, approval of new chemicals; storage and handling of raw materials; waste water treatment; management of contractors; building inspection; pipework inspection; future projects; demolition work; housekeeping; approval of new chemicals; storage and handling of raw materials; recycling; solid waste; energy and water usage.

ABC Company Limited	Procedures Manual	Reference MP 013 Page 4 of 4	
	Operational Planning and Control	Date Released dd/mm/yyyy	Date Reviewed dd/mm/yyyy
Management Process	Approved:	Issue No: 01 Prepared by:	Revision No: 00

	Process Headings	Process Details
11.4	Resource requirements	Resource requirements include equipment, machines, utilities, human resources, raw materials, supplies and others as required by individual procedures. They are addressed through the SP 009 resource provision procedure.
11.5	Communication of operational controls to employees	All Supervisors shall identify employees involved in operations and communicate the operational requirements at training sessions or at brief line meetings just prior to commencing the operations.
11.6	Communication of operational controls to suppliers and contractors	Communication with external providers and management of external procedures are carried out as specified in the external provision procedure (SP 045).
11.7	Change control	Changes are managed in a controlled manner (MP 020).
11.8	Other considerations	1. Controls are implemented to prevent deviations from our policies, objectives and compliance obligations. 2. Ensure that control processes are consistent with life cycle perspective. 3. Environmental requirements are considered for the procurement of products and services (CP 004).
12.0	Records	As described under individual procedures, management review process ensures that product specifications, product data records, process criteria, work instructions, production procedures, flowcharts, forms and checklists are maintained as required by the IQFSE management system.
13.0	Changes made	None.

ABC Company Limited	Procedures Manual	Flowchart MP 013.1 Page 1 of 1	
	Operational Planning	Date Released dd/mm/yyyy	Date Reviewed dd/mm/yyyy
Link MP 013	Approved:	Issue No: 01 Prepared by:	Revision No: 00

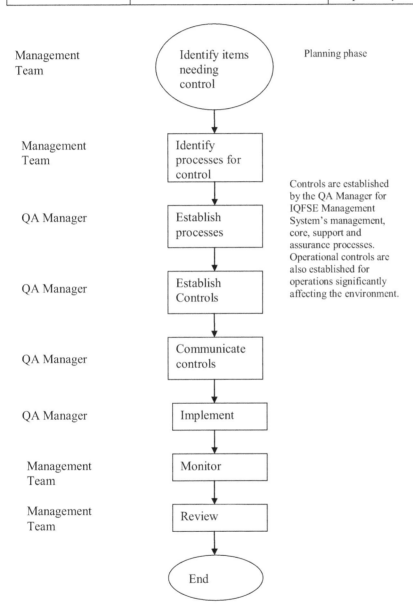

Management Team — Identify items needing control — Planning phase

Management Team — Identify processes for control

QA Manager — Establish processes — Controls are established by the QA Manager for IQFSE Management System's management, core, support and assurance processes. Operational controls are also established for operations significantly affecting the environment.

QA Manager — Establish Controls

QA Manager — Communicate controls

QA Manager — Implement

Management Team — Monitor

Management Team — Review

End

MP 014 Strategic Planning

ABC Company Limited	Procedures Manual	Reference MP 014 Page 1 of 2	
	Strategic Planning	Date Released dd/mm/yyyy	Date Reviewed dd/mm/yyyy
Management Process	Approved:	Issue No: 01 Prepared by:	Revision No: 00

Process Owner		**CEO**
	Process Headings	**Process Details**
1.0	Purpose	To describe the procedure for strategic planning in ABCCL.
2.0	Scope	The strategic plan applies to all the business functions of ABCCL.
3.0	Input	Strengths, weaknesses, opportunities and threats (SWOT) and political, economic, social and technological (PEST) analyses results, goals and objectives, previous plan and results, marketing plan, business plan, internal and external issues, needs of interested parties, environmental aspects and impacts.
4.0	Output	Strategic plan, performance indicators, implementation plan and communication.
5.0	Competency requirements	Knowledge of ABCCL's operations, vision, mission, objectives, goals, competition, financial projections and regulatory requirements and influence of external and internal environment.
6.0	Responsibility	Defined in Flowchart MP 014.1.
7.0	Associated documents	Internal and external issues (Form 002) Balanced score card (Figure MP 014.2) Strategy map (Figure MP 014.1) SWOT analysis report (Form 005) PEST analysis (Form 004) Strategic plan template (Form 032).
8.0	Resources	Planning module.
9.0	Measures/controls	Extent of completion of activities within the timeframe Financial measures Competition Environmental performance Customer feedback.
10.0	Definitions	**Strategy:** A broad programme for designing and achieving the objectives of the organisation and its response to its environment over time.
11.0	System description	Flowchart MP 014.1 shows the strategic planning process.
11.1	Preparation	Identify key decision makers who should be involved. Perform a preliminary stakeholder analysis, identify relevant regulations, policies, ordinances, charters, articles and contracts and their impact. Establish the process, purpose, form and timing of reports; roles; responsibilities; resources and limitations.

ABC Company Limited	Procedures Manual	Reference MP 014 Page 2 of 2	
	Strategic Planning	Date Released dd/mm/yyyy	Date Reviewed dd/mm/yyyy
Management Process	Approved:	Issue No: 01 Prepared by:	Revision No: 00

	Process Headings	Process Details
11.2	External and internal analysis	Refer to MP 001.
11.3	Formulate strategies	Using the results of SWOT analysis, formulate strategies and select the best. Decide on how to allocate resources, expand or diversify operations; whether to enter international markets; merge or enter into joint ventures and how to avoid hostile takeovers.
11.4	Risk analysis	Assess risks and opportunities associated with each strategy and the potential impact on the achievement of objectives. This is the creative step of developing strategies that will deliver the organisation's goals and objectives, mission and vision without exposing it to unacceptable risks.
11.5	Implementation plan	Pay attention to goals, interests and concerns of internal and external stakeholders. Include the anticipated changes and the role the organisation plays. Identify risks and integrate risk minimisation strategies into the implementation plan. Develop policies, practices and systems. Ensure staff have the necessary competencies. Define roles and responsibilities.
12.0	Records	Strategic plan Action plan.
13.0	Changes made	None.

Mission: *We are dedicated to producing premium wines to satisfy all market segments by working with our grape growers to improve the quality of grapes, adopting modern wine technology, enhancing the image of our products while focusing on social values of the community and minimising environmental impact.*

Vision: *ABC Company limited will be the largest exporter of premium quality wines while maintaining high ethical standards and providing employment to local staff.*

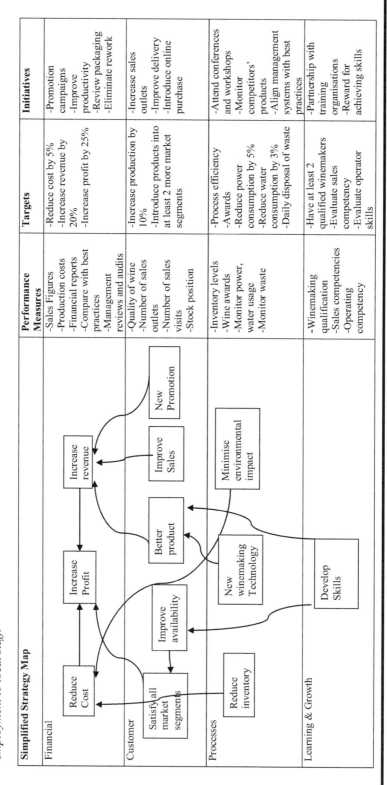

Simplified Strategy Map		Performance Measures	Targets	Initiatives
Financial		-Sales Figures -Production costs -Financial reports -Compare with best practices -Management reviews and audits	-Reduce cost by 5% -Increase revenue by 20% -Increase profit by 25%	-Promotion campaigns -Improve productivity -Review packaging -Eliminate rework
Customer		-Quality of wine -Number of sales outlets -Number of sales visits -Stock position	-Increase production by 10% -Introduce products into at least 2 more market segments	-Increase sales outlets -Improve delivery -Introduce online purchase
Processes		-Inventory levels -Wine awards -Monitor power, water usage -Monitor waste	-Process efficiency -Awards -Reduce power consumption by 5% -Reduce water consumption by 3% -Daily disposal of waste	-Attend conferences and workshops -Monitor competitors' products -Align management systems with best practices
Learning & Growth		-Winemaking qualification -Sales competencies -Operating competency	-Have at least 2 qualified winemakers -Evaluate sales competency -Evaluate operator skills	-Partnership with training organisations -Reward for achieving skills

Figure MP 014.1   Strategy map.

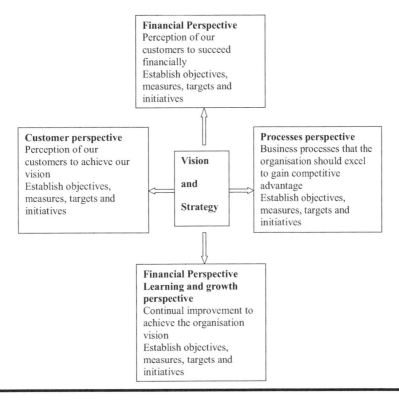

Figure MP 014.2 Balanced score card.

ABC Company Limited	Procedures Manual		Flowchart MP 014.1 Page 1 of 2	
	Strategic Planning		Date Released dd/mm/yyyy	Date Reviewed dd/mm/yyyy
Link MP 014	Approved:		Issue No: 01 Prepared by:	Revision No: 00

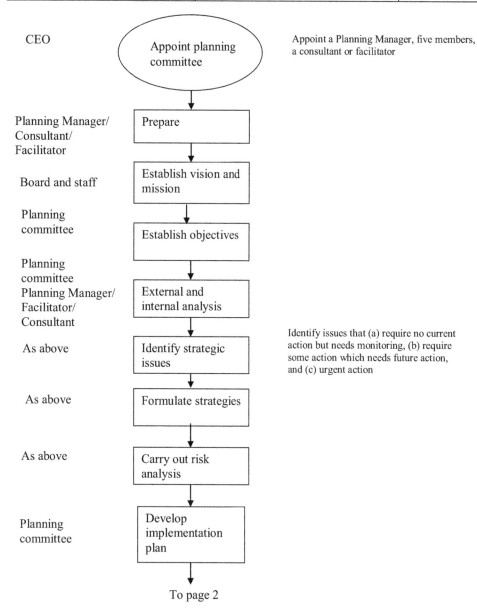

CEO — Appoint planning committee — Appoint a Planning Manager, five members, a consultant or facilitator

Planning Manager/ Consultant/ Facilitator — Prepare

Board and staff — Establish vision and mission

Planning committee — Establish objectives

Planning committee Planning Manager/ Facilitator/ Consultant — External and internal analysis

As above — Identify strategic issues — Identify issues that (a) require no current action but needs monitoring, (b) require some action which needs future action, and (c) urgent action

As above — Formulate strategies

As above — Carry out risk analysis

Planning committee — Develop implementation plan

To page 2

ABC Company Limited	**Procedures Manual**		**Flowchart MP 014.1** Page 2 of 2	
	Strategic Planning		Date Released dd/mm/yyyy	Date Reviewed dd/mm/yyyy
Link MP 014	Approved:		Issue No: 01 Prepared by:	Revision No: 00

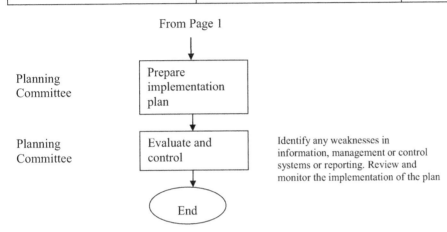

From Page 1

Planning Committee — Prepare implementation plan

Planning Committee — Evaluate and control

Identify any weaknesses in information, management or control systems or reporting. Review and monitor the implementation of the plan

End

MP 015　Production Planning

ABC Company Limited	Procedures Manual	Reference MP 015 Page 1 of 2	
	Production Planning	Date Released dd/mm/yyyy	Date Reviewed dd/mm/yyyy
Management Process	Approved:	Issue No: 01 Prepared by:	Revision No: 00

Process Owner	Production Planner
Process Headings	**Process Details**
1.0　Purpose	To describe the procedure for generating a long-range production plan, production schedule and a daily work schedule for ABBCL activities.
2.0　Scope	This procedure shall apply production and service operations of ABCCL.
3.0　Input	Previous production plan, raw material inventory levels, production capacities, work-in-progress inventory, finished goods inventory, short-term and long-term sales plan, marketing programme, pending orders, set-up times, lead times and workforce requirements.
4.0　Output	Short-term and long-term production plan and work schedule.
5.0　Competency requirements	Production planning skills, materials management and the ability to use the software module on production planning.
6.0　Responsibility	Defined in Flowchart MP 015.1. Additional responsibilities are: Engineering Manager shall: • Provide information on the status of equipment and machinery. Purchasing Manager shall: • Provide information on inventory levels of components.
7.0　Associated documents	Forecast Inventory levels of components and finished goods Production requirements and capacities Daily production data.
8.0　Resources	Production planning programme.
9.0　Measures/controls	Percentage completed according to the planning schedule.
10.0　System description	The procedure for planning for production is shown in Flowchart MP 015.1.
10.1　Demand forecast	Demand forecast is generated by the key marketing and sales personnel using standard forecasting techniques and tools such as sales growth, competitors' performance, published surveys (e.g. Neilsen report), market position and brand image. The data is broken down into individual product families and products for planning purposes.

ABC Company Limited	Procedures Manual	Reference MP 015 Page 2 of 2	
	Production Planning	Date Released dd/mm/yyyy	Date Reviewed dd/mm/yyyy
Management Process	Approved:	Issue No: 01 Prepared by:	Revision No: 00

	Process Headings	Process Details
10.2	Long-range planning meeting	Long-range planning meeting is held monthly between marketing, sales and production personnel. Key marketing and sales personnel, Production Planner, Purchasing Manager and the Engineering Manager shall attend the meeting. The purpose of the meeting is to generate a long-term demand forecast for each product and product family. The annual long-range forecast which has been established is reviewed at each meeting and amended as necessary.
10.3	Production planning meeting	The purpose of the production planning meeting is to discuss the production work schedule at each weekly meeting. The Plant Manager, Purchasing Manager, QA Manager, Engineering Manager, Food Safety Manager, Environment Manager and Line Supervisor shall attend the meeting. Previous weekly schedule is discussed and compared with production figures. The information provides the basis for the next weekly production schedule.
10.4	Daily work schedule	The daily work schedule meeting is a brief meeting held at the end of each day to evaluate the production performance against the weekly schedule, inventory levels and labour requirements for the next day's production. Amendments are made, if necessary, to the work schedule. The meeting is attended by the Production Planner, Purchasing Manager, Inward Goods Officer, Plant Manager, QA Manager, Engineering Manager, Food Safety Manager, Environment Manager and Line Supervisor.
11.0	Records	Daily work schedule Short-term and long-term plans.
12.0	Changes made	None.

ABC Company Limited	Procedures Manual	Flowchart MP 015.1 Page 1 of 2	
	Production Planning	Date Released dd/mm/yyyy	Date Reviewed dd/mm/yyyy
Link MP 015	Approved:	Issue No: 01 Prepared by:	Revision No: 00

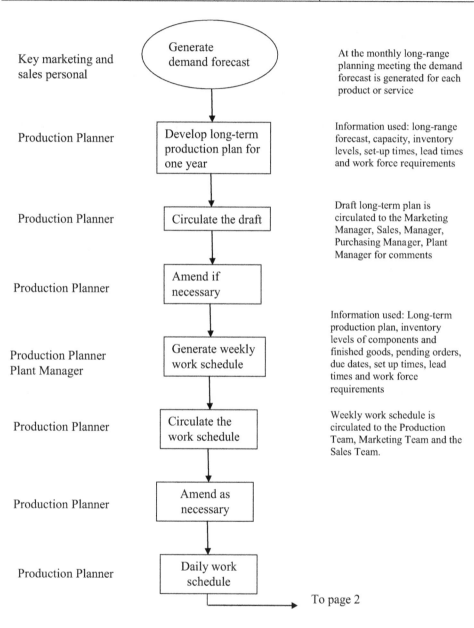

Key marketing and sales personal	Generate demand forecast	At the monthly long-range planning meeting the demand forecast is generated for each product or service
Production Planner	Develop long-term production plan for one year	Information used: long-range forecast, capacity, inventory levels, set-up times, lead times and work force requirements
Production Planner	Circulate the draft	Draft long-term plan is circulated to the Marketing Manager, Sales, Manager, Purchasing Manager, Plant Manager for comments
Production Planner	Amend if necessary	
Production Planner Plant Manager	Generate weekly work schedule	Information used: Long-term production plan, inventory levels of components and finished goods, pending orders, due dates, set up times, lead times and work force requirements
Production Planner	Circulate the work schedule	Weekly work schedule is circulated to the Production Team, Marketing Team and the Sales Team.
Production Planner	Amend as necessary	
Production Planner	Daily work schedule	

To page 2

ABC Company Limited	Procedures Manual	Flowchart MP 015.1 Page 2 of 2	
	Production Planning	Date Released dd/mm/yyyy	Date Reviewed dd/mm/yyyy
Link MP 015	Approved:	Issue No: 01 Prepared by:	Revision No: 00

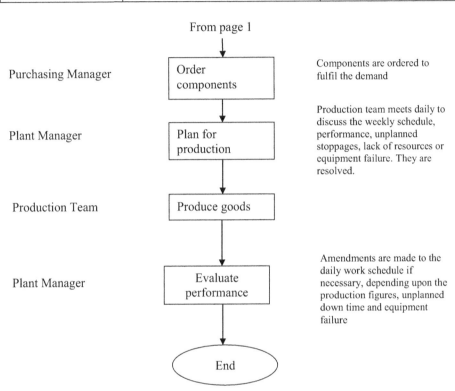

From page 1

Purchasing Manager   Order components   Components are ordered to fulfil the demand

Plant Manager   Plan for production   Production team meets daily to discuss the weekly schedule, performance, unplanned stoppages, lack of resources or equipment failure. They are resolved.

Production Team   Produce goods

Plant Manager   Evaluate performance   Amendments are made to the daily work schedule if necessary, depending upon the production figures, unplanned down time and equipment failure

End

MP 016 Looking After Our Customers

ABC Company Limited	Procedures Manual		Reference MP 016 Page 1 of 2	
	Looking After Our Customers		Date Released dd/mm/yyyy	Date Reviewed dd/mm/yyyy
Management Process	Approved:		Issue No: 01 Prepared by:	Revision No: 00

Process Owner		**Customer Relations Manager**
	Process Headings	**Process Details**
1.0	Purpose	To describe how we focus on customers' needs and expectations.
2.0	Scope	This procedure applies to activities aimed at satisfying our customers' requirements.
3.0	Input	Customer needs and expectations, resource management and customer relations management.
4.0	Output	Satisfied customers and good customer relations and expansion of customer base.
5.0	Competency requirements	Customer relations skills and communication skills.
6.0	Responsibility	Responsibilities are defined under individual procedures.
7.0	Associated documents	CP 016 Customer requirements MP 003 Legal and other requirements MP 007 Risk management SP 046 Customer satisfaction.
8.0	Resources	Necessary resources are described under individual procedures.
9.0	Measures/controls	See control measures under individual procedures.
10.0	System description	ABCCL has developed and implemented procedures for: a. Determining customer requirements and applicable regulatory and statutory requirements; b. Determining risks and opportunities related to products, services and customer satisfaction and taking appropriate action and c. Focusing on customer satisfaction.
10.1	Determining customer requirements and applicable regulatory and statutory requirements	This is achieved through the customer requirements procedure (CP 016). The procedure defines: (a) staffing positions, roles and responsibilities for customer service and sales; (b) customer communication training; (c) developing and implementing procedures for taking orders and (d) reviewing customer requirements for accuracy and completeness. The procedure also covers the determination of statutory and regulatory requirements that relate to the products.

ABC Company Limited	**Procedures Manual**		**Reference MP 016** Page 2 of 2	
	Looking After Our Customers		Date Released dd/mm/yyyy	Date Reviewed dd/mm/yyyy
Management Process	Approved:		Issue No: 01 Prepared by:	Revision No: 00

	Process Headings	Process Details
10.2	Determination of risks and opportunities affecting products, services and customer satisfaction	Risk management procedure (MP 007) defines the application of the risk management principle to products, services and customer satisfaction. When processes or products are developed, the ABCCL Integrated Quality, Food Safety and Environmental (IQFSE) management system identifies the risks and opportunities that can affect the conformity of the products and services or the ability to affect customer satisfaction. Strategic planning process ensures that they are adequately addressed.
10.3	Focus on creating customer satisfaction	Focus on customer satisfaction is maintained through the customer satisfaction procedure (SP 046) by receiving and analysing information and communicating it to relevant parties.
10.4	Focus on consistently providing products and services	ABCCL is able to consistently provide products and services that meet customer requirements and statutory and regulatory requirements by inspecting and verifying the process requirements and through internal audits.
10.5	Customer needs and expectations	Customer needs and expectations are implemented through two processes: the marketing process and the sales process. Marketing processes are concerned with finding out what the customer wants to attract them to our company. The sales process is concerned with making contact with customers for existing products and services and converting enquiries into firm orders.
11.0	Records	Defined under individual procedures.
12.0	Changes made	None.

MP 017 Management of Emergencies

ABC Company Limited	Procedures Manual		Reference MP 017 Page 1 of 4	
	Management of Emergencies	Date Released dd/mm/yyyy		Date Reviewed dd/mm/yyyy
Management Process	Approved:	Issue No: 01 Revision No: 00 Prepared by:		

Process Owner	**Emergency Coordinator**
Process Headings	**Process Details**
1.0 Purpose	To describe the procedure for identifying potential emergency situations and generating appropriate responses.
2.0 Scope	This procedure applies to all emergency situations that can arise due to internal and external causes, which can be accidental or deliberate.
3.0 Input	Potential emergency situations, environmental and food safety impact, risk analysis and regulatory requirements.
4.0 Output	Primary and secondary solutions.
5.0 Competency requirements	Knowledge of the company's operational controls related to significant environmental aspects and food safety hazards, emergency situations, emergency response plan and response planning skills.
6.0 Responsibility	CEO shall: • Appoint the Emergency Coordinator • Invoke the business continuity plan after the emergency. Emergency Coordinator shall: • Appoint the Emergency Response Team (ERT) • Invoke emergency response plan. Plant Manager shall: • Provide necessary training to employees on emergency situations and responses • Coordinate emergency activities • Appoint a Chemical Response Team (CRT). The ERT shall: • Develop the emergency response plan • Implement the response plan in case of an emergency • Identify and assess the impact of potential emergencies on food safety and the environment • Prioritise the emergency situation on the basis of seriousness and probability • Submit results and recommendations for prevention and/or contingency actions to the Management Team.

ABC Company Limited	Procedures Manual	Reference MP 017 Page 2 of 4	
	Management of Emergencies	Date Released dd/mm/yyyy	Date Reviewed dd/mm/yyyy
Management Process	Approved:	Issue No: 01 Revision No: 00 Prepared by:	

	Process Headings	Process Details
		Chemical Response Team shall: • Be aware of health hazards, physical hazards and personnel protective gear required for cleaning up spillages • Know the location, purpose and application techniques for effective spill response equipment, materials and the maintenance of supplies to clean spillages • Request external consultant on dealing with chemical hazards, if needed. Supervisors shall: • Lead emergency response activities in their areas. All employees shall: • Be aware of the emergency response plan • Follow the directives in the plan • Follow the instructions given by the Supervisor.
7.0	Associated documents	Potential emergency situations and impacts (Form 033) Primary and secondary solutions.
8.0	Resources	Statutory regulations Appropriate equipment for emergencies.
9.0	Measures/controls	Unforeseen emergencies Awareness of emergency response plan amongst employees Response time, if applicable Delay in attending to injured person.
10.0	Definitions	**Emergency:** An event or circumstance that may have a significant impact on food safety, company's operations, company's personnel, customers, facilities, assets and records. Emergency situations include sudden, unanticipated occurrence, natural or man-made.
11.0	System description	
11.1	Information and procedures	1. Emergency response plan shall include the information presented in Form 034 and internal and external contact details (Form 035, Form 036).

ABC Company Limited	Procedures Manual	Reference MP 017 Page 3 of 4	
	Management of Emergencies	Date Released dd/mm/yyyy	Date Reviewed dd/mm/yyyy
Management Process	Approved:	Issue No: 01 Revision No: 00 Prepared by:	

Process Headings	Process Details
	2. Emergency protocols:
	(a) ERT shall develop emergency protocols for these activities:
	• Fire and evacuation
	• Medical emergency
	• Terrorist threat
	• Utility failure
	• Suspicious package
	• Flood
	• Gas leak
	• Civil disturbance
	• Nuclear threat
	• Hurricane
	• Hazardous materials release
	• Chemical spillage
	• Sabotage
	• Bioterrorism; and
	(b) Procedures for:
	• Emergency operation, shut-down and securing of critical processes and equipment
	• Recovery and start-up of critical operations and equipment after an emergency
	• For containment and clean-up of spillages.
11.2 Assessment of emergency situations	ERT shall consider the following regarding emergency situations:
	• Probability and the ability to predict the occurrence
	• Estimated period between the prediction and the actual onset of the event
	• Estimated period between the occurrence of the emergency and any impact on food safety and the environment
	• Possibility of controlling or minimising the impact
	• Duration of the emergency and impact.
	Consideration for assessing the impact:
	• Impact on food safety and environment
	• Health effects, injuries and the working environment

ABC Company Limited	**Procedures Manual**	**Reference MP 017** Page 4 of 4	
	Management of Emergencies	Date Released dd/mm/yyyy	Date Reviewed dd/mm/yyyy
Management Process	Approved:	Issue No: 01 Revision No: 00 Prepared by:	

	Process Headings	Process Details
		• Company's reputation and customer confidence • Security measures to protect fixed and movable assets and personnel • Legal issues and insurance cover • Ability to recover lost data • Recovery period after the emergency • Damage to equipment • Losses due to contamination, spoilage and damage • Effect on related functions.
11.3	Generating responses	After potential emergency situations have been identified and prioritised, the ERT shall: (a) establish short-term and long-term solutions to prevent or mitigate the consequences; (b) select the most appropriate solution; (c) test and evaluate these solutions and (d) include them in the emergency response plan and training material. The ERT shall consider the following when solutions are established: • Previous emergency situations response plan and action taken to prevent or mitigate the risk • Requirement for personnel safety equipment • Preventive measures taken to prevent unsafe conditions and unsafe acts • Generate potential long-term and short-term solutions • Determine the most effective primary and secondary solutions • Test and evaluate solutions and equipment for effectiveness • Review insurance policies and contractual agreements with contractors and suppliers • Statutory and legal requirements.
12.0	Records	Potential emergency situations Actions to prevent or mitigate consequences.
13.0	Changes made	None.

MP 018 Emergency Response Planning

ABC Company Limited	Procedures Manual	Reference MP 018 Page 1 of 4	
	Emergency Response Planning	Date Released dd/mm/yyyy	Date Reviewed dd/mm/yyyy
Management Processes	Approved:	Issue No: 01 Prepared by:	Revision No: 00

Process Owner		**Emergency Coordinator**
	Process Headings	**Process Details**
1.0	Purpose	To describe the procedure for emergency response planning.
2.0	Scope	The procedure applies to emergency situations that impact significantly on the environment and food safety and to all personnel at the site of the organisation.
3.0	Input	Potential emergency situations, emergency warnings, responses, regulatory requirements and evacuation procedures.
4.0	Output	Appropriate response to emergency situations, emergency response plan and recall procedure.
5.0	Competency requirements	Knowledge of the company's operational controls related to significant environmental aspects and food safety hazards, emergency situations, emergency response plan and emergency response planning skills.
6.0	Responsibility	Emergency Response Team (ERT) shall: • Develop the emergency response plan. Chemical Response Team shall: • Provide input to the ERT. Supervisors shall: • Direct emergency response activities. All employees shall: • Be aware of the emergency response plan • Follow instructions given by Supervisors.
7.0	Associated documents	Emergency response plan (Form 034) Management of emergencies procedure (MP 017) Chemical clean-up plan Emergency protocols.
8.0	Resources	Equipment for handling emergencies.
9.0	Measures/controls	Emergency drill log Awareness of the emergency response plan among all employees Period to initiate response.
10.0	Definitions	**Material Safety Data (MSD) sheets:** Document describing the physical and chemical properties of the chemical, required protection systems, emergency response and disposal method. **Hazardous material inventory statement:** Information on area-specific chemical inventories and hazards during an emergency.

ABC Company Limited	Procedures Manual		Reference MP 018 Page 2 of 4	
	Emergency Response Planning	Date Released dd/mm/yyyy		Date Reviewed dd/mm/yyyy
Management Processes	Approved:	Issue No: 01 Prepared by:		Revision No: 00

	Process Headings	**Process Details**
11.0	System description	
11.1	Preparation for emergency	The preparation for accidents and emergencies can be managed through several methods. These may include, but are not limited to:

11.1 Preparation for emergency — The preparation for accidents and emergencies can be managed through several methods. These may include, but are not limited to:

- Orientation classes at induction of new employees
- Hazard evaluation training
- Emergency systems evaluation and surveys
- Training to respond to emergencies
- Departmental meetings
- Emergency scenarios and implementation of appropriate training.

11.2 Action plans

11.2.1 Notification

As soon as an emergency has been detected, the Emergency Coordinator shall authorise the notification and immediate response of appropriate personnel. Communication shall be made by phone, in person or through the public address system according to the level of threat.

Level 3: Stand-by mode:

At this level of emergency, appropriate personnel are notified and instructed to remain in stand-by mode ready for action:

- Critical operations and/or equipment are prepared for emergency operation and shut-down according to emergency protocols
- All appropriate records, equipment and documents are prepared for transfer to a secure location.

Level 2: Minimum response:

Only selected personnel are notified to respond immediately, and others are instructed to remain on stand-by:

- All personnel are to remain in current locations until instructed to leave
- All appropriate records, equipment and documents are transferred to a secure location

ABC Company Limited	Procedures Manual	Reference MP 018 Page 3 of 4	
	Emergency Response Planning	Date Released dd/mm/yyyy	Date Reviewed dd/mm/yyyy
Management Processes	Approved:	Issue No: 01 Prepared by:	Revision No: 00

Process Headings	Process Details
	• Business operations with customers are discontinued • Other functions continue until further notification. Level 1: Maximum response: All designated personnel shall respond as instructed. All sections of the facility may be closed and all personnel authorised to deal with the emergency are to remain in current locations or evacuated according to the response plan: • All business operations are discontinued • All appropriate records, equipment and documents are secured • Employees and other personnel remain in current locations until escorted by assigned personnel in the emergency response plan. ERT shall consider the following when considering the appropriate response: detection, reaction, assessment, notification, mobilisation, recovery and resumption.
11.2.2　Responding to emergency situations	(a) When an emergency situation has been declared: • All employees shall remain calm waiting for instructions from the Supervisor. No action shall be taken that might compromise the safety of personnel • Emergency response plan shall be invoked by the Emergency Coordinator • If possible, emergency response activity record shall be maintained • As instructed by the Plant Manager, the Supervisors assist in controlling the impact of the emergency on employees, visitors and other personnel on-site. (b) After the emergency: • Team Leader shall assess the impact of the emergency and report to the Management Team • Perform recovery activities, clean-up procedures according to emergency protocols

ABC Company Limited	**Procedures Manual**	**Reference MP 018** Page 4 of 4	
	Emergency Response Planning	Date Released dd/mm/yyyy	Date Reviewed dd/mm/yyyy
Management Processes	Approved:	Issue No: 01 Prepared by:	Revision No: 00

	Process Headings	**Process Details**
		• Refer media requests to the Plant Manager • Complete the emergency response activity record.
11.3	Review	After every emergency situation and response, the ERT shall review the response activity log and review and modify the emergency response plan as necessary. In the absence of emergency situations, the ERT shall review the plan at least annually.
11.4	Emergency drills and tests	1. Whenever a new emergency situation has been identified, the Emergency Coordinator shall provide appropriate responses and conduct the necessary training and tests required to prevent or mitigate the risk. 2. Emergency Coordinator shall conduct quarterly drills to test various aspects the emergency response plan. 3. The results of such drills are documented in the emergency response activity record (Form 037).
12.0	Records	Emergency training records Emergency response plan (Form 034).
13.0	Changes made	None.

MP 019 Actions to Address Risks and Opportunities

ABC Company Limited	Procedures Manual	Reference MP 019 Page 1 of 3	
	Actions to Address Risks and Opportunities	Date Released dd/mm/yyyy	Date Reviewed dd/mm/yyyy
Management Processes	Approved:	Issue No: 01 Prepared by:	Revision No: 00

Process Owner	QA Manager

	Process Headings	Process Details
1.0	Purpose	To describe the scheme for planning to address significant risks, significant environmental aspects and legal risks.
2.0	Scope	This procedure applies to the risks, environmental aspects and legal risks associated with ABCCL's products, processes and services.
3.0	Input	Significant risks, significant environmental aspects, risk register and action plan.
4.0	Output	Methods to manage risks and opportunities and new practices using new technology and other techniques to address the needs of consumers.
5.0	Competency requirements	Knowledge of risk analysis process, identification of environmental aspects and ABCCL's operations.
6.0	Responsibility	The responsibilities are described under these procedures: MP 007 Risk management CP 031 Environmental aspects and impacts MP 003 Statutory and regulatory requirements.
7.0	Associated documents	Described under the individual procedures.
8.0	Resources	None.
9.0	Measures/controls	Internal audits Management reviews.
10.0	System description	The scheme for planning for action is shown in Flowchart MP 019.1.
10.1	Interrelation between Integrated Quality, Food Safety and Environmental (IQFSE) management systems and risks and opportunities	Organisation and its context – input to risks and opportunities process. Needs and expectations of interested parties – input to risks and opportunities process Corrective actions – input to risks and opportunities process Analysis and evaluation – input to risks and opportunities process and output of actions to address risks and opportunities Management review – input to risks and opportunities process and output of actions to address risks and opportunities Leadership – output of actions to address risks and opportunities Customer focus – output of actions to address risks and opportunities IQFSE processes – input to risks and opportunities process.

ABC Company Limited	Procedures Manual	Reference MP 019 Page 2 of 3	
	Actions to Address Risks and Opportunities	Date Released dd/mm/yyyy	Date Reviewed dd/mm/yyyy
Management Processes	Approved:	Issue No: 01 Prepared by:	Revision No: 00

	Process Headings	Process Details
10.2	Planning for action	1. Inputs to risks and opportunities are converted to an action plan to address risks and opportunities through the generation of objectives. 2. When objectives are generated, significant risks, significant environmental aspects and legal risks are taken into consideration along with the needs of interested parties, policy, strategic plan, internal and external issues and other factors. 3. The action plan (Form 027) is implemented through: P – Procedures and operating instructions O – Organisationally controlled training S – Supervision T – Technology. The implementation programme considers the financial, technological and business requirements when action is planned.
10.3	Integration into the IQFSE management system	(a) Procedures and operating instructions are integrated through the document control procedure; (b) Organisationally controlled training programmes are integrated through the training and development procedure; (c) Supervision – supervisory activities necessary to address actions generated from risks and opportunities are integrated through the training and development procedure and (d) Technology – technology necessary to implement the actions is integrated through the information technology procedure.
10.4	Significance of risks and opportunities	The actions generated through objectives are proportional to the significance of risk and opportunities. The most significant risks generate the most significant actions and the most significant opportunities have major project plans.
10.5	Evaluation of effectiveness	The effectiveness of the programme is monitored at predefined intervals through control procedures and reviewed at management review meetings.

ABC Company Limited	Procedures Manual		Reference MP 019 Page 3 of 3	
	Actions to Address Risks and Opportunities	Date Released dd/mm/yyyy		Date Reviewed dd/mm/yyyy
Management Processes	Approved:	Issue No: 01 Prepared by:	Revision No: 00	

	Process Headings	**Process Details**
11.0	Records	Action plan.
12.0	Changes made	None.

ABC Company Limited	Procedures Manual	Flowchart MP 019.1 Page 1 of 1	
	Actions to Address Risks and Opportunities	Date Released dd/mm/yyyy	Date Reviewed dd/mm/yyyy
Link MP 019/CP 032	Approved:	Issue No: 01 Prepared by:	Revision No: 00

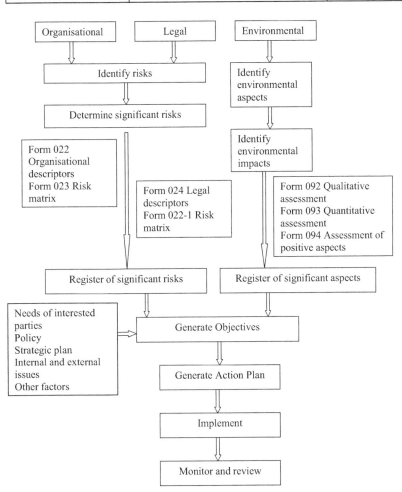

MP 020 Change Management

ABC Company Limited	Procedures Manual	Reference MP 020 Page 1 of 4	
	Change Management	Date Released dd/mm/yyyy	Date Reviewed dd/mm/yyyy
Management Processes	Approved:	Issue No: 01 Prepared by:	Revision No: 00

Process Owner	QA Manager	
	Process Headings	Process Details
1.0	Purpose	To describe the procedure for making changes in our Integrated Quality, Food Safety and Environmental (IQFSE) management system that may affect quality, operations, environment and safety in a controlled manner.
2.0	Scope	This procedure applies to changes to specifications, processes, products and others that are necessary for effective operations of ABCCL's IQFSE management system.
3.0	Input	Change request, process, product, customer request, regulatory changes, improvement opportunities, corrective actions and company/industry changes.
4.0	Output	New or updated document, effective and efficient process or product and customer satisfaction.
5.0	Competency requirements	Knowledge of the IQFSE management system and appropriate skills relating to the proposed change.
6.0	Responsibility	Defined in Flowchart MP 020.1.
7.0	Associated documents	Change request (Form 109) Document control procedure (SP 001) Record control procedure (SP 002).
8.0	Resources	IQFSE management system.
9.0	Measures/controls	Internal audits Management reviews Performance measures.
10.0	Definitions	**Change:** Alteration to: (a) processes; (b) documents, equipment, hardware and software; (c) roles, responsibilities and training; (d) supplier selection and management and (e) other changes such as changes to inputs, resources, persons, activities, controls, measurements and outputs. **Excluded:** Changes such as changing employees, editorial changes to forms, flowcharts and documents.
11.0	System description	Flowchart MP 020.1 shows the process for making changes. A change may be triggered by: • Customer feedback or customer complaint • Product, process and/or service failure • Process needs to be updated in response to external or internal changes or customer requirements

ABC Company Limited	Procedures Manual	Reference MP 020 Page 2 of 4	
	Change Management	Date Released dd/mm/yyyy	Date Reviewed dd/mm/yyyy
Management Processes	Approved:	Issue No: 01 Prepared by:	Revision No: 00

	Process Headings	Process Details
		• New processes are introduced into the management system • The need to comply with regulatory requirements • Innovation and opportunity for improvement • An emergency situation • Request from employees and other stakeholders • Results of audits and management reviews • Corrective actions • Identified risk • Deemed necessary by the management.
11.1	Consideration when making changes	(a) Methods to address unintended consequences of change; (b) Methods of monitoring the effectiveness of change and identify risks and opportunities associated with the change and (c) Preventing obstacles to achieve objectives.
11.2	Who can make a change request?	A change may be requested by any employee, a customer or a regulatory authority.
11.3	Prioritising change control	Method of assigning priority shall consider: (a) consequences of change; (b) impact on customers and relevant interested parties; (c) impact on quality, food safety and environmental objectives and (d) effectiveness of processes. (a) Emergency: Emergency changes require immediate response; (b) High priority: Changes which are necessary to address potential failure have to be dealt with high priority; (c) Medium priority: Changes which are necessary for improvement and innovation and require no timeframe are categorised as medium priority changes and (d) Low priority: These changes are desirable but not necessary.
11.4	Changes to process outputs	Product or service output: Consider the feasibility, resources and skills needed for the product or service. Documents and records output: Document control and record control procedures.

ABC Company Limited	Procedures Manual	Reference MP 020 Page 3 of 4	
	Change Management	Date Released dd/mm/yyyy	Date Reviewed dd/mm/yyyy
Management Processes	Approved:	Issue No: 01 Prepared by:	Revision No: 00

	Process Headings	Process Details
11.5	Changes to orders and contracts	When changes are initiated by the customer, the amended order or contract shall undergo the same procedure. If the initial order is in the process of being fulfilled, negotiated settlement shall be made with the customer.
11.6	Potential consequences of change	The Management Team shall determine the consequences of change, which can be positive or negative, and how they are addressed. These changes can be related to any process, any part of a process such as inputs, resources, people, activities, controls and measurements, outputs, products itself and/or recipes. New risks and opportunities associated with the change shall also be considered.
11.7	Environmental aspects, food safety aspects and other impacts of changes	When changes are planned or done, consideration shall be given to environmental aspects and impacts as described in procedure CP 031. QA Manager shall ensure that environmental concerns, quality issues and food safety issues are addressed when the project is reviewed. Any change to input, processing methods, outputs, storage and delivery shall not compromise safety of food.
11.8	Maintaining the integrity of the IQFSE management system during change	Some typical IQFSE management system considerations during the change include: Change, revision or retention of documentation (SP 001: Document control) Awareness of the change and the need for further training (SP 014) Review of objectives and goals (MP 008) Review the infrastructure (SP 010) New or revised monitoring and inspection (AP 003).
11.9	Emergency changes	Employees are allowed to take appropriate action urgently to protect the health and safety employees, the environment or a food item during an emergency or unplanned event. However, such changes shall be followed up with appropriate documentation at the earliest opportunity.

ABC Company Limited	Procedures Manual		Reference MP 020 Page 4 of 4	
	Change Management	Date Released dd/mm/yyyy		Date Reviewed dd/mm/yyyy
Management Processes	Approved:	Issue No: 01 Prepared by:		Revision No: 00

	Process Headings	**Process Details**
11.10	Resources	The Management Team shall determine the resources needed with description of relevant specifications and how they will be obtained. The expenditure for acquiring such resources has to be approved as follows: Changes that do not involve additional costs: Approval by the Management Team Changes that cost between [*state the limits here*] – approval by the Plant Manager Changes that cost between [*state the limits here*] – approval by the Managing Director.
11.11	Assigning responsibilities and authorities	The Management Team shall determine if responsibilities and authorities have to be reassigned, and if so, the team shall define the responsibilities and authorities related to each change.
11.12	Implementation of change	QA Manager shall be responsible for implementing the change(s) and monitoring in order to ensure that it has the intended effect. However, during the implementation phase, if further assessment is deemed necessary, the revised changes shall be reviewed by the Management Team. Further progress shall only be made after the approval of the revised change.
12.0	Records	Change management request (Form 109).
13.0	Changes made	None.

ABC Company Limited	Procedures Manual		Flowchart MP 020.1 Page 1 of 1	
	Change Management	Date Released dd/mm/yyyy		Date Reviewed dd/mm/yyyy
Link MP 020/MP 021	Approved:	Issue No: 01 Prepared by:		Revision No: 00

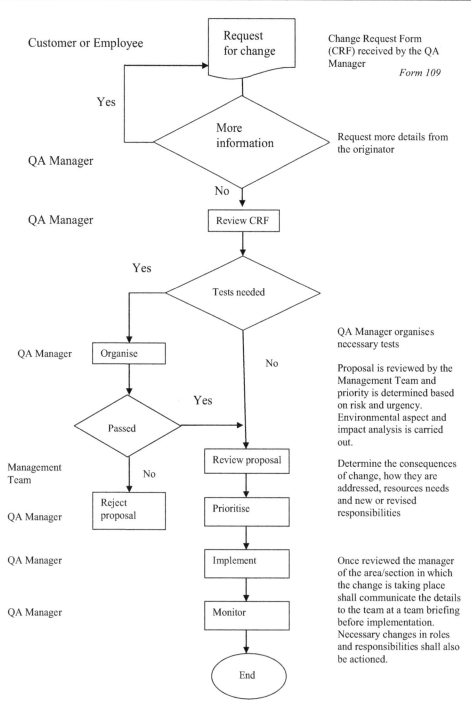

MP 021 Control of Product and Service Changes

ABC Company Limited	Procedures Manual	Reference MP 021 Page 1 of 2	
	Control of Product and Service Changes	Date Released dd/mm/yyyy	Date Reviewed dd/mm/yyyy
Management Process	Approved:	Issue No: 01 Prepared by:	Revision No: 00

Process Owner		QA Manager
	Process Headings	**Process Details**
1.0	Purpose	To describe the procedure for controlling product and service changes. It is a subset of the change management procedure (MP 020).
2.0	Scope	This procedure applies to production and service operations.
3.0	Input	Change request and production and service operations.
4.0	Output	Changed procedure, better performance, reduced unplanned downtime and staff satisfaction.
5.0	Competency requirements	Knowledge of products and processes, problem-solving skills and change management skills.
6.0	Responsibility	As defined in Flowchart MP 020.1.
7.0	Associated documents	Change request form (Form 109) Change management procedure (MP 020).
8.0	Resources	Resources needed to manage change.
9.0	Measures/controls	Performance after change Unplanned downtime Breakdown log.
10.0	Definitions	**Planned change:** Deliberate decision to make a change and is managed to ensure that it is effectively implemented to achieve desired outcome. **Unplanned change:** Immediate change that must be done because of unexpected circumstances, but it must still be controlled. **Unintended change:** Unexpected outcome as a result of a change and action may be required to minimise undesired results.
11.0	System description	The process of making changes is shown in Flowchart MP 020.1.
11.1	Need for change	Numerous factors can contribute to the need to make a product or service change. Some of them are: <ul><li>Customer feedback</li><li>Product failure</li><li>Unsafe product or process</li><li>Employee feedback</li><li>Innovation</li><li>Identified risk</li><li>Internal audit result of management review</li></ul>

ABC Company Limited	Procedures Manual		Reference MP 021 Page 2 of 2	
	Control of Product and Service Changes		Date Released dd/mm/yyyy	Date Reviewed dd/mm/yyyy
Management Process	Approved:		Issue No: 01 Prepared by:	Revision No: 00

	Process Headings	Process Details
		• Identified non-compliance • Ineffective change.
11.2	Change request	Form 109 shall be made to request a change.
11.3	Review of change	1. Management Team shall review the request and determine whether further tests, validation and verification are required. QA Manager shall organise necessary activities to evaluate the change. 2. Management Team shall consider this at the review: • Consequences of the change • Probability of occurrence • Impact on customers, interested parties including employees and objectives • Effectiveness of the process • Other issues. 3. Following the review, the Management Team has two options: Reject the proposal: If the change does not have the intended effect, no change is made. Accept the proposal: If the change leads to continual improvement.
11.4	Control of changes	1. The change shall not compromise the safe use of the product, its safety or the performance. 2. The change shall be communicated to the customer by the sales or Marketing Team, and the customer's views shall be considered carefully by the team. 3. Approval of the proposal: If the change has been effective, QA Manager shall update specification, revise applicable documents, train employees and communicate the change.
11.5	Monitor the change	QA Team shall monitor the impact of the change and take necessary action as outlined in Sections 11.3 and 11.4.
12.0	Records	Change request form Test results Records of reviews.
13.0	Changes made	None.

CORE PROCEDURES

CP 001 Approval of Suppliers

ABC Company Limited	Procedures Manual	Reference CP 001 Page 1 of 4	
	Approval of Suppliers	Date Released dd/mm/yyyy	Date Reviewed dd/mm/yyyy
Core Process	Approved:	Issue No: 01 Prepared by:	Revision No: 00

Process Owner	Management Team
Process Headings	**Process Details**

	Process Headings	Process Details
1.0	Purpose	To describe the procedure for the selection and evaluation of suppliers for purchasing products, services and raw materials for ABC Company Limited (ABCCL).
2.0	Scope	This procedure shall apply to all suppliers categorised as critical under Section 6.0, those identified by ABCCL and those who have requested to be considered for the selection and evaluation process.
3.0	Input	Information on suppliers and purchasing requirements.
4.0	Output	Approved Supplier List (ASL).
5.0	Competency requirements	Knowledge of purchasing procedure, requirements, supplier categories, management systems and audit skills.
6.0	Responsibility	See Flowchart CP 001.1. Additional responsibilities are set out below. Purchasing Manager shall: <ul><li>Communicate with suppliers</li><li>Approve and remove suppliers from the ASL when necessary.</li></ul> Environment Manager shall: <ul><li>Verify that the supplier has the necessary environmental permits and is managing waste according to regulatory requirements</li><li>Evaluate Material Safety Data (MSD) sheets and communicate any hazard information to the Management Team.</li></ul> QA Manager and Food Safety Manager shall: <ul><li>Ensure that the supplier as a certified food safety programme in place.</li></ul> Supplier shall: <ul><li>Comply with or exceed all applicable regulatory requirements and any related material specifications for the supplied material</li><li>Provide evidence of documented management systems as applicable to the supplier's operation which shall be reviewed, evaluated and audited.</li></ul>

ABC Company Limited	Procedures Manual	Reference CP 001 Page 2 of 4	
	Approval of Suppliers	Date Released dd/mm/yyyy	Date Reviewed dd/mm/yyyy
Core Process	Approved:	Issue No: 01 Prepared by:	Revision No: 00

	Process Headings	Process Details
7.0	Associated documents	Supplier evaluation sheet (Form 038) ASL (Form 039) Supplier performance (Form 040) Risk analysis (Form 041).
8.0	Resources	Software module.
9.0	Measures/controls	Supplier performance measurement Audits.
10.0	Definitions	**Critical suppliers:** Suppliers are categorised as critical if one or more of these conditions apply: • Essential for production and/or parts • Manufacture of custom design and/or parts • Manufacture of items with extended lead times • High cost • Provide services that have direct impact on product quality and safety. **Non-critical suppliers:** Suppliers are categorised as non-critical if one or more of these conditions apply: • No negative impact on product quality, safety or customer requirements • Infrequent purchases (annually) • Low cost.
11.0	System description	The process is shown in Flowchart CP 001.1.
11.1	Categories of products and services	These categories of products and services are managed by the purchasing process: • Raw materials and ingredients • Products and services provided to a customer by ABCCL but actually produced by a supplier • Outsourced processes including testing services • Packaging material • Machinery and equipment • Critical spare parts • Transportation services • Calibration services • Contract labour. As and when the need arises, the Purchasing Manager may add other items to this list.

ABC Company Limited	Procedures Manual	Reference CP 001 Page 3 of 4	
	Approval of Suppliers	Date Released dd/mm/yyyy	Date Reviewed dd/mm/yyyy
Core Process	Approved:	Issue No: 01 Prepared by:	Revision No: 00

	Process Headings	Process Details
11.2	Identification and short listing of suppliers	Purchasing Manager identifies potential suppliers and short lists possible suppliers through a combination of sources which include: • Recommendations from business acquaintances and business partners • Recommendations from current suppliers and customers • Local business organisations such as Chamber of Commerce • Exhibitions • World Wide Web. A short list of possible suppliers is prepared taking into consideration: • Ability to deliver what we want and when we want • Financial viability • History of the business • Recommendation from business partners who have used the supplier • Evidence of being included in an ASL in a trade association or government organisation.
11.3	Criteria for selection	The criteria for selections are set out in Form 038. Selection is based on individual block score and total rating. If a supplier is selected whose score is less than 2, they should be considered for development.
11.4	Supplier performance	1. Performance of the supplier shall be measured at intervals agreed between ABCCL and the supplier. It shall be measured on quality, food safety, delivery, price, service and cooperation. Form 040 shall be used for scoring the performance. Performance shall be reviewed at each quarterly meeting with suppliers. 2. Quality, food safety and environmental concerns include conditions on receipt, test and inspections of data and achievement of requirements. Delivery items considered are timeliness of delivery and delivery location. Factors considered for service are courtesy, ease of communication and problem-solving.

ABC Company Limited	Procedures Manual	Reference CP 001 Page 4 of 4	
	Approval of Suppliers	Date Released dd/mm/yyyy	Date Reviewed dd/mm/yyyy
Core Process	Approved:	Issue No: 01 Prepared by:	Revision No: 00

	Process Headings	Process Details
11.5	Re-evaluation of suppliers	Suppliers in the ASL shall be re-evaluated at least annually or as required on the basis of their performance. Some situations that may lead to re-evaluation are: (a) repeat problems; (b) not addressing ABCCL's require-ments; (c) unethical conduct by the supplier; (d) pricing issues; (e) disregarding regulatory requirements; (f) environmental requirements and food safety requirements; (g) bad reputation and (h) adverse media reports.
11.6	Visit to the supplier's facility	Purchasing Manager shall make suitable arrangement with the supplier to visit the facility and perform an audit. The team shall include, but is not limited to, the Purchasing Manager, Plant Manager, Quality Manager, Environment Manager, Food Safety Manager and Plant Engineer.
11.7	ASL	The ASL shall contain, but is not limited to, the information presented in Form 039.
11.8	Exemptions	Non-critical items may be purchased as and when necessary from sup-pliers who have provided the service previously or from any commercial establishment.
11.9	Removal from the ASL	The Purchasing Manager shall discuss the performance of suppliers at the management review meeting. Based on their performance, suppliers who in the opinion of the Management Team have failed to meet the requirements of ABCCL shall be removed from the ASL. The decision shall be communi-cated to the suppliers. Suppliers who have been deleted from the ASL will have to follow the selec-tion and evaluation procedure if they wish to be included in the ASL.
12.0	Records	Supplier evaluation results Supplier performance results Re-evaluation results Any corrective actions.
13.0	Changes made	None.

ABC Company Limited	Procedures Manual	Flowchart CP 001.1 Page 1 of 2	
	Approval of Suppliers	Date Released dd/mm/yyyy	Date Reviewed dd/mm/yyyy
Link CP 001	Approved:	Issue No: 01 Prepared by:	Revision No: 00

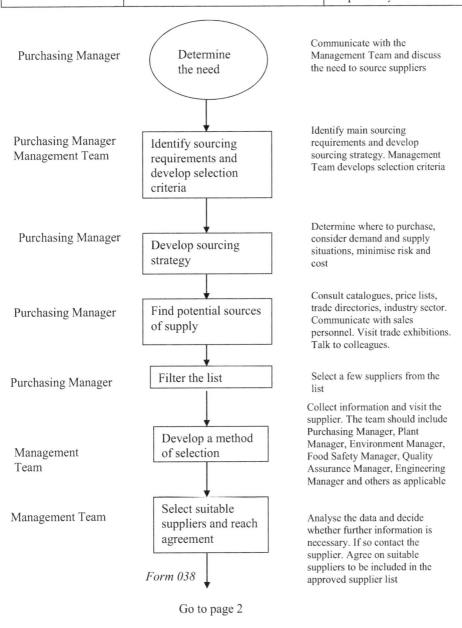

Purchasing Manager — Determine the need — Communicate with the Management Team and discuss the need to source suppliers

Purchasing Manager Management Team — Identify sourcing requirements and develop selection criteria — Identify main sourcing requirements and develop sourcing strategy. Management Team develops selection criteria

Purchasing Manager — Develop sourcing strategy — Determine where to purchase, consider demand and supply situations, minimise risk and cost

Purchasing Manager — Find potential sources of supply — Consult catalogues, price lists, trade directories, industry sector. Communicate with sales personnel. Visit trade exhibitions. Talk to colleagues.

Purchasing Manager — Filter the list — Select a few suppliers from the list

Management Team — Develop a method of selection — Collect information and visit the supplier. The team should include Purchasing Manager, Plant Manager, Environment Manager, Food Safety Manager, Quality Assurance Manager, Engineering Manager and others as applicable

Management Team — Select suitable suppliers and reach agreement — Analyse the data and decide whether further information is necessary. If so contact the supplier. Agree on suitable suppliers to be included in the approved supplier list

Form 038

Go to page 2

ABC Company Limited	Procedures Manual	Flowchart CP 001.1 Page 2 of 2	
	Approval of Suppliers	Date Released dd/mm/yyyy	Date Reviewed dd/mm/yyyy
Link CP 001	Approved:	Issue No: 01 Prepared by:	Revision No: 00

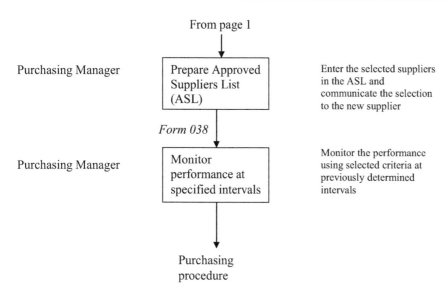

From page 1

Purchasing Manager — Prepare Approved Suppliers List (ASL)

Enter the selected suppliers in the ASL and communicate the selection to the new supplier

Form 038

Purchasing Manager — Monitor performance at specified intervals

Monitor the performance using selected criteria at previously determined intervals

Purchasing procedure

CP 002 Offering Contracts

ABC Company Limited	Procedures Manual	Reference CP 002 Page 1 of 3	
	Offering Contracts	Date Released dd/mm/yyyy	Date Reviewed dd/mm/yyyy
Core Process	Approved:	Issue No: 01 Prepared by:	Revision No: 00

Process Owner		**Purchasing Manager**
	Process Headings	**Process Details**
1.0	Purpose	To describe the procedure for offering a contract to suppliers.
2.0	Scope	This procedure shall apply to external providers of products and services to ABC Company Limited (ABCCL).
3.0	Input	Approved Supplier List (ASL), request for products or services from external providers and current contracts.
4.0	Output	Negotiated contract and supply of products and services.
5.0	Competency requirements	Knowledge of products and services to be contracted out and negotiating skills.
6.0	Responsibility	Purchasing Manager shall: • Identify potential suppliers who are already enlisted in the ASL and deliver a unique product or service regularly. • Jointly with the Plant Manager negotiate the terms of contract. • Arrange a visit to the supplier's facility. Plant Manager shall: • Jointly with the Purchasing Manager negotiate the terms of contract.
7.0	Associated documents	Terms of contract.
8.0	Resources	None.
9.0	Measures/controls	Supplier's performance against the contract.
10.0	System description	Flowchart CP 002.1 shows the process of offering contracts.
10.1	Selection of potential contractors	Contractors shall be selected from the ASL.
10.2	Essential elements of a contract	1. Contracts can be verbal, written or both. A written contract usually consists of a standard from or agreement or a letter confirming the agreement. Verbal contracts such as those involved in emergency situation limit the financial considerations and rely on the good faith of all the parties involved. 2. Essential elements of a contract are an offer of a product or service, acceptance of the offer, legal relationship and a financial consideration.

ABC Company Limited	Procedures Manual	Reference CP 002 Page 2 of 3	
	Offering Contracts	Date Released dd/mm/yyyy	Date Reviewed dd/mm/yyyy
Core Process	Approved:	Issue No: 01 Prepared by:	Revision No: 00

	Process Headings	Process Details
10.3	General terms of contract	Contract terms shall be negotiated by the Plant Manager and the Purchasing Manager and shall be clearly defined and agreed to by both parties. Contracts can include, but are not limited to, these items: • Details of the parties including sub-contracting arrangements • Validity period of the contract • Definitions of key terms in the contract • Description of goods and services to be received by ABCCL • Financial details include the payment terms and interest (if applicable) • Required insurance and indemnity cover • Guarantee provisions including director's guarantee • Renegotiation or renewal terms • Damages or penalty clauses • Complaints and dispute resolution process • Termination conditions • Any special conditions or terms.
10.4	Before signing the contract	• Read carefully including fine print (if necessary), seek legal advice • Ensure that all terms and conditions entered into are included in the contact • Never sign a contract in a hurry – take sufficient time to absorb the contents • Never submit to pressure from the provider – seek legal advice • Do not leave blank spaces in the contract. Always ensure both parties initial changes with date • Obtain a signed copy of the contract.
10.5	Termination of contract	• Agreement by both parties before the end of contract • Consider unexpected circumstances beyond the control of the provider that prevent the continuation of the contract • By agreement allowing one party to terminate by giving notice to the other party • Breach of contract – violating the terms and conditions of the contract.

ABC Company Limited	Procedures Manual	Reference CP 002 Page 3 of 3	
	Offering Contracts	Date Released dd/mm/yyyy	Date Reviewed dd/mm/yyyy
Core Process	Approved:	Issue No: 01 Prepared by:	Revision No: 00

	Process Headings	Process Details
11.0	Records	Negotiated contract Documents related to the contracted.
12.0	Changes made	None.

ABC Company Limited	Procedures Manual	Flowchart CP 002.1 Page 1 of 1	
	Offering Contracts	Date Released dd/mm/yyyy	Date Reviewed dd/mm/yyyy
Link CP 002	Approved:	Issue No: 01 Prepared by:	

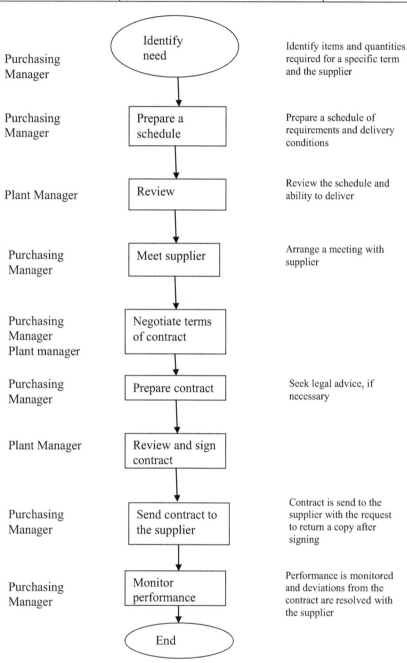

Purchasing Manager	**Identify need**	Identify items and quantities required for a specific term and the supplier
Purchasing Manager	Prepare a schedule	Prepare a schedule of requirements and delivery conditions
Plant Manager	Review	Review the schedule and ability to deliver
Purchasing Manager	Meet supplier	Arrange a meeting with supplier
Purchasing Manager Plant manager	Negotiate terms of contract	
Purchasing Manager	Prepare contract	Seek legal advice, if necessary
Plant Manager	Review and sign contract	
Purchasing Manager	Send contract to the supplier	Contract is send to the supplier with the request to return a copy after signing
Purchasing Manager	Monitor performance	Performance is monitored and deviations from the contract are resolved with the supplier
	End	

CP 003 Purchasing Information

ABC Company Limited	Procedures Manual		Reference CP 003 Page 1 of 2	
	Purchasing Information		Date Released dd/mm/yyyy	Date Reviewed dd/mm/yyyy
Core Process	Approved:		Issue No: 01 Prepared by:	

Process Owner		**Purchasing Manager**
	Process Headings	**Process Details**
1.0	Purpose	To describe the procedure for providing purchasing information when orders are placed with suppliers.
2.0	Scope	This procedure shall apply to all orders placed with suppliers.
3.0	Input	Purchasing data.
4.0	Output	Verified purchasing information.
5.0	Competency requirements	Knowledge of processes and materials, potential
6.0	Responsibility	Department Managers shall: • Generate purchasing information • Communicate the information to the Purchasing Manager. Purchasing Manager shall: • Check the adequacy of purchasing information • Generate the purchase order using the purchasing information • Resolve issues relating to the purchase order or purchasing information.
7.0	Associated documents	Specifications, drawings or any other printed matter related to the document Purchase requisition (Form 042)
8.0	Resources	Reference specifications, drawing and reference samples, and software.
9.0	Measures/controls	Purchasing data errors Number of reorders of the same product.
10.0	System description	
10.1	Preparation of purchasing information	Department Managers shall prepare purchasing information, which shall clearly describe the ordered product. The information shall include, but is not limited, to the following (as necessary): • Address to bill • Delivery address • Special delivery requirements • Requested delivery date • Contact details of the supplier • Product specifications (reference to standards, drawings, grade, etc.) or service specifications • Quantity required

ABC Company Limited	Procedures Manual	Reference CP 003 Page 2 of 2	
	Purchasing Information	Date Released dd/mm/yyyy	Date Reviewed dd/mm/yyyy
Core Process	Approved:	Issue No: 01 Prepared by:	

	Process Headings	Process Details
		• Estimated price • Quality system requirements • Packaging/shipping instructions • Provision for verification • Acceptance criteria • Qualification of personnel • Certification requirements • Environmental requirements • Preferred supplier • Need for verification at the supplier's facility.
10.2	Standard items	If the product is a standard item of the supplier, communication of the part number or catalogue number is sufficient information.
10.3	Communication with the Purchasing Manager	All purchasing information shall be recorded in the purchase requisition form (Form 042) and communicated to the Purchasing Manager.
10.4	Review of purchasing information requirements	1. Purchasing Manager shall check the purchasing information for completeness and adequacy before the purchase order is created. All queries shall be resolved with the Department Manager who raised the information. 2. If verification is required at the supplier's facility, the Purchasing Manager shall make arrangements with the supplier. The arrangements shall be communicated to the appropriate Department Manager.
10.5	Budget provision	The Purchasing Manager shall check budget provision before placing the order. If there is no budget provision, justification shall be submitted to the Plant Manager.
11.0	Records	Purchasing information.
12.0	Changes made	None.

CP 004 Purchasing

ABC Company Limited	Procedures Manual		Reference CP 004 Page 1 of 3	
	Purchasing		Date Released dd/mm/yyyy	Date Reviewed dd/mm/yyyy
Core Process	Approved:		Issue No: 01 Prepared by:	Revision No: 00

Process Owner		Purchasing Manager
	Process Headings	**Process Details**
1.0	Purpose	To describe the procedure for purchasing raw materials, products and/or services required by ABCCL.
2.0	Scope	This procedure applies to all purchases made by ABCCL.
3.0	Input	Purchasing request, Approved Supplier List (ASL), pricing document, specifications and inventory levels
4.0	Output	Completed purchase order sent to the supplier.
5.0	Competencies	Knowledge of order processing module, suppliers and inventory control.
6.0	Responsibilities	Defined in Flowchart CP 004.1. Additional responsibilities are set out below. Department Managers shall: <ul><li>Prepare purchasing information for products, raw materials and/or services required by the department</li></ul> Communicate the requirements to the Purchasing Manager. Environment Manager shall: <ul><li>Ensure that the supplier has the necessary environment permits and is managing waste according to the regulatory requirements</li><li>Evaluate Material Safety Data (MSD) sheets and communicate any hazard information to the Management Team</li><li>Ensure proper storage of material</li><li>Ensure shelf-life considerations are addressed</li><li>Ensure proper labelling and packaging of the material is addressed.</li></ul>
7.0	Associated documents	Purchase requisition (Form 042) Purchase order (Form 043) ASL.
8.0	Resources	Enterprise resource planning (ERP) software Internet for research on suppliers and products.
9.0	Measures and controls	Purchase order errors Inventory turnover ratio Cost savings.
10.0	Definitions	**Critical item:** An item whose supply disruption will adversely affect ABCCL's production or sale.

ABC Company Limited	Procedures Manual	Reference CP 004 Page 2 of 3	
	Purchasing	Date Released dd/mm/yyyy	Date Reviewed dd/mm/yyyy
Core Process	Approved:	Issue No: 01 Prepared by:	Revision No: 00

	Process Headings	Process Details
11.0	System description	The procedure for purchasing is shown in Flowchart CP 004.1.
11.1	Standard items	Purchasing Manager shall determine reorder quantities of standard production inventory items (e.g. standard raw materials and ingredients) by monitoring the current inventory levels and estimating required quantities for production. Purchase orders for such items are generated directly from the computer.
11.2	Specifications	Specifications can refer to external standards such as British Pharmacopeia (BP), United States Pharmacopeia (USP), MSD sheets, or can be generated in-house in consultation with the supplier.
11.3	General environmental impact requirements	1. The supplier shall provide MSD for each shipment of material (as applicable). 2. The supplier shall demonstrate compliance to applicable regulatory requirements before the material can be produced. 3. The product shall not contain any Ozone-Depleting Substances (ODSs). 4. All waste generated at the supplier's facility shall be disposed of or recycled by the supplier in accordance with regulatory requirements.
11.4	General food safety requirements	The supplier shall: 1. Purchase food ingredients and raw materials used in production from second tier suppliers who have effective food safety management programmes in place. In the absence of an effective food safety management programme at the second tier supplier's facility, the supplier shall provide evidence of a food safety audit conducted by them at the second tier supplier's facility. 2. Have controls in place to prevent microbiological, chemical and physical contamination during processing and storage. 3. Have procedures in place to control the presence of physical, chemical and microbiological contaminants in raw materials and packaging that come into direct contact with the product.
11.5	Exemptions	For purchases over [*state the limit here*] seek the approval of the Plant Manager. For purchases under [*state the limit here*] a purchase order is not necessary and the order may be purchased from petty cash.

ABC Company Limited	Procedures Manual	Reference CP 004 Page 3 of 3	
	Purchasing	Date Released dd/mm/yyyy	Date Reviewed dd/mm/yyyy
Core Process	Approved:	Issue No: 01 Prepared by:	Revision No: 00

	Process Headings	Process Details
11.6	Urgent requirements	In the event of an emergency situation for materials or services that cannot be fulfilled by an approved supplier, Purchasing Manager can place orders with a supplier not on the ASL for a period of 30 days.
11.7	Amendments to purchase orders	Amendments to purchase orders shall be made by the Purchasing Manager in consultation with the supplier with whom the purchase order was placed. Amendment shall be recorded and transmitted to the supplier by fax, phone or email. Copies of the amendment shall be sent to the managers to whom the original copies of the purchase order were sent. A request shall be made to the supplier for confirmation of receipt.
11.8	Purchasing review	QA Manager shall issue a non-conformance report in the event that a purchased product fails to meet ABCCL and regulatory requirements. QA Manager shall periodically audit the purchasing process at least annually to ensure its continuing suitability, adequacy and effectiveness, conformance to various requirements, and the ability to deliver products that meet these requirements.
12.0	Records	Purchase order Purchase requisition Communications with the supplier.
13.0	Changes made	None.

ABC Company Limited	Procedures Manual	Flowchart CP 004.1 Page 1 of 1	
	Purchasing Procedure	Date Released dd/mm/yyyy	Date Reviewed dd/mm/yyyy
Link CP 004	Approved:	Issue No: 01 Prepared by:	Revision No: 00

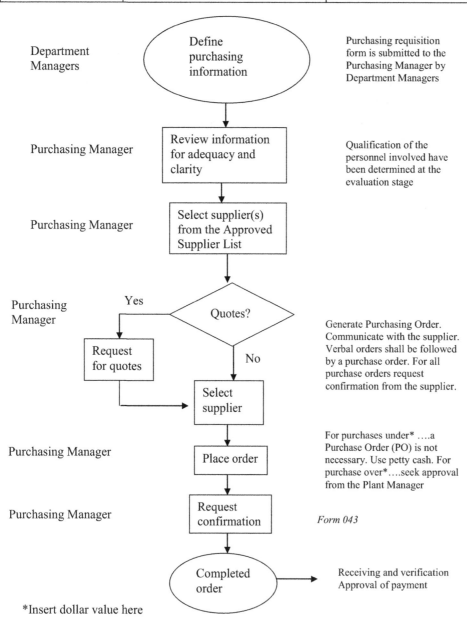

Department Managers — Define purchasing information — Purchasing requisition form is submitted to the Purchasing Manager by Department Managers

Purchasing Manager — Review information for adequacy and clarity — Qualification of the personnel involved have been determined at the evaluation stage

Purchasing Manager — Select supplier(s) from the Approved Supplier List

Purchasing Manager — Quotes? — Yes → Request for quotes — No

Generate Purchasing Order. Communicate with the supplier. Verbal orders shall be followed by a purchase order. For all purchase orders request confirmation from the supplier.

Select supplier

Purchasing Manager — Place order — For purchases under* ....a Purchase Order (PO) is not necessary. Use petty cash. For purchase over*....seek approval from the Plant Manager

Purchasing Manager — Request confirmation — *Form 043*

Completed order — Receiving and verification Approval of payment

*Insert dollar value here

CP 005 Purchasing Engineering Items

ABC Company Limited	Procedures Manual		Reference CP 005 Page 1 of 1	
	Purchasing Engineering Items		Date Released dd/mm/yyyy	Date Reviewed dd/mm/yyyy
Management Processes	Approved:		Issue No: 01 Prepared by:	Revision No: 00

Process Owner		Engineering Manager
	Process Headings	**Process Details**
1.0	Purpose	To describe the procedure for purchasing engineering items such as equipment, machinery, machine parts.
2.0	Scope	This procedure shall apply to machinery, equipment and spare parts necessary for the production process.
3.0	Input	Engineering item details and justification.
4.0	Output	Fully operational item.
5.0	Competency requirements	Knowledge of engineering equipment, production processes, and validation and verification methods.
6.0	Responsibility	Defined in Flowchart CP 005.1.
7.0	Associated documents	Specifications and/or related drawings Purchase order (Form 043).
8.0	Resources	Budget provision.
9.0	Measures/controls	Verification of the machinery, equipment and parts for suitability and conformance with purchasing information.
10.0	System description	See Flowchart CP 005.1
10.1	Approval	For machinery, equipment or parts not exceeding [*state the limit here*], the Plant Manager shall approve or reject the proposal. For machinery, equipment or parts exceeding [*state the limit here*], the General Manager shall approve or reject the proposal. If a visit to the supplier's facility is a necessity, the justification report shall include how the funds can be met.
11.0	Records	Purchase order Confirmation of purchase order.
12.0	Changes made	None.

ABC Company Limited	Procedures Manual		Flowchart CP 005.1 Page 1 of 1	
	Purchasing Engineering Equipment		Date Released dd/mm/yyyy	Date Reviewed dd/mm/yyyy
Link CP 005	Approved:		Issue No: 01 Prepared by:	Revision No: 00

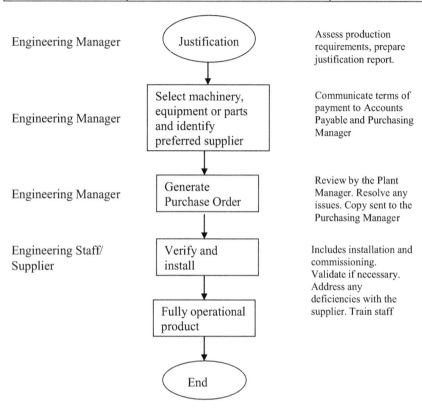

Engineering Manager — Justification — Assess production requirements, prepare justification report.

Engineering Manager — Select machinery, equipment or parts and identify preferred supplier — Communicate terms of payment to Accounts Payable and Purchasing Manager

Engineering Manager — Generate Purchase Order — Review by the Plant Manager. Resolve any issues. Copy sent to the Purchasing Manager

Engineering Staff/ Supplier — Verify and install — Includes installation and commissioning. Validate if necessary. Address any deficiencies with the supplier. Train staff

Fully operational product

End

CP 006 Purchasing Technology Resources

ABC Company Limited	Procedures Manual		Reference CP 006 Page 1 of 2	
	Purchasing Technology Resources		Date Released dd/mm/yyyy	Date Reviewed dd/mm/yyyy
Core Process	Approved:		Issue No: 01 Prepared by:	Revision No: 00

Process Owner		IT Manager
	Process Headings	**Process Details**
1.0	Purpose	To describe the procedure for purchasing information technology (IT) equipment, software and services.
2.0	Scope	This procedure shall apply to all hardware, software and services.
3.0	Input	Request for IT.
4.0	Output	Fully operational IT item.
5.0	Competency requirements	IT skills, knowledge of operations and IT equipment.
6.0	Responsibility	Defined in Flowchart CP 006.1.
7.0	Associated documents	Purchase order (Form 043) Request for the item Approval of suppliers (CP 001) Purchasing information (CP 003) Purchasing process (CP 004).
8.0	Resources	IT equipment, software and services.
9.0	Measures/controls	Budget provision Check on delivered items.
10.0	System description	The process of purchasing IT items is shown in Flowchart CP 006.1.
10.1	Type of IT required	IT equipment, software and services: • Network equipment and services • Telephone equipment, cabling, phone, data circuits and fax machines • Computers, printers, scanners • Video equipment and digital imaging systems • Other electronic devices. Software: • Applications for business, network, phone and voicemail. Services: • Telecommunication • Internet.
10.2	IT office initiated purchases	IT office may purchase equipment, software and services for company wide business activities. IT Staff shall research the needs, reviews and recommends the desired equipment, software and services to the appropriate department.

ABC Company Limited	Procedures Manual	Reference CP 006 Page 2 of 2	
	Purchasing Technology Resources	Date Released dd/mm/yyyy	Date Reviewed dd/mm/yyyy
Core Process	Approved:	Issue No: 01 Prepared by:	Revision No: 00

	Process Headings	Process Details
10.3	Trials of software needs	Employees, with the approval of the department. Manager may request business-related software applications for the department's use for an initial trial. The staff shall obtain the appropriate software and conduct a trial with the user. If the user is satisfied he or she may identify it as a need.
11.0	Records	Purchase order.
12.0	Changes made	None.

ABC Company Limited	Procedures Manual	Flowchart CP 006.1 Page 1 of 1	
	Purchasing IT Equipment, Software and Services	Date Released dd/mm/yyyy	Date Reviewed dd/mm/yyyy
Link CP 006	Approved:	Issue No: 01 Prepared by:	Revision No: 00

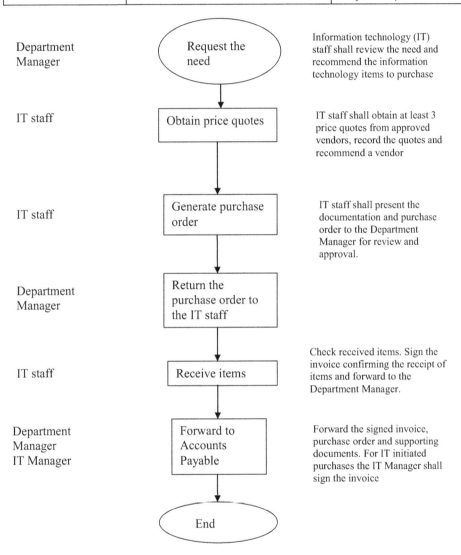

Department Manager — Request the need — Information technology (IT) staff shall review the need and recommend the information technology items to purchase

IT staff — Obtain price quotes — IT staff shall obtain at least 3 price quotes from approved vendors, record the quotes and recommend a vendor

IT staff — Generate purchase order — IT staff shall present the documentation and purchase order to the Department Manager for review and approval.

Department Manager — Return the purchase order to the IT staff

IT staff — Receive items — Check received items. Sign the invoice confirming the receipt of items and forward to the Department Manager.

Department Manager IT Manager — Forward to Accounts Payable — Forward the signed invoice, purchase order and supporting documents. For IT initiated purchases the IT Manager shall sign the invoice

End

CP 007 Inward Goods Receipt

ABC Company Limited	Procedures Manual		Reference CP 007 Page 1 of 3	
	Inward Goods Receipt		Date Released dd/mm/yyyy	Date Reviewed dd/mm/yyyy
Core Process	Approved:		Issue No: 01 Prepared by:	Revision No: 00

Process Owner	**Purchasing Manager**
Process Headings	**Process Details**
1.0 Purpose	To describe the general procedure for the receipt of inward goods from the supplier.
2.0 Scope	This procedure shall apply to all deliveries of inward goods from a supplier. CP 041 shall cover the receipt of food items.
3.0 Input	Goods received, packaging and delivery documents, and inward goods log.
4.0 Output	Verified product and updated inventory.
5.0 Competency requirements	Warehousing skills, technical skills for verification, and knowledge of products.
6.0 Responsibility	Inward Goods Person shall:

Inward Goods Person shall:

- Inspect all incoming trucks for cleanliness
- Unload the shipment and inspect the condition of the shipment
- Check the quantity, description and lot numbers against the details on the packing slip
- Enter the information in the inwards goods log
- Store the goods in the HOLD area for inspection by Quality Control (QC)
- Store inspected goods and those not requiring QC inspection in the allocated location
- Inform QC about verification
- Fill out a material identification label (MIL) – several may be required
- Transfer the goods after verification to the allocated area as soon as possible and attach MIL to the product. If palletised, stick the label on the bottom layer of every pallet
- Sign off the packing slip or pallet docket
- Communicate with the supplier about reject goods, apply HOLD stickers, store in quarantine bay, and make an entry in the computer to ensure that the lot cannot be picked
- Update the inventory.

QC staff shall:

- Verify the items in terms of the test procedures.

Warehouse Administration Staff:

- Allocate locations for passed or rejected goods and those awaiting inspection
- Make appropriate entries to ensure that rejected or HOLD goods cannot be picked.

ABC Company Limited	Procedures Manual	Reference CP 007 Page 2 of 3	
	Inward Goods Receipt	Date Released dd/mm/yyyy	Date Reviewed dd/mm/yyyy
Core Process	Approved:	Issue No: 01 Prepared by:	Revision No: 00

	Process Headings	**Process Details**
7.0	Associated documents	Packing slip (Form 044) Inward goods log book (Form 045) Inspection report (Form 046) Material Identification Label (Form 047).
8.0	Resources	Handling equipment Warehouse computer programme Transport facilities.
9.0	Measures/Controls	Timely processing of incoming material including inspection Availability of material for production Segregation of non-conforming goods Accuracy of receiving record.
10.0	System description	Flowchart CP 007.1 shows the process for the receipt of inward goods.
10.1	Receiving	Inward Goods Person shall check the consignment and enter it into the log book (Form 045). In the inventory control module enter the description under each raw material. The computer assigns a unique inventory control number for each consignment of product for each batch number. This number is recorded in the MIL
10.2	Signs of damage	1. If the shipment shows signs of damage, Inward Goods Person shall inform the QA Manager. If the QA Manager rejects the material, it shall be processed according to the Non-conforming Goods Procedure. 2. Purchasing Manager shall communicate with the supplier regarding the disposal of non-conforming goods.
10.3	Receiving towards the end of the shift	All receipts of inwards goods delivered to the site until 30 minutes prior to the end of the shift shall be processed and moved to the location before the end of the shift. Receipts of inward goods at the site within 30 minutes before the end of the shift shall be stored in the receiving area provided all storage conditions have been met.

ABC Company Limited	Procedures Manual	Reference CP 007 Page 3 of 3	
	Inward Goods Receipt	Date Released dd/mm/yyyy	Date Reviewed dd/mm/yyyy
Core Process	Approved:	Issue No: 01 Prepared by:	Revision No: 00

	Process Headings	Process Details
10.4	Verification	1. For inward goods that require special storage conditions, the Inward Goods Person shall verify the transporter's log book to ensure correct storage conditions have been maintained.
		2. The packing slip is sent to the QA Department for necessary verification of received items and QA Staff shall decide whether verification is required (Inspection of Inward Goods Procedure, CP 008).
11.0	Records	Inwards good log Inventory control database.
12.0	Changes made	None.

ABC Company Limited	Procedures Manual		Flowchart CP 007.1 Page 1 of 1	
	Receiving Goods		Date Released dd/mm/yyyy	Date Reviewed dd/mm/yyyy
Link CP 007/CP 041	Approved:		Issue No: 01 Prepared by:	Revision No: 00

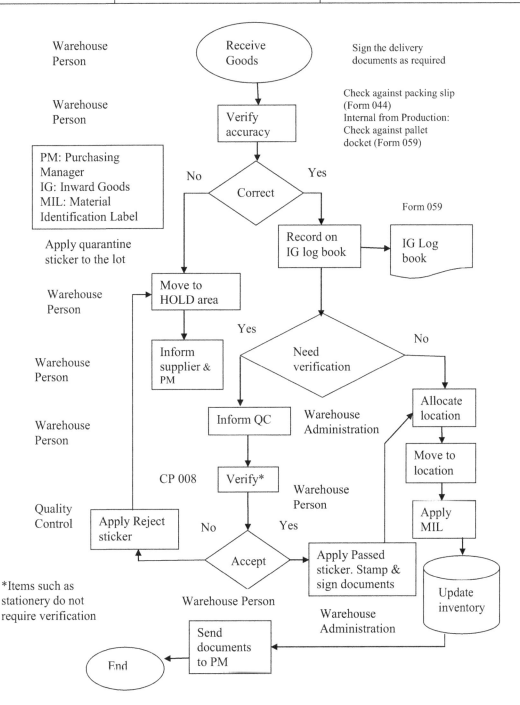

CP 008 Inward Goods Inspection

ABC Company Limited	Procedures Manual	Reference CP 008 Page 1 of 3	
	Inward Goods Inspection	Date Released dd/mm/yyyy	Date Reviewed dd/mm/yyyy
Core Process	Approved:	Issue No: 01 Prepared by:	Revision No: 00

Process Owner		QA Manager
	Process Headings	**Process Details**
1.0	Purpose	To describe the procedure for verifying the purchased product for conformance to ABCCL's requirements.
2.0	Scope	This procedure shall apply to all purchases received by ABCCL.
3.0	Input	Received items, documentation, specifications and test methods.
4.0	Output	Verified product.
5.0	Competency requirements	Technical skills sampling skills.
6.0	Responsibility	Defined in Flowchart CP 008.1. Additional responsibilities are set out below. Purchasing Manager shall: • Approve the invoice for payment • Negotiate with the supplier about rejected goods, goods on hold, or incomplete delivery. Environment Manager shall: • Check the documents about environmental aspects of raw material to ensure that they meet ABCCL's requirements. Accounts Payable: • Make payment to the supplier.
7.0	Associated documents	Packing slip (Form 044) Invoice (Form 048) Test methods manual Test reports (Form 046, Form 049).
8.0	Resources	Computer system Laboratory equipment.
9.0	Measures/Controls	Timely processing of incoming material including inspection Availability of material for production Segregation of non-conforming goods Accuracy of receiving records Payment to the supplier in terms of the agreement with them.
10.0	System description	The process of inspecting inward goods is shown on CP 008.1.

ABC Company Limited	Procedures Manual	Reference CP 008 Page 2 of 3	
	Inward Goods Inspection	Date Released dd/mm/yyyy	Date Reviewed dd/mm/yyyy
Core Process	Approved:	Issue No: 01 Prepared by:	Revision No: 00

	Process Headings	Process Details
10.1	Verification levels	There are five levels of verification: 1. Certificate of conformance: Materials require only a certificate of conformance, e.g. outer packaging, raw materials from previous suppliers with a good history of supplies. 2. Visual inspection: Materials require visual inspection, e.g. promotion material. 3. Partial inspection, e.g. for microbiological contamination: Materials require only partial inspection, e.g. random samples of food ingredients for physical, chemical and/or microbiological contamination. 4. Complete inspection of random samples of the product: Materials require complete inspection at ABCCL, e.g. random samples of machine parts, labels and raw materials. 5. Inspection during processing at supplier's facility: The products that are delivered to the customer direct shall be inspected during the processing phase at the supplier's facility. For example, materials such as 3 litre plastic bags for filling wine that cannot be inspected without destructing the product.
10.2	Test methods	The test methods needed for (1) laboratory; (2) packaging material; (3) chemicals; and (4) food processing material are stipulated in the Hazard Analysis and Critical Control Point (HACCP) plan. The test methods specify acceptance criteria.
10.3	Environmental aspects	The supplier shall submit at a minimum these documents (as applicable) to enable ABCCL to monitor the environmental aspects of raw materials: • Process failure mode and effect Analysis (FMEA) • Design FMEA • Material Safety Data (MSD) sheets • Labelling and product identification • Declaration that no Ozone-Depleting Substances (ODSs) have been used in the production of raw materials • Physical and chemical characteristics • Test reports • Hazard warnings. All reports shall be retained by the Quality Control Officer.

ABC Company Limited	Procedures Manual	Reference CP 008 Page 3 of 3	
	Inward Goods Inspection	Date Released dd/mm/yyyy	Date Reviewed dd/mm/yyyy
Core Process	Approved:	Issue No: 01 Prepared by:	Revision No: 00

	Process Headings	Process Details
11.0	Records	Test reports.
12.0	Changes made	None.

ABC Company Limited	Procedures Manual		Flowchart CP 008.1 Page 1 of 1	
	Inspection of Inward Goods		Date Released dd/mm/yyyy	Date Reviewed dd/mm/yyyy
Link CP 008	Approved:		Issue No: 01	
	Prepared by:			

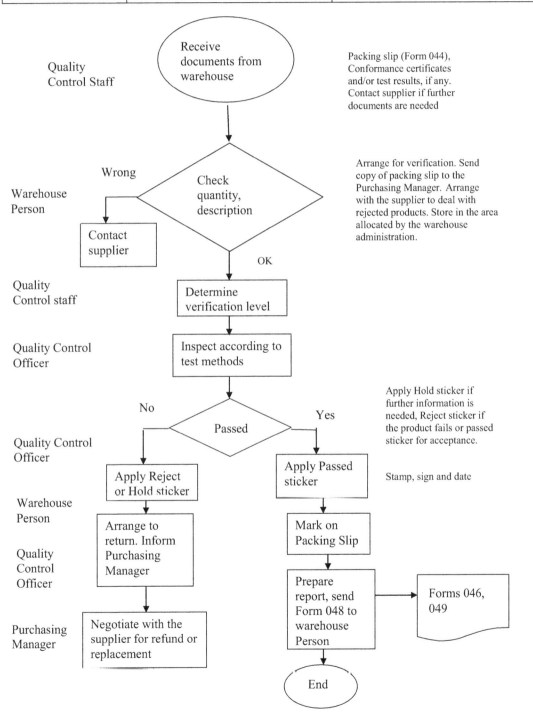

Quality Control Staff — Receive documents from warehouse

Packing slip (Form 044), Conformance certificates and/or test results, if any. Contact supplier if further documents are needed

Warehouse Person — Wrong — Check quantity, description — Contact supplier

Arrange for verification. Send copy of packing slip to the Purchasing Manager. Arrange with the supplier to deal with rejected products. Store in the area allocated by the warehouse administration.

OK

Quality Control staff — Determine verification level

Quality Control Officer — Inspect according to test methods

No — Passed — Yes

Apply Hold sticker if further information is needed, Reject sticker if the product fails or passed sticker for acceptance.

Stamp, sign and date

Quality Control Officer — Apply Reject or Hold sticker / Apply Passed sticker

Warehouse Person — Arrange to return. Inform Purchasing Manager / Mark on Packing Slip

Quality Control Officer — Prepare report, send Form 048 to warehouse Person — Forms 046, 049

Purchasing Manager — Negotiate with the supplier for refund or replacement

End

CP 009 Issue of Inward Goods

ABC Company Limited	Procedures Manual	Reference CP 009 Page 1 of 1	
	Issue of Inward Goods	Date Released dd/mm/yyyy	Date Reviewed dd/mm/yyyy
Core Process	Approved:	Issue No: 01 Prepared by:	Revision No: 00

Process Owner		Inward Goods Person
	Process Headings	**Process Details**
1.0	Purpose	To describe the procedure for issuing inward good components for production.
2.0	Scope	This procedure shall apply to items necessary to produce goods.
3.0	Input	Components, raw materials, ingredients, inventory levels, production schedule and specification sheet.
4.0	Output	Right items in right quantity delivered to production.
5.0	Competency requirements	Knowledge of components and inventory levels management.
6.0	Responsibility	Defined in Flowchart CP 009.1. Additional responsibilities are set out below. Quality Control Officer shall: • Issue the correct specification form to the Line Supervisor.
7.0	Associated documents	Packaging specification form (Form 050).
8.0	Resources	Computer programme.
9.0	Measures/Controls	Verification of items and quantities received by the Line Supervisor Record of items used and unused during production.
10.0	System description	The procedure for issuing inward goods for production is shown in Flowchart CP 009.1.
11.0	Records	Updated inventory levels Completed specification sheet.
12.0	Changes made	None.

ABC Company Limited	Procedures Manual	Flowchart CP 009.1 Page 1 of 2	
	Issue of Inward Goods	Date Released dd/mm/yyyy	Date Reviewed dd/mm/yyyy
Link CP 009	Approved:	Issue No: 01 Prepared by:	

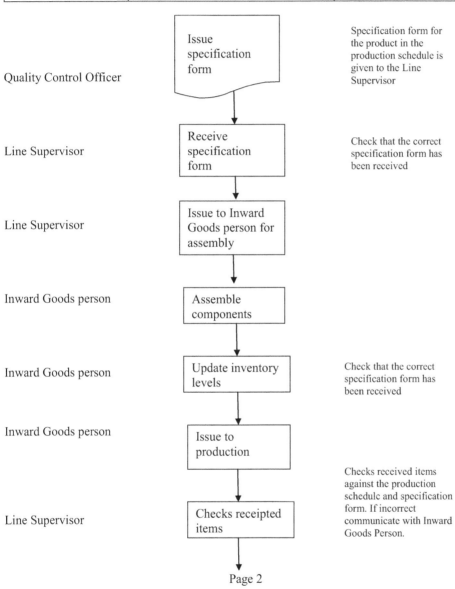

Quality Control Officer — Issue specification form — Specification form for the product in the production schedule is given to the Line Supervisor

Line Supervisor — Receive specification form — Check that the correct specification form has been received

Line Supervisor — Issue to Inward Goods person for assembly

Inward Goods person — Assemble components

Inward Goods person — Update inventory levels — Check that the correct specification form has been received

Inward Goods person — Issue to production

Line Supervisor — Checks receipted items — Checks received items against the production schedule and specification form. If incorrect communicate with Inward Goods Person.

Page 2

ABC Company Limited	Procedures Manual	Flowchart CP 009.1 Page 2 of 2	
	Issue of Inward Goods	Date Released dd/mm/yyyy	Date Reviewed dd/mm/yyyy
Link CP 009	Approved:	Issue No: 01 Prepared by:	Revision No: 00

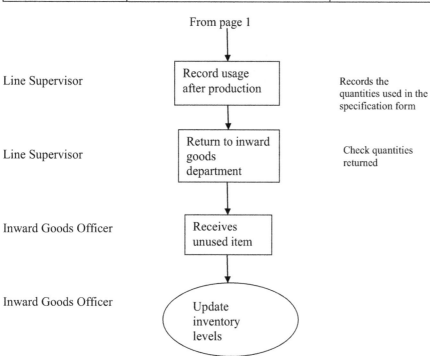

From page 1

Line Supervisor — Record usage after production — Records the quantities used in the specification form

Line Supervisor — Return to inward goods department — Check quantities returned

Inward Goods Officer — Receives unused item

Inward Goods Officer — Update inventory levels

CP 010 Inspection and Test Status

ABC Company Limited	Procedures Manual		Reference CP 010 Page 1 of 3	
	Inspection and Test Status		Date Released dd/mm/yyyy	Date Reviewed dd/mm/yyyy
Core Process	Approved:		Issue No: 01 Prepared by:	Revision No: 00

Process Owner		QA Manager
	Process Headings	**Process Details**
1.0	Purpose	To describe the procedure for inspection and determining the test status.
2.0	Scope	This procedure applies to inward goods, goods in-process and finished goods manufactured by ABCCL.
3.0	Input	Test results, inward goods, in-process goods, finished goods and goods at work-in-progress stage.
4.0	Output	Identified status of items.
5.0	Competency requirements	Knowledge of requirements necessary for the identification of status.
6.0	Responsibility	Line Staff shall: • Carry out inspection and testing during processing, identify the inspection status of the product and release conforming product to the next operation • Label and segregate non-conforming product for inspection by the QA Team. Inward Goods Supervisor shall: • Identify all incoming goods for inspection by the QA Team or Engineers. QA Team shall: • Ensure that all tests are performed during processing and on finished goods • Apply status stickers as appropriate • Inspect non-conforming products and determine their status.
7.0	Associated documents	Status stickers In-process control methods Laboratory manual Finished goods inspection.
8.0	Resources	Tools for inspection Reference samples.
9.0	Measures/controls	In-process controls and finished goods test records Non-conforming products Status unidentified items.
10.0	System description	

ABC Company Limited	Procedures Manual	Reference CP 010 Page 2 of 3	
	Inspection and Test Status	Date Released dd/mm/yyyy	Date Reviewed dd/mm/yyyy
Core Process	Approved:	Issue No: 01 Prepared by:	Revision No: 00

	Process Headings	Process Details
10.1	Categories of inspection	(a) Inward goods; (b) In-process controls; (c) Laboratory tests; (d) Finished good inspection; and (e) Inspection at supplier's premises.
10.2	Types of inspection	(a) Observations: Applicable to the observation of physical features such as form, finish, design and packaging integrity; (b) Comparison with a 'standard': The standard may be an internal standard such as a colour standard or an external standard, e.g. checking labels against a standard sample; (c) Go-No Go gauges: For example, assessment of a diameter of an item or the size of a perforation. All gauges shall have a calibration check identity; (d) Absolute measurement using measurement tools such as calibrated rulers, measurement devices such as a CO_2 tester. All such devices shall carry a calibration identity; and (e) Laboratory methods include chemical, instrumental and microbiological test methods;
10.3	Manuals	(a) The company shall maintain an in-process control manual and a laboratory manual that specify the competency requirements, references to validation (if applicable), resources required and the method of carrying out the test; (b) The QA Manager shall maintain and update the manuals as necessary; and (c) British Pharmacopoeia (BP), AOAC or other published test methods do not require validation. In-house developed test methods shall be validated and verified before being introduced. Records of such validation and verification shall be maintained by the QA Manager.
10.4	Training	The QA Manager shall provide the necessary training to carry out the tests. Competencies shall be assessed by the QA Manager and recorded in skill charts and displayed in appropriate locations.

ABC Company Limited	**Procedures Manual**	**Reference CP 010** Page 3 of 3	
	Inspection and Test Status	Date Released dd/mm/yyyy	Date Reviewed dd/mm/yyyy
Core Process	Approved:	Issue No: 01 Prepared by:	Revision No: 00

	Process Headings	**Process Details**
10.5	Status of products	All conforming products shall bear the green PASSED sticker on the bottom row of a column of pallets. All products pending inspection shall bear the yellow QUARANTINE sticker. All reject goods shall bear the red REJECT sticker. All goods that require further investigation shall bear the blue HOLD sticker with the reason written on the label.
10.6	Non-conforming products	All non-conforming products shall be handled according to the procedure AP 008: Handling Non-conformances. Non-compliances during production shall be brought to the attention of the Supervisor who shall apply a HOLD sticker, isolate the product in question and take remedial action.
10.7	Inspection at supplier's premises	If a product supplied by the supplier needs to be inspected by ABCCL, the type of tests to be carried out and the tools required shall be negotiated with the supplier.
11.0	Records	Records relating to inspection status.
12.0	Changes made	None.

CP 011 Management of Customers' and Suppliers' Property

ABC Company Limited	Procedures Manual		Reference CP 011 Page 1 of 2	
	Management of Customers' and Suppliers' Property	Date Released dd/mm/yyyy	Date Reviewed dd/mm/yyyy	
Core Process	Approved:	Issue No: 01 Prepared by:	Revision No: 00	

Process Owner		Purchasing Manager
	Process Headings	**Process Details**
1.0	Purpose	To describe the procedure for managing the property of customers in the custody of ABCCL.
2.0	Scope	This procedure shall apply to items that are in use, storage or production in an ABCCL facility belonging to customers.
3.0	Input	All items belonging to customers and external providers under the custody of ABCCL.
4.0	Output	Safe custody of items belonging to customers and external providers.
5.0	Competency requirements	Knowledge of customers' and external providers' items and knowledge of storage requirements.
6.0	Responsibility	Department Manager shall: • Maintain a record of the item(s) belonging to the supplier and the condition in which it has been received • If the item has to be returned, the Department Manager shall arrange for this.
7.0	Associated documents	Record of the receipted items.
8.0	Resources	None.
9.0	Measures/controls	Verification of the item received Number of loss or damaged items.
10.0	System description	
10.1	Identification of items	1. Property can include materials, components, tools, equipment, intellectual property, hardware and software, personal data including customer supplied data used for design, production and/or inspection. 2. Purchasing Manager shall maintain a log under each customer or external provider giving the name of the item, its description, date received, received condition, any identifiable markings and to which department it has been transferred.
10.2	Verification of property	1. QA Officers shall inspect the product on arrival to ensure that it is correct and usable for the intended activity. He or she may call upon a Department Manager for verification. Verification of such property shall be included in the internal audit programme.

ABC Company Limited	Procedures Manual	Reference CP 011 Page 2 of 2	
	Management of Customers' and Suppliers' Property	Date Released dd/mm/yyyy	Date Reviewed dd/mm/yyyy
Core Process	Approved:	Issue No: 01 Prepared by:	Revision No: 00

	Process Headings	Process Details
10.3	Protection of property	1. All staff who are in possession of or using a customer's property shall exercise care while it is under the control of ABCCL. 2. The Department Manager who is responsible for the property shall be aware of any special environmental conditions for storing and using the item, storage procedures, operating conditions and maintenance.
10.4	Lost, damaged or unsuitable property	If the customer's property is lost, damaged or otherwise found to be unsuitable for use while in the custody of ABCCL, it shall be recorded and reported to the customer for disposal. Purchasing Manager shall make an entry in the log book.
11.0	Records	Customer property log book.
12.0	Changes made	None.

CP 012 Production Process Control

ABC Company Limited	Procedures Manual	Reference CP 012 Page 1 of 4	
	Production Process Control	Date Released dd/mm/yyyy	Date Reviewed dd/mm/yyyy
Core Process	Approved:	Issue No: 01 Prepared by:	Revision No: 00

Process Owner	Production Manager
Process Headings	**Process Details**
1.0 Purpose	To describe the procedure for controlling the operations to maintain quality and food safety and protect the environment during the operations.
2.0 Scope	This procedure shall apply to all operations in the facility.
3.0 Input	Work schedule, operating procedures, raw materials and ingredients, samples, drawings, test methods and inspection forms.
4.0 Output	Requirements necessary to control production operations.
5.0 Competency requirements	Knowledge of operating procedures, hygiene requirements and skills for operating equipment and conducting tests.
6.0 Responsibility	Defined in Flowchart CP 012.3: Production process control. Additional responsibilities are set out below. Quality Assurance Manager shall: • Monitor inspection results • Issue the relevant reference sample or the standard for comparison during production. Production Supervisor shall: • Ensure that devices and equipment necessary for the operations have been calibrated and made available • Ensure the working environment is clean and the appropriate protection equipment is worn by the operators. Engineering Team shall: • Carry out necessary repairs and maintenance during production. Environment Manager shall: • Monitor and record environmental aspects such as energy use, water use, spillages, waste disposal, recycling, noise, emissions and other items that affect the environment during production • Communicate with authorities about the necessary environmental permits • Train all operating personnel on all • environmental requirements.

ABC Company Limited	Procedures Manual	Reference CP 012 Page 2 of 4	
	Production Process Control	Date Released dd/mm/yyyy	Date Reviewed dd/mm/yyyy
Core Process	Approved:	Issue No: 01 Prepared by:	Revision No: 00

	Process Headings	Process Details
		Food Services Manager shall: • Ensure that all equipment is cleaned and sanitised as required • Ensure that the environment is clean at all times • Ensure that pest management programmes are effective • Ensure that waste disposal is carried out as specified • Monitor the health of workers in the production area. Operators shall: • Carry out cleaning and sanitising activities as specified in the procedures • Isolate non-conforming goods.
7.0	Associated documents	Specifications form (Form 050) Hazard Analysis and Critical Control Point (HACCP) worksheet (Form 052: Control schedule) In-process control (Form 051) Environmental records Pre-requisite Programmes (PRPs) HACCP plan Production schedule Production records Reference samples Skill chart Palletising pattern.
8.0	Measures/Controls	In-process checks for quality and food safety Final product checks.
9.0	Definitions	**Operational control**: Operating conditions necessary to carry out the operations of the facility.
10.0	System description	Flowchart CP 012.3 shows process control operations.
10.1	Availability of documentation	1. Documented information that defines product or service characteristics and activities to be performed is included in individual procedures, flowcharts, forms, figures, work instructions, specifications, samples, test methods, process control operations, PRPs, hazard analysis, work orders and documents for contracts with external providers. 2. Results to be achieved are embedded in specifications, control charts, as outputs and measures and controls in individual procedures.

ABC Company Limited	Procedures Manual		Reference CP 012 Page 3 of 4	
	Production Process Control	Date Released dd/mm/yyyy		Date Reviewed dd/mm/yyyy
Core Process	Approved:	Issue No: 01 Prepared by:		Revision No: 00

	Process Headings	Process Details
10.2	Availability of monitoring and measuring devices	1. The availability of suitable monitoring and measuring (MM) devices is described in the Resource Management Procedure (SP 009), Measurement and Analysis Procedure (AP 003) and Control of Monitoring and Measuring Devices (AP 002). 2. Defective testing and inspection equipment and suspect results shall be immediately brought to the attention of the QA Manager and Production Supervisor. 3. QA Manager may decide to stop further production until the problem is resolved and isolate the finished product for investigation (if necessary).
10.3	Implementation of monitoring and measurement activities	1. MM activities are carried out at various stages from receipt of inward goods to dispatch of goods in order to verify that control of processes or outputs and acceptance criteria for products and services have been met. Documented information in test methods, in-process control sheets and specifications defines acceptance/rejection criteria and/or control limits, points at which verifications are to be performed, and MM device to be used with operating procedures. 2. If samples are drawn during process operations, number of samples to be taken and the frequency of sampling is defined in specification sheets.
10.4	Availability of skilled personnel	Training and Development Procedure (SP 014) addresses this requirement.
10.5	Validation of processes	Validation and periodic re-validation necessary to achieve planned results for production and service provision when resulting outputs cannot be verified by subsequent monitoring and measurement are addressed in Validation and Verification Procedure (AP 010, AP 011).
10.6	Avoidance of human error	Production Manager shall provide satisfactory work environment, including breaks at regular intervals, and monitor the welfare of staff to prevent human error. Other methods used to prevent human error are: adequate labelling of products during all stages of production; isolating non-conforming items; and regular monitoring of test results.

ABC Company Limited	Procedures Manual	Reference CP 012 Page 4 of 4	
	Production Process Control	Date Released dd/mm/yyyy	Date Reviewed dd/mm/yyyy
Core Process	Approved:	Issue No: 01 Prepared by:	Revision No: 00

	Process Headings	**Process Details**
10.7	Release, delivery and post-delivery activities	They are controlled through these procedures: CP 014 Release of finished goods CP 021 Delivery CP 022 Post-delivery.
10.8	Monitoring environmental aspects	ABCCL shall monitor the items identified as significant in the environmental aspects and impacts evaluation, e.g. emissions to air, hazardous waste, recycling, solid waste and utilities.
10.9	Food safety requirements	1. ABCCL shall develop and implement PRPs, which serve as a foundation for conducting a HACCP study. Critical Control Points (CCPs) identified in the HACCP plan shall be monitored to assure food safety. ABCCL shall monitor (e.g. sanitation, pest management, environment cleanliness and waste disposal) as required by the PRPs. 2. The flowchart for food production is shown in CP 012.4.
10.10	Control of outsourced production	Outsourced production is controlled through procedure SP 045.
10.11	Infrastructure	A suitable infrastructure and environment are provided for effective operations (SP 010).
10.12	Samples	The flowchart for sparkling wine production is shown in CP 012.1. The flowchart for wine bottling process is shown in CP 012.2. Form 051 shows process controls for wine bottling operations.
11.0	Records	Test results and control records.
12.0	Changes made	None.

ABC Company Limited	Procedures Manual	Flowchart CP 012.1 Page 1 of 1	
	Sparkling Wine Production	Date Released dd/mm/yyyy	Date Reviewed dd/mm/yyyy
Link CP 012 Form 051	Approved:	Issue No: 01 Prepared by:	Revision No: 00

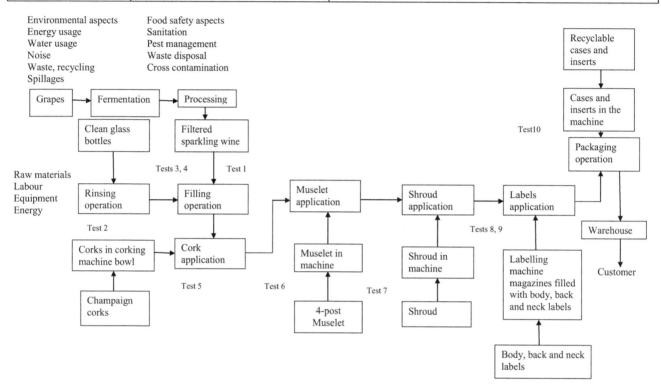

ABC Company Limited	Procedures Manual	Flowchart CP 012.2 Page 1 of 1	
	Wine Bottling Process	Date Released dd/mm/yyyy	Date Reviewed dd/mm/yyyy
Link CP 012 Form 051	Approved:	Issue No: 01 Prepared by:	Revision No: 00

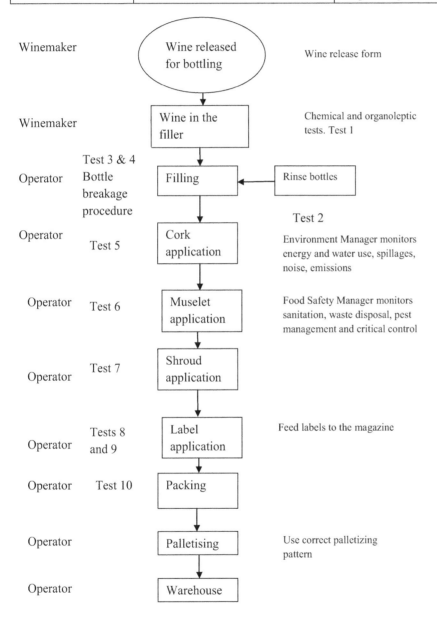

Winemaker   Wine released for bottling   Wine release form

Winemaker   Wine in the filler   Chemical and organoleptic tests. Test 1

Operator   Test 3 & 4 Bottle breakage procedure   Filling ← Rinse bottles

Test 2

Operator   Test 5   Cork application   Environment Manager monitors energy and water use, spillages, noise, emissions

Operator   Test 6   Muselet application   Food Safety Manager monitors sanitation, waste disposal, pest management and critical control

Operator   Test 7   Shroud application

Operator   Tests 8 and 9   Label application   Feed labels to the magazine

Operator   Test 10   Packing

Operator   Palletising   Use correct palletizing pattern

Operator   Warehouse

ABC Company Limited	Procedures Manual	Flowchart CP 012.3 Page 1 of 1	
	Generic Production Process	Date Released dd/mm/yyyy	Date Reviewed dd/mm/yyyy
Link CP 012/AP 007	Approved:	Issue No: 01 Prepared by:	Revision No: 00

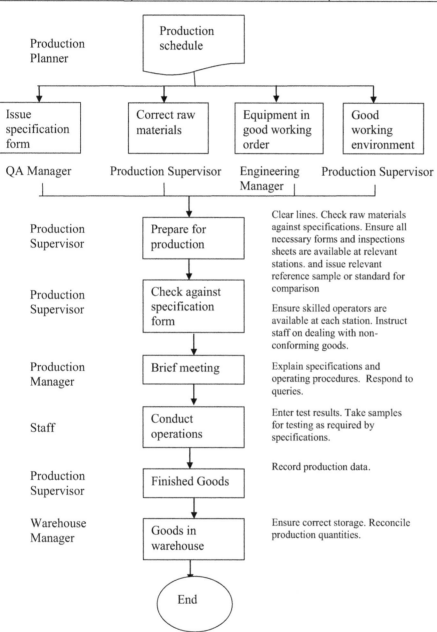

Production Planner — Production schedule

Issue specification form
Correct raw materials
Equipment in good working order
Good working environment

QA Manager — Production Supervisor — Engineering Manager — Production Supervisor

Production Supervisor — Prepare for production — Clear lines. Check raw materials against specifications. Ensure all necessary forms and inspections sheets are available at relevant stations. and issue relevant reference sample or standard for comparison

Production Supervisor — Check against specification form — Ensure skilled operators are available at each station. Instruct staff on dealing with non-conforming goods.

Production Manager — Brief meeting — Explain specifications and operating procedures. Respond to queries.

Staff — Conduct operations — Enter test results. Take samples for testing as required by specifications.

Production Supervisor — Finished Goods — Record production data.

Warehouse Manager — Goods in warehouse — Ensure correct storage. Reconcile production quantities.

End

ABC Company Limited	Procedures Manual	Flowchart CP 012.4 Page 1 of 1	
	Food Production Process	Date Released dd/mm/yyyy	Date Reviewed dd/mm/yyyy
Link CP 012/AP 007	Approved:	Issue No: 01 Prepared by:	Revision No: 00

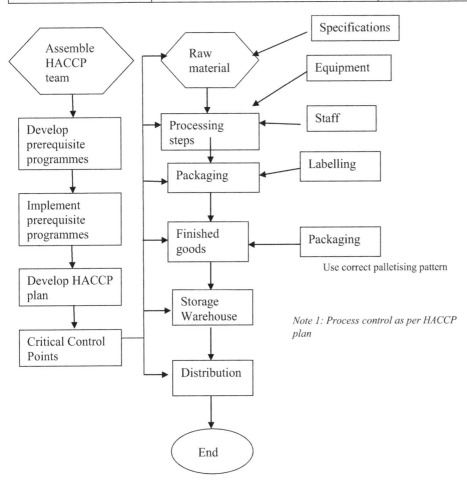

Use correct palletising pattern

Note 1: Process control as per HACCP plan

CP 013 Design and Development

ABC Company Limited	Procedures Manual	Reference CP 013 Page 1 of 6	
	Design and Development	Date Released dd/mm/yyyy	Date Reviewed dd/mm/yyyy
Core Process	Approved:	Issue No: 01 Prepared by:	Revision No: 00

Process Owner		Management Team
	Process Headings	**Process Details**
1.0	Purpose	To describe the procedure for new product development by our company.
2.0	Scope	This procedure shall apply to all products and services designed and developed by our company.
3.0	Input	See section 10.3.
4.0	Output	See section 10.9.
5.0	Competency requirements	Project management skills and competencies specified in this document.
6.0	Responsibility	Defined in Flowchart CP 013.1 and Form 053.
7.0	Associated documents	Specifications and standards Market requirements Test methods and results Environmental review Form 054 Design and Development Plan (DDP) Form 053 Risk assessment Form 055.
8.0	Resources	Project planning software Designing software Test equipment Manufacturing equipment.
9.0	Measures/Controls	Completion of the project as scheduled Performance of the product Market performance.
10.0	System description	The design and development process is shown in Flowchart CP 013.1.
10.1	Design concept	• General Manager shall appoint a Project Manager for each design and development project • Engineering and production shall adhere to this documented procedure that assures all design/development solutions (hardware, software, services, etc.) meet market requirements and performance criteria.
10.2	Design and Development Plan	Form 053 is used as the DDP. 1. Reviews shall be conducted at the end of each phase and action taken to resolve any issues. 2. Design Team shall define organisational and technical interfaces between different functions that contribute to the design and development process and the necessary information is documented, transmitted and regularly reviewed.

ABC Company Limited	Procedures Manual		Reference CP 013 Page 2 of 6	
	Design and Development		Date Released dd/mm/yyyy	Date Reviewed dd/mm/yyyy
Core Process	Approved:		Issue No: 01 Prepared by:	Revision No: 00

	Process Headings	Process Details
10.3	Design and development input	1. Marketing and sales personnel shall identify and document the market's needs for the new product or service. The contents of this document shall serve as the input for design and development work. This document shall contain at least this information: • The product or service required including the desired features and functions • The reason for the demand (customer demand) • Information from previous designs • When it is needed • Market segment • Detailed product requirements including performance standards, customer requirements, reliability, applicable regulatory requirements, codes and product life needs • Potential consequences of failure • Target price. 2. When a new service has to be designed or an existing service has to be modified, marketing and sales personnel shall provide the customer requirements. 3. The Design Team shall document the design and development input and it can be in any form including data sheets, drawings and specifications, photographs, samples, reference standards, etc. 4. Marketing, sales, engineering, production, quality and purchasing functions (as applicable) shall review and approve the design order document before release. 5. Project Manager shall carry out a risk analysis according to Form 055.
10.4	Specific considerations	
10.4.1	Health and safety	Project Manager shall be aware of health and safety regulatory requirements and he or she shall: • Identify relevant safety standards that make a product more effective • Carry out at specified stages design evaluation tests and prototype testing for safety • Review instructions, warnings, labels and maintenance manuals, etc. to minimise misinterpretation • Establish a means of traceability to enable a product to be recalled for safety reasons.

ABC Company Limited	Procedures Manual	Reference CP 013 Page 3 of 6	
	Design and Development	Date Released dd/mm/yyyy	Date Reviewed dd/mm/yyyy
Core Process	Approved:	Issue No: 01 Prepared by:	Revision No: 00

	Process Headings	Process Details
10.4.2	Environmental considerations	Environment Manager (EMS Manager) shall evaluate environmental impact of the materials and processes used in the manufacture of the product (Form 054). He or she shall consider the energy and water requirements and the impact of materials and processes on the environment. Some of the factors to be considered are emissions, waste water, solid waste, noise, radiation, odour and land use. The Design Team shall discuss the findings in the report and resolve any issues.
10.4.3	Food safety	For food products, the Food Safety Manager shall conduct a hazard analysis plan, identify Critical Control Points (CCPs) and establish controls as necessary. Food Safety Manager shall provide instructions for packaging, labelling and storage of the product and carry out necessary tests to assure food safety during all stages of development.
10.5	Design and development controls	Design and development controls define the requirements for design review, design verification and design validation. It includes: • Results to be achieved • Conducting design reviews • Conducting design verification • Conducting design validation • Resolution of problems identified during reviews, verification and validation activities • Documented information on these activities.
10.6	Design review	The Project Team shall conduct a formal documented design and development review at predetermined stages. The review serves two purposes: (a) to assess the ability of the design process to meet requirements and (b) to identify and resolve any problems. Form 056 shows typical topics for the review.

ABC Company Limited	Procedures Manual	Reference CP 013 Page 4 of 6	
	Design and Development	Date Released dd/mm/yyyy	Date Reviewed dd/mm/yyyy
Core Process	Approved:	Issue No: 01 Prepared by:	Revision No: 00

	Process Headings	Process Details
10.7	Design and development verification	Engineering, production and quality personnel shall devise methods for verification and validation. Verification may be performed once near the end of the project or during multiple stages of the project. Verification and validation test methods shall be documented. The methods for verification shall include, but are not limited to: • Alternative calculations to verify the correctness of original calculations and analyses • Comparison with other sample designs • Confirmation of basic attributes • Verification of performance properties and/or third party evaluation • Periodic evaluation of sample production models and prototypes • Feedback from previous similar designs and from customer • Information gained during manufacture, assembly, installation, commissioning, service and field use • Safety and health issues • Environmental impact applied to the full life-cycle • Marketing review • Legal review.
10.8	Design and development validation	Where possible, validation tests should be performed before the delivery or installation of the product. Tests performed are: • Evaluation of functions such as performance, durability, safety, reliability and maintainability of the product under normal handling, storage and operational conditions • Inspection methods to verify all design features are as they were originally intended, approved design changes have been incorporated, and these changes have been recorded • Validation of associated computer systems and software (if applicable).

ABC Company Limited	Procedures Manual	Reference CP 013 Page 5 of 6	
	Design and Development	Date Released dd/mm/yyyy	Date Reviewed dd/mm/yyyy
Core Process	Approved:	Issue No: 01 Prepared by:	Revision No: 00

	Process Headings	Process Details
10.9	Design output	1. Design output (Form 057) defines specifications that describe how the product is built. At this stage, all design specifications are developed by the Design Team and QA, and reviewed to verify that they exist and meet the specifications established in the input phase. 2. The Project Manager shall identify and provide skilled individuals, tools and equipment for the project.
10.10	Design changes	1. Changes to design shall be documented, reviewed and revisions controlled by the Design Team. The changes from the previous version shall include but not limited to release notes, critical dimensions and features, critical assembly requirements, performance criteria and functional and operational requirements. Design changes can occur during any design and development phase. All affected documentation shall be revised to reflect the change. 2. When any aspect of the design changes the QA Manager shall conduct a new risk analysis to determine whether the change has caused new hazards and eliminated the mitigations. 3. The output of design change process consists of a design change checklist – a list of changes, revised documents and a change notice. 4. Quality functions shall verify that all design features meet specified requirements and that the necessary development changes have been implemented. Quality function shall maintain all records of validation n and verification activities. Engineering function shall incorporate the new requirements into design and development activities and schedules. 5. Requests for design changes to released products shall be submitted to the engineering function for review. Major changes are evaluated by the Design Team. 6. All requests shall be documented and serve as inputs to design and development change projects.

ABC Company Limited	**Procedures Manual**		**Reference CP 013** Page 6 of 6	
	Design and Development		Date Released dd/mm/yyyy	Date Reviewed dd/mm/yyyy
Core Process	Approved:		Issue No: 01 Prepared by:	Revision No: 00

	Process Headings	**Process Details**
10.11	Design transfer	After verification and validation the design shall be transferred into production and service. Project Manager shall ensure that all training materials are ready. A product inventory is created. QA Manager shall ensure that necessary regulatory clearances have been obtained. Final stage of the transfer phase is production and product launch.
10.12	Design and development resources and techniques	1. Engineering functions shall validate tools used in calculations and other design and development activities. Standard commercial software may be used without validation. Software documentation includes validation specifications established by the Engineering Manager and validation records. Software that has been used successfully by the company in previous design and development activities may also be used for one year without validation testing. 2. Design and development reference material such as standards, catalogues, samples and records of such reference material shall be maintained by the Engineering Manager.
10.13	Customer involvement	1. At various stages specified by the Design Team, consumer response shall be obtained and recorded. 2. Engineering function shall prepare the necessary models or prototypes. 3. QA Manager shall specify the test methods. 4. Marketing Manager shall prepare a plan for testing to be conducted by the sales staff.
10.14	Before delivery or implementation of the product	Validation may require evaluation under realistic conditions.
11.0	Records	All documents specified in Form 057.
12.0	Changes made	None.

ABC Company Limited	Procedures Manual	Flowchart CP 013.1 Page 1 of 2	
	Design and Development	Date Released dd/mm/yyyy	Date Reviewed dd/mm/yyyy
Link CP 013	Approved:	Issue No: 01 Prepared by:	Revision No: 00

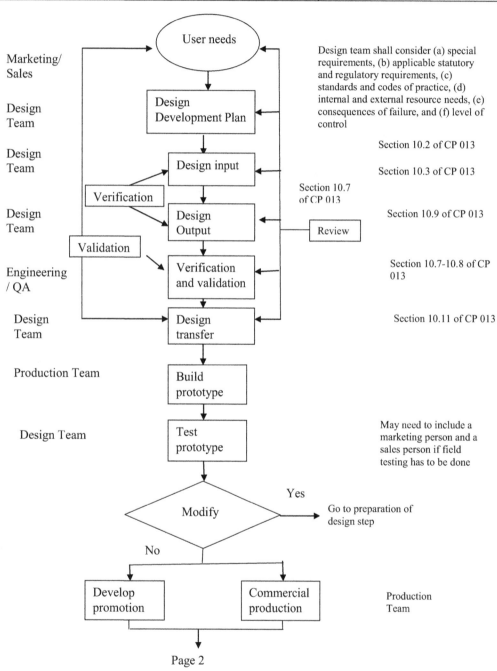

ABC Company Limited	Procedures Manual	Flowchart CP 013.1 Page 2 of 2	
	Design and Development	Date Released dd/mm/yyyy	Date Reviewed dd/mm/yyyy
Link CP 013	Approved:	Issue No: 01 Prepared by:	Revision No: 00

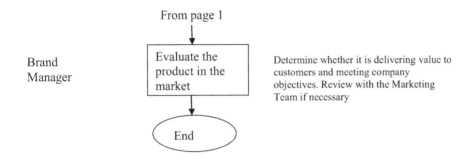

Brand Manager

From page 1

Evaluate the product in the market

Determine whether it is delivering value to customers and meeting company objectives. Review with the Marketing Team if necessary

End

CP 014 Release of Finished Products

ABC Company Limited	Procedures Manual		Reference CP 014 Page 1 of 3	
	Release of Finished Products	Date Released dd/mm/yyyy		Date Reviewed dd/mm/yyyy
Core Process	Approved:	Issue No: 01 Prepared by:		Revision No: 00

Process Owner	QA Manager
Process Headings	**Process Details**
1.0 Purpose	To describe the procedure for releasing finished products for sale and delivery.
2.0 Scope	This procedure applies to all finished goods manufactured by ABCCL or on its behalf.
3.0 Input	Product ready to be monitored and tested, testing methods, monitoring and measuring (MM) tools and in-process controls records.
4.0 Output	Product released for dispatch, then held for further investigation if non-conforming product or service.
5.0 Competency requirements	Knowledge of MM requirements and skill in testing methods.
6.0 Responsibility	Quality Control Officer shall: <ul><li>Ensure that all relevant tests are performed and recorded</li><li>Obtain samples of finished goods for final tests in the laboratory</li><li>Ensure that only products that meet planned arrangements and specifications are released for sale and delivery</li><li>Identify released material by applying a status sticker (PASSED)</li><li>Identify materials for rework and rejection by applying HOLD stickers with the reason stated on the sticker</li><li>Remove QUARANTINE stickers (as applicable).</li></ul> Line Supervisor shall: <ul><li>Apply QUARANTINE stickers on all pallets of finished goods before transporting to the warehouse for storage.</li></ul> Warehouse Manager shall: <ul><li>Store all finished goods according to the instructions stated on the pallet label. Update the stock position of finished goods in the computer system on release.</li></ul>
7.0 Associated documents	Testing methods Non-forming work procedure Release goods form (Form 058).
8.0 Resources	Nil.

ABC Company Limited	Procedures Manual	Reference CP 014 Page 2 of 3	
	Release of Finished Products	Date Released dd/mm/yyyy	Date Reviewed dd/mm/yyyy
Core Process	Approved:	Issue No: 01 Prepared by:	Revision No: 00

	Process Headings	Process Details
9.0	Measures/controls	Verification of documents before release.
10.0	System description	
10.1	Verification activities of product and service requirements before release	ABCCL shall measure and monitor the characteristics of products and services at various stages to verify that planned arrangements have been met. Critical items and activities shall be identified and ensured that they are controlled and monitored in accordance with procedures described in this manual.
10.1.1	MM activities	MM activities take place: (a) when goods and items are received; (b) during defined stages of production and (c) before release for despatch. The procedures specify: • The points at which MM takes place • The responsibilities for MM • The types of MM, e.g. visual, comparison with a sample or standard, measurement using tools and equipment and chemical and microbiological analysis • The measuring equipment • The acceptance criteria • Records to be maintained. Products shall not be allowed to progress to the next operation until the required verification and tests have been successfully completed.
10.1.2	Sampling for tests	Samples of products shall be obtained during production and on completion of production as specified in the product specification form.
10.1.3	MM methods	MM methods may include, but are not limited to: (a) Laboratory tests; (b) Automated monitoring by a machine; (c) In-process inspection by operators; (d) Sensory evaluation; (e) Comparison with a sample or standard; (f) Inviting customer feedback of service; (g) Observation of a service against predefined criteria; (h) External inspection and test service; (i) Supplier certificates of conformance and (j) Inspection and testing random samples.
10.2	Tests for finished goods	All finished goods shall be tested according to the test methods in the Laboratory Test Methods Manual.

ABC Company Limited	Procedures Manual	Reference CP 014 Page 3 of 3	
	Release of Finished Products	Date Released dd/mm/yyyy	Date Reviewed dd/mm/yyyy
Core Process	Approved:	Issue No: 01 Prepared by:	Revision No: 00

	Process Headings	Process Details
10.3	Verification of test results	The QA Manager/Food Safety Manager shall inspect all records pertaining to the product and batch to determine whether the results comply with specified requirements (Form 058).
		1. The QA Team shall ensure that finished products are stored under specified conditions and products bearing REJECT, QUARANTINE or HOLD stickers are segregated from released products.
		2. On release, the QA Team shall apply PASSED stickers on the bottom row of each column of pallets so that they are clearly visible to the Picking Team in the warehouse.
		3. Warehouse Administration Staff shall obtain the product release form from the QA Department and remove allocation restriction so that the product is available for picking.
11.0	Records	All test results Final release from Inventory level.
12.0	Changes made	None.

CP 015 Handling and Storage of Goods

ABC Company Limited	Procedures Manual		Reference CP 015 Page 1 of 6	
	Handling and Storage of Goods		Date Released dd/mm/yyyy	Date Reviewed dd/mm/yyyy
Core Process	Approved:		Issue No: 01 Prepared by:	Revision No: 00

Process Owner		**Department Managers**
	Process Headings	**Process Details**
1.0	Purpose	To describe the procedure for identification, handling, packaging, storage, transport and protection of raw materials, ingredients and finished products during receiving, processing, storage and delivery operations.
2.0	Scope	This procedure applies to all goods handled and operations of ABCCL.
3.0	Input	All goods, all operations affecting the quality, food safety and the environment and regulatory requirements.
4.0	Output	Preserved product and safe operations.
5.0	Competency requirements	Knowledge of goods handling and operations.
6.0	Responsibility	Production Supervisor shall: • Palletise the product and label the pallets for transport to the warehouse • Keep a record of pallet numbers for reconciliation. Fork Hoist Driver shall: • Check pallet details • Transport pallets to the warehouse • Store the pallets safely in the designated location. Warehouse Administration shall: • Assign a location for storage • Make entries in the warehouse computer module • Update inventory levels • Make stock "unallocable" until released by QA.
7.0	Associated documents	Pallet record Stock transfer record Pallet label (Form 059) Cleaning records.
8.0	Resources	Warehousing computer module Fork hoist.
9.0	Measures/controls	Pallet numbers Warehouse temperature monitors Damaged goods.
10.0	System description	

ABC Company Limited	**Procedures Manual**	**Reference CP 015** Page 2 of 6	
	Handling and Storage of Goods	Date Released dd/mm/yyyy	Date Reviewed dd/mm/yyyy
Core Process	Approved:	Issue No: 01 Prepared by:	Revision No: 00

	Process Headings	**Process Details**
10.1	Identification and preservation	1. Product preservation is maintained through identification, handling, contamination control, packaging, storage, transmission, transport and storage. Preservation shall also be applicable to constituent parts of a product. AP 007 describes the procedure for product identification and traceability. 2. Preservation methods applicable to specifications, regulatory requirements and customer requirements include, but are not limited to, cleaning and sanitation, prevention, detection and removal of foreign objects, prevention of cross-contamination, pest control, special handling and storage of sensitive products, marking and suitable labelling including safety warnings and cautions, shelf-life management, inventory control, safe movement and transport of products, inspection requirements for transport equipment and vehicles, prevention of dropping and shaking of product, palletising and loading patterns for shipping containers and truck trailers, handling to prevent electro-static discharge, use of approved packaging material and suppliers, hygiene requirements for personnel who handle product and special handling and storage of hazardous materials.
10.2	Handling	Handling is involved in numerous activities of ABCCL. Department Managers shall instruct all employees who handle goods on safe handling procedures to prevent damage, deterioration and loss or contamination of product. Such instructions may be in the form of memos, work instructions, training programmes or briefings at department meetings.
10.3	Packaging	1. QA Manager shall review packaging requirements regularly or in response to changes and ensure that they are adequate, in good condition and are effective for maintaining the integrity of the product through receipt, processing, transporting, storage, shipping and delivery to destinations. Packaging materials include, but are not limited to, outer packaging, inserting sections, packaging graphics, inner packaging, labels and bar codes, shrink wrapping, packaging information and documents attached to packaging. 2. QA Manager shall specify the requirements for packaging cleanliness and work with the design team to design effective packaging. 3. Production Supervisor shall palletise the product according to the assigned palletising pattern, complete the pallet labels and attach them to all four sides of the bottom row of the pallet. All products shall be packaged to prevent damage during storage and delivery. 4. Product being prepared for shipment shall have an indication of release or passed for shipment.

ABC Company Limited	Procedures Manual	Reference CP 015 Page 3 of 6	
	Handling and Storage of Goods	Date Released dd/mm/yyyy	Date Reviewed dd/mm/yyyy
Core Process	Approved:	Issue No: 01 Prepared by:	Revision No: 00

	Process Headings	Process Details
10.4	Storage	1. Storage conditions shall apply to products maintained in the facility as well as to those in contractors' warehouse and outsourced warehouses. Warehouse Manager shall consider these environmental conditions when storing products in the warehouse: storage area; access to product; security requirements; pest control programme; house-keeping requirements; inspection and monitoring requirements to detect and damage; location of waste containers and First-in-First-Out (FIFO) requirements. 2. Fork Hoist Driver shall check the pallet label, transport to the warehouse and obtain a storage location from Warehouse Administration Staff. Warehouse Administration Staff shall assign a location for the goods awaiting release and make the inventory "unallocable" in the computer system to prevent picking up in error. All those goods designed to be tested should bear a quarantine label unless advised by the QA Staff. 3. All products should be stacked safely and checked periodically for structural integrity. Where appropriate, corner posts should be used to make the corner stand out visually and to protect the product from accidental impact damage by fork hoists or pallet trucks. 4. On completion of stacking, the Fork Hoist Driver shall communicate the details to the Warehouse Administration Staff for updating the records. If there is a discrepancy in pallet numbers between the records of the Supervisor and the Fork Hoist Driver, the matter shall be resolved before the final count is communicated to the Warehouse Administration Staff.

ABC Company Limited	Procedures Manual	Reference CP 015 Page 4 of 6	
	Handling and Storage of Goods	Date Released dd/mm/yyyy	Date Reviewed dd/mm/yyyy
Core Process	Approved:	Issue No: 01 Prepared by:	Revision No: 00

	Process Headings	Process Details
10.5	Storage of food items and ingredients	1. Warehouse conditions shall be maintained and controlled in a manner so as to assure product integrity. 2. Products that require refrigeration or frozen storage shall be stored in controlled areas. Rooms and temperature control areas are monitored at least daily to ensure that appropriate temperatures are maintained (<42° F for refrigeration and −10° F for frozen). 3. Slip sheets shall be used when double stacking to protect the material from dirty or damaged pallets. 4. Finished goods, packaging material, ingredients or equipment shall not be stored in close proximity to cleaning products, pesticides or other non-food items. Such non-food items shall be stored in separate locations with restricted access. 5. Damaged, leaking or unsecured products shall be immediately isolated and placed on hold for evaluation by QA personnel. 6. Partially used or previously opened ingredient containers shall not be stored with finished goods. 7. Allergen-containing ingredients shall be stored separately from non-allergen-containing ingredients. Physical barriers shall separate allergen and non-allergen ingredients. 8. Ingredients shall not be stored on the floor.
10.6	Storage of sensitive and toxic ingredients	1. All restricted, sensitive and toxic material shall be stored separately under strict controlled conditions to prevent accidental contamination. 2. Toxic and sensitive material and inflammable solvents shall be stored as required by the regulations. They shall be stored away from packaging material with access restricted to designated personnel. Records of usage and disposal shall be kept as required by law. 3. Sensitive and toxic material shall be clearly identified. Material Safety Data (MSD) sheets shall be available in the location. 4. Physical barriers shall separate inflammable products from non-inflammable products.

ABC Company Limited	Procedures Manual	Reference CP 015 Page 5 of 6	
	Handling and Storage of Goods	Date Released dd/mm/yyyy	Date Reviewed dd/mm/yyyy
Core Process	Approved:	Issue No: 01 Prepared by:	Revision No: 00

	Process Headings	Process Details
10.7	Storage of returned product	1. Returned products shall be segregated and properly identified. Disposing of such products shall be determined by the Plant Manager. 2. All such items shall bear a HOLD sticker. 3. Warehouse Manager shall maintain records of returned products. 4. Details of products returned due to quality or food safety issues shall be promptly communicated to the QA Manager for investigation and the necessary action.
10.8	Storage of equipment	1. All equipment shall be stored indoors protected from adverse environmental conditions. 2. The condition of such equipment shall be regularly inspected by the Engineering Manager. Necessary repairs or maintenance work shall be carried out before use.
10.9	Storage of liquid waste	Liquid waste shall be stored in designated areas and regularly inspected by the Environment Manager for any damage such as leakages, spillages and corrosion.
10.10	Preserving the product	1. Warehouse Manager shall manage the inventory to ensure that product conformity is preserved during storage, internal processing and delivery to the final destination. 2. Components, ingredients and products are handled and stored in a manner to prevent damage or deterioration pending use or delivery. 3. Warehouse Staff shall ensure that conforming and non-conforming products are not stored in the same location. 4. Packaging ensures the integrity of the product during storage and transport. 5. Temperature of temperature-controlled items shall be maintained and kept in good condition.

ABC Company Limited	Procedures Manual	Reference CP 015 Page 6 of 6	
	Handling and Storage of Goods	Date Released dd/mm/yyyy	Date Reviewed dd/mm/yyyy
Core Process	Approved:	Issue No: 01 Prepared by:	Revision No: 00

	Process Headings	Process Details
10.11	Maintenance of storage area	1. ABCCL shall maintain product monitoring and product status through the use of both physical identification tags/labels and electronic records. Further, physical location in a clearly designated hold area is an indication of the product status. 2. Warehouse storage areas shall be maintained in clean and orderly manner and shall have adequate space round the periphery for access, inspection and cleaning. Walls shall be maintained in a clear and clean manner to allow for pest management inspection and sanitation/housekeeping requirements. Warehouse Manager shall ensure that spilled, damaged and exposed products are not stored in the receiving area. 3. Stacking shall not block blowers or vents to prevent the circulation of air. 4. Items shall be stacked at least 6" above the floor. 5. Floors and walls shall be maintained in good condition to prevent the access of pests. 6. Effective cleaning shall be carried out at specified intervals according to the cleaning schedule.
10.12	Training	1. All Fork Hoist Drivers shall successfully complete a training programme approved by the Warehouse Manager. 2. Department Managers shall provide the necessary training to operators who carry out activities for which Department Managers are responsible.
11.0	Records	Pallet numbers Stock locations Goods inventory.
12.0	Changes made	None.

CP 016 Customer Requirements

ABC Company Limited	Procedures Manual	Reference CP 016 Page 1 of 4	
	Customer Requirements	Date Released dd/mm/yyyy	Date Reviewed dd/mm/yyyy
Management Processes	Approved:	Issue No: 01 Prepared by:	Revision No: 00

Process Owner	Sales Manager	
	Process Headings	**Process Details**
1.0	Purpose	To describe the procedure for the identification and review of product and service requirements and communicating with the customer.
2.0	Scope	This procedure applies to product and service requirements of customers.
3.0	Input	Product and service catalogue, customer needs, pricing schedule, customer's payment history and resource requirements.
4.0	Output	Clearly defined customer requirements.
5.0	Competency requirements	Clearly defined customer requirements.
6.0	Responsibility	Sales Team shall: • Determine product and service requirements • Clarify the requirements • Take the order. QA Manager/Production Team shall: • Determine the feasibility of producing and delivering the product or service • Ensure that adequate resources are available.
7.0	Associated documents	External communication procedure SP 006 Take orders procedure CP 017.
8.0	Resources	Order processing software.
9.0	Measures/controls	Customer satisfaction Number of incorrect requirements Number of orders that could not be fulfilled.
10.0	System description	There are three categories of customer requirements: 1. Finished products offered by ABCCL. 2. A product to be made according to specified requirements. 3. A service.
10.1	Requirements for a finished products	Defined in CP 017 Take order, CP 018 Processing orders and SP 007 Customer communication.
10.2	Requirements for a product to be made	CP 013 Design and development See Section 10.5.

ABC Company Limited	Procedures Manual	Reference CP 016 Page 2 of 4	
	Customer Requirements	Date Released dd/mm/yyyy	Date Reviewed dd/mm/yyyy
Management Processes	Approved:	Issue No: 01 Prepared by:	Revision No: 00

	Process Headings	Process Details
10.3	Requirements for a service	1. Customer Relations Manager shall communicate with the customer and determine the details of the service required including the timeframe for the delivery of service. 2. The information shall be communicated to the Sales Manager. 3. The Sales Manager may enter into a contract when the details of the service have been agreed between the customer and ABCCL (CP 002).
10.4	Communication with customers	See Procedure SP 007.
10.5	Determining the requirements	1. The Sales Team or the Orders Entry Team shall record this information about the product or service requested by the customer: • Product and service requirements specified by the customer including the requirements for availability, delivery and post-delivery support • Product requirements not specified by the customer but necessary for intended or specified use • Statutory and regulatory requirements related to the product • Post-delivery requirements such as warranty provisions, contractual obligations, servicing requirements, recycling and final disposal requirements • Any other requirements considered necessary by ABCCL.
10.6	Determining the statutory requirements	QA Manager shall determine the statutory and regulatory requirements related to the product or service at the time of review.
10.7	Determining the ability to deliver the requirements	The Production Team shall ensure that ABCCL can meet the claims for products and services that it offers, determine the special requirements of products and services and identify operational risks such as the need for new technology and the ability and capacity to meet short delivery times. It may be necessary to perform a failure mode and effects analysis (FMEA) on the processes as a form of risk assessment.

ABC Company Limited	Procedures Manual	Reference CP 016 Page 3 of 4	
	Customer Requirements	Date Released dd/mm/yyyy	Date Reviewed dd/mm/yyyy
Management Processes	Approved:	Issue No: 01 Prepared by:	Revision No: 00

	Process Headings	Process Details
10.8	Review of requirements	1. The review is conducted by the Production Team: (a) before the commitment to produce the product or deliver the service; (b) to resolve product or service order; (c) to resolve order requirements that may differ from those previously defined and (d) to confirm the requirements not defined by the customer. These items shall be reviewed: 1. Requirements defined by the customer. 2. Applicable requirements for the product or service. 3. Resolution of discrepancy between 1 and 2. 4. R&D activities that may be involved. 5. Applicable statutory and regulatory requirements. 6. Competencies of personnel responsible for production and delivery. 7. Materials and infrastructure needed. 8. Lead time for delivery. 9. Costs involved. 10. Ability to meet the demands. 11. Evaluation of risk. 12. Special requirements.
10.9	Review of contract before acceptance	Production Team shall: 1. Determine whether there is a difference between original quote and contract. 2. Ensure that codes, standards and specifications are current. 3. Check schedules. 4. Check quality objectives. 5. Lines of communication. Any discrepancies between the original quote and the contract shall be brought to the attention of the customer. No order or contract shall be accepted until the discrepancies have been satisfactorily resolved. Requirements communicated verbally by the customer shall be confirmed and documented.
10.10	Amendments to the requirements	1. Changes can be amended by either party. Those requested by the customer shall undergo the same review procedure. Impact on the cost and the schedule shall be clearly communicated to the customer and documented. 2. Changes initiated by ABCCL shall also be communicated to the customer along with the impact on cost and schedule. All changes and communications shall be documented.

ABC Company Limited	Procedures Manual	Reference CP 016 Page 4 of 4	
	Customer Requirements	Date Released dd/mm/yyyy	Date Reviewed dd/mm/yyyy
Management Processes	Approved:	Issue No: 01 Prepared by:	Revision No: 00

	Process Headings	**Process Details**
10.11	Internal requirements	QA Manager shall establish internal requirements for products and services such as the use of logo, safety requirements, packaging and promotion material.
11.0	Records	All documents related to product and service requirements.
12.0	Changes made	None.

CP 017 Take Order

ABC Company Limited	Procedures Manual		Reference CP 017 Page 1 of 2	
	Take Order	Date Released dd/mm/yyyy		Date Reviewed dd/mm/yyyy
Core Process	Approved:	Issue No: 01 Prepared by:		Revision No: 00

Process Owner		Sales Manager
	Process Headings	**Process Details**
1.0	Purpose	To describe the procedure for taking orders.
2.0	Scope	This procedure shall apply to all sales orders
3.0	Input	Products or services, product information, order form, inventory level and customer payment history.
4.0	Output	Confirmed order.
5.0	Competency requirements	Product knowledge, knowledge of sales process and the ability to convince the customer.
6.0	Responsibility	Defined in Flowchart CP 017.1. Additional responsibilities are set out below. Sales Manager shall: • Allocate Sales Team to territories • Review activity schedule • Provide resources • Analyse sales activities. Sales Person shall: • Take order • Communicate the order for supply and delivery.
7.0	Associated documents	Order book Customer requirements (CP 016).
8.0	Resources	Software programme for sales activities.
9.0	Measures/controls	Number of closed sales per visit.
10.0	System description	Flowchart CP 017.1 shows the process for taking orders. ABCCL offers four types of orders: 1. Customer orders: Orders placed by customers themselves influenced by the Sales Person. Orders may be placed with the Sales Person or with the Orders Entry Staff. 2. Indirect orders: Customer places orders through a distributor. Record on the sales activity module in the computer. Confirm the acceptance of the order. 3. Direct orders: These are orders placed by the Sales Person on behalf of the customer after a sales visit. Record on the sales activity module in the computer. Hand over the copy of the order to the customer. 4. "Off car" orders: Ideal for immediate sale of core product range.

ABC Company Limited	Procedures Manual	Reference CP 017 Page 2 of 2	
	Take Order	Date Released dd/mm/yyyy	Date Reviewed dd/mm/yyyy
Core Process	Approved:	Issue No: 01 Prepared by:	Revision No: 00

	Process Headings	Process Details
10.1	Changes to orders	Changes to orders shall be carried out according to the customer requirements procedure (CP 016).
11.0	Records	Confirmed order.
12.0	Changes made	None.

ABC Company Limited	Procedures Manual	Flowchart CP 017.1 Page 1 of 1	
	Take Order	Date Released dd/mm/yyyy	Date Reviewed dd/mm/yyyy
Link CP 017/CP 018	Approved:	Issue No: 01 Prepared by:	Revision No: 00

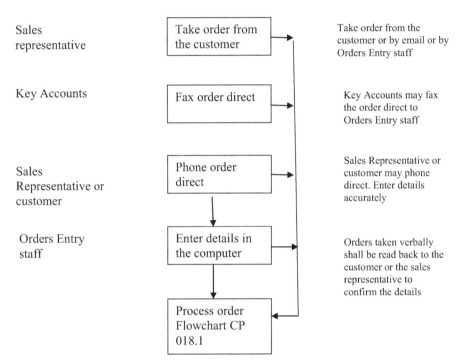

Sales representative — Take order from the customer — Take order from the customer or by email or by Orders Entry staff

Key Accounts — Fax order direct — Key Accounts may fax the order direct to Orders Entry staff

Sales Representative or customer — Phone order direct — Sales Representative or customer may phone direct. Enter details accurately

Orders Entry staff — Enter details in the computer — Orders taken verbally shall be read back to the customer or the sales representative to confirm the details

Process order Flowchart CP 018.1

Notes:

If the order cannot be fulfilled in full:
Production: Refer to Warehouse Manager
Limited line: Check commitments

Warehouse action:
Ship overnight out of current city, same
Day delivery, local orders, urgent orders
Liaise with Warehouse Manager

Changes to above:
Request by Warehouse Manager to orders
Entry staff to contact the customer

CP 018 Processing Orders

ABC Company Limited	Procedures Manual		Reference CP 018 Page 1 of 1	
	Processing Orders	Date Released dd/mm/yyyy		Date Reviewed dd/mm/yyyy
Core Process	Approved:	Issue No: 01 Prepared by:		Revision No: 00

Process Owner		Warehouse Manager
	Process Headings	**Process Details**
1.0	Purpose	To describe the procedure for processing orders from customers.
2.0	Scope	This procedure shall apply to all orders received by the Sales Staff or Orders Entry Staff.
3.0	Input	Order from the customer, inventory level and goods released note.
4.0	Output	Pick list and adjusted inventory levels.
5.0	Competency requirements	Managing orders entry module, warehousing skills and fork hoist driving skills.
6.0	Responsibility	Orders Entry Staff shall: • Receive and code the orders • Input the information in the computer • Resolve any differences in the order • Update the entries in the out-of-stock board. Sales Manager or Key Accounts Manager Staff shall: • Prepare and update the price list • Authorise the price list • Issue order pads to the customer. Credit Controller shall: • Authorise new accounts • Resolve any differences of credit type.
7.0	Associated documents	Order form (Form 060) Price list (Form 061) Pick list (Form 062).
8.0	Resources	Orders entry system.
9.0	Measures/controls	Number of orders entry errors.
10.0	System description	The procedure for receiving and processing customer orders is shown in Flowcharts CP 017.1 and CP 018.1.
11.0	Records	Customer orders. Pick list.
12.0	Changes made	None.

ABC Company Limited	**Procedures Manual**	**Flowchart CP 018.1** Page 1 of 2	
	Processing Orders	Date Released dd/mm/yyyy	Date Reviewed dd/mm/yyyy
Link CP 018	Approved:	Issue No: 01 Prepared by:	Revision No: 00

1.0 Stock available

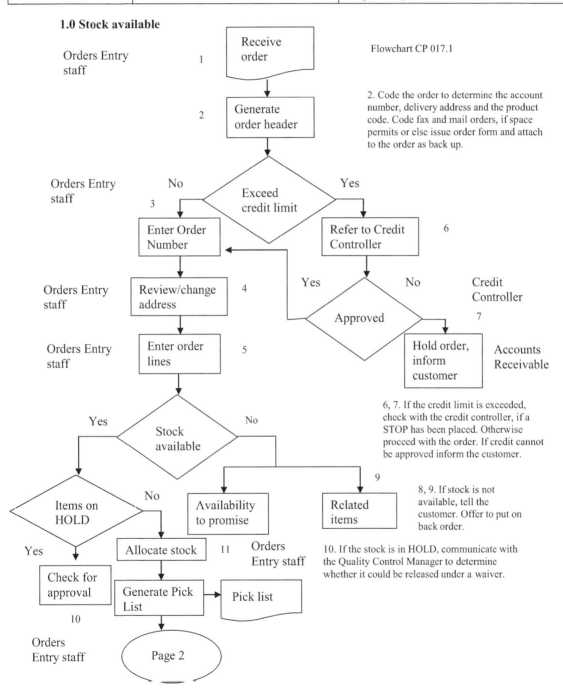

Orders Entry staff

Flowchart CP 017.1

2. Code the order to determine the account number, delivery address and the product code. Code fax and mail orders, if space permits or else issue order form and attach to the order as back up.

Orders Entry staff

Orders Entry staff

Orders Entry staff

Credit Controller

Accounts Receivable

6, 7. If the credit limit is exceeded, check with the credit controller, if a STOP has been placed. Otherwise proceed with the order. If credit cannot be approved inform the customer.

8, 9. If stock is not available, tell the customer. Offer to put on back order.

10. If the stock is in HOLD, communicate with the Quality Control Manager to determine whether it could be released under a waiver.

Orders Entry staff

Orders Entry staff

ABC Company Limited	Procedures Manual	Flowchart CP 018.1 Page 2 of 2	
	Processing Orders	Date Released dd/mm/yyyy	Date Reviewed dd/mm/yyyy
Link CP 018	Approved:	Issue No: 01 Prepared by:	Revision No: 00

2.0 Out of stock　　　　　　From page 1

Orders Entry staff

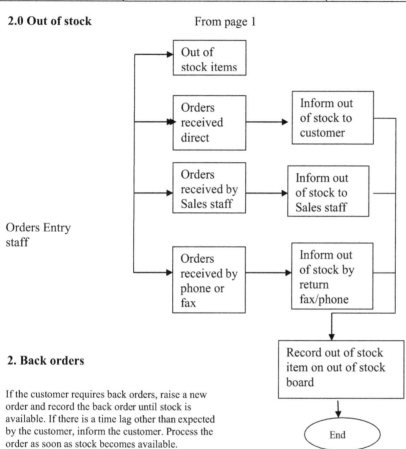

2. Back orders

If the customer requires back orders, raise a new order and record the back order until stock is available. If there is a time lag other than expected by the customer, inform the customer. Process the order as soon as stock becomes available.

Note 1 – All special pricing and discounts shall be approved by the Sales Manager and shall be entered in the computer before orders are entered so that all orders will be automatically priced.
Note 2 – All communications with the customer shall be followed up by the Orders Entry staff in order to resolve any outstanding issues
Note 3 – All free of charge orders shall be authorised by the Manager responsible for the orders or by the National Sales Manager or the Chief Financial Controller.

>

CP 019 Picking Orders

ABC Company Limited	Procedures Manual	Reference CP 019 Page 1 of 1	
	Picking Orders	Date Released dd/mm/yyyy	Date Reviewed dd/mm/yyyy
Core Process	Approved:	Issue No: 01 Prepared by:	Revision No: 00

Process Owner	**Warehouse Manager**
Process Headings	**Process Details**
1.0 Purpose	To describe the procedure for picking orders from customers.
2.0 Scope	This procedure shall apply to all orders received by the Sales Staff or Orders Entry Staff.
3.0 Input	Pick list, inventory levels and product release note.
4.0 Output	Picked order ready for delivery.
5.0 Competency requirements	Managing order processing module, product knowledge and fork hoist driving skills.
6.0 Responsibility	Orders Entry Staff shall: <ul><li>Generate pick lists for picking</li><li>Communicate with the customer to resolve issues</li><li>Generate shipping documents.</li></ul> Warehouse Administration Staff shall: <ul><li>Pick items from the pick list</li><li>Check items before shipment</li><li>Package items for delivery</li><li>Generate invoices</li><li>Arrange for delivery</li><li>Communicate with the customer about the delivery</li><li>Load the goods into the vehicle.</li></ul>
7.0 Associated documents	Pick list (Form 062) Packing slip (Form 044) Address label Invoice (Form 048).
8.0 Resources	Orders entry system Equipment for moving stock.
9.0 Measures/controls	Accuracy of picking.
10.0 System description	The flowchart for picking items is shown in CP 019.1.
11.0 Records	Adjusted inventory level. Back order list.
12.0 Changes made	None.

ABC Company Limited	Procedures Manual	Flowchart CP 019.1 Page 1 of 2	
	Picking Orders	Date Released dd/mm/yyyy	Date Reviewed dd/mm/yyyy
Link CP 019	Approved:	Issue No: 01 Prepared by:	Revision No: 00

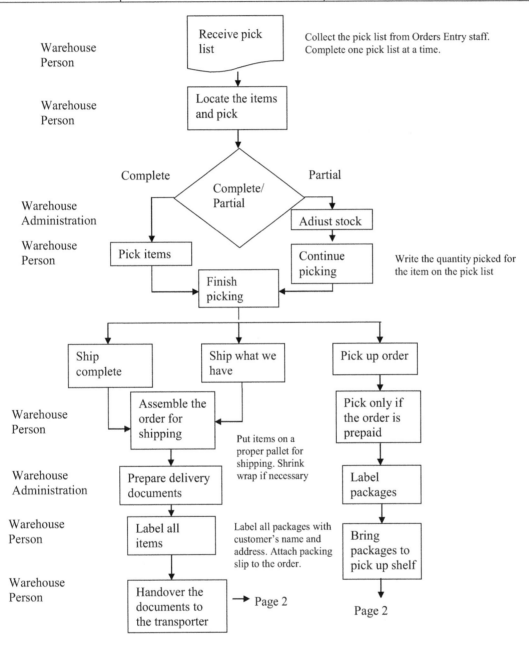

Warehouse Person — Receive pick list
Collect the pick list from Orders Entry staff. Complete one pick list at a time.

Warehouse Person — Locate the items and pick

Warehouse Administration — Complete/Partial

Complete / Partial

Adjust stock

Warehouse Person — Pick items / Continue picking
Write the quantity picked for the item on the pick list

Finish picking

Ship complete / Ship what we have / Pick up order

Warehouse Person — Assemble the order for shipping / Pick only if the order is prepaid
Put items on a proper pallet for shipping. Shrink wrap if necessary

Warehouse Administration — Prepare delivery documents / Label packages

Warehouse Person — Label all items / Bring packages to pick up shelf
Label all packages with customer's name and address. Attach packing slip to the order.

Warehouse Person — Handover the documents to the transporter → Page 2

Page 2

ABC Company Limited	**Procedures Manual**	**Flowchart CP 019.1** Page 2 of 2	
	Picking Orders	Date Released dd/mm/yyyy	Date Reviewed dd/mm/yyyy
Link CP 019	Approved:	Issue No: 01 Prepared by:	Revision No: 00

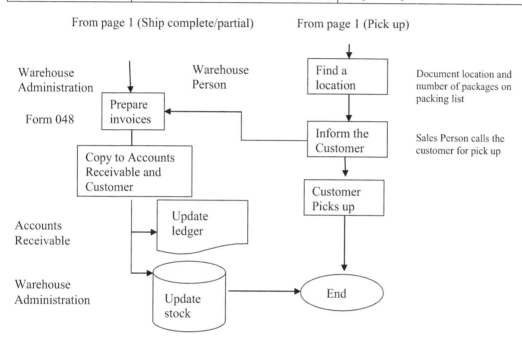

From page 1 (Ship complete/partial)   From page 1 (Pick up)

Warehouse
Administration

Warehouse
Person

Find a
location — Document location and number of packages on packing list

Form 048 — Prepare invoices

Inform the Customer — Sales Person calls the customer for pick up

Copy to Accounts Receivable and Customer

Accounts Receivable — Update ledger

Customer Picks up

Warehouse Administration — Update stock — End

CP 020 New Product Development

ABC Company Limited	Procedures Manual	Reference CP 020 Page 1 of 2	
	New Product Development	Date Released dd/mm/yyyy	Date Reviewed dd/mm/yyyy
Core Process	Approved:	Issue No: 01 Prepared by:	Revision No: 00

Process Owner		Marketing Manager
	Process Headings	**Process Details**
1.0	Purpose	To describe the procedure for new product development by our company.
2.0	Scope	This procedure shall apply to all products designed and developed by our company.
3.0	Input	Functional performance, safety requirements, applicable regulatory requirements, information relating to previous designs, risk analysis and other requirements essential for design and development.
4.0	Output	Information for purchasing, manufacturing and service, product acceptance criteria and features of the product for safe and proper use.
5.0	Competency requirements	Appropriate technical skills, project management skills, problem-solving skills, communication skills and the ability to work as a team.
6.0	Responsibility	Brand Manager shall: • Identify opportunities for new product development • Gather market information • Test market the product • Evaluate the product in the market. Marketing Manager shall: • Approve the concept for the new product • Plan product development activities and approve market authorisation • Monitor the progress of the product development programme • Provide the necessary resources for the product • Communicate with the Production Department about the progress of the project. Purchasing Manager shall: • Identify purchasing requirements and select suppliers • Purchase the requirements. Engineering Manager shall: • Evaluate the manufacturing feasibility of the proposed product • Evaluate the performance of the product • Prepare the design and develop specifications in collaboration with the Production Team • Develop a prototype (if necessary) • Make recommendations for modifications (if necessary).

ABC Company Limited	Procedures Manual		Reference CP 020 Page 2 of 2	
	New Product Development		Date Released dd/mm/yyyy	Date Reviewed dd/mm/yyyy
Core Process	Approved:		Issue No: 01 Prepared by:	Revision No: 00

	Process Headings	Process Details
7.0	Associated documents	Design requirements Market information Test methods and results.
8.0	Resources	Project planning software Designing software Test equipment Manufacturing equipment.
9.0	Measures/controls	Completion of the project as scheduled Performance of the product Market performance.
10.0	System description	The new product development process is shown in Flowchart CP 020.1 and Procedure CP 013.
11.0	Records	Specifications Purchasing requirements Customer requirements.
12.0	Changes made	None.

ABC Company Limited	Procedures Manual		Flowchart CP 020.1 Page 1 of 2	
	New Product Development		Date Released dd/mm/yyyy	Date Reviewed dd/mm/yyyy
Link CP 020	Approved:		Issue No: 01 Prepared by:	Revision No: 00

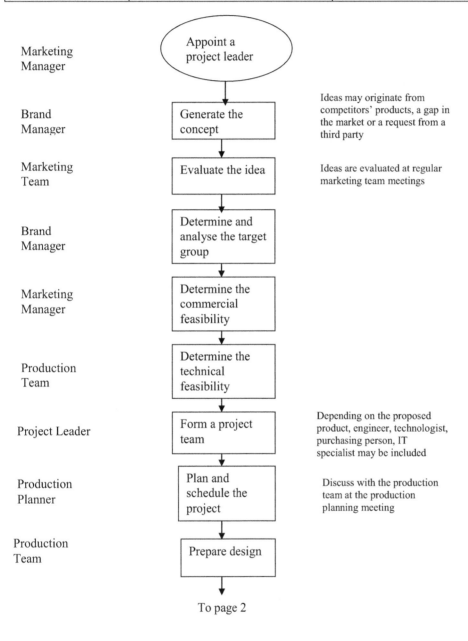

Marketing Manager — Appoint a project leader

Brand Manager — Generate the concept — Ideas may originate from competitors' products, a gap in the market or a request from a third party

Marketing Team — Evaluate the idea — Ideas are evaluated at regular marketing team meetings

Brand Manager — Determine and analyse the target group

Marketing Manager — Determine the commercial feasibility

Production Team — Determine the technical feasibility

Project Leader — Form a project team — Depending on the proposed product, engineer, technologist, purchasing person, IT specialist may be included

Production Planner — Plan and schedule the project — Discuss with the production team at the production planning meeting

Production Team — Prepare design

To page 2

ABC Company Limited	Procedures Manual	Flowchart CP 020.1 Page 2 of 2	
	New Product Development	Date Released dd/mm/yyyy	Date Reviewed dd/mm/yyyy
Link CP 020	Approved:	Issue No: 01 Prepared by:	Revision No: 00

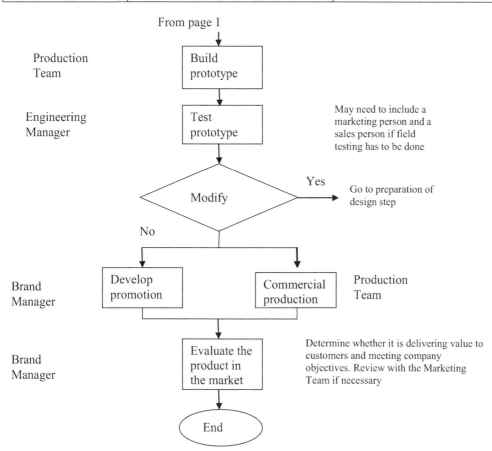

From page 1

Production Team — Build prototype

Engineering Manager — Test prototype — May need to include a marketing person and a sales person if field testing has to be done

Modify — Yes → Go to preparation of design step

No

Brand Manager — Develop promotion

Commercial production — Production Team

Brand Manager — Evaluate the product in the market — Determine whether it is delivering value to customers and meeting company objectives. Review with the Marketing Team if necessary

End

CP 021 Delivery

ABC Company Limited	Procedures Manual		Reference CP 021 Page 1 of 2	
	Delivery		Date Released dd/mm/yyyy	Date Reviewed dd/mm/yyyy
Core Process	Approved:		Issue No: 01 Prepared by:	Revision No: 00

Process Owner	Warehouse Manager
Process Headings	**Process Details**
1.0 Purpose	To describe the procedure for the delivery of orders to customers.
2.0 Scope	This procedure shall apply to all filled orders to be delivered to customers.
3.0 Input	Customer order, inventory levels, product release, shipping document and delivery method.
4.0 Output	Product delivered to customer, delivery note and receipt by the customer.
5.0 Competency requirements	Fork hoist driving skills, knowledge of hygiene requirements for transport and product knowledge.
6.0 Responsibility	Defined in Flowchart CP 021.1. Additional responsibilities are set out below. Warehouse Manager shall: • Ensure that all documents are correct and ready. Warehouse Person shall: • Hand over delivery documents to the transporter • Communicate with the customer about the delivery.
7.0 Associated documents	Address label Packing slip (Form 044) Approved transport carrier list Carrier's cleaning log Pallet docket (Form 059) Delivery note (Form 063).
8.0 Resources	Equipment for moving stock.
9.0 Measures/controls	Number of orders shipped Transport damage.
10.0 System description	The delivery process is shown in Flowchart CP 021.1.
10.1 Release for shipment	• Products shall not be shipped until all activities in the quality and food safety management plans have been successfully completed • Products manufactured under mandatory regulatory Hazard Analysis and Critical Control Point (HACCP) programmes shall have a signed release by the Food Safety Manager verifying that all HACCP records are complete, properly signed and that there are no Critical Control Point (CCP) deficiencies before shipment.

ABC Company Limited	Procedures Manual		Reference CP 021 Page 2 of 2	
	Delivery		Date Released dd/mm/yyyy	Date Reviewed dd/mm/yyyy
Core Process	Approved:		Issue No: 01 Prepared by:	Revision No: 00

	Process Headings	Process Details
10.2	Transportation	1. Warehouse Manager shall schedule transportation in the most economical way. Warehouse Manager shall keep a list of acceptable carriers who can meet the requirements of ABCCL.
		2. All delivery vehicles shall be checked and inspected for condition, odour, sanitation and potential contamination sources. Inspection results shall be recorded on shipping documents. Carrier's cleaning log shall also be examined.
		3. All temperature-controlled trucks shall be inspected for proper operation and temperature settings to ensure that units are running when loading and the vehicle has been pre-cooled before loading the container.
		4. Transport vehicles shall not be cleaned in the facility as it can create a warehouse sanitation problem and a potential for pest access.
		5. Slip sheets shall be used when double-stacking palletised finished product to prevent potential contamination from dirty and damaged pallets.
		6. Several orders may be scheduled to be delivered.
		7. Warehouse Person shall marshal together the items to form vehicle loads in the dispatch area and then load them onto outbound vehicles for onward dispatch to the next point in the supply chain – a distributor, a port or airport – for the next transport leg or to the final customer.
11.0	Records	Invoice Inventory level Details of delivery.
12.0	Changes made	None.

ABC Company Limited	**Procedures Manual**	**Flowchart CP 021.1** Page 1 of 1	
	Delivery of Orders	Date Released dd/mm/yyyy	Date Reviewed dd/mm/yyyy
Link CP 021	Approved:	Issue No: 01 Prepared by:	Revision No: 00

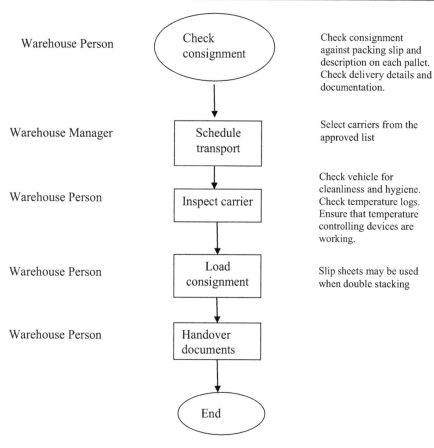

Warehouse Person — Check consignment — Check consignment against packing slip and description on each pallet. Check delivery details and documentation.

Warehouse Manager — Schedule transport — Select carriers from the approved list

Warehouse Person — Inspect carrier — Check vehicle for cleanliness and hygiene. Check temperature logs. Ensure that temperature controlling devices are working.

Warehouse Person — Load consignment — Slip sheets may be used when double stacking

Warehouse Person — Handover documents

End

CP 022 Post-Delivery Activities

ABC Company Limited	Procedures Manual		Reference CP 022 Page 1 of 4	
	Post-Delivery Activities		Date Released dd/mm/yyyy	Date Reviewed dd/mm/yyyy
Core Process	Approved:		Issue No: 01 Prepared by:	Revision No: 00

Process Owner		**Customer Relations Manager**
	Process Headings	**Process Details**
1.0	Purpose	To describe the activities necessary to support the customer in the use of products and/or services after delivery to ensure continuing customer satisfaction.
2.0	Scope	The procedure applies to all products and services offered by ABCCL.
3.0	Input	User manuals; contract/warranty documents; legal requirements, quality, food safety and environmental risk; service schedule and replacement parts.
4.0	Output	Safe disposal of product after use, equipment in good working order, customer satisfaction and improvement opportunities.
5.0	Competency requirements	Knowledge of products and services, equipment maintenance and service skills, customer relation skills and legal requirements.
6.0	Responsibility	Engineering Manager shall: • Plan service and maintenance activities • Assign staff for service, maintenance and repair • Analyse and organise action to resolve product-related issues. Customer Relations Manager shall: • Respond to customer queries • Direct queries and requests to appropriate functions. Legal Officer shall: • Deal with warranty issues • Investigate and take appropriate action on liability and compensation issues.
7.0	Associated documents	CP 016 Customer requirements MP 003 Legal and other requirements SP 046 Customer satisfaction Risk management (MP 007) Service and maintenance schedule User manuals Maintenance report (Form 064) Work order (Form 065).
8.0	Resources	Equipment parts.

ABC Company Limited	Procedures Manual	Reference CP 022 Page 2 of 4	
	Post-Delivery Activities	Date Released dd/mm/yyyy	Date Reviewed dd/mm/yyyy
Core Process	Approved:	Issue No: 01 Prepared by:	Revision No: 00

	Process Headings	Process Details
9.0	Measures/controls	Customer satisfaction Number of product failures Number of maintenance and service activities not completed on time Number of warranty claims.
10.0	Definitions	**Warranty:** A written guarantee issued to a purchaser of an item by its manufacturer promising to repair or replace it (if necessary) within a specified period of time.
11.0	System description	
11.1	Statutory and legal requirements	Legal Officer shall determine whether there are statutory and legal requirements for post-delivery activities relating to products and services. If so, the Sales Manager shall organise such activities. The activity may be related to the safe disposal of product after use or safe operation of equipment.
11.2	Potential for misuse	1. Results of the risk management process identify risks including safety issues, environmental issues and food safety issues associated with the product/service and its use. 2. Product literature shall include all safety issues, proper use of the equipment and applicable storage conditions. The proposed action in case of harm to an individual as a result of using the equipment or consuming the product shall be clearly stated in the product literature. When such a report is received, a representative at an executive level shall visit the customer to investigate and provide whatever support is necessary.
11.3	Installation	1. The purchase order from the client shall specify whether installation is required. If installation is specified in the purchase order, the Engineering Manager shall assign staff and schedule the task for installation. Installation is defined as completed when the equipment has been shown to be capable of performing as expected by the client after finishing all applicable tests such as validation and verification. 2. Installation of equipment and items not supplied by the organisation: Requests for installation of equipment, hardware and software may be received from customers who have purchased the items from a third party. When such a request is received, the Engineering Manager shall review the request for the ability to provide the service. If skills are available, the Engineering Manager shall assign staff and schedule the work. The payment for such services shall be agreed between the service provider and the customer.

ABC Company Limited	Procedures Manual		Reference CP 022 Page 3 of 4	
	Post-Delivery Activities	Date Released dd/mm/yyyy		Date Reviewed dd/mm/yyyy
Core Process	Approved:	Issue No: 01 Prepared by:		Revision No: 00

	Process Headings	**Process Details**
11.4	Maintenance and service	1. Engineering Manager shall ensure that the customer has a service agreement with the organisation. If no such agreement is available, the payment for such services shall be agreed between the service provider and the customer before the work begins. Engineering Manager shall assign staff and schedule the work. For regular maintenance and services, Form 064 shall be completed by the Service Engineer. 2. Repair work: Engineering Manager shall review the request for the ability to provide the repair work. Service Engineer shall discuss with the customer, the details of repair work necessary and ascertain whether spare parts are available. If they are available, the Engineering Manager shall assign staff and schedule the work. Service Engineer shall provide a quote for the repair work, and only when the customer has given their approval to go ahead, should the work begin.
11.5	Warranty information	Our organisation shall provide warranty information when we sell [*specify the items here*]. Warranty information shall include these details: • Warranty period • Contact for warranty service repair action if and when equipment, hardware and software fail • Parts and repair problems covered by the warranty • Whether consequential damage is included in the warranty • Conditions and limitations on the warranty. When a request for a warranty issue is received, the Service Engineer shall evaluate the claim and inform the decision to the customer. If there is disagreement, the issue shall be escalated to the Engineering Manager who shall resolve the issue. If warranty service is accepted, the procedure under 11.4 shall be followed.

ABC Company Limited	Procedures Manual	Reference CP 022 Page 4 of 4	
	Post-Delivery Activities	Date Released dd/mm/yyyy	Date Reviewed dd/mm/yyyy
Core Process	Approved:	Issue No: 01 Prepared by:	Revision No: 00

	Process Headings	**Process Details**
11.6	Liability issues	All issues related to compensation or liability shall be handled by the Legal Officer.
11.7	End-of-life support	Appropriate recycling and safe disposal methods shall be included in the product literature when products which could cause environmental issues are delivered. This includes items such as batteries, glass containers and tyres.
12.0	Records	Work orders Sales visits.
13.0	Changes made	None.

CP 023 Business Continuity

ABC Company Limited	Procedures Manual		Reference CP 023 Page 1 of 3	
	Business Continuity		Date Released dd/mm/yyyy	Date Reviewed dd/mm/yyyy
Core Process	Approved:		Issue No: 01 Prepared by:	Revision No: 00

Process Owner		Business Continuity Plan Coordinator (BCPC)
	Process Headings	**Process Details**
1.0	Purpose	To describe the procedure for continuing critical business activities and resuming normal operations following a major disruptive event.
2.0	Scope	This procedure shall apply to all ABCCL's operations identified as critical for business continuity.
3.0	Input	Results of risk analysis, list of critical operations, list of essential resources and key suppliers, legal issues, essential staff positions, financial resources, contact details and hardware and software requirements.
4.0	Output	Business continuity plan and business resumption.
5.0	Competency requirements	Ability to analyse critical situations, communication skills and a good knowledge of business operations.
6.0	Responsibility	CEO and the Financial Manager shall: • Appoint a Business Continuity Plan Coordinator (BCPC) • Identify the critical business activities • Provide the necessary resources for the plan. BCPC shall: • Develop the plan and establish strategies and actions to ensure the operation of critical activities • Prepare the business continuity plan kit • Establish a single point of contact for business continuity arrangements • Provide the leadership to business unit managers • Obtain necessary resources for business continuity arrangements • Coordinate the business continuity activities • Review the business continuity plan in consultation with Chief Risk Officer.
7.0	Associated documents	Key contact details (Form 066) List of essential activities business (Continuity Plan Section 1) (Form 067) List of essential resources (Continuity Plan Section 2) (Form 068) Requirements for business continuity (Continuity Plan Section 3) (Form 069)

ABC Company Limited	Procedures Manual	Reference CP 023 Page 2 of 3	
	Business Continuity	Date Released dd/mm/yyyy	Date Reviewed dd/mm/yyyy
Core Process	Approved:	Issue No: 01 Prepared by:	Revision No: 00

	Process Headings	Process Details
8.0	Resources	Resources for relocation and resumption of business Hardware and software.
9.0	Measures/controls	Monitor the accuracy, relevance and effectiveness of the business continuity plan.
10.0	System description	The flowchart for operating a business continuity plan is CP 023.1.
10.1	Identify critical business activities	1. Determine the impact on fulfilling the objectives, service delivery, financial activities, stakeholders' expectations, ABCCL's reputation and compliance to regulatory requirements. 2. Determine the Maximum Acceptable Outage (MAO) in business days: 1–2 days 3–5 days 6–15 days Longer than 16 days. 3. Categorise the level of impact as major, critical or MAO of greater than 15 days. 4. Prioritise critical business activities with similar MAOs.
10.2	Identify response strategies	(a) Use all hazards approach: • No access to buildings or infrastructure • No access to information technology (IT) • Significant number of staff unavailable • Any combination of these. (b) Identify response strategies to re-establish business activities: • Select the most appropriate action using appropriate resources and coordinate business continuity activities.
10.3	Develop the business continuity plan	Consolidate the individual business continuity plans into one major plan for ABCCL. Consolidate the resources and prepare an action plan. Chart the process for activation including governance arrangements, assign roles and responsibilities and provide information to make strategic decisions and prioritise resources.
10.4	Prepare business continuity kit	The kit shall consist of business continuity plans, contact details for staff and other stakeholders and the resources necessary to carry out business activities.

ABC Company Limited	Procedures Manual	Reference CP 023 Page 3 of 3	
	Business Continuity	Date Released dd/mm/yyyy	Date Reviewed dd/mm/yyyy
Core Process	Approved:	Issue No: 01 Prepared by:	Revision No: 00

	Process Headings	**Process Details**
10.5	Maintain the business continuity plan and kit	Test the plan by stepping through an activation of the plan to ensure that it is fit for the purpose, practicable and can be easily activated, response and recovery results are within MAOs and the staff are skilled to use the plan.
10.6	Response log	BCPC shall complete a log of key events in response to interruptions including when warnings are received, decisions to evacuate and return, request for assistance and actions taken (Form 070).
11.0	Records	Response log.
12.0	Changes made	None.

ABC Company Limited	Procedures Manual	Flowchart CP 023.1 Page 1 of 1	
	Business Continuity	Date Released dd/mm/yyyy	Date Reviewed dd/mm/yyyy
Link CP 023	Approved:	Issue No: 01 Prepared by:	Revision No: 00

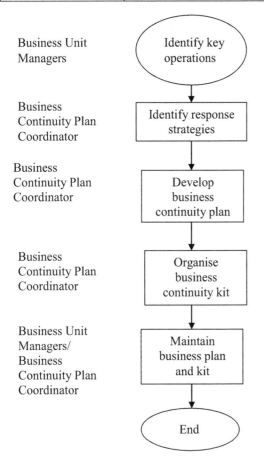

Business Unit Managers

Business Continuity Plan Coordinator

Business Continuity Plan Coordinator

Business Continuity Plan Coordinator

Business Unit Managers/ Business Continuity Plan Coordinator

Identify key operations

Identify response strategies

Develop business continuity plan

Organise business continuity kit

Maintain business plan and kit

End

Assess the impact on department's activities, determine the maximum acceptable outage, identify the level of impact and prioritise critical business activities

Use all hazards approach, identify response strategies for business continuity, select the best option and identify the resources

Prepare individual plans for each business unit, consolidate the plans and prioritise actions and obtain CEO's approval

Kit consists of business continuity plans, contact details for staff, shareholders, customers and data and information for re-establishing business activities

Test the kit, prepare the report and review biannually

CP 024 Preparation for Hazard Analysis

ABC Company Limited	Procedures Manual		Reference CP 024 Page 1 of 3	
	Preparation for Hazard Analysis		Date Released dd/mm/yyyy	Date Reviewed dd/mm/yyyy
Core Process	Approved:		Issue No: 01 Prepared by:	Revision No: 00

Process Owner		Food Safety Manager
	Process Headings	**Process Details**
1.0	Purpose	To describe the procedure for preparing for analysing food safety hazards associated with our food products in preparation for establishing Critical Control Points (CCPs).
2.0	Scope	This procedure applies to all our food products and processes related to food safety.
3.0	Input	Codex Alimentarius, process operations, legal requirements and Pre-requisite programmes (PRPs).
4.0	Output	List of ingredients and raw materials, product description and flow diagram.
5.0	Competency requirements	Knowledge of Hazard Analysis and Critical Control Point (HACCP) principles, biological, physical and chemical hazards, risk analysis and management, company's food products and recipes and food microbiology.
6.0	Responsibility	Food Safety Manager shall: <ul><li>Supervise hazard analysis</li><li>Report results to the Management Team</li><li>Review food processes</li><li>Ensure hazards are controlled</li><li>Organise food safety training</li><li>Appoint external consultants when required.</li></ul> Food Safety Team (FST) shall: <ul><li>Conduct hazard analysis</li><li>Seek external help when required.</li></ul> Management Team shall: <ul><li>Implement food safety hazard controls</li><li>Review food processes as necessary</li><li>Implement revisions.</li></ul> QA Manager shall: <ul><li>Ensure continuous improvement of the food safety system</li><li>Support the staff in implementing food safety controls.</li></ul>
7.0	Associated documents	Flow diagram List of ingredients and raw materials Sanitation procedures.
8.0	Resources	None.
9.0	Measures/Controls	Accuracy of plant layout, product description and the flow diagram.

ABC Company Limited	Procedures Manual	Reference CP 024 Page 2 of 3	
	Preparation for Hazard Analysis	Date Released dd/mm/yyyy	Date Reviewed dd/mm/yyyy
Core Process	Approved:	Issue No: 01 Prepared by:	Revision No: 00

	Process Headings	Process Details
10.0	Definitions	**Flow diagram:** A logical sequence of steps involved in processing a food product. **Food safety hazard:** A biological, physical or a chemical agent that has the potential to cause the production food unsafe for consumption.
11.0	System description	
11.1	The Food Safety Team	The team shall at least consist of the Food Safety Manager, an employee who has had HACCP training and the QA Manager. Food Safety Manager may include employees from production, sanitation, quality control, engineering and employees directly involved in food processing activities. Responsibilities and authorities of team members are defined by the Food Safety Manager.
11.2	Preliminary documented information	Includes (a) applicable statutory, regulatory and customer requirements; (b) ABCCL's products, processes and equipment; (c) customer requirements and (d) relevant food safety hazards.
11.3	Raw materials, ingredients, packaging material and end product	(a) Specifications have been set out for all raw materials, ingredients and product contact packaging material. The description of the safety of the product category considers the food chain ranging from raw materials through to the distribution of the end product. (b) Specifications include (as applicable): • Product identification and product description • Raw materials and ingredients used and their composition • General product specifications according to applicable legal requirements • Control of biological, chemical and physical hazards • Packaging material, storage conditions and labelling • Identification of potential mishandling or misuse.
11.4	Intended use	For each product, the method of distribution, intended use and consumers of the food are defined. The intended use is continually reviewed.

ABC Company Limited	Procedures Manual	Reference CP 024 Page 3 of 3	
	Preparation for Hazard Analysis	Date Released dd/mm/yyyy	Date Reviewed dd/mm/yyyy
Core Process	Approved:	Issue No: 01 Prepared by:	Revision No: 00

	Process Headings	Process Details
11.5	Flow diagram	(a) The FST shall prepare a flow diagram for each food product or food product category. Standard symbols shall be used in the flow diagram to facilitate understanding. Flow diagram shall be verified by walking through the steps by the Food Safety Manager [see Volume 1, Chapters 15 and 13 for guidance]. (b) The flow diagram shows processing steps and control points.
11.6	Description of layout and processes	(a) All facilities which are part of the infrastructure such as production lines, warehouse storage areas and staff facilities are shown in the plant layout. The processes which include the necessary PRPs, operational pre-requisite programmes (oPRPs), processing steps and control measures are described under individual procedures. (b) Control measures take into consideration legal requirements applicable to the product or process.
11.7	Observation of operations	1. The FST shall observe the actual operating practices, employee practices where raw or contaminated products could cross-contaminate hands, gloves or equipment used for finished/post-process products. 2. Study the traffic pattern and handling operations past any kill step to determine potential for cross-contamination.
11.8	Information sources	Company complaints file Scientific research and review papers Epidemiological data on foodborne illnesses and diseases The World Wide Web Statutory regulations Sector-specific codes of practices.
12.0	Records	Specifications Procedures Flow diagram Plant layout.
13.0	Changes made	None.

CP 025 Hazard Analysis: Assessment of Hazards

ABC Company Limited	Procedures Manual		Reference CP 025 Page 1 of 4	
	Hazard Analysis: Assessment of Hazards		Date Released dd/mm/yyyy	Date Reviewed dd/mm/yyyy
Core Process	Approved:		Issue No: 01 Prepared by:	Revision No: 00

Process Owner	Food Safety Manager
Process Headings	**Process Details**
1.0 Purpose	To describe the procedure for the assessment of hazards.
2.0 Scope	This procedure applies to ingredients, other raw materials, processes, products and end use of our products.
3.0 Input	Codex Alimentarius, process operations, pre-requisite programmes (PRPs), risk analysis matrix and CP 024 Preparation for hazard analysis.
4.0 Output	List of significant hazards, corrective actions.
5.0 Competency requirements	Knowledge of biological, physical and chemical hazards, risk analysis and management, food microbiology and PRPs.
6.0 Responsibility	Defined in Flowchart CP 025.1. Additional responsibilities are set out below. Food Safety Manager shall: • Review the hazards • Review control measures • Appoint the Food Safety Team (FST) (CP 024 Preparation for hazard analysis). FST shall: • Establish the necessary PRPs • Determine their significance.
7.0 Associated documents	Assessment of raw materials (Form 071) Assessment of processes (Form 072) Assessment of product (Form 073) Assessment of end use (Form 074) Preventive measures (Form 075) Matrix for the assessment of significant hazards (Form 076) Hazard analysis (Form 077).
8.0 Resources	None.
9.0 Measures/Controls	List of significant hazards Effectiveness of preventive measures.

ABC Company Limited	Procedures Manual		Reference CP 025 Page 2 of 4	
	Hazard Analysis: Assessment of Hazards		Date Released dd/mm/yyyy	Date Reviewed dd/mm/yyyy
Core Process	Approved:		Issue No: 01 Prepared by:	Revision No: 00

	Process Headings	Process Details
10.0	Definitions	**Acceptable level:** The level of a particular hazard in the end product that is acceptable to ensure food safety. **Hazard analysis:** Identification of biological, physical, chemical or other hazards associated with ingredients, production practices, processing, storage, distribution, retailing and end use. **PRP:** Control measures applicable across the food chain aimed at maintaining a safe and hygienic environment supporting the Hazard Analysis and Critical Control Point (HACCP) plan. **Preventive measures:** Physical, chemical or other means that can be used to control identified food safety hazards. **Risk:** Estimate of the probability of a hazard occurring. **Severity:** Seriousness of consequence of exposure to the hazard.
11.0	System description	The procedure for the assessment of hazards is presented in Flowchart CP 025.1.
11.1	PRPs and standard operating procedures (SOPs)	Identify and develop the necessary PRPs and SOPs.
11.2	Initial review	Food Safety Manager shall review the product description, list of ingredients and raw materials and the flow diagram.
11.3	Types of hazards	The FST shall identify: • Biological hazards – microorganisms, viruses and parasites including spore-forming bacteria • Physical hazards – metal fragments, glass, hair, jewellery, etc. • Chemical hazards – sanitisation chemicals, pesticide residues, mercury, etc.

ABC Company Limited	Procedures Manual	Reference CP 025 Page 3 of 4	
	Hazard Analysis: Assessment of Hazards	Date Released dd/mm/yyyy	Date Reviewed dd/mm/yyyy
Core Process	Approved:	Issue No: 01 Prepared by:	Revision No: 00

	Process Headings	Process Details
11.4	Hazard identification	FST shall apply appropriate tools and knowledge to identify food safety hazards that may occur in relation to the product, type of process and processing methods. Here are some of the means of identifying food safety hazards: 1. Preliminary information identified in the Procedure CP 024 Preparation for hazard analysis. 2. FST members' knowledge. 3. Information from external sources such as epidemiological, historical, legal and other data. 4. Information from the supply chain that is relevant to the safety of ABCCL products and operations and the food at the end of the supply chain. 5. Flowcharts showing the operations from receiving raw materials and ingredients to the end use of the product. 6. The absence of a hazard is indicated by a minus (−) sign and the efficacy of a hazard removal process or the extent to which the hazard can occur is shown by the number of plus (+) signs (e.g. +++ for high, ++ for moderate, + for low and − for none). For example, cooked food items have a low risk compared to uncooked food. Even if the hazard is eliminated at a later stage, any risk associated with raw materials should not be ignored. This analysis provides the level of risk associated with raw materials, ingredients, processing steps, delivery and end use that can pose a threat to food safety.
11.4.1	Hazards associated with ingredients and raw materials	Raw materials and ingredients are evaluated on the basis of microbial contamination, potential for microbial growth, presence of foreign matter, chemical contamination, transportation and storage. A suitable layout for assessing raw materials and ingredients is shown in Form 071.
11.4.2	Hazards associated with processes	For each step in the flow diagram, evaluate the potential hazards. Consideration shall be given to: • Efficacy of microbial destruction • Microbial contamination and growth (e.g. during handling) • Foreign matter removal/destruction • Foreign matter introduction • Equipment • Usage of returned or reworked product • Degree of control necessary to eliminate or reduce the hazard is classified as high, moderate or low. If the hazard is not eliminated downstream, a high degree of control is necessary. A template for the assessment of processes is presented in Form 072.

ABC Company Limited	Procedures Manual		Reference CP 025 Page 4 of 4	
	Hazard Analysis: Assessment of Hazards		Date Released dd/mm/yyyy	Date Reviewed dd/mm/yyyy
Core Process	Approved:		Issue No: 01 Prepared by:	Revision No: 00

	Process Headings	Process Details
11.4.3	Hazards associated with the product	The product is evaluated on the basis of hazards associated with its stability. Consideration is given to storage conditions, packaging requirements and delivery instructions necessary to prevent the product from undergoing deterioration or spoilage. A layout for the assessment of the product is shown in Form 073.
11.4.4	Hazards associated with end use	When assessing the end use, consider the possibility of inappropriate usage, mishandling and abuse in the hands of the consumer. Form 074 shows a suitable template for assessing the hazards associated with end use.
11.5	Assessment of the significance of hazards	The FST shall consider the level of risk and the degree of control associated with raw materials, ingredients, products, processes and end use and determine the significance of identified hazards using the 4×4 matrix shown in Form 076.
11.6	Acceptable levels and control measures	1. The FST shall establish acceptable levels for each identified hazard and define control measures to reduce the level of hazard to an acceptable level. They are typically defined by: (a) food safety code; (b) regulatory requirements; (c) industry codes of practice; (d) Codex Alimentarius and (e) customer requirements including intended use. 2. Effective preventive measures shall be introduced to control raw materials, processes, plant and machinery, storage and distribution, premises and personnel. FST shall establish preventive measures to control identified hazards using scientific and technical information. Supervisors shall explain the control measures to food processing operators and ensure their successful implementation.
12.0	Records	Scientific and technical information Hazard analysis form Assessment records shown under associated documents.
13.0	Changes made	None.

ABC Company Limited	Procedures Manual	Flowchart CP 025.1 Page 1 of 2	
	Overview of HACCP Planning	Date Released dd/mm/yyyy	Date Reviewed dd/mm/yyyy
Link CP 025	Approved:	Issue No: 01 Prepared by:	Revision No: 00

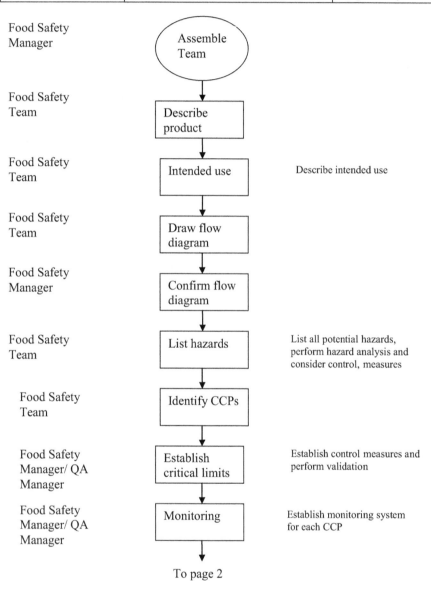

Food Safety Manager — Assemble Team

Food Safety Team — Describe product

Food Safety Team — Intended use — Describe intended use

Food Safety Team — Draw flow diagram

Food Safety Manager — Confirm flow diagram

Food Safety Team — List hazards — List all potential hazards, perform hazard analysis and consider control, measures

Food Safety Team — Identify CCPs

Food Safety Manager/ QA Manager — Establish critical limits — Establish control measures and perform validation

Food Safety Manager/ QA Manager — Monitoring — Establish monitoring system for each CCP

To page 2

ABC Company Limited	Procedures Manual	Flowchart CP 025.1 Page 2 of 2	
	Overview of HACCP Planning	Date Released dd/mm/yyyy	Date Reviewed dd/mm/yyyy
Link CP 025	Approved:	Issue No: 01 Prepared by:	Revision No: 00

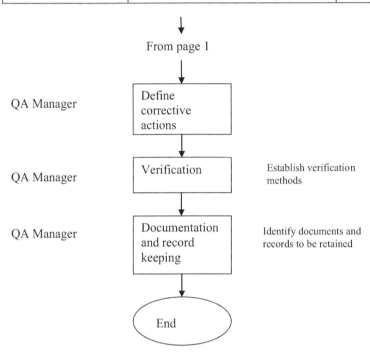

From page 1

QA Manager — Define corrective actions

QA Manager — Verification — Establish verification methods

QA Manager — Documentation and record keeping — Identify documents and records to be retained

End

CP 026 Hazard Analysis: CCPs and Control Measures

ABC Company Limited	Procedures Manual		Reference CP 026 Page 1 of 5	
	Hazard Analysis: CCPs and Control Measures		Date Released dd/mm/yyyy	Date Reviewed dd/mm/yyyy
Core Process	Approved:		Issue No: 01 Prepared by:	Revision No: 00

Process Owner		Food Safety Manager
	Process Headings	Process Details
1.0	Purpose	To describe the procedure for identifying Critical Control Points (CCPs) and establishing control activities for hazards identified as significant.
2.0	Scope	This procedure applies to significant hazards associated with food processing activities.
3.0	Input	Significant hazards, control measures, pre-requisite programmes (PRPs), operational pre-requisite programmes (oPRPs), process operations and control measures.
4.0	Output	List of CCPs and control activities, safe food products for consumption and consumer satisfaction.
5.0	Competency requirements	Knowledge of Hazard Analysis and Critical Control Point (HACCP) principles, biological, physical and chemical hazards, risk analysis and management, company's food products and recipes, food microbiology, PRPs, oPRPs and critical limits.
6.0	Responsibility	Food Safety Manager shall: • Review and approve the CCPs • Establish critical limits for CCPs • Appoint the Food Safety Team (FST) (CP 024 Preparation for hazard analysis) • Verify the control schedule. FST shall: • Establish CCPs for each hazard identified as significant • Establish controls for identified hazards.
7.0	Associated documents	Hazard analysis (Form 077) CCP identification using decision tree (Form 078) Control schedule (Form 083) Decision tree (Form 079) Risk analysis (Form 080) Matrix for the assessment of CCPs (Form 081).
8.0	Resources	None.
9.0	Measures/controls	CCPs Verification Validation Audits.

ABC Company Limited	Procedures Manual	Reference CP 026 Page 2 of 5	
	Hazard Analysis: CCPs and Control Measures	Date Released dd/mm/yyyy	Date Reviewed dd/mm/yyyy
Core Process	Approved:	Issue No: 01 Prepared by:	Revision No: 00

	Process Headings	Process Details
10.0	Definitions	**Control point (CP):** An operational step in a manufacturing or distribution process that could be controlled to ensure quality, food safety and regulatory compliance. **CCP:** A step at which a control can be applied and is essential to prevent or eliminate a food safety hazard or reduce it to an acceptable level. **Critical limit:** One or more specified tolerances that must be met to ensure that controls at a CCP are effective in eliminating or reducing the hazard to an acceptable level. They are expressed as numbers or specific parameters based on visual observations such as time/temperature, humidity, water activity, pH, salt concentration and chlorine level. **Hazard analysis:** Identification of biological, physical, chemical or other hazards associated with ingredients, production practices, processing, storage, distribution, retailing and end use. **HACCP:** A scientific, rational and systemic approach to identification, assessment and control of hazards throughout the food chain to ensure that food is safe for consumption. **PRP:** Control measures applicable across the food chain aimed at maintaining a safe and hygienic environment supporting the HACCP plan. **oPRP:** A form of PRP identified by the hazard analysis as essential to control introduction food safety hazards and prevent contamination or proliferation of food safety hazards in the product(s) or the processing environment. **Risk:** Estimate of the probability of a hazard occurring. **Severity:** Seriousness of consequence of exposure to the hazard.
11.0	System description	
11.1	Gather information	Collect the list of significant hazards, the flow diagram and block diagram. [Refer Volume 1 Chapter 15 for guidance on preparing the flow diagram and block diagram.]

ABC Company Limited	Procedures Manual	Reference CP 026 Page 3 of 5	
	Hazard Analysis: CCPs and Control Measures	Date Released dd/mm/yyyy	Date Reviewed dd/mm/yyyy
Core Process	Approved:	Issue No: 01 Prepared by:	Revision No: 00

	Process Headings	Process Details
11.2	Assessment of CCPs	The decision tree or the risk analysis may be used to establish the CCPs.
11.2.1	Using the decision tree	The decision tree is based on a series of questions (Form 079).
11.2.2	Risk analysis	This approach is a semi-quantitative method using the likelihood of occurrence of a hazard and the severity of consequences (Form 080). The risk matrix in Form 081 shows the scoring system. Hazards with scores less than 10 are considered CCPs.
11.3	Critical limits	HACCP Team shall establish critical limits for each CCP. Critical limits are criteria that separate acceptability from unacceptability. They define the boundaries that are used to determine whether an operation is yielding a safe product. The limits may be derived through various sources: experiments through validation, regulatory requirements, codes of practice and other valid sources. If the information needed to set critical limits is not available, a conservative value or regulatory limit should be selected. 1. Include for each CCP check if there is a regulatory critical limit which has been specified to ensure food safety. As an alternative establish a critical limit based on scientific evidence. 2. Retaining supporting evidence such as regulatory requirements, expert opinions, letters from processing authorities and scientific evidence.
11.4	Control measures	Control measures are established by monitoring and measurement (MM) or observation monitoring. MM involves instrumentation and can be automated. Observation monitoring involves the use of checklists customised to each operational area. They include sensory and visual checks (sight, small, taste), visual observations for physical characteristics (presence of foreign objects, package integrity) and checks for hygiene and cleanliness. Form 082 shows some examples of measures used in critical limits. 1. For each CCP, identify the best control measure 2. Determine the frequency of monitoring. 3. Define how random monitoring will be done. Make provision to select a good sample representing every shift operation. 4. Determine the test procedure that needs to be performed for each monitoring function (e.g. chlorine levels or temperature). 5. Communicate control measures and train food processing staff on food safety and monitoring requirements. 6. Ensure that operators record the findings at the time of monitoring. 7. Statutory, regulatory and customer requirements that can have an impact on control measures also shall be documented.

ABC Company Limited	Procedures Manual		Reference CP 026 Page 4 of 5	
	Hazard Analysis: CCPs and Control Measures		Date Released dd/mm/yyyy	Date Reviewed dd/mm/yyyy
Core Process	Approved:		Issue No: 01 Prepared by:	Revision No: 00

	Process Headings	**Process Details**
11.5	Operating limits	An operating limit is a form of interference to adjust the deviation when there is a trend towards lack of control at a CCP. The operators shall take action to prevent the loss of control of the CCP before the critical limit is exceeded. Operating limits shall be established by the QA Manager.
11.6	Corrective actions	(a) When a deviation from critical limits is observed, the operator shall be trained to adjust the process to bring the process within critical limits using operating limits. (b) When corrective action is taken after the process has exceeded critical limits, affected product processed during this time period shall be isolated and the cause of deviation investigated. (c) Demonstrate that the CCP is again under control following corrective action. (d) If corrective action is taken which is not listed in the HACCP plan, it should be recorded and brought to the attention of the QA Manager for review.
11.7	Record-keeping	Necessary records are listed under associated documents under each procedure. 1. FST shall review the records currently maintained and determine which ones adequately address the monitoring requirements of the HACCP plan or develop records for this information. 2. Establish forms to record corrective actions and those needed for the HACCP system. 3. Enter the record number/name against the CCP in the control schedule.

ABC Company Limited	Procedures Manual		Reference CP 026 Page 5 of 5	
	Hazard Analysis: CCPs and Control Measures		Date Released dd/mm/yyyy	Date Reviewed dd/mm/yyyy
Core Process	Approved:		Issue No: 01 Prepared by:	Revision No: 00

	Process Headings	**Process Details**
12.0	Records	CCP identification form Control schedule.
13.0	Changes made	None.

CP 027 Management of HACCP Plan

ABC Company Limited	Procedures Manual	Reference CP 027 Page 1 of 5	
	Management of HACCP Plan	Date Released dd/mm/yyyy	Date Reviewed dd/mm/yyyy
Core Process	Approved:	Issue No: 01 Prepared by:	Revision No: 00

Process Owner		Food Safety Manager
	Process Headings	**Process Details**
1.0	Purpose	To define the steps needed to develop, implement and maintain Hazard Analysis and Critical Control Point (HACCP) plans for the company's products and meet regulatory and customer requirements.
2.0	Scope	This procedure applies to all processes that directly or indirectly affect the safety of our food products.
3.0	Input	Codex Alimentarius, process operations and pre-requisite programmes (PRPs).
4.0	Output	HACCP plan, food safety hazards and Critical Control Points (CCPs).
5.0	Competency requirements	Knowledge of HACCP principles, biological, physical and chemical hazards of risk analysis and management, company's food products and recipes and food microbiology.
6.0	Responsibility	Food Safety Manager shall:

Food Safety Manager shall:
- Appoint the Food Safety Team (FST)
- Organise food safety training for all employees involved in food processing operations
- Approve the HACCP plan
- Define critical limits to CCPs
- Communicate the plan to those who need the information.

FST shall:
- Develop, ensure implementation, maintain and review the company's HACCP system
- Identify food safety hazards and verify the flow diagram
- Identify the CCPs
- Define training requirements for employees
- Review HACCP-related documents.

All employees involved in food processing operations shall:
- Implement HACCP plans
- Be aware of food safety hazards and personal hygiene requirements
- Bring unsafe operations or products to the immediate attention of the supervisor
- Implement any corrective actions.

Top management shall:
- Demonstrate the commitment to the plans
- Provide resources for the development, implementation and maintenance of plans.

ABC Company Limited	Procedures Manual		Reference CP 027 Page 2 of 5	
	Management of HACCP Plan		Date Released dd/mm/yyyy	Date Reviewed dd/mm/yyyy
Core Process	Approved:		Issue No: 01 Prepared by:	Revision No: 00

	Process Headings	Process Details
7.0	Associated documents	HACCP plan template (Form 084) Product description (Form 085).
8.0	Resource	None.
9.0	Measures/controls	Corrective actions Product recalls Customer complaints Regulatory compliance.
10.0	Definitions	**Hazard:** Unacceptable biological (growth or survival of microorganisms), physical (glass fragments, metal pieces, hair, jewellery) or chemical (pesticide residues, cleaning chemicals, heavy metals) contamination that renders the food unsafe and unfit for consumption. **HACCP:** A scientific, rational and systemic approach to identification, assessment and control of hazards throughout the food chain to ensure that food is safe for consumption. **HACCP plan:** A document that defines the processes based on the principles of HACCP to be followed to assure food safety. **HACCP system:** Organisational structure, procedures, processes and resources required to implement the HACCP plan.
11.0	System description	
11.1	FST	See Procedure CP 024 Preparation for hazard analysis. The first task of the FST is to define the scope of the study.
11.2	Product description and intended use	For each product, the FST shall establish a product description which includes, but is not limited to, this information: • Product name • Important product features such as pH, preservatives and colour • Intended use of the product • Type of packaging • Shelf life • Distribution outlets • Storage conditions • Special handling requirements • Target population • Sensitive population • Allergen declaration.

ABC Company Limited	Procedures Manual	Reference CP 027 Page 3 of 5	
	Management of HACCP Plan	Date Released dd/mm/yyyy	Date Reviewed dd/mm/yyyy
Core Process	Approved:	Issue No: 01 Prepared by:	Revision No: 00

	Process Headings	Process Details
11.2.1	Input materials	FST shall describe: (a) all ingredients and raw materials used in processing the product; (b) packaging materials used in the product and (c) any processing aids.
11.3	Flow diagram	FST shall prepare a flow diagram for each product or product category to provide a basis for identifying all food safety hazards. Each flow diagram should include the following (as appropriate): • Process steps in sequence • Outsourced and contracted out processes • Entry of raw materials, ingredients and intermediate products • Points of any recycling or rework • Exit points of finished products, intermediate products, by-products and waste.
11.4	Flow diagram confirmation	FST shall perform an on-site confirmation of the flow diagram.
11.5	HACCP plan	FST shall prepare the HACCP plan on the basis of seven principles of HACCP: Principle 1 – List all food safety hazards and control measures for each step in the flow diagram (CP 024, CP 025). Principle 2 – Identify CCPs associated with the processes (CP 026). Principle 3 – Establish critical limits (CP 026). Principle 4 – Establish monitoring procedures for each CCP (CP 026). Principle 5 – Establish corrective actions to be taken when a process is approaching critical limits or exceeding critical limits (CP 026). Principle 6 – Establish validation and verification methods for each monitoring activity (AP 010, AP 011). Principle 7 – Maintain records associated with HACCP activities.

ABC Company Limited	Procedures Manual	Reference CP 027 Page 4 of 5	
	Management of HACCP Plan	Date Released dd/mm/yyyy	Date Reviewed dd/mm/yyyy
Core Process	Approved:	Issue No: 01 Prepared by:	Revision No: 00

	Process Headings	Process Details
11.6	Plan implementation	
11.6.1	Gain management commitment	FST shall ensure that the senior management provides visible support and commitment to the programme. The QA Manager shall introduce the plan to all employees involved in food processing.
11.6.2	Identify the implementation team	The implementation is multidisciplinary and may include members from manufacturing, quality control, engineering, sanitation, laboratory, R&D, etc. The QA Manager shall introduce the plan to all employees involved in food processing operations.
11.6.3	Provide training	Food Safety Manager shall approve the plan for implementation, identify any gaps in food safety knowledge requirements and organise relevant training. QA Manager shall conduct a mock implementation trial to identify any deficiencies. Necessary changes shall be made and implemented.
11.7	Updating the HACCP plan	After hazard analysis and verification or when changes occur, it may be necessary to update the preliminary information specifying the PRPs and the HACCP plan. FST shall update as necessary: <ul><li>Product features</li><li>Intended use</li><li>Flow diagram</li><li>Process steps</li><li>Control measures.</li></ul> If necessary, the HACCP plan and the procedures and instructions specifying the PRPs shall also be amended.
11.8	HACCP plan review	FST shall review the plan at specified intervals (at least annually) to determine whether it meets company, customer and statutory requirements. The plan shall also be reviewed when product, process, ingredient or equipment changes occur.
11.9	HACCP plan revision	FST shall revise and update the plan (as necessary) and submit the revised plan for verification and implementation as above).

ABC Company Limited	Procedures Manual	Reference CP 027 Page 5 of 5	
	Management of HACCP Plan	Date Released dd/mm/yyyy	Date Reviewed dd/mm/yyyy
Core Process	Approved:	Issue No: 01 Prepared by:	Revision No: 00

	Process Headings	Process Details
12.0	Records	HACCP plan.
13.0	Changes made	None.

CP 028 Pre-Requisite Programmes

ABC Company Limited	Procedures Manual	Reference CP 028 Page 1 of 4	
	Pre-requisite Programmes	Date Released dd/mm/yyyy	Date Reviewed dd/mm/yyyy
Core Process	Approved:	Issue No: 01 Prepared by:	Revision No: 00

Process Owner		Food Safety Manager
	Process Headings	**Process Details**
1.0	Purpose	To describe the procedure for establishing pre-requisite programmes (PRPs) for the food safety management system.
2.0	Scope	This procedure applies to employees for managing the food safety management programme.
3.0	Input	Control schedule, relevant standard operating procedures (SOPs), PRPs and operational pre-requisite programmes (oPRPs), ISO 22000:2018 standard and applicable statutory and legal requirements.
4.0	Output	Control of food safety hazards, safe food products for consumption and PRP and oPRP completed records.
5.0	Competency requirements	Knowledge of the company's food safety management programmes, HACCP, food safety operations and Good Manufacturing Practices (GMPs).
6.0	Responsibility	Food Safety Manager shall: • Appoint a team to identify and develop necessary PRPs • Organise necessary training on food safety to those who have an impact on food safety directly or indirectly • Seek external assistance if necessary • Review all PRPs • Communicate PRPs and oPRPs accurately and thoroughly to employees responsible for implementing them in a timely manner. Food Safety Team (FST) shall: • Develop the necessary PRPs. Supervisors shall: • Assign PRP-related tasks to employees in their department • Ensure that employees have the necessary training and skill to carry out PRP-related activities • Review PRP records to identify non-compliances and take corrective actions. Employees shall: • Perform PRP-related activities • Report findings.

ABC Company Limited	Procedures Manual		Reference CP 028 Page 2 of 4	
	Pre-requisite Programmes		Date Released dd/mm/yyyy	Date Reviewed dd/mm/yyyy
Core Process	Approved:		Issue No: 01 Prepared by:	Revision No: 00

	Process Headings	**Process Details**
7.0	Associated documents	Control schedule (Form 083) PRP verification example (Form 086).
8.0	Resources	Codex Alimentarius
9.0	Measures/controls	PRP logs filled in correctly Evidence of completion of tasks Review of PRPs.
10.0	Definitions	**PRPs:** Programmes that support the food safety management system, specifying basic conditions and tasks necessary to maintain a clean hygienic environment throughout the food supply chain to ensure that food is safe for consumption. **oPRPs:** A form of PRP identified by the hazard analysis as essential to control the introduction of food safety hazards and prevent contamination or proliferation of food safety hazards in the product(s) or in the processing environment. **Material Safety Data (MSD) sheets:** Documents that describe the properties of the substance and procedures for safe handling or using the substance.
11.0	System description	
11.1	Preliminary information	ABCCL has its own set of PRPs. As far as possible, PRPs shall be based on established "good practices". Some examples are: Good Agriculture Practice Good Distribution Practice Good Manufacturing Practice Good Sanitation Practice. The FST shall consult good practice documents applicable to the operation. PRPs shall be established before hazard analysis.
11.2	PRP planning	FST shall consult regulatory authorities, industry sector personnel and QA specialists to enhance the knowledge required to establish PRPs. When PRPs are developed, the FST shall ensure that they are appropriate to ABCCL's operations and implemented across all its production processes.

ABC Company Limited	Procedures Manual	Reference CP 028 Page 3 of 4	
	Pre-requisite Programmes	Date Released dd/mm/yyyy	Date Reviewed dd/mm/yyyy
Core Process	Approved:	Issue No: 01 Prepared by:	Revision No: 00

	Process Headings	Process Details
11.2.1	Identify the PRPs	The FST shall identify the PRPs required for the operation of the food safety management system. Form 087 may be used to assist the identification. 1. **Contents of a PRP:** Each PRP shall consist of: • Procedure(s) describing the manner of performing the task • Training requirements • Records and documents to be completed. 2. **Identify oPRPs:** oPRPs are identified during the hazard analysis stage (Form 079). The FST shall base their judgement on their experience in the industry, the organisation's products and services, specific programmes and the food sector codes of practice. Form 087 shall be used to document oPRPs. (a) **Contents of oPRPs:** An oPRP shall consist of: • The food safety hazard to be controlled and control measures • Methods to monitor its effective implementation • Corrective actions to be taken when necessary • Responsibilities and authorities • Necessary records to be maintained.
11.3	Implementation of PRPs and oPRPs	(a) The Supervisor shall assign primary responsibility to conduct PRP and oPRP activities; (b) The appointed person shall carry out the tasks according to the control schedule and report to the Supervisor at least once a day on all PRP and oPRP activities. Deviations are identified and addressed according to AP 003 measurement and analysis; (c) Non-conforming product shall be identified and segregated. The affected production during this period shall be held in quarantine until a decision is taken by the QA Manager and (d) The Supervisor shall ensure that Food Processing Operators are adequately trained to perform their work.

ABC Company Limited	Procedures Manual		Reference CP 028 Page 4 of 4	
	Pre-requisite Programmes		Date Released dd/mm/yyyy	Date Reviewed dd/mm/yyyy
Core Process	Approved:		Issue No: 01 Prepared by:	Revision No: 00

	Process Headings	Process Details
11.4	Monitoring	QA Manager shall review the logs, records and documents daily to ensure that they have been carried out effectively and non-compliances are identified.
11.5	Review of PRPs and oPRPs	Food Safety Manager shall review the PRPs and oPRPS at least six monthly or more frequently to ensure that they comply with company, regulatory and customer requirements. PRPs and oPRPs shall also be subjected to periodic third-party audits.
11.6	Verification of PRPs	See Procedure AP 011 Verification. The FST shall confirm through methods specified in AP 011 that all PRPs have been implemented effectively.
12.0	Records	PRPs (e.g. PRP 01 Pest control) oPRPs Monitoring records (e.g. Form 086 Daily sanitation log (PRP); Form 088 Food delivery monitoring record).
13.0	Changes made	None.

CP 029 Recall Procedure

ABC Company Limited	Procedures Manual	Reference CP 029 Page 1 of 3	
	Recall Procedure	Date Released dd/mm/yyyy	Date Reviewed dd/mm/yyyy
Core Process	Approved:	Issue No: 01 Prepared by:	Revision No: 00

Process Owner	Food Safety Manager

	Process Headings	Process Details
1.0	Purpose	To describe the procedure for recalling a food product that is unsafe for consumption in order prevent harm to the consumer.
2.0	Scope	This procedure applies to all food products that have the potential to cause harm or ill health to consumers.
3.0	Input	Customer complaints, harmful incidents or ill health associated with a food product, operation failure and requisition by regulatory authorities.
4.0	Output	Recall plan, media release, corrective action, disposal of non-conforming product and report on the cause of failure.
5.0	Competency requirements	Knowledge of food safety, food operations, food recipes, hazard analysis and the ability to respond to emergency situations.
6.0	Responsibility	Responsibilities are defined Flowcharts CP 29.1, CP 29.2 and CP 29.3. Additional responsibilities are set out below. Chief Executive Officer (CEO) shall: • Nominate a person for approval in his or her absence. Food Safety Manager shall: • Initiate a recall with assistance from the Food Safety Team (FST) • Supervise the recall and ensure adequate implementation and effectiveness. QA Manager shall: • Establish the scope of recall • Establish the status and disposal of recalled product. Customer Relations Manager shall: • Communicate with customers, regulatory authorities and media. All employees involved with food operation activities shall: • Identify non-conforming product or non-conforming situations • Inform the supervisor on such issues. Financial Manager shall: • Deal with any compensations or reimbursements identified by the Legal Officer • Maintain all records of financial transactions associated with the recall.

ABC Company Limited	Procedures Manual	Reference CP 029 Page 2 of 3	
	Recall Procedure	Date Released dd/mm/yyyy	Date Reviewed dd/mm/yyyy
Core Process	Approved:	Issue No: 01 Prepared by:	Revision No: 00

	Process Headings	Process Details
7.0	Associated documents	Complaint report or incident report Reports on investigations and tests Communications about the incident Recall notice (Form 089) Corrective action reports.
8.0	Resources	Access to media.
9.0	Measures/controls	Response time between receiving safety incident report and initiating the recall Time to complete the recall Number of reported incidents before initiating the recall.
10.0	Definitions	**Recall:** Removal of unsafe product from the distribution chain that extends to consumers. **Withdrawal:** Removal of product from the distribution chain that does not extend to consumers.
11.0	System description	
11.1	Part One: Recall initiation	The flow diagram for the process of initiating a recall response is shown in Flowchart CP 029.1. During this stage, the Recall Team prepares media information and the Customer Relations Manager communicates with media, regulatory agencies and others as necessary.
11.2	Part Two: Recall operation	Flow diagram for the process of operating a recall is shown in Flowchart CP 029.2. • Ensure that all items of affected product are returned to the designation within 24 hours of initiating the recall • Warehouse Manager shall identify the returned stock with appropriate status stickers, isolate the stock and adjust inventory levels • All items are destroyed as recommended by the Recall Team under the supervision of the Warehouse Manager.
11.3	Part Three: Post-recall activities	Post-recall procedure is shown in Flowchart CP 29.3.

ABC Company Limited	Procedures Manual	Reference CP 029 Page 3 of 3	
	Recall Procedure	Date Released dd/mm/yyyy	Date Reviewed dd/mm/yyyy
Core Process	Approved:	Issue No: 01 Prepared by:	Revision No: 00

	Process Headings	Process Details
11.4	Verification of recall procedure	Mock recall shall be performed by the Food Safety Manager to verify that the procedure is effective. This may be done by tracking a product from production to delivery of stock to individual customers through the warehousing programme. This audit shall be documented.
12.0	Records	All records and documentation related to the recall.
13.0	Changes made	None.

ABC Company Limited	Procedures Manual	Flowchart CP 029.1 Page 1 of 2	
	Recall Initiation	Date Released dd/mm/yyyy	Date Reviewed dd/mm/yyyy
Link CP 029	Approved:	Issue No: 01 Prepared by:	Revision No: 00

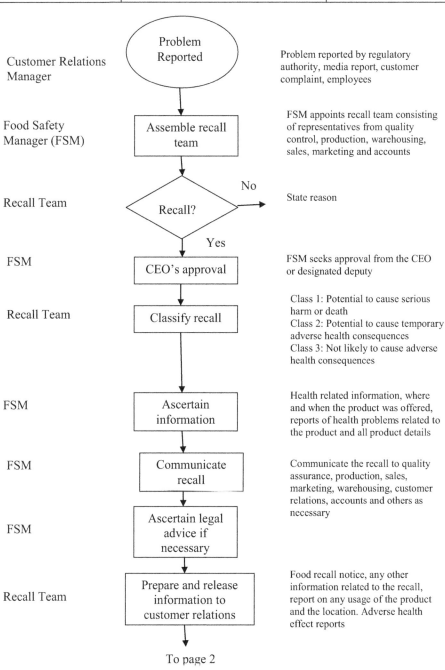

Customer Relations Manager — Problem Reported

Problem reported by regulatory authority, media report, customer complaint, employees

Food Safety Manager (FSM) — Assemble recall team

FSM appoints recall team consisting of representatives from quality control, production, warehousing, sales, marketing and accounts

Recall Team — Recall?

No — State reason

Yes

FSM — CEO's approval

FSM seeks approval from the CEO or designated deputy

Recall Team — Classify recall

Class 1: Potential to cause serious harm or death
Class 2: Potential to cause temporary adverse health consequences
Class 3: Not likely to cause adverse health consequences

FSM — Ascertain information

Health related information, where and when the product was offered, reports of health problems related to the product and all product details

FSM — Communicate recall

Communicate the recall to quality assurance, production, sales, marketing, warehousing, customer relations, accounts and others as necessary

FSM — Ascertain legal advice if necessary

Recall Team — Prepare and release information to customer relations

Food recall notice, any other information related to the recall, report on any usage of the product and the location. Adverse health effect reports

To page 2

ABC Company Limited	Procedures Manual	Flowchart CP 029.1 Page 2 of 2	
	Recall Initiation	Date Released dd/mm/yyyy	Date Reviewed dd/mm/yyyy
Link CP 029	Approved:	Issue No: 01 Prepared by:	Revision No: 00

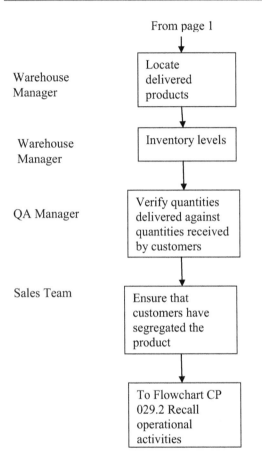

Warehouse Manager — Locate delivered products

Identify and record whether any product was received by customers. Locate delivered product and verify that product bears details listed in the recall notice.

Warehouse Manager — Inventory levels

Check inventory levels in stock of affected product from every customer including quantities used or sold

QA Manager — Verify quantities delivered against quantities received by customers

The product is segregated and put on HOLD. It is made unallocable to prevent unintentional or intentional pick up

Sales Team — Ensure that customers have segregated the product

To Flowchart CP 029.2 Recall operational activities

ABC Company Limited	Procedures Manual		Flowchart CP 029.2 Page 1 of 1	
	Recall Process		Date Released dd/mm/yyyy	Date Reviewed dd/mm/yyyy
Link CP 029	Approved:		Issue No: 01 Prepared by:	Revision No: 00

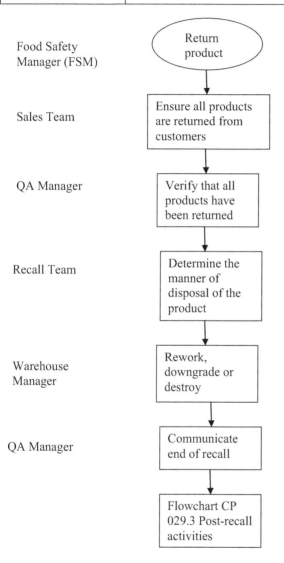

Food Safety Manager (FSM)

Return product

FSM issues instructions through the Sales Team to recall the product to a designated location

Sales Team

Ensure all products are returned from customers

Warehouse Manager identifies and isolates the returned stock and stock in hand with appropriate status stickers

QA Manager

Verify that all products have been returned

QA Manager verifies the quantities of returned stock against inventory levels and instructs the Sales Team to follow up. Ensures that all items are isolated and made unallocable to prevent intentional or unintentional pick up.

Recall Team

Determine the manner of disposal of the product

The affected product may be reworked, downgraded or destroyed depending on the nature of the problem

Warehouse Manager

Rework, downgrade or destroy

If the product has to be reworked or downgraded inventory levels are adjusted and product is reclassified with appropriate status stickers. Product destined to be destroyed should be done under the supervision of the Warehouse Manager

QA Manager

Communicate end of recall

Flowchart CP 029.3 Post-recall activities

ABC Company Limited	Procedures Manual	Flowchart CP 029.3 Page 1 of 1	
	Post-Recall Activities	Date Released dd/mm/yyyy	Date Reviewed dd/mm/yyyy
Link CP 029	Approved:	Issue No: 01 Prepared by:	Revision No: 00

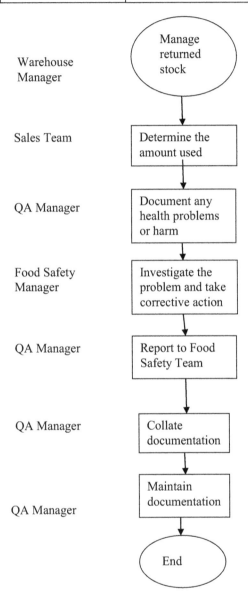

Warehouse Manager — Manage returned stock

Label all returned stock as HOLD with reason
Adjust inventory levels
Isolate the stock
Make stock unallocable

Sales Team — Determine the amount used

Consolidate the quantities: quantity delivered = returned stock + used stock

QA Manager — Document any health problems or harm

If there are reports of adverse health effects, direct affected persons to medical attention. Document details of people affected by the consumption of the product, reported symptoms, physical illness and actions taken

Food Safety Manager — Investigate the problem and take corrective action

Investigate the problem and take corrective action. Report to the Food Safety Team

QA Manager — Report to Food Safety Team

- Amount of used stock, returned stock and current inventory
- Manner of segregation and prevention from further use
- Reports of health problems
- compensations, if any

QA Manager — Collate documentation

Collate all documentations relating to the incident

- Copies of communication on food recall
- Documentation showing the food recall procedures were followed
- Manner of return
- Manner of segregation
- Manner of disposal
- Recall notice and communications about the product
- Records of returns and destructions, if applicable
- Compensations
- Reports issued to media
- Adverse health reports

QA Manager — Maintain documentation

End

CP 030 Initial Environmental Review (IER)

ABC Company Limited	Procedures Manual	Reference CP 030 Page 1 of 2	
	Initial Environmental Review	Date Released dd/mm/yyyy	Date Reviewed dd/mm/yyyy
Core Process	Approved:	Issue No: 01 Prepared by:	Revision No: 00

Process Owner		Environment Manager
	Process Headings	**Process Details**
1.0	Purpose	To describe the procedure for conducting the Initial Environmental Review (IER) of ABCCL.
2.0	Scope	This procedure applies to all activities of the organisation.
3.0	Input	Company's activities and products, usage of utilities (energy, water), emissions and discharges, waste generation and disposal, chemicals usage and disposal, transport information, raw material specifications and legal and other requirements.
4.0	Output	Awareness of environmental issues, input to aspect and impact assessment and continuous improvement, environmental impact caused by the activities and IER report.
5.0	Competency requirements	Understanding of basic environmental business issues, organisation's activities, key drivers for environmental management, analytical skills and requirements to ensure legal compliance and communications skills.
6.0	Responsibility	Environment Manager shall: • Appoint a team to conduct the review • Review and approve the report • Appoint a specialist (if and when required) • Specify data collection methods • Communicate the report to the Management Team. Engineering Manager shall: • Submit data on utilities usage, waste generation and disposal. QA Manager shall: • Present information from third parties about environmental issues complaints.
7.0	Associated documents	IER report template (Form 090) Material necessary for initial review (Form 091).
8.0	Resources	Specialist (if needed).
9.0	Measures/controls	Environmental costs.
10.0	System description	
10.1	Formation of the team	Environment Manager shall appoint a team comprising of representatives from each department and brief them on their mission. He or she shall appoint a specialist from an external agency if expertise is not available in-house.

ABC Company Limited	Procedures Manual	Reference CP 030 Page 2 of 2	
	Initial Environmental Review	Date Released dd/mm/yyyy	Date Reviewed dd/mm/yyyy
Core Process	Approved:	Issue No: 01 Prepared by:	Revision No: 00

	Process Headings	Process Details
10.2	Issues to be covered	1. Applicable legislation. 2. Environmental issues associated with company's products, services and processes. 3. Review of existing management practices and procedures. 4. Evaluate previous emergency situations and accidents.
10.3	Approach	The IER shall be carried out by one or more of these methods: • Discussions/interviews with relevant people in the area • Site visits to study the operations • Reference material.
10.4	Data collection	Each department shall record information on usage of resources and environmental issues associated with their activities in their respective departments.
10.5	Review findings	Environment Manager shall review the presented information by walking through the plant before the report is approved.
10.6	Communication	Environment Manager shall communicate the report to the management and a session is held with employees to create awareness of environmental issues associated with their activities.
11.0	Records	IER Utilities usage Waste products records.
12.0	Changes made	None.

CP 031 Identification of Environmental Aspects and Impacts

ABC Company Limited	Procedures Manual		Reference CP 031 Page 1 of 4	
	Identification of Environmental Aspects and Impacts		Date Released dd/mm/yyyy	Date Reviewed dd/mm/yyyy
Core Process	Approved:		Issue No: 01 Prepared by:	Revision No: 00

Process Owner	**Management Team**
Process Headings	**Process Details**
1.0 Purpose	To describe the method for the identification of environmental aspects relating to our operations and product life cycle.
2.0 Scope	The procedure applies to products, activities and services offered by our organisation.
3.0 Input	Customer requirements, areas of concern, statutory and legal requirements, organisational context, needs and expectations of interested parties, risks and opportunities, Initial Environmental Review (IER) and significant impacts.
4.0 Output	Process improvement, Integrated Quality, Food Safety and Environmental (IQFSE) Management System improvement, conforming processes, control of impacts, enhancing desirable effects, register of environmentally significant aspects, legally compliant environmental programme and new practices and integrated actions.
5.0 Competency requirements	Understanding the scope and activities of the organisation, key environmental issues of the business, broad environmental issues, analysis of information and management judgement.
6.0 Responsibility	Defined in Flowchart CP 031.1. Additional responsibilities are set out below. Environment Manager shall: • Appoint a Cross-Functional Team (CFT) representing all appropriate functional areas and departments • Provide the necessary training to carry out the procedure described here • Update environmental aspects at predetermined intervals (or as necessary). CFT shall: • Establish procedures • Update the register (as and when necessary).
7.0 Associated documents	Register of legal and other requirements Emergency preparedness and response procedure Monitoring and measurement (MM) of environmental operational controls Form 090 Initial Environmental Review Customer complaints about environmental issues Communications with regulatory bodies (SP 006).

ABC Company Limited	Procedures Manual		Reference CP 031 Page 2 of 4	
	Identification of Environmental Aspects and Impacts		Date Released dd/mm/yyyy	Date Reviewed dd/mm/yyyy
Core Process	Approved:		Issue No: 01 Prepared by:	Revision No: 00

	Process Headings	Process Details
8.0	Resources	IQFSE Management System ISO 14001:2015 standard Policy commitments.
9.0	Measures/controls	Level of compliance Regulatory audits Number of customer concerns Emergency incidents and effectiveness of responses.
10.0	Definitions	**Environmental aspect:** Element of ABCCL's activities, products or services that can interact with the environment. **Environmental impact:** Any change to the environment, whether detrimental or beneficial, wholly or partly resulting from ABCCL's environmental aspects. **Environmental targets:** Detailed performance measurement related to environmental objectives. **Environmental team:** A CFT selected by the Environmental Manager to review aspects, impacts and other responsibilities assigned by the Environment Manager. **Prevention of pollution:** Action to eliminate, mitigate or control the creation or discharge of any type of pollutant or waste to reduce adverse environmental effects. **Significance criteria:** A set of measures used to quantify and prioritise environmental aspects and potential impacts of ABCCL's activities, products and services. **Significant environmental aspect:** An environmental aspect of ABCCL's activities, products and services that has (or may have) a significant environmental impact.
11.0	System description	Flowchart CP 031.1 shows the procedure for identifying environmental aspects and impacts.
11.1	Identify key operations	1. CFT shall formulate a list of activities, products, services, new or changed activities, all raw materials, chemicals and utilities used as inputs and all outputs produced as products and by-products that have environmental aspects resulting in potentially beneficial or adverse environmental impacts. To identify the activities, major operations may be classified under functional departments. 2. CFT shall also identify outsourced processes that have environmental impact and can be influenced so as to control them.

ABC Company Limited	Procedures Manual	Reference CP 031 Page 3 of 4	
	Identification of Environmental Aspects and Impacts	Date Released dd/mm/yyyy	Date Reviewed dd/mm/yyyy
Core Process	Approved:	Issue No: 01 Prepared by:	Revision No: 00

	Process Headings	**Process Details**
11.2	Criteria for the identification of environmental aspects	1. The IER provides the basis for identification. The categories of activities and products listed as inputs are considered and reviewed to identify environmental aspects. 2. Each aspect is identified for: • Discharges to sewer • Contamination of soil and water • Disposal of electrical items • Resource usage – electricity and water • Housekeeping rubbish • Raw material usage • Community issues • Fire • Hazardous waste • Control of suppliers and contractors • Air conditioning • Compressed air • Oil usage • Emissions to air • Generation of noise • Usage of forklift trucks. 3. Identify as many aspects as possible associated with the selected item. Consider normal, abnormal and emergency situations when aspects are evaluated. Table CP 31.1 shows some examples of abnormal and emergency situations.
11.3	Classification of aspects	Aspects may be classified into: (a) potentially polluting and regulatory aspects (MP 007 Environmental risk analysis) and (b) positive aspects (non-polluting regulatory aspects with potential for energy/cost saving and environmental benefits).

ABC Company Limited	Procedures Manual		Reference CP 031 Page 4 of 4	
	Identification of Environmental Aspects and Impacts		Date Released dd/mm/yyyy	Date Reviewed dd/mm/yyyy
Core Process	Approved:		Issue No: 01 Prepared by:	Revision No: 00

	Process Headings	Process Details
11.4	Evaluation of impacts	Impacts include, but are not limited to: • Pollution of soil, water and air through discharges, emissions, radiation, particulate matter, toxic substances, pesticides, heavy metals, industrial chemicals and by-products and noise • Depletion of natural resources • Global warming • Ozone depletion • Acidification of soil and water.
11.4.1	Life Cycle Analysis (LCA)	LCA refers to the evaluation of impacts throughout a product's lifespan including: 1. Extraction and processing of raw materials. 2. Design and manufacture of the product. 3. Storage, transport and distribution. 4. End use and maintenance. 5. Disposal/recycling.
12.0	Records	Register of environmental aspects Records used for identifying environmental aspects and impacts.
13.0	Changes made	None.

ABC Company Limited	Procedures Manual	Flowchart CP 031.1 Page 1 of 1	
	Identification of Environmental Aspects and Impacts	Date Released dd/mm/yyyy	Date Reviewed dd/mm/yyyy
Link CP 031	Approved:	Issue No: 01 Prepared by:	Revision No: 00

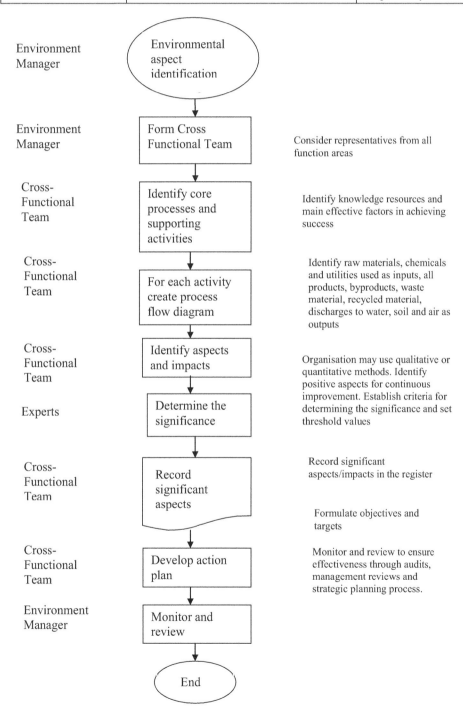

Environment Manager — Environmental aspect identification

Environment Manager — Form Cross Functional Team
Consider representatives from all function areas

Cross-Functional Team — Identify core processes and supporting activities
Identify knowledge resources and main effective factors in achieving success

Cross-Functional Team — For each activity create process flow diagram
Identify raw materials, chemicals and utilities used as inputs, all products, byproducts, waste material, recycled material, discharges to water, soil and air as outputs

Cross-Functional Team — Identify aspects and impacts

Experts — Determine the significance
Organisation may use qualitative or quantitative methods. Identify positive aspects for continuous improvement. Establish criteria for determining the significance and set threshold values

Cross-Functional Team — Record significant aspects
Record significant aspects/impacts in the register

Formulate objectives and targets

Cross-Functional Team — Develop action plan
Monitor and review to ensure effectiveness through audits, management reviews and strategic planning process.

Environment Manager — Monitor and review

End

Table CP 31.1   Examples of Abnormal and Emergency Situations

Aspect	Abnormal	Emergency
Packaging waste	Usage of excessive amounts	Placed in the wrong bin
Discharge to sewer	Large amount	Spillage to foul drain
Usage of natural gas	Appliances not turned off when not in use	Major gas leak
Electricity usage	Used when not required	Power failure
Water usage	Tap left turned on after cleaning	Major pipe rupture
Waste disposal	Contractor or labour dispute	Drains blocked
Hazardous waste	Not collected	Major spillage
Compressed air	Compressed air leak	Compressor failure

CP 032 Assessment of the Significance of Environmental Aspects and Impacts

ABC Company Limited	Procedures Manual		Reference CP 032 Page 1 of 5	
	Assessment of the Significance of Environmental Aspects and Impacts	Date Released dd/mm/yyyy		Date Reviewed dd/mm/yyyy
Core Process	Approved:	Issue No: 01 Prepared by:		Revision No: 00

Process Owner   **Environment Manager**

	Process Headings	Process Details
1.0	Purpose	To describe the method for determining the significance of related aspects that have actual or may have potential significant impacts on the environment.
2.0	Scope	The procedure applies to products, activities and services offered by our organisation.
3.0	Input	Aspects and impacts identified in CP 031.
4.0	Output	Register of environmentally significant aspects, legally compliant environmental programme, new practices and integrated actions.
5.0	Competency requirements	Understanding the scope and activities of the organisation, key environmental issues of the business, broad environmental issues, analysis of information and management judgement.
6.0	Responsibility	Defined in CP 031.
7.0	Associated documents	Register of legal and other requirements Emergency preparedness and response procedure Monitoring and measurement (MM) of environmental operational controls Form 092 Qualitative assessment template Form 093 Quantitative assessment template Form 094 Evaluation of positive aspects Form 095 Register of environmental aspects.
8.0	Resources	IQFSE management system ISO 14001:2015 standard Policy commitments.
9.0	Measures/controls	Level of compliance Regulatory audits Number of customer concerns Emergency incidents and effectiveness of responses.
10.0	Definitions	See Procedure CP 031.
11.0	System description	
11.1	Assessment of impacts	

ABC Company Limited	Procedures Manual	Reference CP 032 Page 2 of 5	
	Assessment of the Significance of Environmental Aspects and Impacts	Date Released dd/mm/yyyy	Date Reviewed dd/mm/yyyy
Core Process	Approved:	Issue No: 01 Prepared by:	Revision No: 00

	Process Headings	Process Details
11.1.1	Criteria for qualitative assessment (Form 092)	These situations are considered significant and do not require further evaluation: 1. (a) Environmental regulations specify controls and conditions; (b) information on particular aspects have to be submitted to regulatory bodies or (c) if there are periodic inspections or enforcement actions taken by the authorities. 2. Community concerns: Include noise, air pollution, complaints from public and awards from environmental agencies. 3. Resource use: High levels of renewable or non-renewable resource use. 4. Potential impact on the environment: Impact on the environment due to: (a) toxicity; (b) large amounts of emissions, waste or release; (c) consumption of large amounts of non-renewable resources and (d) the frequency and severity of impacts that may require a local emergency service.
11.1.2	Criteria for quantitative assessment (Form 093)	Environmental impacts that do not fall into the above categories are subjected to quantitative assessment: 1. **Probability:** 4 – Very often: More than 4 times per year 3 – Occasional: Happens 1–4 times per year 2 – Rare: Less than once per year 1 – Never happened: But possible. 2. **Severity of the impact:** The impact on the environment can be either detrimental or beneficial. 4 – High: Significant impact – damages the environment, produces hazardous waste, likely interruptions to normal operations 3 – Moderate: Localised – containable, likely interruptions to normal operations but operation can be resumed without adverse effects 2 – Minor: Temporary – operation can be resumed without adverse effects 1 – Low: Interruptions to normal operations are unlikely or consequences are minor and can be easily remedied. 3. **Scale of impact:** 4 – Major: Significant disturbance to particular environmental components and ecosystems. Some environmental components lose the ability to recover

ABC Company Limited	Procedures Manual		Reference CP 032 Page 3 of 5	
	Assessment of the Significance of Environmental Aspects and Impacts		Date Released dd/mm/yyyy	Date Reviewed dd/mm/yyyy
Core Process	Approved:		Issue No: 01 Prepared by:	Revision No: 00

	Process Headings	Process Details
		3 – Moderate: Environmental changes exceed limits of natural variation and cause damage to separate environmental components but natural environment is self-recoverable
		2 – Environmental changes exceed limits of natural variation but natural environment is completely self-recoverable
		1 – Environmental changes do not exceed existing limits of natural variation.
		4. Duration of impact:
		4 – Multiyear and permanent: Impact observed for more than 3 years
		3 – Long term: Impact observed for 1–3 years
		2 – Medium term: Impact observed for 3 months to 1 year
		1 – Short term: Impact observed for less than 3 months.
		Significance score = Probability + Severity + Scale + Duration
		A score > 18 is considered significant.
11.2	Recording	Record in the environmental aspects register (Form 095).
11.3	Develop an action plan	When controls or modifications to existing controls are established, the CFT shall use the following guide to formulate an action plan:
		(a) No actions: Environmental aspects with extremely limited impact and/or which the organisation cannot influence including non-significant aspects;
		(b) Control or maintain: Significant environmental aspects with an acceptable risk that comply with legal requirements. Continue to maintain operational controls to achieve objectives and targets;
		(c) Improve: Environmental aspects with a high or unacceptable risk and not in compliance with legal requirements. Improvement programmes can also be applied to reduce the energy and water use which is not controlled by law but fall within our commitment to reduce pollution;
		(d) Study or investigate: Improvement is beneficial, but further study is needed to ascertain financial, technological and logistic feasibility.

ABC Company Limited	Procedures Manual		Reference CP 032 Page 4 of 5	
	Assessment of the Significance of Environmental Aspects and Impacts		Date Released dd/mm/yyyy	Date Reviewed dd/mm/yyyy
Core Process	Approved:		Issue No: 01 Prepared by:	Revision No: 00

	Process Headings	Process Details
11.4	Communicate the plan	1. Internal communication about environmental aspects and impacts is carried out through quarterly company meeting of the Management Team chaired by the Environment Manager. It may be included as a part of management review meetings. 2. Requests by external organisations shall be directed to the Managing Director who is authorised to release an uncontrolled copy of the document.
11.5	Training	Training shall be organised by the Environment Manager and shall include the purpose and implication of identifying aspects and impacts and general training on environmental management systems (EMSs) and ISO 14001.
11.6	Review	The review shall be conducted by the Environment Manager. Review the continuing suitability of aspects and impacts at least annually or after: • MM of the EMS • Work practice, equipment, products and services changes • Regulatory changes • Audit results and regulatory feedback. Significant aspects of the review are added to the record of significant aspects.
11.7	Link to IQFSE management system (Flowchart MP 019.1)	Significant aspects and impacts will be used in setting environmental objectives, targets and programmes. When objectives and targets are developed, the Management Team shall consider: (a) compliance assurance; (b) pollution prevention; (c) waste minimisation; (d) energy management and (e) waste reduction.

ABC Company Limited	**Procedures Manual**		**Reference CP 032** Page 5 of 5	
	Assessment of the Significance of Environmental Aspects and Impacts		Date Released dd/mm/yyyy	Date Reviewed dd/mm/yyyy
Core Process	Approved:		Issue No: 01 Prepared by:	Revision No: 00

	Process Headings	**Process Details**
11.8	Degree of control	Only those aspects that are under the control of ABCCL and those the company can influence are considered in this procedure. The aspects over which ABCCL has no control or influence include these: (a) product features when the organisation cannot influence its design and development activities; (b) manufacture and delivery of purchased materials, products or services when ABCCL has no influence on these activities and when no alternatives are available and (c) a process technology or when there is technology that cannot be modified for financial or competitive reasons.
12.0	Records	Register of environmental aspects Records used for identifying environmental aspects and impacts.
13.0	Changes made	None.

CP 033 Managing Environmental Impact of Sales and Marketing

ABC Company Limited	Procedures Manual		Reference CP 033 Page 1 of 2	
	Managing Environmental Impact of Sales and Marketing	Date Released dd/mm/yyyy		Date Reviewed dd/mm/yyyy
Core Process	Approved:	Issue No: 01 Prepared by:		Revision No: 00

Process Owner		Environment Manager
	Process Headings	**Process Details**
1.0	Purpose	To describe the procedure for managing environmental aspects of sales and marketing functions.
2.0	Scope	This procedure shall apply to sales and marketing activities.
3.0	Input	Sales and marketing activities.
4.0	Output	List of environmental activities and proposals to minimise the consequences.
5.0	Competency requirements	Knowledge of environmental concerns and regulations affecting sales activities.
6.0	Responsibility	All sales and marketing staff shall be aware of the activities that have a significant impact on the environment.
7.0	Associated documents	Energy use reports Fuel consumption reports Waste or recyclable packaging reports.
8.0	Resources	Energy utilisation monitors Power consumption monitors.
9.0	Measures/controls	Energy, power consumption Waste and/or recyclable material.
10.0	System description	
10.1	Impact of sales activities	Environmental impact of sales activities is presented in Form 096.
10.2	Impact of marketing activities	Marketing personnel shall communicate environmental issues relating to the environmental management system (EMS) to customers, receive feedback and communicate environmental issues with stakeholders. 1. Green design: ABCCL shall carry out Life Cycle Analysis (LCA) to incorporate into the eco-design process to minimise environmental impact. 2. Green positioning: ABCCL shall promote its environmental activities to customers through its logo and other promotional media. 3. Green pricing: ABCCL shall disclose existing energy saving features of our product and make prices affordable and competitive. 4. Green promotion: ABCCL shall ensure that eco-benefits are always included in promotional material. 5. Green alliance: ABCCL shall form alliances with other environmental protection groups.

ABC Company Limited	Procedures Manual	Reference CP 033 Page 2 of 2	
	Managing Environmental Impact of Sales and Marketing	Date Released dd/mm/yyyy	Date Reviewed dd/mm/yyyy
Core Process	Approved:	Issue No: 01 Prepared by:	Revision No: 00

	Process Headings	Process Details
11.0	Records	Actions to reduce environmental impact.
12.0	Changes made	None.

CP 034 Managing Food Safety Issues in Sales and Marketing

ABC Company Limited	Procedures Manual		Reference CP 034 Page 1 of 2	
	Managing Food Safety Issues in Sales and Marketing	Date Released dd/mm/yyyy		Date Reviewed dd/mm/yyyy
Core Process	Approved:	Issue No: 01 Prepared by:		Revision No: 00

Process Owner	Food Safety Manager
Process Headings	**Process Details**
1.0 Purpose	To describe the procedure for managing food safety issues in sales and marketing roles.
2.0 Scope	This procedure shall apply to sales and marketing of food products.
3.0 Input	Sales and marketing activities.
4.0 Output	List of environmental activities and proposals to minimise the consequences.
5.0 Competency requirements	Knowledge of food safety concerns and regulations affecting sales activities.
6.0 Responsibility	All sales and marketing staff shall be aware of food safety practices in sales and marketing roles.
7.0 Associated documents	Food safety programme.
8.0 Resources	None.
9.0 Measures/controls	Outdated and returned stock records. Customer complaints log.
10.0 System description	
10.1 Sales activities	1. ABCCL sales staff shall ensure that products are stored on the basis of First-In-First-Out (FIFO). Outdated and returned stocks shall be removed from the shelves. 2. Returned products log and returned products shall be examined and sent for analysis to the plant laboratory. 3. Ensure that products are stored at the correct temperature. Temperature log in the premises shall also be examined. 4. Customer complaints shall be investigated and ensure follow-up action. 5. If there is a promotion of a new product and samples are issued to customers for tasting, ensure that all utensils containing the food item are clean and kept covered to prevent the entry of insects. 6. Ensure that products such as meat or bakery goods are not handled with bare hands.

ABC Company Limited	Procedures Manual		Reference CP 034 Page 2 of 2	
	Managing Food Safety Issues in Sales and Marketing	Date Released dd/mm/yyyy		Date Reviewed dd/mm/yyyy
Core Process	Approved:	Issue No: 01 Prepared by:		Revision No: 00

	Process Headings	Process Details
10.2	Marketing activities	1. Ensure that all regulatory requirements for labelling products are adhered to.
		2. If food items have to be reconstituted, ensure that instructions are clear on the label.
		3. Advertising and promotion material shall reflect food safety practices and product characteristics.
11.0	Records	Action plan to address food safety issues.
12.0	Changes made	None.

CP 035 Managing Environmental Impact of IT

ABC Company Limited	Procedures Manual		Reference CP 035 Page 1 of 1	
	Managing Environmental Impact of IT	Date Released dd/mm/yyyy	Date Reviewed dd/mm/yyyy	
Core Process	Approved:	Issue No: 01 Prepared by:	Revision No: 00	

Process Owner		Manager Information Systems
	Process Headings	**Process Details**
1.0	Purpose	To describe the guidelines for managing the environmental impact of information technology (IT) equipment.
2.0	Scope	This procedure shall apply to IT equipment.
3.0	Input	IT equipment and environmental requirements.
4.0	Output	Impact list.
5.0	Competency requirements	Knowledge of IT equipment and environmental requirements applicable to them.
6.0	Responsibility	All users shall be aware of the impact of IT equipment on the environment.
7.0	Associated documents	Environmental aspect and impact assessment.
8.0	Resources	None.
9.0	Measures/controls	Energy use Disposal records of IT equipment.
11.0	System description	
11.1	Impact of IT equipment and their usage	Form 097 shows the impact of IT equipment on the environment. Manager information systems shall address these requirements when IT equipment is procured.
12.0	Records	List of environmental requirements.
13.0	Changes made	None.

CP 036 Sales Process

ABC Company Limited	Procedures Manual		Reference CP 036 Page 1 of 1	
	Sales Process	Date Released dd/mm/yyyy		Date Reviewed dd/mm/yyyy
Management Processes	Approved:	Issue No: 01 Prepared by:		Revision No: 00

Process Owner		Sales Manager
	Process Headings	**Process Details**
1.0	Purpose	To describe the procedure for the sales process.
2.0	Scope	This procedure shall apply to all products and services offered by the ABCCL.
3.0	Input	Sales target, price list, inventory levels and customer base.
4.0	Output	Sales order, new customers and customer satisfaction.
5.0	Competency requirements	Sales qualifications, sales experience, communication skills, computer skills and negotiation skills.
6.0	Responsibility	Sales Manager shall: • Allocate Sales Team to territories • Review activity schedule • Provide resources • Analyse sales activities. Sales Person shall: • Prepare visit schedule. • Visit customers • Enter data • Take orders • Review the activities against the objectives.
7.0	Associated documents	Schedule planner Sales targets.
8.0	Resources	Software programme for sales activities.
9.0	Measures/controls	Success rate (number of orders against the number of visits).
10.0	System description	The flowchart for the sales process is shown in CP 036.1.
10.1	Visit plan	Procedure CP 037 (visit planning)
10.2	Visit store	Procedure CP 038 (in-store procedure)
10.3	Take orders	Procedure CP 017 (take order)
10.4	Offer of samples	Procedure CP 039 (offer of samples)
10.5	Sales meetings	Procedure CP 040 (sales meetings).
11.0	Records	Customer base Sales targets and sales.
12.0	Changes made	None.

ABC Company Limited	Procedures Manual	Flowchart CP 036.1 Page 1 of 1	
	Sales Process	Date Released dd/mm/yyyy	Date Reviewed dd/mm/yyyy
Link CP 036	Approved:	Issue No: 01 Prepared by:	Revision No: 00

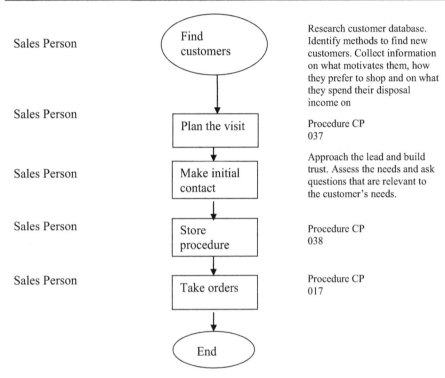

Sales Person	Find customers	Research customer database. Identify methods to find new customers. Collect information on what motivates them, how they prefer to shop and on what they spend their disposal income on
Sales Person	Plan the visit	Procedure CP 037
Sales Person	Make initial contact	Approach the lead and build trust. Assess the needs and ask questions that are relevant to the customer's needs.
Sales Person	Store procedure	Procedure CP 038
Sales Person	Take orders	Procedure CP 017
	End	

CP 037 Visit Planning

ABC Company Limited	Procedures Manual		Reference CP 037 Page 1 of 2	
	Visit Planning		Date Released dd/mm/yyyy	Date Reviewed dd/mm/yyyy
Core Process	Approved:		Issue No: 01 Prepared by:	Revision No: 00

Process Owner		**Sales Manager**
	Process Headings	**Process Details**
1.0	Purpose	To describe the procedure for visits to customers.
2.0	Scope	This procedure shall apply to all sales activities.
3.0	Input	Price list, samples and other sales materials.
4.0	Output	New customers, sales orders and customer satisfaction.
5.0	Competency requirements	Sales qualifications, sales experience, communication skills, computer skills and negotiation skills.
6.0	Responsibility	Sales Manager shall: • Allocate Sales Team to territories • Review activity schedule • Provide resources. • Analyse sales activities. Sales Person shall: • Prepare visit schedule • Enter data • Review the activities against the objectives.
7.0	Associated documents	Schedule planner Sales activity lot (Form 098) Field visit log (Form 099).
8.0	Resources	Software programme for sales activities.
9.0	Measures/controls	Number of visits Completion according to the activity schedule.
10.0	System description	The flowchart for visit planning is shown in CP 037.1.
10.1	Visit preparation	Set clear measurable objectives that you can use to evaluate the success of your visit.

ABC Company Limited	Procedures Manual	Reference CP 037 Page 2 of 2	
	Visit Planning	Date Released dd/mm/yyyy	Date Reviewed dd/mm/yyyy
Core Process	Approved:	Issue No: 01 Prepared by:	Revision No: 00

	Process Headings	Process Details
10.2	Visit requirements	Ensure that you have all the necessary material before you visit your customer. Some of the items are: • Sales folders including samples, data, planogram proposals • Promotional material • Products and price list • Order forms • Product information • Planogram requisitions • Mobile phone, camera • Merchandising tools knife, staples, etc.
11.0	Records	Visit log.
12.0	Changes made	None.

ABC Company Limited	Procedures Manual	Flowchart CP 037.1 Page 1 of 1	
	Visit Planning	Date Released dd/mm/yyyy	Date Reviewed dd/mm/yyyy
Link CP 037	Approved:	Issue No: 01 Prepared by:	

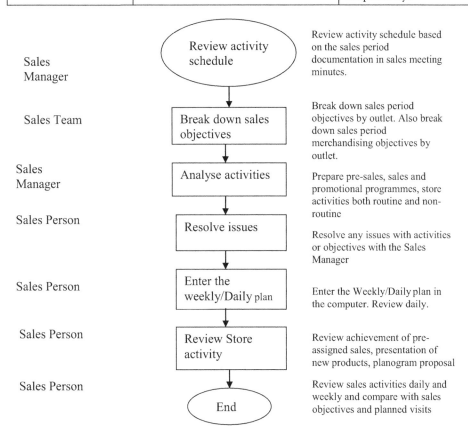

Sales Manager	Review activity schedule	Review activity schedule based on the sales period documentation in sales meeting minutes.
Sales Team	Break down sales objectives	Break down sales period objectives by outlet. Also break down sales period merchandising objectives by outlet.
Sales Manager	Analyse activities	Prepare pre-sales, sales and promotional programmes, store activities both routine and non-routine
Sales Person	Resolve issues	Resolve any issues with activities or objectives with the Sales Manager
Sales Person	Enter the weekly/Daily plan	Enter the Weekly/Daily plan in the computer. Review daily.
Sales Person	Review Store activity	Review achievement of pre-assigned sales, presentation of new products, planogram proposal
Sales Person	End	Review sales activities daily and weekly and compare with sales objectives and planned visits

CP 038 In-Store Procedure

ABC Company Limited	Procedures Manual		Reference CP 038 Page 1 of 1	
	In-Store Procedure		Date Released dd/mm/yyyy	Date Reviewed dd/mm/yyyy
Management Processes	Approved:		Issue No: 01 Prepared by:	Revision No: 00

Process Owner		Sales Manager
	Process Headings	**Process Details**
1.0	Purpose	To describe the in-store procedure.
2.0	Scope	This procedure shall apply to all Sales Staff visits to customer's premise.
3.0	Input	Price list, samples, product information, visit plan.
4.0	Output	New customers, orders and customer satisfaction.
5.0	Competency requirements	Sales qualification, time management skills, computer skills, communication skills and selling skills.
6.0	Responsibility	Sales Manager shall: • Allocate Sales Team to territories • Review activity schedule • Provide resources • Analyse sales activities. Sales Person shall: • Plan store visit • Communicate with the customer • Review the activities against the objectives.
7.0	Associated documents	Schedule planner.
8.0	Resources	Software programme for sales activities.
9.0	Measures/controls	Number of visits Completion according to the activity schedule.
10.0	System description	The flowchart for the in-store procedure is shown in CP 038.1.
10.1	Food safety	Check the storage conditions of your food products. Check temperature logs where necessary. Remove outdated and damaged products from the shelf. Handle any customer complaints.
10.2	Environmental issues	Discuss recycling opportunities and green packaging.
11.0	Records	Visit log Sales orders Returned products list Complaints.
12.0	Changes made	None.

ABC Company Limited	Procedures Manual		Flowchart CP 038.1 Page 1 of 1	
	In-Store Procedure	Date Released dd/mm/yyyy	Date Reviewed dd/mm/yyyy	
Link CP 038	Approved:	Issue No: 01 Prepared by:		

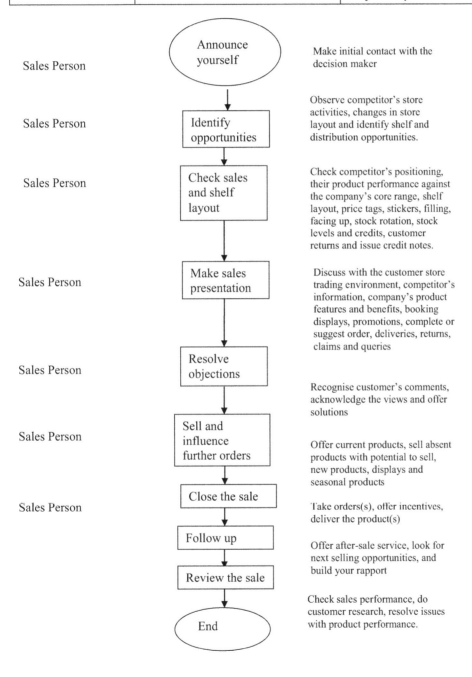

Sales Person — Announce yourself — Make initial contact with the decision maker

Sales Person — Identify opportunities — Observe competitor's store activities, changes in store layout and identify shelf and distribution opportunities.

Sales Person — Check sales and shelf layout — Check competitor's positioning, their product performance against the company's core range, shelf layout, price tags, stickers, filling, facing up, stock rotation, stock levels and credits, customer returns and issue credit notes.

Sales Person — Make sales presentation — Discuss with the customer store trading environment, competitor's information, company's product features and benefits, booking displays, promotions, complete or suggest order, deliveries, returns, claims and queries

Sales Person — Resolve objections — Recognise customer's comments, acknowledge the views and offer solutions

Sales Person — Sell and influence further orders — Offer current products, sell absent products with potential to sell, new products, displays and seasonal products

Sales Person — Close the sale — Take orders(s), offer incentives, deliver the product(s)

Follow up — Offer after-sale service, look for next selling opportunities, and build your rapport

Review the sale — Check sales performance, do customer research, resolve issues with product performance.

End

CP 039 Offer of Samples

ABC Company Limited	Procedures Manual		Reference CP 039 Page 1 of 2	
	Offer of Samples		Date Released dd/mm/yyyy	Date Reviewed dd/mm/yyyy
Core Process	Approved:		Issue No: 01 Prepared by:	Revision No: 00

	Process Owner	Sales Manager
	Process Headings	**Process Details**
1.0	Purpose	To describe the procedure for promoting a new or modified product by offering samples to customers.
2.0	Scope	This procedure shall apply to new products or modified products.
3.0	Input	Customers, request for samples and samples.
4.0	Output	Offer of samples, customer feedback and customer satisfaction.
5.0	Competency requirements	Sales qualifications and selling skills.
6.0	Responsibility	Sales Manager shall: • Approve the sampling plan • Designate a sales person for promotion • Provide resources • Evaluate feedback. Sales Person shall: • Organise samples • Prepare information leaflets/promotion material • Select an appropriate location and get approval.
7.0	Associated documents	Information leaflets/brochures.
8.0	Resources	Material required for offering samples (as required).
9.0	Measures/controls	Feedback from customers.
10.0	System description	1. The Sales Person shall organise samples, utensils and assistants required for the promotion. 2. Select a location for the promotion depending on the product. A shopping mall is ideal for promoting cosmetics. A better location to promote a food product is a supermarket. 3. Place the promotion material in a high traffic density area. 4. Ask customer's permission to offer samples. Start a conversation and describe the benefits of the product. 5. If samples of food products are offered, ensure that all utensils are clean. Never reuse disposable items. 6. Place a bin to collect used disposable items. 7. Get feedback from customers.

ABC Company Limited	Procedures Manual	Reference CP 039 Page 2 of 2	
	Offer of Samples	Date Released dd/mm/yyyy	Date Reviewed dd/mm/yyyy
Core Process	Approved:	Issue No: 01 Prepared by:	Revision No: 00

	Process Headings	Process Details
11.0	Records	New customers Customer feedback.
12.0	Changes made	None.

CP 040 Sales Meetings

ABC Company Limited	Procedures Manual		Reference CP 040 Page 1 of 2	
	Sales Meetings		Date Released dd/mm/yyyy	Date Reviewed dd/mm/yyyy
Core Process	Approved:		Issue No: 01 Prepared by:	Revision No: 00

Process Owner		Sales Manager
	Process Headings	**Process Details**
1.0	Purpose	To describe the procedure for organising and conducting monthly/weekly sales meetings.
2.0	Scope	This procedure shall apply to weekly and monthly sales meetings.
3.0	Input	Meeting agenda, sales reports and notice of meeting.
4.0	Output	Current status of sales, future expected sales and actions arising out of the meetings.
5.0	Competency requirements	Knowledge of sales activities, decision-making skills and communication skills.
6.0	Responsibility	Sales Manager shall: • Circulate the agenda and the minutes of the previous meeting • Select an appropriate location • Send invitations to people outside the sales department, e.g. marketing and production • Evaluate feedback. Sales Person shall: • Prepare for the meeting • Present a summary of sales activities.
7.0	Associated documents	Sales activity log (Form 098) Field visit log (Form 099) Agenda.
8.0	Resources	None.
9.0	Measures/controls	Attendance Duration of the meeting Feedback.
10.0	System description	
10.1	Notice of meeting	1. The Sales Manager shall inform the date and time of the meeting and distribute the minutes of the previous meeting. 2. The Sales Manager shall invite marketing personnel and production personnel (as and when necessary). It is a good practice to include them so that issues raised by the Sales People can be clarified.

ABC Company Limited	Procedures Manual	Reference CP 040 Page 2 of 2	
	Sales Meetings	Date Released dd/mm/yyyy	Date Reviewed dd/mm/yyyy
Core Process	Approved:	Issue No: 01 Prepared by:	Revision No: 00

	Process Headings	Process Details
10.2	Agenda	Welcome – Sales Manager: • The Sales Manager welcomes the attendees and briefly comments on the efforts of the Sales Team • Discuss issues from the previous meeting • Share stories. Each Sales Representative to present: • Results of sales activities and field visits • Performance of demonstrations and promotions • Performance of products and services • Competitors' activities • Prospecting • Qualifying prospects • Issues to be addressed • Closing remarks by the Sales Manager.
11.0	Records	Minutes of the meetings Sales reports.
12.0	Changes made	None.

CP 041 Receiving and Storing Food Items

ABC Company Limited	Procedures Manual	Reference CP 041 Page 1 of 4	
	Receiving and Storing Food Items	Date Released dd/mm/yyyy	Date Reviewed dd/mm/yyyy
Core Process	Approved:	Issue No: 01 Prepared by:	Revision No: 00

Process Owner		Purchasing Manager
	Process Headings	**Process Details**
1.0	Purpose	To describe the procedure for the receiving and storing of food items from the supplier.
2.0	Scope	This procedure shall apply to all deliveries of food items from a supplier.
3.0	Input	Goods received, packaging and delivery documents and inward goods log.
4.0	Output	Verified product and updated inventory.
5.0	Competency requirements	Warehousing skills, technical skills for verification and food safety knowledge.
6.0	Responsibility	Warehouse Person shall:

Warehouse Person shall:
- Keep receiving area clean and well lit
- Inspect the delivery truck for cleanliness and organisation to minimise cross-contamination
- Check the temperatures of refrigerated trucks or trucks delivering refrigerated products
- Check frozen food items to ensure that they are frozen solid and show no signs of thawing (check the bottom of the carton for ice crystals)
- Identify the items against the description on the packing slip
- Record the delivery in the inward goods log book
- Store the goods in the HOLD area for inspection by Quality Control (QC) Staff
- Check the temperature of refrigerated food products:
  - Fresh meat and poultry 5°C or below
  - Packaged products 5°C or below
  - Milk and eggs 7°C or below
- Check packaging to ensure the integrity of sealing and that cans are free from dents, bulges or other signs of deterioration
- Inform QC about verification
- Check dates of milk, eggs and other perishable items
- Fill out a Material Identification Label (MIL) – several may be required

ABC Company Limited	Procedures Manual		Reference CP 041 Page 2 of 4	
	Receiving and Storing Food Items		Date Released dd/mm/yyyy	Date Reviewed dd/mm/yyyy
Core Process	Approved:		Issue No: 01 Prepared by:	Revision No: 00

	Process Headings	**Process Details**
		• Transfer the goods after verification to the allocated area as soon as possible and attach MIL to the product. If palletised, stick the label on the bottom layer of every row • Sign off the packing slip. QC Staff shall: • Verify the items in terms of the test procedures. Warehouse Administration Staff: • Allocate locations for passed or rejected goods and those awaiting inspection • Make appropriate entries to ensure that rejected or HOLD goods cannot be picked • Update the inventory.
7.0	Associated documents	Packing slip (Form 044) Inward goods log book (Form 045) Food items inspection report (Form 049) MIL (Form 047).
8.0	Resources	Handling equipment Warehouse computer programme Transport facilities.
9.0	Measures/controls	Description and quantity of delivered item Number of rejected items.
10.0	System description	Flowchart CP 007.1 shows the process for the receipt of inward goods. All received goods that require verification shall be stored in the HOLD area. The computer system does not permit goods stored in the HOLD area to be picked for orders.
10.1	General requirements	• Store items using First-In-First-Out (FIFO) principle • Store food items and chemicals and other items in separate areas • Date foods and place new foods behind current stock • Keep food products in clean, sturdy containers to prevent pest and rodent access • Keep food off the floor and away from the walls

ABC Company Limited	Procedures Manual	Reference CP 041 Page 3 of 4	
	Receiving and Storing Food Items	Date Released dd/mm/yyyy	Date Reviewed dd/mm/yyyy
Core Process	Approved:	Issue No: 01 Prepared by:	Revision No: 00

	Process Headings	Process Details
10.2	Dry food storage	• Keep a clean environment and monitor regularly. Store dry foods in a well-ventilated area at least 15 cm above the floor and away from walls • Maintain a temperature between 10°C and 15°C • Do not store foods under exposed waste or sewer lines • Store open packages in closed, clean, sturdy, labelled containers • Always keep shelving and floors clean.
10.3	Frozen food storage	• Store food between 0°C and – 18°C • Wrap food properly to prevent freezer burn • Defrost freezer as needed • Keep shelving and floors clean at all times.
10.4	Refrigerated food storage	• Store at 4.5°C or below • Store raw meat on the bottom shelf in a close, clean container away from other foods • Store dairy products away from foods that produce a strong odour • Allow air circulation • Check the temperature regularly • Keep the refrigerator doors closed • Keep the shelving and floors clean at all times.
10.5	Rejection criteria	• Frozen foods showing signs of thawing and/or deterioration • Cans that show dents, rust, defective seals or seams and bulging sides or ends • Torn or punctured packages • Outdated products • Refrigerated products that have been in storage above the required temperature.

ABC Company Limited	Procedures Manual	Reference CP 041 Page 4 of 4	
	Receiving and Storing Food Items	Date Released dd/mm/yyyy	Date Reviewed dd/mm/yyyy
Core Process	Approved:	Issue No: 01 Prepared by:	Revision No: 00

	Process Headings	Process Details
11.0	Records	Inward good log Inventory control database.
12.0	Changes made	None.

Unites States Department of Agriculture. (2005). *Food safety standard operating procedures (SOPs)*. Institute of Child Nutrition. Retrieved May 15, 2020 from https://theicn.org/icn-resources-a-z/standard-operating-procedures/

CP 042 Product and Service Requirements

ABC Company Limited	Procedures Manual	Reference CP 042 Page 1 of 2	
	Product and Service Requirements	Date Released dd/mm/yyyy	Date Reviewed dd/mm/yyyy
Core Process	Approved:	Issue No: 01 Prepared by:	Revision No: 00

Process Owner		Sales Manager
	Process Headings	**Process Details**
1.0	Purpose	To describe the procedure for the identification and review of product and service requirements and communicating with the customer.
2.0	Scope	This procedure applies to requirements relating to finished products and products to be made for the customer and service requests.
3.0	Input	Product and service catalogue, customer needs, pricing schedule, customer's payment history and resource requirements
4.0	Output	Clearly defined customer requirements
5.0	Competency requirements	Products and service knowledge, sales competency and communication skills
6.0	Responsibility	Defined in CP 016 Customer requirements
7.0	Associated documents	External communication procedure SP 006 Take orders procedure CP 017
8.0	Resources	Order processing software
9.0	Measures/controls	Customer satisfaction Number of incorrect requirements Number of orders which could not be fulfilled.
10.0	System description	There are three categories of customer requirements: 1. For finished products offered by ABCCL. 2. For a product to be made according to specified requirements. 3. For a service.
10.1	Requirements for a finished products	Defined in CP 017 Take order, CP 016 Customer requirements, CP 018 Processing orders and SP 007 Customer communication
10.2	Requirements for a product to be made	Defined in CP 016 Customer requirements and CP 013 Design and development
10.3	Requirements for a service	1. Customer Relations Manager shall communicate with the customer and determine the details of the service required including the timeframe for the delivery of service. 2. The information shall be communicated to the Sales Manager (see CP 016 Customer requirements procedure). 3. The Sales Manager may enter into a contract when the details of the service have been agreed between the customer and ABCCL (CP 002).

ABC Company Limited	Procedures Manual	Reference CP 042 Page 2 of 2	
	Product and Service Requirements	Date Released dd/mm/yyyy	Date Reviewed dd/mm/yyyy
Core Process	Approved:	Issue No: 01 Prepared by:	Revision No: 00

	Process Headings	Process Details
11.0	Records	Details of the service Customer feedback (SP 046 Customer satisfaction).
12.0	Changes made	None.

SUPPORT PROCEDURES

SP 001 Document Control

ABC Company Limited	Procedures Manual	Reference SP 001 Page 1 of 7	
	Document Control	Date Released dd/mm/yyyy	Date Reviewed d/mm/yyyy
Support Process	Approved:	Issue No: 01 Prepared by:	Revision No: 00

	Process Owner	Department Managers	
	Process Headings	Process Details	
1.0	Purpose	To describe the procedure for the creation, review, approval, distribution, use and revision of ABCCL's Integrated Quality Food Safety and Environmental (IQFSE) management system documents.	
2.0	Scope	This procedure applies to all documents within the quality, environmental and food safety management systems of the organisation, including documents of internal and external origin.	
3.0	Input	Draft document, test or measurement results, if applicable, regulations and IQFSE manual.	
4.0	Output	New or updated document, effective and efficient process or product, regulatory compliance.	
5.0	Competency requirements	Knowledge of the IQFSE management system, operations and regulatory requirements.	
6.0	Responsibility	As defined in Flowchart SP 001.1 and in this procedure.	
7.0	Associated documents	IQFSE management system Distribution list of documents (Form 100) Document change control form (Form 101) Procedure template (Form 019) List of external documents (Form 102) Master list of documents (Form 103) Master list of changes (Form 104).	
8.0	Resources	Document control database.	
9.0	Measures/Controls	No obsolete documents in use, number of re-issued documents, documentation errors, average time to release document changes.	
10.0	Definitions	**Document:** Information and the medium used for recording the information including paper, magnetic, electronic, optical computer disc, photograph, image or a sample. **Controlled document:** A document that provides information necessary to perform the work specified in a procedure and stamped (or water marked) "Master Copy" or "Controlled Copy". **Uncontrolled document:** A photocopy of a master copy of a document or a written document, which is given to a person or a department for reference purpose only. They are not controlled documents and therefore not retrieved.	

ABC Company Limited	Procedures Manual	Reference SP 001 Page 2 of 7	
	Document Control	Date Released dd/mm/yyyy	Date Reviewed dd/mm/yyyy
Support Processes	Approved:	Issue No: 01 Prepared by:	Revision No: 00

	Process Headings	Process Details
		External document: Document originating outside the organisation that provides information or direction for the performance of business activities within the scope of ABCCL's management systems. It includes customer drawings or specifications, industry standards, international standards, regulations, user manuals, maintenance manuals etc. **Internal document:** Document developed by ABCCL and used for the performance of business activities within the scope of the company's management systems.
11.0	system description	Document control process is shown in Flowchart SP 001.1.
11.1	Document types	(a) Procedures required to comply with ISO 9001, ISO 14001 and ISO 22000 standards; (b) other procedures needed for the operation and control of operations; and (c) documents maintained for communicating the information such as flowcharts, forms, tables, specifications, production plans, approved supplier list, inspections plans, test methods, material safety data sheets, surveys, hazard plans, control schedule, etc. necessary for performing the operations; and (d) documents required to be retained for the provision of results achieved (records).
11.2	Document structure	ABCCL maintains two levels of documents: Procedures manual which contains procedures and work instructions.
11.2.1	Document numbering system	Procedure document, work instructions, laboratory manual documents and flowcharts are created with a header shown in this document. IQFSE management system procedure documents contain the specific requirements of all three standards: quality, environment and food safety. Management requirements carry the prefix MP – management processes, CP – core processes, SP – support processes and AP – assurance processes. A procedure is formatted as shown in Form 019.

ABC Company Limited	Procedures Manual		Reference SP 001 Page 3 of 7	
	Document Control		Date Released dd/mm/yyyy	Date Reviewed dd/mm/yyyy
Support Process	Approved:		Issue No: 01 Prepared by:	Revision No: 00

	Process Headings	**Process Details**
		Flowcharts, figures and tables are linked to individual procedures and numbered accordingly.
11.2.2	Document identification	All procedures, flowcharts have these identifying features shown in the heading: Document title, reference number, page number, date released, date reviewed, issue number and revision number. All other documents shall have a reference to trace the author, title, date and other particulars.
11.2.3	Issue numbers and revision numbers	For issue number 01 the revision number is 00. The revision number increases in ascending order 01, 02, 03, etc. whenever changes are made. The issue number is increased: (a) when there is a major change in ISO standard requirements or company organisation and/or (b) when the revision number increases above 09 (issue number is increased by 1 and the revision number reverts to 00 status).
11.3	Document status	Master copy: The original copy stamped "Master Copy" (hard copies) or with a "Master Copy" watermark in electronic documents. Controlled copy: A legitimate copy of the master copy stamped "Controlled Copy". Obsolete copy: A document no longer is use and stamped "Obsolete" or "Obsolete Legal", with hard copies or documents bearing the watermark "Obsolete" or "Obsolete Legal" in electronic documents moved to a different location in the computer system.
11.4	Document creation	1. A document is drafted by the QA Manager (for quality-related issues), Environment Manager (for environment-related issues) or Food Safety Manager (for food safety-related issues) and circulated to affected departments or managers for comments. Comments are reviewed and incorporated into the final version of the document. The new document is then checked and incorporated into the system by the QA Manager. 2. When documents are reviewed the following shall be considered: (a) the suitability, relevance, and adequacy to the activity in the organisation; (b) areas for improvement; (c) effectiveness in achieving the desired outcomes; and (d) compliance with regulatory requirements.

ABC Company Limited	Procedures Manual	Reference SP 001 Page 4 of 7	
	Document Control	Date Released dd/mm/yyyy	Date Reviewed dd/mm/yyyy
Support Process	Approved:	Issue No: 01 Prepared by:	Revision No: 00

	Process Headings	Process Details
11.5	Document approval	Food Safety Systems Manager or the Environment Systems Manager shall sign the final version of the relevant document under "Prepared by" and submit it to the QA Manager for approval. The QA Manager shall review and approve all documents. Documents prepared by the QA Manager shall be approved by the Plant Manager.
11.6	Distribution	1. QA Manager shall ascertain the requirements of documents from Department Managers and ensure that current versions of necessary documents are made available at locations where they are needed for the performance of activities. 2. The QA Manager shall maintain a distribution list of documents. 3. Department Managers are responsible for maintaining the controlled copies and returning obsolete copies to the QA Manager. 4. Access: Controlled copy holders shall make the relevant procedures, work instructions and any other documents available in suitable locations to employees working under Department Managers. 5. Retrieval: Department Managers shall educate all employees in the organisation about the document structure to enable easy access and retrieval. 6. Use: Department Managers shall ensure that the contents of documents are understood by the employees so they can take effective action.
11.7	Storage and preservation	Documents are protected by keeping them in a secure setting to minimise damage or loss. If they are used in moist or wet environments, it may be necessary to insert them in plastic sleeves.
11.8	Management of controlled copies	1. Controlled hard copies shall not be altered or modified by users and must remain legible and readily identifiable. This includes hard mark-ups by unauthorised personnel. 2. Controlled hard copies shall not be photocopied unless for the purpose of sending to a client who is approved to receive uncontrolled versions. Such copies shall bear the stamp "Uncontrolled Copy".

ABC Company Limited	Procedures Manual		Reference SP 001 Page 5 of 7	
	Document Control		Date Released dd/mm/yyyy	Date Reviewed dd/mm/yyyy
Support Process	Approved:		Issue No: 01 Prepared by:	Revision No: 00

	Process Headings	Process Details
11.9	Document changes and revisions	1. The request for changing the contents of a document can be initiated by any employee. The request shall be made to the QA Manager by completing the document change form. The QA Manager shall assign a change control number and review the request with the Department Manager and the Food Safety Manager and/or the Environment Systems Manager as appropriate. If the request is approved, the procedure under section 11.4 shall be followed. 2. If the request is rejected, QA Manager shall communicate the decision to the person who made the request giving the reasons for rejection. 3. The QA Manager shall coordinate with Department Managers who own the procedures to revise all procedures and standard operating procedures (SOPs) at least annually and update them as necessary to ensure documents remain current.
11.10	Temporary changes	1. For uninterrupted performance of business activities, temporary changes to documents may be necessary. The originator shall submit the request by completing the document change form, stating the reasons and the criteria for the duration of the change such as "until item x is received" or "until the export order is completed". 2. The request for change shall be reviewed by the team reviewing document changes and, if acceptable, the change is made under a waiver. 3. They remain legible and identifiable. 4. No other changes to documents are made. 5. If the temporary change needs to be made permanent, the change control procedure shall be followed.
11.11	Electronic documents	1. When documents are processed electronically, they are subject to IT procedures. 2. Electronic version of the document shall carry the initials of the person who prepared it and the person who approved it. Read and write access shall be granted to the signatories and all others shall be granted read access only.

ABC Company Limited	Procedures Manual	Reference SP 001 Page 6 of 7	
	Document Control	Date Released dd/mm/yyyy	Date Reviewed dd/mm/yyyy
Support Process	Approved:	Issue No: 01 Prepared by:	Revision No: 00

	Process Headings	Process Details
		3. If documents are available only via the company network system, QA Manager shall maintain an electronic distribution list. 4. The IT department shall conduct training sessions on access, retrieval and use of electronic documents.
11.12	Managing obsolete documents	1. Obsolete hard copies of all documents shall be filed away in a folder marked "Obsolete". If obsolete copies have to be retained for legal or for any other purpose, they shall be filed away in the same folder but using a divider marked "Obsolete Legal". 2. Obsolete copies of electronic documents in the computer or network shall be stamped "Obsolete" with the watermark and archived with access granted only to the QA Manager, Environment Manager and the Food Safety Systems Manager. Obsolete electronic copies that are required for legal or for any other purpose shall also be archived separately with access rights shown above. 3. Permanent removal and destruction of obsolete documents can only be done with the approval of the QA Manager.
11.13	Managing documents of external origin	1. Department Managers, Quality, Environment and Food Safety Managers shall determine what external documents are needed to perform business activities. These include, but are not limited to, standards, statutory regulations, customers' standards, industry standards etc. 2. QA Manager shall ensure that relevant versions of documents are available where needed, they are identifiable, remain legible, their distribution is controlled and that obsolete documents are not in use. 3. QA Manager shall monitor the status of external documents and publications held at least annually and ensure that current versions of external documents are made available to ABCCL through subscription, information from websites or by communicating with the originator.

ABC Company Limited	Procedures Manual	Reference SP 001 Page 7 of 7	
	Document Control	Date Released dd/mm/yyyy	Date Reviewed dd/mm/yyyy
Support Process	Approved:	Issue No: 01 Prepared by:	Revision No: 00

	Process Headings	Process Details
		4. QA Manager shall maintain a list of all external documents held including international standards, technical standards, codes of practice, regulations, etc. 5. QA Manager shall review impact of changes on IQFSE management system documents and introduce changes according to this procedure. 6. Controls specified in sections 11.7 to 11.9 are also applicable to documents of external origin.
11.14	Control of business sensitive documents	Business sensitive documents such as financial performance, mergers and acquisitions shall be created by appropriate Department Managers and circulated to personnel authorised by the Managing Director.
11.15	Retention period	All documents shall be retained for a period of seven years from the date of creation or as required by regulatory requirements.
12.0	Records	Change control forms Test results, if applicable.
13.0	Changes made	None.

ABC Company Limited	Procedures Manual	Flowchart SP 001.1 Page 1 of 1	
	Document Control	Date Released dd/mm/yyyy	Date Reviewed dd/mm/yyyy
Link SP 001	Approved:	Issue No: 01 Prepared by:	Revision No: 00

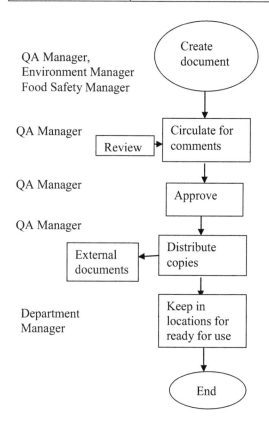

QA Manager, Environment Manager Food Safety Manager

Create document

Need may arise due to regulatory changes, system failure, audits, reviews, changes to business activities, industry sector, best practice initiatives, need to change existing documents, suggestions from employees. Section 11.4, SP 001

QA Manager

Review

Circulate for comments

Circulate the draft to those affected by the contents for comments (Form 136)

QA Manager

Approve

One print out is stamped "Master Copy". Copies to be distributes stamped "Controlled Copy" Section 11.5, SP 001

QA Manager

External documents

Distribute copies

Copies are distributed and recorded in the distribution list. Obsolete copies are stamped 'Obsolete', removed and filed. External documents are managed by the QA Manager. Update the master list and changes made section. Section 11.6, SP 001

Department Manager

Keep in locations for ready for use

Documents are reviewed at least annually

End

SP 002 Record Control

ABC Company Limited	Procedures Manual	Reference SP 002 Page 1 of 3	
	Record Control	Date Released dd/mm/yyyy	Date Reviewed dd/mm/yyyy
Suppport Processes	Approved:	Issue No: 01 Prepared by:	Revision No: 00

Process Owner		Department Managers
	Process Headings	**Process Details**
1.0	Purpose	To describe the procedure for controlling ABCCL records.
2.0	Scope	This procedure applies to all records generated by ABCCL (hand-written, hard copy and electronic) as well as those generated by external parties and sub-contractors for the use of ABCCL.
3.0	Input	Data preserved on records for regulatory requirements.
4.0	Output	New or updated record, updated master list, new data and index of records.
5.0	Competency requirements	Knowledge of the IQFSE management system, operations, requirements of relevant ISO standards, operational controls relative to quality, food safety and environment standards and regulatory requirements.
6.0	Responsibility	Department Managers shall: • Create records for conducting the activities in the department • Ensure accuracy of information in the record • File the records in the department for identifications and easy retrieval • Inform the QA Manager whenever new records are created. QA Manager shall: • Keep a master list of all records with details from regulatory agencies. All users shall: • Record the information accurately and legibly.
7.0	Associated documents	Master list of records (Form 105).
8.0	Resources	Record management software.
9.0	Measures/Controls	Internal audits.
10.0	Definitions	**Record:** Any document (see definition under SP 001) providing evidence of or information about past events.
11.0	System description	
11.1	Record types	Records provide the following information: (a) results of activities performed; (b) minutes of meetings; (c) product or process evaluation for

ABC Company Limited	Procedures Manual	Reference SP 002 Page 2 of 3	
	Record Control	Date Released dd/mm/yyyy	Date Reviewed dd/mm/yyyy
Support Processes	Approved:	Issue No: 01 Prepared by:	Revision No: 00

Process Headings		Process Details
		meeting acceptance criteria; (d) test results of inspecting components, ingredients, processes, etc.; (e) records relating to personnel, material or equipment qualification; and (f) applicable records from contractors or external agencies.
11.2	Record generation	1. Each department or business unit is responsible for creating records to demonstrate the effective performance of activities as defined in each procedure and compliance to regulatory requirements. 2. The information shall be filled in accurately and legibly. Hand-written records shall be completed using a ballpoint pen to protect them from unauthorised change. 3. Corrections are made out by crossing out with a single line, signing the correction (initials) and dating the correction. Correcting fluid or correcting tape shall not be used. Activity logs shall demonstrate changes in electronic records.
11.3	Record identification	Records are identified by: (a) the title of the record and a unique number, if applicable, e.g. the purchase order and purchase order number; (b) the date of creation; and (c) the location and/or owner
11.4	Master list of records	Company shall maintain a master list of records.
11.5	Record maintenance	1. Records are maintained in the department where it was created. Department Manager shall ensure the integrity and safety of records within his or her responsibility. Action shall be taken to prevent damage or deterioration or loss during storage. 2. Hard copies of electronic records shall be protected by controlling access to the records by authorised personnel. 3. Electronic records are protected by granting access rights. They are managed by IT procedures described in this manual. 4. Externally generated records and their distribution shall be maintained by the QA Manager.
11.6	Retrieval of records	1. Any person requiring access to a record shall initially make the request to the Department Manager responsible for managing the record. If the request is denied he or she may approach the QA Manager whose decision shall be final. The retrieval for reasonable use shall not be denied.

ABC Company Limited	Procedures Manual		Reference SP 002 Page 3 of 3	
	Record Control		Date Released dd/mm/yyyy	Date Reviewed dd/mm/yyyy
Support Processes	Approved:		Issue No: 01 Prepared by:	Revision No: 00

	Process Headings	Process Details
		2. Paper records are retrieved on the basis of the title of the record (and a number, if applicable), location area and the date of creation of the record. 3. Electronic records shall be made retrievable by keywords under search criteria. 4. Managers from whom records are requested shall be aware of applicable data protection acts. 5. Retrieval of archived records shall be made to the QA Manager.
11.7	Statutory requirements	QA Manager, Environment Manager and the Food Safety Systems Manager shall be familiar with applicable regulations and be able to demonstrate compliance to federal, state, local and tribal laws applicable to record-keeping.
11.8	Control of record keeping	QA Manager or his or her staff shall ensure that records are being filled in correctly and legibly by record holders through daily inspections and observations.
11.9	Storage and preservation	Records are protected by keeping them in containers such as file cabinets or storage boxes to minimise damage or loss after use. If they are used in moist or wet environments, it may be necessary to insert them in plastic sleeves.
11.10	Retention of records	Unless otherwise specified, records shall be maintained for a period of seven years.
11.11	Disposal of records	1. All paper records after the retention period shall be stamped with "Obsolete" awaiting destruction. Obsolete electronic records shall be archived to a separate location. If a watermark can be used the word "Obsolete" should appear on every page of the record. 2. After the retention period documents are destroyed. Confidential records shall be shredded.
12.0	Records	Master list of records.
13.0	Changes made	None.

SP 003 Maintenance Management

ABC Company Limited	Procedures Manual	Reference SP 003 Page 1 of 2	
	Maintenance Management	Date Released dd/mm/yyyy	Date Reviewed dd/mm/yyyy
Support Process	Approved:	Issue No: 01 Prepared by:	Revision No: 00

Process Owner	Engineering Manager
Process Headings	**Process Details**
1.0 Purpose	To describe the procedure for maintaining machinery and equipment for effective performance and safety.
2.0 Scope	This procedure shall apply to all machinery and equipment used in the facility.
3.0 Input	Maintenance schedule, manuals and operating instruction, necessary tools, spare parts and calibration equipment.
4.0 Output	Skilled staff, properly maintained equipment, reduced unplanned downtime, reliable and accurate measurements and staff satisfaction.
5.0 Competency requirements	Planning skills, effective labour utilisation skills and technical skills.
6.0 Responsibility	Engineering Manager shall: • Determine the manpower and skills necessary for maintenance activities • Ensure availability of proper tools, tackles, spares, consumables, special equipment, jigs, fixtures, lifting and handling equipment, cranes, structural and other required materials • Ensure availability of external contractors and their capabilities • Prepare maintenance schedule plan • Evaluate necessary equipment and suppliers of engineering items. Engineering Team shall: • Carry out maintenance work as scheduled • Keep records of maintenance work.
7.0 Associated documents	Maintenance schedule Record of maintenance work SP 010 Managing infrastructure.
8.0 Resources	Engineering tools for maintenance Maintenance programme.
9.0 Measures/Controls	Machine breakdown log Timely completion of tasks.
10.0 System description	The procedure for maintenance management is described in Flowchart SP 003.1.
10.1 Maintenance process	1. Maintenance of equipment, facilities and support services is performed as per original equipment manufacturer's recommendations and is recorded in the maintenance log for each item of equipment.

ABC Company Limited	Procedures Manual		Reference SP 003 Page 2 of 2	
	Maintenance Management		Date Released dd/mm/yyyy	Date Reviewed dd/mm/yyyy
Support Process	Approved:		Issue No: 01 Prepared by:	Revision No: 00

	Process Headings	Process Details
		2. The accuracy and performance of the equipment is continuously monitored and special attention is given to items of key equipment that contribute to the product's quality characteristics.
10.2	Types of maintenance	ABCCL carries out four types of maintenance: 1. Planned maintenance: This is a proactive approach in which maintenance work such as checking, adjusting and replacement is scheduled to take place regularly. 2. Preventive maintenance: Maintenance work is carried out at pre-determined intervals to reduce the possibility of equipment failure or performance degradation. 3. Corrective maintenance: This is a reactive approach where maintenance work is carried out after a failure to restore the item for effective performance. 4. Predictive maintenance: It is a planned preventive maintenance programme, which depends on predicted equipment failure. Parts may have to be replaced, e.g. after a certain number of hours of operation.
11.0	Records	Maintenance log.
12.0	Changes made	None.

ABC Company Limited	Procedures Manual	Flowchart SP 003.1 Page 1 of 1	
	Maintenance Management	Date Released dd/mm/yyyy	Date Reviewed dd/mm/yyyy
Link SP 003	Approved:	Issue No: 01 Prepared by:	Revision No: 00

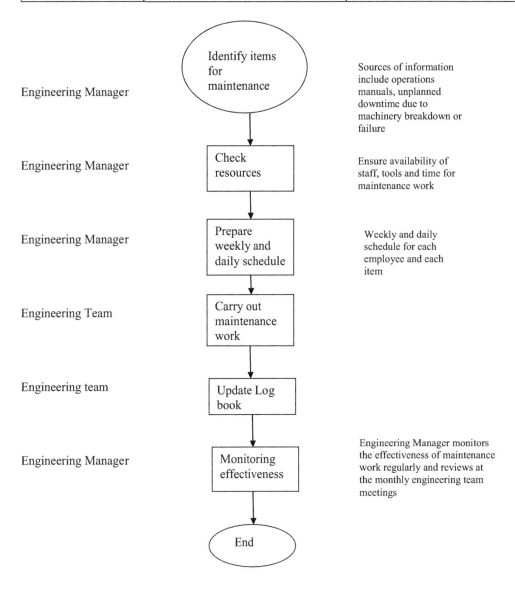

Engineering Manager — Identify items for maintenance

Sources of information include operations manuals, unplanned downtime due to machinery breakdown or failure

Engineering Manager — Check resources

Ensure availability of staff, tools and time for maintenance work

Engineering Manager — Prepare weekly and daily schedule

Weekly and daily schedule for each employee and each item

Engineering Team — Carry out maintenance work

Engineering team — Update Log book

Engineering Manager — Monitoring effectiveness

Engineering Manager monitors the effectiveness of maintenance work regularly and reviews at the monthly engineering team meetings

End

SP 004 Set-up Procedure

ABC Company Limited	Procedures Manual	Reference SP 004 Page 1 of 2	
	Set-up Procedure	Date Released dd/mm/yyyy	Date Reviewed dd/mm/yyyy
Management Processes	Approved:	Issue No: 01 Prepared by:	Revision No: 00

Process Owner		Engineering Manager
	Process Headings	**Process Details**
1.0	Purpose	To describe the procedure for setting up machinery for effective operation.
2.0	Scope	This procedure shall apply to all machinery and equipment used in the facility.
3.0	Input	Equipment and machinery, tools, set-up procedures, engineering manuals, and user manuals.
4.0	Output	Equipment and machinery set up for effective performance, reduced unplanned downtime, operator satisfaction and better production output.
5.0	Competency requirements	Knowledge of operation of equipment and machinery, engineering skills and ability to find root causes of problems.
6.0	Responsibility	Engineering Manager shall: • Allocate an engineer for each item that requires set up • Ensure the Engineering Team has the necessary skills to carry out the tasks • Monitor the production work schedule and plan set up as necessary. Engineering Team shall: • Carry out set up as scheduled • Ensure availability of spares required for routine work.
7.0	Associated documents	Operations manuals Work schedule Tacit knowledge repository.
8.0	Resources	Engineering tools and equipment.
9.0	Measures/Controls	Unplanned downtime due to equipment/machinery breakdown or failure Operation failures of the item after set up.
10.0	System description	The procedure for set up is shown in Flowchart SP 004.1. The Engineering Team shall set up the machinery or equipment according to the procedure described in each operation manual. Any deviations from the described procedure, which have been customised to suit the operation in the facility, shall be recorded in the tacit knowledge repository for future use. A reference to this data shall be recorded in the operations manual. All deviations are communicated to the Engineering Team at the monthly meeting.

ABC Company Limited	Procedures Manual	Reference SP 004 Page 2 of 2	
	Set-up Procedure	Date Released dd/mm/yyyy	Date Reviewed dd/mm/yyyy
Management Processes	Approved:	Issue No: 01 Prepared by:	Revision No: 00

	Process Headings	Process Details
11.0	Records	Set-up log Maintenance log.
12.0	Changes made	None

ABC Company Limited	Procedures Manual	Flowchart SP 004. 1 Page 1 of 1	
	Set-up Procedure	Date Released dd/mm/yyyy	Date Reviewed dd/mm/yyyy
Link SP 004	Approved:	Issue No: 01 Prepared by:	Revision No: 00

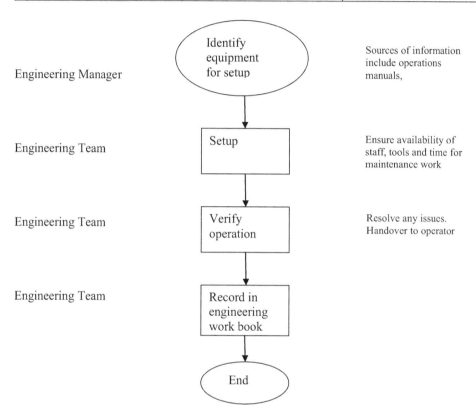

Engineering Manager — Identify equipment for setup

Sources of information include operations manuals,

Engineering Team — Setup

Ensure availability of staff, tools and time for maintenance work

Engineering Team — Verify operation

Resolve any issues. Handover to operator

Engineering Team — Record in engineering work book

End

SP 005 Internal Communication

ABC Company Limited	Procedures Manual	Reference SP 005 Page 1 of 2	
	Internal Communication	Date Released dd/mm/yyyy	Date Reviewed dd/mm/yyyy
Support Processes	Approved:	Issue No: 01 Prepared by:	Revision No: 00

Process Owner		QA Manager, Environment Manager and Food Safety Manager
	Process Headings	**Process Details**
1.0	Purpose	To describe the process for internal communication within ABCCL.
2.0	Scope	This procedure shall apply to all staff within the organisation and covers quality, environmental and food safety issues.
3.0	Input	Relevant information and communication media.
4.0	Output	Delivered message and the creation of awareness and understanding.
5.0	Competency requirements	Listening, observation, motivation, translation, written and verbal communication skills.
6.0	Responsibility	Defined in Form 106 – communication matrix.
7.0	Associated documents	Communication matrix.
8.0	Resources	Customer relationship module Communication media.
9.0	Measures/controls	Staff surveys, audience perception measurement, interviews and compliance with requirements.
10.0	Definitions	**Communication:** Exchange of information between two or more parties, documenting and responding to the information.
11.0	System description	
11.1	Communication methods and delivery	**Verbal communication:** (a) direct speech – meetings, consultations, training and informal meetings; and (b) telephone – information. **Written communication:** (a) delivery by employees – reports, messages, records and documents; and (b) information services – notice board and message board. **Electronic communication:** (a) IT – files on computer network, email messages and files, and shared files on network discs; (b) portable media – electronic media such as DVD, USB, FD and CG; and (c) fax – copies of documents, maintenance of communication tools, particularly electronic media, is the responsibility of the IT department.
11.2	Communication matrix Form 106	When information is prepared, the originator shall consider the needs and skill levels of the intended audience. The originator shall ensure that the information is accurate and consistent with management system requirements by checking available resources.

ABC Company Limited	Procedures Manual	Reference SP 005 Page 2 of 2	
	Internal Communication	Date Released dd/mm/yyyy	Date Reviewed dd/mm/yyyy
Support Processes	Approved:	Issue No: 01 Prepared by:	Revision No: 00

	Process Headings	Process Details
11.3	Upward communication	Individual Department Managers regularly provide data and information relative to customer satisfaction, quality, environmental and food safety expectations of and services, quality, environment and food safety performance of products and processes, opportunities for improvement and the effectiveness of management systems to the Management Team.
11.4	Special communications	At times, it may be necessary for the CEO or a senior executive to communicate the status of the business performance. The communications are delivered on a need to know basis to prevent the spread of rumours through the grapevine.
11.5	Communication from employees	Communication from employees on quality, food safety or environmental issues shall be received by the Plant Manager in coordination with the Department Manager. The information provided by employees shall be considered for continual improvement projects at management review meetings.
11.6	Other information	At times, it may be necessary to convey information not captured in the communication matrix. In such instances, procedure in Flowchart SP 005.1 shall be followed.
11.7	Further action	Management Team ensures that the information is included in updating the IQFSE management system and the relevant information is included as input to the management review meeting.
12.0	Records	All communications shall be recorded and retained by the originator for a period specified under record management procedure.
13.0	Changes made	None.

ABC Company Limited	Procedures Manual	Flowchart SP 005.1 Page 1 of 1	
	Internal Communication	Date Released dd/mm/yyyy	Date Reviewed dd/mm/yyyy
Link CP 005	Approved:	Issue No: 01 Prepared by:	Revision No: 00

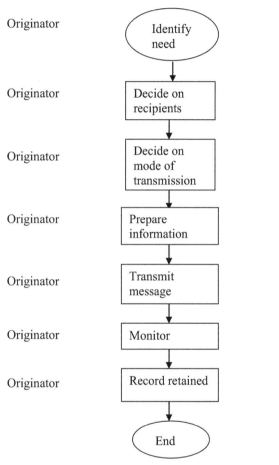

Originator — Identify need

Communication need is determined by considering (a) tasks to be performed by employees, (b) statutory, customer and other requirements, and (c) the need to create an awareness of quality, environment and food safety management elements.

Originator — Decide on recipients

Decide on the parties to whom the message is intended.

Originator — Decide on mode of transmission

Originator — Prepare information

Originator — Transmit message

Information shall be communicated at the earliest opportunity in order to prevent the spread of rumours.

Originator — Monitor

Originator — Record retained

End

SP 006 External Communication

ABC Company Limited	Procedures Manual		Reference SP 006 Page 1 of 2	
	External Communication	Date Released dd/mm/yyyy		Date Reviewed dd/mm/yyyy
Support Processes	Approved: Prepared by:	Issue No: 01		Revision No: 00

Process Owner		QA Manager, Environment Manager and Food Safety Manager
	Process Headings	**Process Details**
1.0	Purpose	To describe the procedure for communicating quality, environmental and food safety issues with external agencies.
2.0	Scope	This procedure shall apply to external agencies that communicate with the organisation and covers quality, environmental and food safety issues.
3.0	Input	Relevant information and communication media.
4.0	Output	Delivered message and the creation of awareness and understanding.
5.0	Competency requirements	Listening, observation, motivation, translation, written and verbal communication skills.
6.0	Responsibility	Defined in the external communication matrix.
7.0	Associated documents	External communication record (Form 107) External communication matrix (Form 108).
8.0	Resources	Communication media.
9.0	Measures/Controls	Customer satisfaction surveys, response to queries and complaints.
10.0	System description	
10.1	Interested parties	Interested parties include regulators, community groups, suppliers, contractors, stakeholders, insurers, banks, customers, etc.
10.2	Communication methods and delivery (external communication matrix)	Letters, email, verbal, open houses, media conferences, informal discussions with interested parties, awareness programmes, telephone, verbal, etc.
10.3	Soliciting views of interested parties	Organisation may use additional techniques such as advisory panels, newsletters or informal meetings with external groups to solicit their views that affect the IQFSE management system.
10.4	Message criteria	The information shall be clearly presented and verifiable.
10.5	Communications about emergency situations and accidents	External communication required during emergency situations and accidents is handed by the emergency response team and recorded in the emergency response plan.
10.6	Communications about product recall (CP 029)	Recall procedure.
10.7	Time for communication	Response to external communication shall be made at the earliest opportunity to prevent the spread of rumours through the grapevine.

ABC Company Limited	Procedures Manual	Reference SP 006 Page 2 of 2	
	External Communication	Date Released dd/mm/yyyy	Date Reviewed dd/mm/yyyy
Support Processes	Approved:	Issue No: 01 Prepared by:	Revision No: 00

	Process Headings	Process Details
10.8	Receiving communications	Communication received shall be directed to the personnel specified in the external communication matrix. Person receiving communication shall be able to provide further information or direct the originator to other sources of information, if necessary.
10.9	Communication with regulatory agencies	Plant Manager shall review the information, take appropriate action and verify the responses before presenting to the Managing Director for communication with regulators.
10.10	Policies and environmental aspects	1. Quality, environmental and food safety policy shall be made available to external parties on request by the Plant Manager or via the company web page. 2. Requests for significant environmental aspects shall be forwarded to the Managing Director for a decision. If the decision is made to communicate significant environmental aspects, the following information shall also be given: environmental objectives, management programmes and opportunities for mitigation.
10.11	Further action	Management Team ensures that the information is included in updating the IQFSE management system and relevant information is included as input to the management review meeting.
11.0	Records	All communications shall be kept by the originator for a period specified under record control.
12.0	Changes made	None.

SP 007 Communication with Customers

ABC Company Limited	Procedures Manual		Reference SP 007 Page 1 of 3	
	Communication with Customers	Date Released dd/mm/yyyy		Date Reviewed dd/mm/yyyy
Support Process	Approved:	Issue No: 01 Prepared by:		Revision No: 00

Process Owner		**Customer Relations Manager**
	Process Headings	**Process Details**
1.0	Purpose	To describe the procedure for communicating with customers.
2.0	Scope	This procedure relates to customer-related processes.
3.0	Input	Communication material.
4.0	Output	Customer satisfaction and clarification of information.
5.0	Competency requirements	Communication skills.
6.0	Responsibility	Defined in this document.
7.0	Associated documents	Procedures quoted in this document.
8.0	Resources	Customer relations management module.
9.0	Measures/controls	Customer satisfaction.
10.0	System description	
10.1	Methods of communication	Customer communication occurs through these formats, events and processes:
		• Brochures, catalogues, specifications or technical data sheets relating to our products and services
		• Enquiries, quotations and order form, invoices and credit notes
		• Confirmation of approved orders and amended orders
		• Emails, letters and general correspondence
		• Customer feedback and customer compliant processes.
10.2	Customer communication subjects	Customer communication is involved with, but is not limited to, these activities:
		• Determining product and service information
		• Handling enquiries
		• Taking orders (CP 017) and handling contracts (CP 002)
		• Handling amendments (CP 016)
		• Customer feedback (SP 046) and complaints (SP 047)
		• Person-to-person contact with customers (CP 037)
		• Receiving a product schedule
		• Agreeing to a project plan
		• Managing customer property (CP 011)

ABC Company Limited	Procedures Manual	Reference SP 007 Page 2 of 3	
	Communication with Customers	Date Released dd/mm/yyyy	Date Reviewed dd/mm/yyyy
Support Process	Approved:	Issue No: 01 Prepared by:	Revision No: 00

	Process Headings	Process Details
		• Dealing with contingencies when necessary • External communication (SP 006) • Product information to enable the safe handling, display, storage, preparation, distribution and use of the product within the food chain or by the consumer • Identified food safety hazards that need to be controlled by other organisations in the food chain and/or consumer.
10.2.1	Product and service information	Product information is provided by these means: • Advertising materials • Catalogues • Website • Service agreements • Product data sheets • Price lists • Product samples. Sales Team is responsible for communication with customers about the above information.
10.2.2	Handling enquiries	All enquiries shall be directed to the Customer Relations Manager who shall direct the enquiry to the appropriate department or person. Enquiries about business sensitive information shall always be directed to the General Manager. In the absence of the Customer Relations Manager, QA Manager shall deal with the enquiry.
10.2.3	Receiving a product schedule	It may be necessary to communicate with the customer about a product schedule. Plant Manager shall communicate with the customer about this.
10.2.4	Agreeing to a project plan	All enquiries about a project plan shall be discussed with the Plant Manager. A project plan initiated by ABCCL shall be discussed with the customer only after agreement has been reached by the Production Team. A project plan proposed by the customer shall be discussed by the Production Team for approval. If the project is feasible, details shall be communicated to the customer by the Plant Manager.
10.2.5	Dealing with contingencies	Contingencies include, but are not limited to, lost or delayed delivery product failure in the market, urgent deliveries, production failure due to adverse

ABC Company Limited	Procedures Manual		Reference SP 007 Page 3 of 3	
	Communication with Customers		Date Released dd/mm/yyyy	Date Reviewed dd/mm/yyyy
Support Processes	Approved:		Issue No: 01 Prepared by:	Revision No: 00

	Process Headings	Process Details
		weather conditions, labour disputes, fire in the facility, extensive damage to plant and machinery, food safety issues and any other situation that prevents normal business activities. Plant Manager shall discuss the situation with the customer and offer alternative arrangements to meet their demands.
10.2.6	Food safety product information	Food product information such as safe handling, display, storage, preparation, distribution and use of the product within the food chain or by consumer is conveyed via labelling and product literature.
10.3	Customer communication training	Customer Relations Manager shall have gained customer communication skills and organise necessary customer communication training for sales, marketing and other staff who interact with customers.
11.0	Records	Communication records.
12.0	Changes made	None.

SP 008 Organisational Knowledge

ABC Company Limited	Procedures Manual		Reference SP 008 Page 1 of 5	
	Organisational Knowledge		Date Released dd/mm/yyyy	Date Reviewed dd/mm/yyyy
Support Process	Approved:		Issue No: 01 Prepared by:	Revision No: 00

Process Owner		**Manager Information Systems**
	Process Headings	**Process Details**
1.0	Purpose	To describe how the knowledge of our organisation is managed.
2.0	Scope	The procedure applies to knowledge associated with our business activities.
3.0	Input	Knowledge required for operating the processes and for producing products and delivering services to customers.
4.0	Output	Knowledge database, codified knowledge, improved performance and training programmes.
5.0	Competency requirements	IT skills, ability to identify different types of knowledge and knowledge management skills.
6.0	Responsibility	Management Team shall: • Identify the key processes • Identify the knowledge required to perform the activities. QA Manager, Food Safety Manager and Environment Manager shall: • Identify knowledge gaps • Secure required knowledge. Manager Information Systems shall: • Conduct a knowledge management workshop • Create and maintain the knowledge database • Train the staff to retrieve and apply the knowledge • Carry out audits of organisational knowledge and update knowledge when necessary.
7.0	Associated documents	SP 009 Resource management.
8.0	Resources	Knowledge management database.
9.0	Measures/Controls	Knowledge gaps Knowledge audit.
10.0	Definitions	**Knowledge:** Theoretical and practical understanding of a subject. **Competence:** The ability to perform a task and is knowledge put into action. **Organisation knowledge:** Knowledge resources that reside in the organisation, which can be realistically captured by the organisation.

ABC Company Limited	Procedures Manual	Reference SP 008 Page 2 of 5	
	Organisational Knowledge	Date Released dd/mm/yyyy	Date Reviewed dd/mm/yyyy
Support Process	Approved:	Issue No: 01 Prepared by:	Revision No: 00

	Process Headings	Process Details
		Tacit knowledge: Tacit knowledge is the type of knowledge that is not written down or difficult to be shared and is gained through personal experience or working in an organisation. **Explicit knowledge:** Explicit knowledge in the organisation is documented and structured, and exists in the form of procedures, steps and checklists. **Skills:** Proficiency gained through training or experience to carry out a task. **Ability:** The quality of being able to do something. **Codification:** It is the process of making organisational knowledge visible, accessible and usable by converting tacit knowledge into explicit form and documenting it.
11.0	system description	The process of managing organisational knowledge is shown in Flowchart SP 008.1.
11.1	Knowledge sources	(a) Internal sources: Intellectual property, knowledge gained from experience, lessons learnt from failures and successful projects, capturing and sharing undocumented knowledge and experience, results of improvement in processes, product and services; and (b) External sources: Standards, user manuals, conference proceedings, knowledge from customers and clients, benchmarks, industry best practices.
11.2	Identification of knowledge requirements	(a) Manager Information Systems shall hold brainstorming sessions and workshops to identify and define which knowledge is most important, and which knowledge is critical. Regularity with which such brainstorming sessions and workshops are held shall be determined by the QA Manager in consultation with Department Managers; (b) Knowledge required for key processes are identified by examining the procedures, standards and other documents related to the process and interviewing the process owners. Knowledge gaps are identified by comparing the existing knowledge with what is necessary for performing the activity effectively; and

ABC Company Limited	Procedures Manual	Reference SP 008 Page 3 of 5	
	Organisational Knowledge	Date Released dd/mm/yyyy	Date Reviewed dd/mm/yyyy
Support Process	Approved:	Issue No: 01 Prepared by:	Revision No: 00

Process Headings	Process Details
	(c) Manager Information Systems shall source knowledge requirements through the sources identified in section 11.1 (a).
11.3 Codification	1. When tacit knowledge is identified by the Management Team, Manager Information Systems shall determine which tacit knowledge should be converted to explicit form.
	2. Each Department Manager shall have a system to capture tacit knowledge related to the processes. A simple form may be used to capture the tacit knowledge in work instructions.
11.4 Knowledge management database	1. Manager Information Systems shall create a database for managing organisational knowledge. The database shall include, but is not limited to:
	(a) Date of creation;
	(b) Entered by;
	(c) Reference source of the information;
	(d) Description of the information;
	(e) Reviewed person; and
	(f) A short description of the application of knowledge and the key personnel who should have access to it.
	2. Information technology provides the architecture for (i) capturing, (ii) defining, storing, categorising, indexing and linking digital objects, (iii) retrieval and subscribing, and (iv) allowing sufficient flexibility to render it meaningful and applicable across multiple contexts of use.
11.5 Knowledge management architecture	There are three components to knowledge management architecture:
	1. Knowledge repository contains declarative knowledge (concepts, categories and definitions), procedural knowledge (processes, actions and sequence of events), specific contextual knowledge (circumstances and intentions of knowledge development and applications), and linkages among the various types of knowledge.
	2. Knowledge refinery includes the process for acquisition, creation, refining (adding value), storage and retrieval, and distribution the knowledge in the repository.

ABC Company Limited	Procedures Manual	Reference SP 008 Page 4 of 5	
	Organisational Knowledge	Date Released dd/mm/yyyy	Date Reviewed dd/mm/yyyy
Support Process	Approved:	Issue No: 01 Prepared by:	Revision No: 00

	Process Headings	Process Details
		3. Knowledge management roles: Manager Information Systems shall be responsible for our knowledge management architecture. He or she may appoint knowledge champions for each area who are responsible for a particular body of knowledge.
11.6	Access to knowledge	Manager Information Systems shall make the database accessible to all employees. A search facility should be provided to obtain relevant knowledge, e.g. of processes, products, technology, in-house experts, etc.
11.7	Maintaining knowledge	ABCCL shall use the following methods to maintain its knowledge: 1. Provision for feedback to enable users to comment and update knowledge in the knowledge database. 2. Recognising employees who communicate tacit knowledge to the process owner. 3. Learning from experience. 4. Knowledge gained through failures and through successful projects. 5. Rewarding employees for creating useful knowledge. 6. Knowledge audits conducted by the Manager Information Systems. 7. Acquiring knowledge from new employees and those who leave the organisation. 8. Updating knowledge available through external sources which are applicable to the organisation.
11.8	Responding to changing needs	Whenever processes and procedures are updated or created in response to either internal or external changes, the Management Team shall review the existing knowledge with a view to identify knowledge gaps. New knowledge requirements are identified in the change request Form 109.
11.9	Knowledge audit	Manager Information Systems shall carry out a knowledge audit at least annually or as required by changing circumstances and shall assess: • The organisation's knowledge needs tacit and explicit knowledge in the organisation and their location

ABC Company Limited	Procedures Manual	Reference SP 008 Page 5 of 5	
	Organisational Knowledge	Date Released dd/mm/yyyy	Date Reviewed dd/mm/yyyy
Support Process	Approved:	Issue No: 01 Prepared by:	Revision No: 00

Process Headings	Process Details
	• Knowledge flow within the organisation, formally and informally, and to and from clients and relevant organisations • Methods of identification, creation, codification, storage sharing and use • Obstacles to knowledge flows from people and technology • Knowledge gaps.
12.0 Records	Knowledge management database Records of workshops and training sessions.
13.0 Changes made	None.

ABC Company Limited	Procedures Manual	Flowchart SP 008.1 Page 1 of 1	
	Organisational Knowledge	Date Released dd/mm/yyyy	Date Reviewed dd/mm/yyyy
Link SP 008	Approved:	Issue No: 01 Prepared by:	

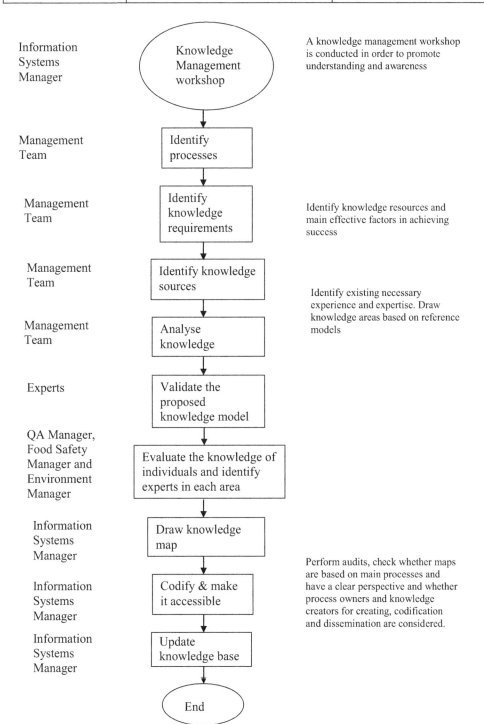

Information Systems Manager — Knowledge Management workshop

A knowledge management workshop is conducted in order to promote understanding and awareness

Management Team — Identify processes

Management Team — Identify knowledge requirements

Identify knowledge resources and main effective factors in achieving success

Management Team — Identify knowledge sources

Management Team — Analyse knowledge

Identify existing necessary experience and expertise. Draw knowledge areas based on reference models

Experts — Validate the proposed knowledge model

QA Manager, Food Safety Manager and Environment Manager — Evaluate the knowledge of individuals and identify experts in each area

Information Systems Manager — Draw knowledge map

Information Systems Manager — Codify & make it accessible

Perform audits, check whether maps are based on main processes and have a clear perspective and whether process owners and knowledge creators for creating, codification and dissemination are considered.

Information Systems Manager — Update knowledge base

End

SP 009 Resource Management

ABC Company Limited	Procedures Manual	Reference SP 009 Page 1 of 4	
	Resource Management	Date Released dd/mm/yyyy	Date Reviewed dd/mm/yyyy
Support Processes	Approved:	Issue No: 01 Prepared by:	Revision No: 00

Process Owner		Plant Manager
	Process Headings	**Process Details**
1.0	Purpose	To describe the procedure for the provision of resources for the establishment, implementation, maintenance and continual improvement of our IQFSE management system.
2.0	Scope	This procedure applies to the products, services and the management system of ABCCL.
3.0	Input	Quality objectives and plans, sales forecasts, production plan, process, product, management system changes, regulatory changes, and new product development.
4.0	Output	Acquired resources, meeting customer needs and regulatory changes and effective performance.
5.0	Competency requirements	Resource management skills, knowledge of particular resources and the ability to identify the impact of changes on resource requirements.
6.0	Responsibility	Defined in Flowchart SP 009.1. Additional responsibilities are: Financial Manager shall: • Monitor the utilisation of funds • Obtain necessary funds to finance the resources.
7.0	Associated documents	Request for resources (Form 110) IT resources, usage, security (SP 021) Purchasing (CP 004) Request for financial resources.
8.0	Resources	Enterprise resource planning module.
9.0	Measures/Controls	Product: Qualification, validation and verification Process: Process controls, as appropriate Equipment: equipment breakdown log, downtime, productivity Human resources (HR): performance review.
10.0	System description	Flowchart SP 009.1 shows the procedure for managing the resources.
10.1	Types of resources	Resources can include, but is not limited to: • Natural resources • Tangible resources, e.g. physical resources such as measuring and monitoring devices • Intangible resources, e.g. intellectual property • Future resources for continual improvement

ABC Company Limited	**Procedures Manual**	**Reference SP 009** Page 2 of 4	
	Resource Management	Date Released dd/mm/yyyy	Date Reviewed dd/mm/yyyy
Support Process	Approved:	Issue No: 01 Prepared by:	Revision No: 00

	Process Headings	**Process Details**
		• Organisational resources • IT resources • HR • Financial resources.
10.2	Identification of resource needs	1. Department Managers shall consider the following when identifying resource needs: • Quality objectives • Quality plans • Sales forecasts • Production plans • Process, product, management system changes • Customer needs • What needs to be obtained from external providers • Regulatory changes • New product development activities • Future resource requirements • Current business opportunities and constraints. Department Managers shall also determine the HR needs for the effective operation of the IQFSE management system and its processes. 2. Department Managers shall identify physical, human and financial resources needed to maintain a high level of performance, continually improve the effectiveness of the management system and enhance customer satisfaction by meeting organisation's objectives. Quality, current resources and their constraints, food safety, environment friendly and delivery requirements are important considerations when selecting resources. 3. QA Manager in consultation with the Engineering Manager and the Laboratory Manager shall identify specific monitoring and measuring devices needed to control the operations. 4. Plant Manager shall review all requests for physical resources. HR Manager shall review all requests for HR. If the request is rejected the Plant Manager/HR Manager shall propose alternative plans.

ABC Company Limited	Procedures Manual	Reference SP 009 Page 3 of 4	
	Resource Management	Date Released dd/mm/yyyy	Date Reviewed dd/mm/yyyy
Support Process	Approved:	Issue No: 01 Prepared by:	Revision No: 00

	Process Headings	Process Details
10.3	Acquisition of resources	Physical resources are acquired through the purchasing process (CP 004). HR are acquired through HR activities (SP 011). Financial resources are obtained through funding sources.
10.4	Maintenance of resources	Maintenance of resources includes the maintenance of sufficient inventory levels, equipment in good condition, skills levels, and competency of staff and facilities of the organisation.
10.5	Deployment of resources	The deployment process involves the mobilisation and preparation of resources for use. Resources such as equipment are considered deployed only when they are installed, commissioned and ready for use. With HR, the Department Manager shall ensure that they are in a position ready to assume duties, i.e. deemed competent and skilled to take up a position under supervision.
10.6	Disposal of resources	Plant Manager shall have plans for the disposal of physical resources after their use, bearing in mind the environmental impact. Plant Manager shall also develop succession planning in case of retirement or loss of personnel.
10.7	Types of changes that affect the provision of resources	• Unplanned changes due to staff leaving or death, equipment obsolescence, major breakdowns, fuel shortage, man-made or natural disasters • An increase in demand • Change in organisational objectives due to new targets, new products or processes • Change imposed by external environment such as regulatory changes, changes in standards, markets and/or customer expectations.
10.8	Classification of resource costs	1. Maintenance costs include the costs of maintaining inventory levels, equipment, people, facilities, etc.

ABC Company Limited	Procedures Manual	Reference SP 009 Page 4 of 4	
	Resource Management	Date Released dd/mm/yyyy	Date Reviewed dd/mm/yyyy
Support Process	Approved:	Issue No: 01 Prepared by:	Revision No: 00

	Process Headings	Process Details
		2. Improvement costs include costs associated with change.
10.9	Managing financial resources	1. Funds can be acquired by cutting costs, eliminating waste, down-sizing, selling surplus equipment, stock and shares and bank loans. 2. Develop financial budget for setting up processes and operating and maintaining them. 3. Establish financial controls. 4. Develop revenue collection mechanisms and invoicing, and debt collection processes. 5. Set up cost accounting mechanisms. 6. Monitor and measure the acquisition and utilisation of financial resources against the budget. 7. Manage surplus resources and recover the cost of surplus or waste physical resources as is practicable. 8. Continually improve the acquisition and utilisation of financial resources.
11.0	Records	Budget proposals Requests for resources.
12.0	Changes made	None.

ABC Company Limited	Procedures Manual	Flowchart SP 009.1 Page 1 of 1	
	Resource Management	Date Released dd/mm/yyyy	Date Reviewed dd/mm/yyyy
Link SP 009	Approved:	Issue No: 01 Prepared by:	Revision No: 00

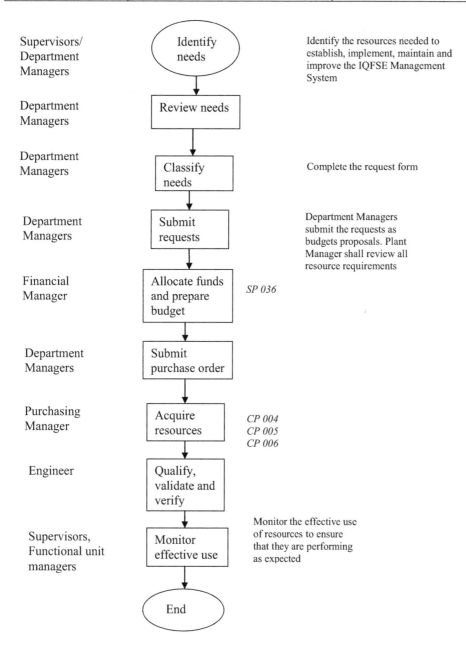

Supervisors/ Department Managers — Identify needs — Identify the resources needed to establish, implement, maintain and improve the IQFSE Management System

Department Managers — Review needs

Department Managers — Classify needs — Complete the request form

Department Managers — Submit requests — Department Managers submit the requests as budgets proposals. Plant Manager shall review all resource requirements

Financial Manager — Allocate funds and prepare budget — SP 036

Department Managers — Submit purchase order

Purchasing Manager — Acquire resources — CP 004 CP 005 CP 006

Engineer — Qualify, validate and verify

Supervisors, Functional unit managers — Monitor effective use — Monitor the effective use of resources to ensure that they are performing as expected

End

SP 010 Managing the Infrastructure and Work Environment

ABC Company Limited	Procedures Manual	Reference SP 010 Page 1 of 6	
	Managing the Infrastructure and Work Environment	Date Released dd/mm/yyyy	Date Reviewed dd/mm/yyyy
Support Process	Approved:	Issue No: 01 Prepared by:	Revision No: 00

Process Owner	Plant Manager
Process Headings	**Process Details**
1.0 Purpose	To describe the procedure for the provision and maintenance of building, suitable facilities, infrastructure and work environment to ensure product compliance, customer satisfaction and staff wellbeing.
2.0 Scope	This procedure applies to the provision, planning and maintenance of employee facilities, workplaces, equipment, buildings, software and services in our organisation.
3.0 Input	IQFSE management system processes, staff health and safety requirements, staff welfare requirements and sales, marketing and production plans.
4.0 Output	Acquired infrastructure, meeting customer needs and regulatory changes and effective performance.
5.0 Competency requirements	Knowledge of various facilities, human resource (HR) requirements, and building, equipment, and facilities and maintenance skills.
6.0 Responsibility	Facilities Managers shall: • Maintain a maintenance schedule • Carry out maintenance activities • Carry out expansion activities • Ensure skilled, competent staff are available for work • Arrange for external service providers, if necessary • Monitor the maintenance and expansion work carried out by the staff or contractors to ensure they are effective • Ensure that the facility is kept in a clean condition to avoid pest infestation • Manage the pest management programme • Manage the disposal of waste and obsolete equipment • Obtain necessary permission or licence for any work, if necessary • Communicate with external regulatory agencies.

ABC Company Limited	**Procedures Manual**		**Reference SP 010** Page 2 of 6	
	Managing the Infrastructure and Work Environment		Date Released dd/mm/yyyy	Date Reviewed dd/mm/yyyy
Support Process	Approved:		Issue No: 01 Prepared by:	Revision No: 00

	Process Headings	**Process Details**
		HR Manager shall: • Ensure the provision of a suitable work environment for the staff • Monitor the working conditions and address any issues • Coordinate with the Facilities Manager for any maintenance or expansion work • Monitor the health and wellbeing of the staff through appropriate health checks such as hearing tests, X-rays, blood tests, etc. Engineering Manager shall: • Identify the equipment for maintenance • Keep a schedule of preventive maintenance • Ensure preventive maintenance is carried out as scheduled • Ensure that the staff are skilled and competent to carry out maintenance work. Logistics Manager shall: • Maintain a schedule of inspection and maintenance of transport vehicles and equipment installed in them • Arrange for the warrant of fitness for each vehicle as scheduled. Supervisors shall: • Identify the need and requirements for new (or modification of existing) facilities in the organisation • Monitor the work environment to maintain the safety and wellbeing of the staff.
7.0	Associated documents	Maintenance schedule Record of maintenance work Pest management record Waste disposal records Regulatory requirements IQFSE management system Facility plans.
8.0	Resources	Engineering tools for maintenance Monitoring and measuring devices.
9.0	Measures/Controls	Machine breakdown log Health issues due to unsafe and unsatisfactory work environment

ABC Company Limited	Procedures Manual	Reference SP 010 Page 3 of 6	
	Managing the Infrastructure and Work Environment	Date Released dd/mm/yyyy	Date Reviewed dd/mm/yyyy
Support Process	Approved:	Issue No: 01 Prepared by:	Revision No: 00

	Process Headings	**Process Details**
		IT service log.
10.0	Definitions	**Infrastructure:** System of facilities, building, equipment and services necessary for the operations at ABCCL. **Work environment:** Set of conditions under which work is performed by the staff. **Quality characteristics:** Inherent characteristics of a product, process or system.
11.0	System description	Facilities described in this document include, but are not limited to, buildings, the workplace and associated facilities, equipment, software and hardware, transport and support services such as telephone, internet, etc.
11.1	Identification of infrastructure	Infrastructure needed for the business is identified and acquired as and when the need arises. Since there is a wide range of infrastructure needed it is not possible to present a comprehensive list. Although the following list is not extensive, it defines the personnel responsible for the identification of major infrastructure items. Major projects and business development: General Manager Production-related activities: Plant Manager Equipment and machinery for production: Engineering Manager Communication and technology, hardware and software: Manager Information Systems Storage, distribution, transport and logistics: Logistics Manager HR activities: HR Manager. These requirements shall be included in the budget proposals for approval.
11.2	Provision of infrastructure	The provision of infrastructure includes acquisition, deployment and disposal. 1. Acquisition: Infrastructure is generally acquired through the purchasing process (CP 004). Special provision has been made for purchasing engineering items (CP 005) and IT resources (CP 006). For major capital works, such as new facilities to provide additional capacity, a complete project proposal shall be submitted to the CEO.

ABC Company Limited	Procedures Manual	Reference SP 010 Page 4 of 6	
	Managing the Infrastructure and Work Environment	Date Released dd/mm/yyyy	Date Reviewed dd/mm/yyyy
Support Process	Approved:	Issue No: 01 Prepared by:	Revision No: 00

	Process Headings	Process Details
11.2.1	Deployment	Once assets are deployed to the unit, the user is responsible for their safe operation and maintenance.
11.2.2	Maintenance	1. Maintenance of buildings Facilities Manager shall identify the work necessary to repair and/or maintain buildings and other facilities. This shall be achieved by regular inspection. Repairs of buildings and other facilities may be contracted out, if necessary. Facilities Manager shall coordinate the work and inspect it after completion to ensure that the work carried out has been satisfactory. 2. Maintenance of equipment See SP 003 Maintenance management. 3. Support facilities maintenance Support facilities maintenance includes regular scheduled maintenance of: • Production environment • Lighting system • Air conditioning and ventilation equipment • Heating system • Landscaping • Cleaning • Pest management. 4. Maintenance of IT resources Manager Information Systems shall carry out audits to maintain the resources in good condition (SP 029).
11.2.4	Disposal of infrastructure	Proposal to dispose of any fixed asset shall be submitted to the General Manager with justification. To maintain production and delivery of services, the user may submit a proposal for disposal and replacement after its expected lifespan. 1. Waste disposal Facilities Managers shall appoint a waste disposal contractor and ensure that the work is carried out regularly according to the contract. Glass and plastics and cardboard shall be recycled and the Facilities Manager shall appoint an agent(s) for this work. Agent's receipt shall be kept as evidence of recycling effort.

ABC Company Limited	Procedures Manual		Reference SP 010 Page 5 of 6	
	Managing the Infrastructure and Work Environment	Date Released dd/mm/yyyy		Date Reviewed dd/mm/yyyy
Support Process	Approved:	Issue No: 01 Prepared by:		Revision No: 00

	Process Headings	Process Details
		2. Pest management programme Facilities Manager shall contract out the pest management programme, ensure that the work is carried out as scheduled and it has been effective. During inspection of buildings and facilities, Facilities Manager shall ensure that all possible pest entry points and locations are sealed. New locations or possible entry points not in the schedule shall be brought to the attention of the contractor.
11.2.5	Managing the work environment	1. Physical factors HR Manager in consultation with the Occupational Health and Safety representative shall define safe limits for exposure to extreme temperature variation, excessive noise, corrosive chemicals, etc. Mitigation measures include limiting exposure time, increasing the frequency of breaks, appropriate personnel protective equipment, automating processes, etc. Occupational Health and Safety representative shall monitor environmental factors in all operational areas including the warehouse such as: Safety and ergonomics • Light • Noise • Cleaning/hygiene • Heat and humidity • Working space. 2. Human factors (a) Motivation: Creation of a good work environment through promoting and encouraging employee participation, creativity and soliciting ideas from employees; (b) Development opportunities: Encouraging participation in education programmes and development programmes. ABCCL encourages professional development and has a policy to send selected employees to fully paid short courses and seminars;

ABC Company Limited	Procedures Manual	Reference SP 010 Page 6 of 6	
	Managing the Infrastructure and Work Environment	Date Released dd/mm/yyyy	Date Reviewed dd/mm/yyyy
Support Process	Approved:	Issue No: 01 Prepared by:	Revision No: 00

	Process Headings	Process Details
		(c) All employees have HR support to help overcome any HR issues;
		(d) ABCCL provides opportunities for developing multi-skills;
		(e) Safety rules and guidance: All employees are provided with a safety manual, which includes the use of protective equipment and facilities; and
		(f) Employee and policy manual: All employees are provided with an employee and policy manual, which outlines expectations about relationship with co-workers, supervisors and customers, inter-cultural issues, disciplinary measures, etc.
11.3	Review	Facilities Manager shall review and report about the infrastructure and facilities to the management review meeting for continual compliance to operational needs with required corrective and preventive actions.
12.0	Records	Maintenance reports Audit reports.
13.0	Changes made	None.

SP 011 Planning for Human Resources

ABC Company Limited	Procedures Manual		Reference SP 011 Page 1 of 1	
	Planning for Human Resources	Date Released dd/mm/yyyy		Date Reviewed dd/mm/yyyy
Support Process	Approved:	Issue No: 01 Prepared by:		Revision No: 00

Process Owner		Human Resources (HR) Manager
	Process Headings	**Process Details**
1.0	Purpose	To describe the procedure for planning for HR.
2.0	Scope	This procedure applies to all the departments of ABCCL when planning for HR in their departments.
3.0	Input	Current HR inventory, external HR sources, promotions, transfers, staff losses due to retirement or death, job enrichment and multi-skills.
4.0	Output	No staff shortages, no overstaffing, skilled staff, effective operations and staff satisfaction.
5.0	Competency requirements	Human resource skills in managing HR activities.
6.0	Responsibility	Department Managers shall: • Identify the HR needs for the operations under his or her control • Assess current and future needs • Determine the type of training required. HR Manager shall: • Provide guidance to identify needs • Plan recruitment and development • Source external training providers • Maintain records relating to HR. Supervisors shall: • Identify special HR needs for individual staff.
7.0	Associated documents	Resource requisition (Form 110) Regulatory requirements Individual HR procedures.
8.0	Resources	Budget provision.
9.0	Measures/Controls	Downtime due to staff unavailability Employee turnover Staff complaints Number of problems due to staff incompetence.
10.0	System description	The planning for HR process is shown in Flowchart SP 011.1.
11.0	Records	Described under individual procedures.
12.0	Changes made	None.

ABC Company Limited	Procedures Manual	Flowchart SP 011.1 Page 1 of 1	
	Planning for Human Resources	Date Released dd/mm/yyyy	Date Reviewed dd/mm/yyyy
Link SP 011	Approved:	Issue No: 01 Prepared by:	Revision No: 00

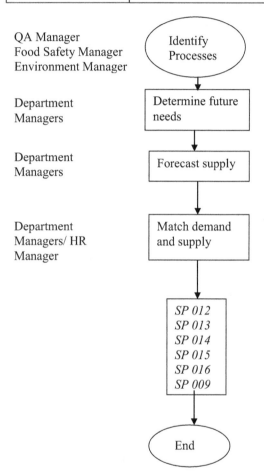

QA Manager
Food Safety Manager
Environment Manager

Department
Managers

Department
Managers

Department
Managers/ HR
Manager

Identify the processes needed to establish, implement, maintain and improve the IQFSE Management System

Determine the future HR needs in terms of quality, quantity using organisation's plans and procedures

Determine the future sources of HR likely to be available from within and outside the organisation. Consider promotions, transfers, job enrichment, multi-skills internally and the recruitment of new candidates who are capable of fulfilling the roles.

Assess supply and demand to resolve staff shortages and overstaffing. This step provides knowledge about requirements and sources of HR

SP 012　Recruitment

ABC Company Limited	Procedures Manual	Reference SP 012 Page 1 of 2	
	Recruitment	Date Released dd/mm/yyyy	Date Reviewed dd/mm/yyyy
Support Process	Approved:	Issue No: 01 Prepared by:	Revision No: 00

Process Owner	Human Resource (HR) Manager
Process Headings	**Process Details**
1.0　Purpose	To describe the procedure for recruiting staff for ABCCL.
2.0　Scope	This procedure shall apply to all grades of staff.
3.0　Input	Job requirements, job description, advertisement for hiring, and budget allocation.
4.0　Output	Hired employee and fulfilment of job requirements.
5.0　Competency requirements	Understanding of job requirements, HR skills of hiring procedure and competence evaluation skills.
6.0　Responsibility	Defined in Flowchart SP 012.1. Additional responsibilities are: • Prepare the letter of appointment or the contract. Financial Manager shall • Allocate financial resources for the position.
7.0　Associated documents	Request form Advertisement Job description.
8.0　Resources	Psychometric test.
9.0　Measures/controls	Interview, reference checks and psychometric tests.
10.0　System description	Flowchart SP 012.1 shows the recruitment process.
10.1　Pre-requirement	1. The Department Manager shall send the request for recruitment to the HR Manager and it shall include the job description, necessary qualifications for the position and the advertisement. If the position is new, the HR manager and the Department Manager carry out the job evaluation. 2. The first offer is made to internal employees who fit the job requirements and the job description. If internal candidates are not available the procedure in 10.2 shall be followed.
10.2　Shortlisting candidates	All applications are received by the HR Manager. HR personnel shall review the applications and reject those that do not comply with stated job specifications. The Department Manager shall then receive all qualified applications. The Department Manager shall shortlist three or four applicants on the basis of requirements. Applicants who were not successful shall be informed accordingly.

ABC Company Limited	Procedures Manual		Reference SP 012 Page 2 of 2	
	Recruitment	Date Released dd/mm/yyyy		Date Reviewed dd/mm/yyyy
Support Process	Approved:	Issue No: 01 Prepared by:		Revision No: 00

	Process Headings	Process Details
10.3	Interview	The HR Manager shall summon the shortlisted candidates for the interview and form the interview panel. One of the interview panel members shall be the Supervisor to whom the candidate will report, if selected. The interview may be conducted by the entire panel or individually on a one-to-one basis with each member of the panel. Notes of the interview shall be recorded.
10.4	Psychometric tests and numeric tests	Each selected candidate shall be subjected to a psychometric test approved by the HR Manager. All floor staff shall be subjected to a numeric test.
10.5	Reference checks and other checks	Referees nominated by the candidates shall be contacted either verbally or in writing. If the check is carried out verbally, the responses shall be recorded on the interview form. If qualification checks are necessary, the HR Manager shall contact the relevant authorities for confirmation.
10.6	Selection	Final selections shall be carried out by the entire panel. Selection package consisting of the letter of appointment or the contract, the company handbook and other relevant information shall be prepared by HR personnel. The Department Manager shall check the details in the package and arrange for delivery.
10.7	Confirmation	If the selected candidate refuses the offer, the position shall be offered to the next candidate selected by the panel.
10.8	Recruitment by agency	If the company decides to nominate a recruitment agency, the procedure shown in Flowchart SP 012.1 shall be followed.
11.0	Records	Job requirement, job description, list of candidates, interviewed candidates, notes of the interview, reference checks, letter of offer and confirmation of acceptance.
12.0	Changes made	None.

ABC Company Limited	Procedures Manual	Flowchart SP 012.1 Page 1 of 2	
	Recruitment	Date Released dd/mm/yyyy	Date Reviewed dd/mm/yyyy
Link SP 012	Approved:	Issue No: 01 Prepared by:	Revision No: 00

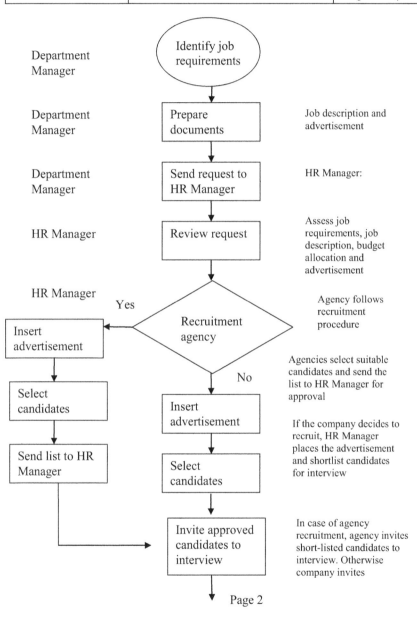

Department Manager — Identify job requirements

Department Manager — Prepare documents — Job description and advertisement

Department Manager — Send request to HR Manager — HR Manager:

HR Manager — Review request — Assess job requirements, job description, budget allocation and advertisement

HR Manager — Recruitment agency — Agency follows recruitment procedure

Yes — Insert advertisement

Agencies select suitable candidates and send the list to HR Manager for approval

No — Insert advertisement

Select candidates

Send list to HR Manager

If the company decides to recruit, HR Manager places the advertisement and shortlist candidates for interview

Select candidates

Invite approved candidates to interview

In case of agency recruitment, agency invites short-listed candidates to interview. Otherwise company invites

Page 2

ABC Company Limited	Procedures Manual	Flowchart SP 012.1 Page 2 of 2	
	Recruitment	Date Released dd/mm/yyyy	Date Reviewed dd/mm/yyyy
Link SP 012	Approved:	Issue No: 01 Prepared by:	Revision No: 00

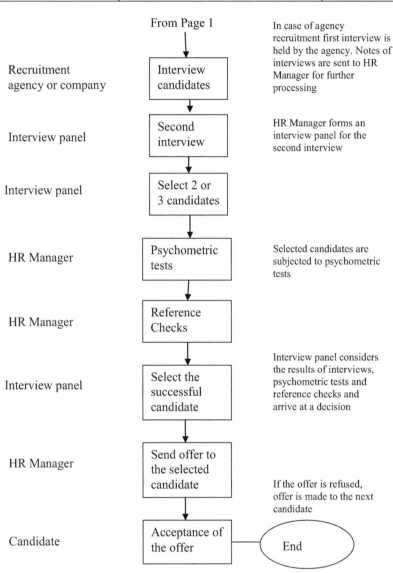

From Page 1

Recruitment agency or company	Interview candidates	In case of agency recruitment first interview is held by the agency. Notes of interviews are sent to HR Manager for further processing
Interview panel	Second interview	HR Manager forms an interview panel for the second interview
Interview panel	Select 2 or 3 candidates	
HR Manager	Psychometric tests	Selected candidates are subjected to psychometric tests
HR Manager	Reference Checks	
Interview panel	Select the successful candidate	Interview panel considers the results of interviews, psychometric tests and reference checks and arrive at a decision
HR Manager	Send offer to the selected candidate	If the offer is refused, offer is made to the next candidate
Candidate	Acceptance of the offer	End

SP 013 Induction

ABC Company Limited	Procedures Manual	Reference SP 013 Page 1 of 3	
	Induction	Date Released dd/mm/yyyy	Date Reviewed dd/mm/yyyy
Support Processes	Approved:	Issue No: 01 Prepared by:	Revision No: 00

Process Owner		Department Manager
	Process Headings	**Process Details**
1.0	Purpose	To describe the procedure for inducting new employees.
2.0	Scope	This procedure shall apply to all new staff.
3.0	Input	New employee, job description, current competence, and IQFSE management system.
4.0	Output	Inducted employee, understanding of job requirements, updated skills and knowledge of IQFSE management system.
5.0	Competency requirements	Knowledge of IQFSE management system and human resource (HR) skills.
6.0	Responsibility	HR Manager shall: • Arrange induction programme and inform the Department Manager • Ensure the availability of Line Supervisors to welcome the new staff member. Department Manager shall: • Appoint a mentor • Introduce the new staff member to the staff.
7.0	Associated documents	Induction pack.
8.0	Resources	Induction pack and checklist.
9.0	Measures/Controls	Completion of the induction programme.
10.0	System description	
10.1	Documentation, training and preparation	1. The HR department shall inform the Line Supervisor and the Department Manager about the induction of the new staff member. 2. The Line Supervisor or the head of department shall confirm the start date, time and the name of the individual who will be meeting the new member of staff on the first day. 3. HR department shall provide a map of the site indicating where and to whom he or she should report.

ABC Company Limited	Procedures Manual		Reference SP 013 Page 2 of 3	
	Induction		Date Released dd/mm/yyyy	Date Reviewed dd/mm/yyyy
Support Processes	Approved:		Issue No: 01 Prepared by:	Revision No: 00

	Process Headings	Process Details
10.2	Preparation of the induction pack	The Line Supervisor shall prepare the induction pack which shall include: • Welcome letter • Organisation chart • Induction programme • Staff diversity programme • Health and safety information • Key contact details • Employee's contact details • Job requirements • Overview of the IQFSE management system including objectives and policies • Pay arrangements • Professional development • Staff welfare programme. Some of the information may be included in the company handbook.
10.3	Induction mentoring	1. The Line Supervisor or the Head of Department shall nominate a mentor/buddy to the new staff member to provide support during the first week. The mentor or the buddy should be someone who is familiar with the working role and the department and should be someone other than the Line Supervisor. 2. The mentor shall help the new staff member understand the working of the new department policies and procedures and support centres.
10.4	Welcome activities	• Ensure the availability of relevant staff to greet the new member and show him or her the working location • Line Supervisor shall go through the information in the induction pack and information guide to ensure that the activities listed for the first day on the induction programme are complete and understood • Demonstrate company web pages and all new information that the new member needs before he or she starts on the first day and during the first few months of employment. The web pages have been constructed to assist new staff to navigate around the company website and obtain relevant information they require quickly and easily • Confirm the major tasks of the job including main activities, responsibilities, working hours and the probation period • Complete the safety induction checklist • Introduce the mentor or the buddy • Take the new member on a tour of the workplace • Set up the computer station and an email account • Introduce the member to the colleagues and workmates.

ABC Company Limited	Procedures Manual	Reference SP 013 Page 3 of 3	
	Induction	Date Released dd/mm/yyyy	Date Reviewed dd/mm/yyyy
Support Processes	Approved:	Issue No: 01 Prepared by:	Revision No: 00

	Process Headings	Process Details
11.0	Records	The Line Supervisor shall record the details of the induction activity in the employee's personal file.
12.0	Changes made	None.

SP 014 Training and Development

ABC Company Limited	Procedures Manual	Reference SP 014 Page 1 of 5	
	Training and Development	Date Released dd/mm/yyyy	Date Reviewed dd/mm/yyyy
Support Process	Approved:	Issue No: 01 Prepared by:	Revision No: 00

Process Owner		**Human Resource (HR) Manager**
	Process Headings	**Process Details**
1.0	Purpose	To identify and provide employees' training needs in quality, food safety of our products and services and environmental aspects relating to our products.
2.0	Scope	This procedure shall apply to all ABCCL employees.
3.0	Input	Procedures, standard operating procedures (SOPs), job descriptions, promotion opportunities, future needs and training resources.
4.0	Output	Skilled and competent employees, job satisfaction, knowledge of policies and plans, and development opportunities.
5.0	Competency requirements	Training and development skills, training evaluation skills and knowledge of roles and responsibilities within the organisation.
6.0	Responsibility	HR Manager shall: • Hire new employees • Organise training and development programmes • Keep records of training and development activities • Evaluate the effectiveness of training. Department Manager or Supervisor shall: • Approve or refuse applications for training and development • Recommend training and development programmes that would benefit employees and improve their performance • Identify the training needs and establish core and specific training requirements • Conduct on-the-job training.
7.0	Associated documents	Company handbook Training needs analysis (Form 111) Training plan (Form 112) Training topics (Form 113) Skill chart (for shop floor staff) (Form 114).
8.0	Resources	Training provider Resources for delivery of training.
9.0	Measures/Controls	Training evaluation Application of learning to the job.

ABC Company Limited	Procedures Manual	Reference SP 014 Page 2 of 5	
	Training and Development	Date Released dd/mm/yyyy	Date Reviewed dd/mm/yyyy
Support Process	Approved:	Issue No: 01 Prepared by:	Revision No: 00

	Process Headings	Process Details
10.0	Definitions	**Training:** Includes all types of training such as on-the-job experience, background education, programmed training, etc. **Awareness:** Refers to awareness of environmental aspects and environmental management system, food safety hazards, hygiene requirements. **Competence:** Competencies are defined by the education, experience and training requirements for each job.
11.0	System description	Flowchart SP 014.1 shows the training process.
11.1	New employee selection	The HR Manager shall follow the recruitment procedure to appoint personnel competent for the job.
11.2	Training needs	1. The Department Manager shall establish the competencies for the jobs in his or her area. The training needs for the roles are defined in terms of educational qualifications, skills and experience. They are reflected in the respective job descriptions. 2. Department Managers shall take an inventory of existing resources and identify competency gaps. 3. Training needs also include training that is related to environmental management, food safety hazards, the effects of environmental management on each area and role, and the potential consequences of departure from established procedures.
11.3	Training plan	HR department in consultation with quality, environment and food safety management representatives shall develop and maintain a training plan in accordance with the company education policy.
11.4	Training and development options	1. Types of training include: (a) job-specific training and development; (b) career development training; and (c) educational development courses offered by recognised institutions. 2. HR function shall periodically review training logs to ensure that all ABCCL employees are receiving the necessary training on a timely basis and to evaluate the training programmes to ensure that they meet business, regulatory and customer requirements.

ABC Company Limited	Procedures Manual	Reference SP 014 Page 3 of 5	
	Training and Development	Date Released dd/mm/yyyy	Date Reviewed dd/mm/yyyy
Support Process	Approved:	Issue No: 01 Prepared by:	Revision No: 00

	Process Headings	Process Details
11.5	Financial provision	Each department shall apply for funds for training and development of their staff from the HR department. Financial requirements for training and development of each department shall be included in the annual HR budget. HR function shall ensure the transparency of the approval process and the distribution of funds.
11.6	HR capacity	The Department Manager shall ensure that operational activities are not interrupted while employees are involved in training activities.
11.7	In-house training	• Peer and support coaching on particular job-related skills • Mentoring with an internal or external mentor on job and career-related skills and abilities • Job rotation to gain multi-skills • Training methods can be classroom training, on-line training, video training and in-house conferences and seminars.
11.8	Training approval process	1. The Department Manager shall consider (a) the number of training days an employee may take within the company policy on educational leave and (b) the positions that must be covered during regular business hours. 2. Employee originated training and development: The employee shall provide all the details of training and development programme, and justification for his or her application to attend. 3. Organisation directed: The Department Manager provides all the information about the training programme that the company has organised. In both instances, the Department Manager shall make arrangements for work while employee is away on training.
11.9	Off-base training	If training is conducted away from the ABCCL premises the Department Manager shall make necessary arrangements. Training certificates or other evidence of training are retained by the employee and a copy submitted to the HR function to update the training log.

ABC Company Limited	Procedures Manual	Reference SP 014 Page 4 of 5	
	Training and Development	Date Released dd/mm/yyyy	Date Reviewed dd/mm/yyyy
Support Process	Approved:	Issue No: 01 Prepared by:	Revision No: 00

	Process Headings	Process Details
11.10	Special training needs	1. When special or other formal training needs are identified, the Department Manager determines whether expertise is available in-house. If no in-house expertise is available, the Department Manager shall make arrangements to outsource the training. 2. If in-house expertise is available, the person is notified of the training arrangements and his or her agreement is obtained.
11.11	Awareness	1. Awareness needs Department Managers provide orientation training to all employees. The employees are made aware of (a) the importance of conforming to the quality, food safety and environment policy and ABCCL's objectives derived to meet the policy; (b) control methods derived to reduce the importance of the significant environmental aspects, food safety hazards and quality problems; (c) potential emergency situations, consequences of departure from SOPs; and (d) environmental impacts and food safety hazards associated with their work and how corrective action(s) can be taken. 2. Provision This is achieved through courses that offer a variety of quality-related information including techniques established for performing verification, validation and preparing reports. Refresher courses are also offered to reinforce quality awareness, knowledge of quality policy, objectives and procedures that contribute to the achievement of conformity to product and service requirements.
11.12	Evaluation of training	Effectiveness of competence can be evaluated using any one or more of the following depending on the type of training: 1. Observation: The performance of the task is observed by the trainer. 2. Inspection: Inspection of a person's work or product over a specified period. 3. Tests and examinations: These are used to ensure competence, especially when the competence is linked to knowledge and facts. 4. Review of training effectiveness evaluation: ABCCL shall consider the cost and time involved in collecting the data, the source of data and its accuracy, and the accuracy required by the organisation. 5. The needs may be assessed annually or as and when required. It may be necessary to review the requirements in response to future needs, competition, regulatory changes, company policy changes, and external or internal environment changes.

ABC Company Limited	Procedures Manual	Reference SP 014 Page 5 of 5	
	Training and Development	Date Released dd/mm/yyyy	Date Reviewed dd/mm/yyyy
Support Process	Approved:	Issue No: 01 Prepared by:	Revision No: 00

	Process Headings	Process Details
12.0	Records	Training records.
13.0	Changes made	None.

ABC Company Limited	Procedures Manual	Flowchart SP 014.1 Page 1 of 1	
	Training and Development	Date Released dd/mm/yyyy	Date Reviewed dd/mm/yyyy
Link SP 014	Approved:	Issue No: 01 Prepared by:	Revision No: 00

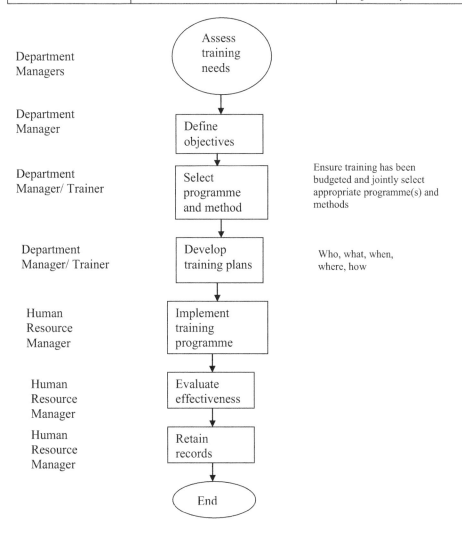

Department Managers — Assess training needs

Department Manager — Define objectives

Department Manager/ Trainer — Select programme and method — Ensure training has been budgeted and jointly select appropriate programme(s) and methods

Department Manager/ Trainer — Develop training plans — Who, what, when, where, how

Human Resource Manager — Implement training programme

Human Resource Manager — Evaluate effectiveness

Human Resource Manager — Retain records

End

SP 015 Leave

ABC Company Limited	Procedures Manual		Reference SP 015 Page 1 of 4	
	Leave	Date Released dd/mm/yyyy		Date Reviewed dd/mm/yyyy
Support Process	Approved:	Issue No: 01 Prepared by:		Revision No: 00

Process Owner		Department Manager
	Process Headings	**Process Details**
1.0	Purpose	To describe the procedure for granting leave.
2.0	Scope	This procedure shall apply to paid and unpaid leave, education leave, professional development leave, compassionate leave and emergency leave.
3.0	Input	Leave application, leave taken and leave available, employees' personal file.
4.0	Output	Leave approved or rejected.
5.0	Competency requirements	Human resource (HR) skills.
6.0	Responsibility	HR Manager shall: • Record all leave taken in personal files Department Manager shall: • Approve or refuse leave • Make arrangements for work during the absence of the employee on leave.
7.0	Associated documents	Company handbook Leave form.
8.0	Resources	HR module.
9.0	Measures/controls	Leave record.
10.0	System description	
10.1	Leave year	The leave year runs from 1 April to 31 March the following year.
10.2	Leave entitlement	**Salaried staff:** The amount of leave a person is entitled to is specified in the conditions of employment. Within the first year of employment, a salaried person is entitled to one-and-a-half days per calendar month. After one year, the entitlement increases to three weeks inclusive of statutory holidays. After 10 years of service, a salaried person is entitled to five weeks of annual leave. **Wages staff:** As defined by the contract.
10.3	Approval	All annual leave must have management approval before being taken. Requests for annual leave must be made using the leave form and given to the immediate Supervisor at the earliest opportunity. Employees are strongly advised not to make any arrangements until written approval has been received. Once approved, it will not be cancelled. However, in exceptional circumstances leave may be cancelled in consultation with the employee involved If the requested period of leave exceeds the normal entitlement, up to two weeks of extra leave may be granted on leave without pay.

ABC Company Limited	Procedures Manual		Reference SP 015 Page 2 of 4	
	Leave	Date Released dd/mm/yyyy	Date Reviewed dd/mm/yyyy	
Support Process	Approved:	Issue No: 01 Prepared by:	Revision No: 00	

	Process Headings	**Process Details**
10.4	Leave carry over	Leave may be carried over for one more year. Accumulated leave cannot be cashed in, except when the employment is terminated.
10.5	Sick leave	1. Employees who are ill during a period of annual leave are entitled to treat this as sick leave and count it against the employee's sick leave entitlement. The employee must provide evidence of illness. Days of annual leave lost through illness may be taken at a later date. 2. If an employee is unable to attend work, the employee or his or her representative shall inform the Line Supervisor on the first day and indicate the expected date of return. An employee who is ill for only three days need not submit a medical certificate on return. However, sick leave for more than three days shall always be supported by a medical certificate. An employee who exceeds the annual sick leave entitlement may be instructed to consult a medical practitioner nominated by the company.
10.6	Late return	An employee who is unable to return to work after the annual leave shall promptly contact the immediate Supervisor about the lateness. Failure to do so may result in disciplinary action for unauthorised absence.
10.7	Leave on termination	Any leave outstanding may be taken during the period prior to termination with the approval of the immediate Supervisor. There is also provision to cash in outstanding leave during termination.
10.8	Casual leave	One or two days of casual leave may be granted with the approval of the immediate Supervisor and the number of days taken will be counted against the annual leave entitlement.
10.9	Education leave	1. Employees may apply for up to 10 days of employee initiated paid education leave per financial year. This leave shall be approved by the immediate Supervisor and will only be considered if it is beneficial to the department and taken when it does not interrupt staffing needs. Benefits must be directly related to the employee's current position and the company. 2. Paid education leave cannot be carried forward or cashed in. Should the professional development opportunity requires more than 10 days, the employee will be required to use his or her annual leave or unpaid leave.

ABC Company Limited	Procedures Manual		Reference SP 015 Page 3 of 4	
	Leave	Date Released dd/mm/yyyy		Date Reviewed dd/mm/yyyy
Support Process	Approved:	Issue No: 01 Prepared by:		Revision No: 00

	Process Headings	Process Details
10.10	No pay leave	A leave of absence may be approved after one year of service at a rate in relation to years of continuous service in one job up. It can be for three months of absence per year of service. The employee will not be entitled to statutory holidays during the period of no pay leave.
10.11	Leave for professional development	1. Company directed: When a staff member is requested to attend a course, seminar or conference by a Supervisor, the company will meet all the expenses related to the professional development programme and, as far as practicable, it shall be taken during regular working hours. 2. Employee directed: An employee may apply to the Supervisor for permission to attend a job-related seminar, a short course, conference, etc. If leave is granted, it shall be with pay provided the Supervisor can justify that such training is appropriate and beneficial to current staff training priorities.
10.12	Compassionate/bereavement leave	Compassionate or bereavement leave up to five days is provided to all employees in case of a death in the family or in exceptional circumstances for other individuals. Compassionate leave may also be granted to visit a relative who is in the final stage of an illness. Compassionate or bereavement leave shall be considered on a case-by-case basis.
10.13	Jury or witness duty	1. Any regular full-time or regular part-time employee who is required to serve as a juror on a regular working day will be released to serve. The employee will be reimbursed by the company for the difference between the pay received for jury duty and the employee's regular salary for the same period of time. Evidence of attendance and the amount received shall be produced. 2. An employee who is required to serve as a witness in a non-work-related legal proceeding will be required to use paid leave or no pay leave. Any request for attendance shall be notified to the Supervisor immediately. On the days when an employee serves less than one full working day, they shall contact the Supervisor to determine whether he or she should return to work.

ABC Company Limited	Procedures Manual	Reference SP 015 Page 4 of 4	
	Leave	Date Released dd/mm/yyyy	Date Reviewed dd/mm/yyyy
Support Process	Approved:	Issue No: 01 Prepared by:	Revision No: 00

	Process Headings	Process Details
11.0	Records	Employee's leave record.
12.0	Changes made	None.

SP 016 Safety and Wellbeing

ABC Company Limited	Procedures Manual		Reference SP 016 Page 1 of 3	
	Safety and Wellbeing	Date Released dd/mm/yyyy		Date Reviewed dd/mm/yyyy
Support Process	Approved:	Issue No: 01 Prepared by:		Revision No: 00

Process Owner		Human Resource (HR) Manager
	Process Headings	**Process Details**
1.0	Purpose	To describe the procedure for managing the safety and wellbeing of our staff.
2.0	Scope	This procedure shall apply to all grades of staff.
3.0	Input	Job description and staff welfare programme.
4.0	Output	Regulatory compliance, dedicated employees and job satisfaction.
5.0	Competency requirements	HR skills.
6.0	Responsibility	HR Manager shall:

HR Manager shall:
- Ensure that bullying and harassment do not take place in the workplace
- Be aware of diversity issues, disclosed and undisclosed disabilities, and offer support
- Appoint a Health and Safety Advisor.

Health and Safety Advisor shall:
- Organise health and safety training programmes
- Communicate the health and safety policy to all employees
- Monitor the health and safety of employees
- Conduct regular health and safety meetings
- Conduct risk assessment with the Supervisor as and when needed
- Be a champion to implement health and safety procedures
- Offer professional support to an employee under stress.

Department Manager shall:
- Conduct a risk assessment in the area under his or her control and implement strategies to eliminate or minimise risks
- Ensure employees are fully trained to perform their duties in a safe manner
- Arrange programmes to educate the employees on health and safety
- Monitor workloads to ensure that employees are not overburdened
- Ensure that employees avail themselves of their leave entitlement
- Ensure that first aiders and first aid facilities are available during all working hours.

Employees shall:
- Minimise excessive pressures and demands by behaving responsibly, acting reasonably and reporting any concerns to the immediate Supervisor
- Implement the findings of any risk assessment in conjunction with the Supervisor
- Avoid bullying other employees. Always follow safe work practices.

ABC Company Limited	**Procedures Manual**	**Reference SP 016** Page 2 of 3	
	Safety and Wellbeing	Date Released dd/mm/yyyy	Date Reviewed dd/mm/yyyy
Support Process	Approved:	Issue No: 01 Prepared by:	Revision No: 00

	Process Headings	**Process Details**
7.0	Associated documents	Company handbook Health and safety records.
8.0	Resources	Health and safety programmes.
9.0	Measures/Controls	Workplace incidents External audit reports Ill health and sickness records.
10.0	System description	
10.1	Smoke-free environment	Communicate the smoke-free policy to all employees at induction. A smoking area shall be assigned away from the operational area. There shall be no smoking in all other areas. Smoking is only allowed during breaks and meal times. No smoking signage shall be displayed prominently in the facility. Smoking policy shall be communicated to all employees.
10.2	First aid	First aid support shall include the availability of qualified first aiders in each area, first aid kits and a first aid facility. Each area shall have a first aider available during all working hours. First aiders shall gain first aid qualifications from a recognised healthcare institution and update this as required at company expense. Health and Safety Advisor shall identify potential causes of workplace injury and illness and assess their risks. Health and Safety Advisor shall review first aid support to ensure its effectiveness.

ABC Company Limited	Procedures Manual	Reference SP 016 Page 3 of 3	
	Safety and Wellbeing	Date Released dd/mm/yyyy	Date Reviewed dd/mm/yyyy
Support Process	Approved:	Issue No: 01 Prepared by:	Revision No: 00

	Process Headings	Process Details
10.3	Health monitoring	1. Health and Safety Advisor shall monitor the health of workers who are at risk such as those handling chemicals, exposed to fumes and dust, exposed to high noise and those carrying out visual inspection, etc. 2. The tests may be carried out by a mobile unit fully equipped to carry out tests by qualified personnel. They may also be conducted at the nearest health centre. 3. Health and Safety Advisor shall analyse the information periodically to determine any trends to address any issues. 4. HR department shall maintain health records in individual's personal file.
10.4	Incident investigation	1. Serious injury causing fatality: Health and Safety Advisor shall immediately notify the CEO and regulatory authorities and appoint a health and safety investigator to conduct an investigation immediately. The site where the incident occurred shall not be disturbed. 2. Non-fatal serious injury: Health and Safety Advisor shall immediately notify the CEO and regulatory authorities and appoint a health and safety investigator to conduct an investigation immediately. 3. In both cases, the organisation may appoint an external specialist to conduct an investigation. Health and Safety Advisor shall inform appropriate authorities as required by law. 4. In all other cases, the Health and Safety Advisor shall communicate whether to conduct an investigation or not.
11.0	Records	Health and safety reports Investigation reports Employees' health records.
12.0	Changes made	None.

SP 017 Promotions and Transfers

ABC Company Limited	Procedures Manual	Reference SP 017 Page 1 of 2	
	Promotions and Transfers	Date Released dd/mm/yyyy	Date Reviewed dd/mm/yyyy
Support Process	Approved:	Issue No: 01 Prepared by:	Revision No: 00

Process Owner		Department Manager
	Process Headings	**Process Details**
1.0	Purpose	To describe the procedure for promoting and transferring employees in our organisation.
2.0	Scope	This procedure shall apply to all promotions and transfers in ABCCL.
3.0	Input	Organisation structure, requirement for promotion, position details and competence requirements.
4.0	Output	Job satisfaction and promoted and motivated employee.
5.0	Competency requirements	Knowledge of requirements for the position, evaluation of current skills and human resource (HR) skills.
6.0	Responsibility	Defined in Flowchart SP 017.1. Additional responsibilities are: • Department Manager shall: • Approve or reject the employee nominated by the Supervisor • Identify and make changes as necessary for the vacancy • Inform the HR department about the vacancy • Request the HR department to advertise the vacancy if it cannot be filled by a person within the department. HR department shall: • Advertise the vacancy if requested by the Department Manager • Prepare a memo about the promotion or transfer, indicating in it any changes in the employment contract. Supervisor shall: • Recommend an employee for the promotion or transfer • Discuss the new conditions of employment with the candidate who has been recommended.
7.0	Associated documents	Company handbook HR department memo Advertisement in Bulletin Board.
8.0	Resources	No new resources are required.

ABC Company Limited	Procedures Manual	Reference SP 017 Page 2 of 2	
	Promotions and Transfers	Date Released dd/mm/yyyy	Date Reviewed dd/mm/yyyy
Support Process	Approved:	Issue No: 01 Prepared by:	Revision No: 00

	Process Headings	Process Details
9.0	Measures/Controls	Number of employees promoted.
10.0	Definitions	**Promotion:** It is a movement of an employee from a position of lower grade to one of higher grade with different duties or increased responsibilities and possibly carrying a higher remuneration, higher status and offering better benefits. It represents an employee's movement up the organisational hierarchy. **Transfer:** Transfer is the movement of an employee from one job to another requiring approximately the same degree of duties and responsibilities without any changes in salary or wages. It gives the employee an opportunity to multi-skill.
11.0	System description	Flowchart SP 017.1 shows the promotions and transfer process.
12.0	Records	Advertisement Letter of appointment.
13.0	Changes made	None.

ABC Company Limited	Procedures Manual		Flowchart SP 017.1 Page 1 of 1	
	Promotions and Transfers		Date Released dd/mm/yyyy	Date Reviewed dd/mm/yyyy
Link SP 017	Approved:		Issue No: 01 Prepared by:	Revision No: 00

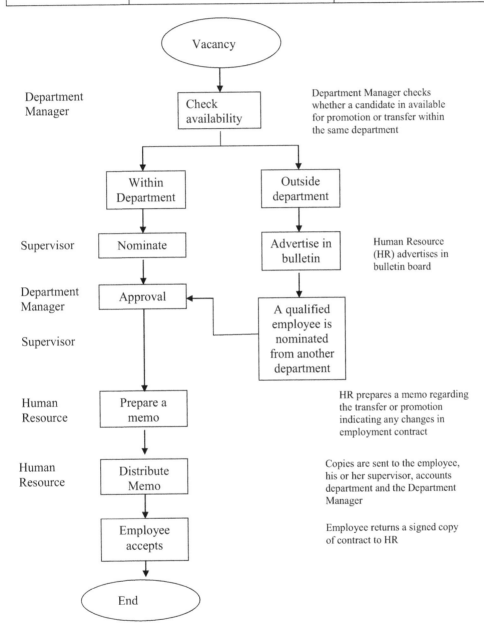

Department Manager — Check availability — Department Manager checks whether a candidate in available for promotion or transfer within the same department

Within Department / Outside department

Supervisor — Nominate / Advertise in bulletin — Human Resource (HR) advertises in bulletin board

Department Manager / Supervisor — Approval / A qualified employee is nominated from another department

Human Resource — Prepare a memo — HR prepares a memo regarding the transfer or promotion indicating any changes in employment contract

Human Resource — Distribute Memo — Copies are sent to the employee, his or her supervisor, accounts department and the Department Manager

Employee accepts — Employee returns a signed copy of contract to HR

End

SP 018 Disciplinary Procedure

ABC Company Limited	Procedures Manual	Reference SP 018 Page 1 of 4	
	Disciplinary Procedure	Date Released dd/mm/yyyy	Date Reviewed dd/mm/yyyy
Support Process	Approved:	Issue No: 01 Prepared by:	Revision No: 00

Process Owner	Human Resource (HR) Manager
Process Headings	**Process Details**

	Process Headings	Process Details
1.0	Purpose	To describe the progressive disciplinary procedure.
2.0	Scope	This procedure shall apply to minor violations of company rules or serious violations.
3.0	Input	Performance review, incident report, employee's personal file, legal requirements about employment, disciplinary procedure and company handbook.
4.0	Output	Disciplinary action.
5.0	Competency requirements	HR skills, knowledge of employment regulations, investigation skills and performance review skills.
6.0	Responsibility	Supervisor shall: Give the employee an opportunity to correct his or her behaviour or actions Give informal warning and written. warnings as appropriate HR department shall: • Initiate an investigation giving the employee every opportunity to respond to the allegation of violating company rules • Inform the employee that he or she can accompany a representative, if necessary • Issue the letter of termination, if necessary. Department Manager shall: • Be present at every stage of the investigation.
7.0	Associated documents	Company handbook Disciplinary action form (Form 115) Letter of termination (Form 116) Relevant employment contract.
8.0	Resources	Employment regulations.
9.0	Measures/Controls	Compliance with statutory and company requirements Number of challenges to disciplinary action.
10.0	System description	Flowchart SP 018.1 shows the disciplinary procedure.

ABC Company Limited	Procedures Manual	Reference SP 018 Page 2 of 4	
	Disciplinary Procedure	Date Released dd/mm/yyyy	Date Reviewed dd/mm/yyyy
Support Process	Approved:	Issue No: 01 Prepared by:	Revision No: 00

	Process Headings	**Process Details**
10.1	Degree of misconduct	1. Minor violations include, but are not limited to, infrequent lateness, carelessness, lack of effort, minor insensitive behaviour with colleagues, etc. 2. Serious violations include, but are not limited to, frequent absenteeism and lateness, dishonesty, refusal to carry our lawful instructions, unreasonable or unacceptable conduct, misuse of company resources, threatening behaviour, breach of company rules, driving under the influence of alcohol, accepting bribes, etc. 3. Gross misconduct includes, but is not limited to, theft, misappropriation of funds, damage to company property, falsifying records, working under the influence of alcohol or using drugs, sexual harassment, false claims of harassment or victimisation, violation of health and safety regulations, unauthorised access to company information, abuse of company resources, etc.
10.2	Informal procedure	Informal procedure is applied in case of minor violations. The Supervisor shall summon the employee and discuss the specific instances of violations. The employee shall be allowed to bring in a representative. The Supervisor gives the employee feedback about performance below expectation and communicates requirements and a reasonable timeframe to fix it. A record of the discussion shall be kept with the Supervisor.
10.3	Formal procedure	A formal procedure is executed when the employee has not shown any improvement as expected or the Supervisor considers that the breach of conduct that is believed to have occurred is too serious (serious violations or gross misconduct) to be dealt with informally.
10.4	Investigation	Before a disciplinary procedure can take place, the HR Manager shall appoint a higher-level manager to conduct the investigation. The person appointed shall have no connection whatsoever to the incident under investigation, be competent to conduct the investigation and be able to complete it within 15 days.
10.5	Disciplinary meeting	1. Before the disciplinary meeting, the HR Manager shall inform the employee in writing stating the purpose of the meeting, details of the incident alleged to have occurred and other issues involved with the incident. The employee shall be given a minimum of five working days' notice of the meeting. The meeting can be rearranged once with mutual consent. 2. Either party may bring witnesses as required. 3. Either party may present evidence including details of previous warnings, witness statements, call witnesses and have the opportunity to clarify.

ABC Company Limited	Procedures Manual		Reference SP 018 Page 3 of 4	
	Disciplinary Procedure	Date Released dd/mm/yyyy		Date Reviewed dd/mm/yyyy
Support Process	Approved:	Issue No: 01 Prepared by:		Revision No: 00

	Process Headings	Process Details
10.6	Report	
10.6.1	Outcome	Five courses of action are available: 1. There is no case to answer, in which case the employee shall be told immediately. 2. The matter can be resolved through guidance, counselling and/or training. 3. Verbal warning: In case of initial or minor issues. 4. The matter is serious enough to issue a letter of warning. If (a) the issue is more serious or (b) a verbal warning is in place with no improvement or (c) a further misconduct has occurred, the first letter of warning shall be issued which remains in place for six months from the date of investigation. 5. Final warning: If (a) the issue is more serious or (b) a first warning is still in place with no improvement or (c) a further misconduct has occurred, a final warning shall be issued which remains valid for at least 12 months from the date of the investigation.
10.6.2	Dismissal	If a further misconduct occurs within 12 months of the issue of final warning, or no improvement has been made, notice of termination shall be offered.
10.6.3	Summary dismissal	In case of gross misconduct, the employee shall be dismissed without notice.
10.6.4	Authority for dismissal	(i) The decision for dismissal or summary dismissal shall be taken jointly by the General Manager, the HR Manager and the Department Manager to whom the employee reports; and (ii) If the intention is to consider dismissal a further disciplinary meeting shall be held as outlined in section 10.5.

ABC Company Limited	Procedures Manual	Reference SP 018 Page 4 of 4	
	Disciplinary Procedure	Date Released dd/mm/yyyy	Date Reviewed dd/mm/yyyy
Support Process	Approved:	Issue No: 01 Prepared by:	Revision No: 00

	Process Headings	Process Details
10.7	Expiry of disciplinary actions	After the specified period of satisfactory service with no subsequent disciplinary issues all records relating to the incident shall be destroyed.
10.8	Right to appeal	1. At any stage of the proceedings, the employee has the right to appeal within 10 days following the investigation. 2. An appeal hearing shall take place within 15 days of receiving the notice of appeal and shall be conducted by a panel consisting of a senior executive nominated by the General Manager and the HR Manager. 3. The decision of the appeal hearing cannot be contested.
10.9	Criminal offence	If an employee has been found guilty of a criminal offence for an offence unrelated to work, the HR Manager shall conduct an enquiry to determine the course of action. Each offence must be carefully considered according to the particular circumstances.
11.0	Records	Warning letters and/or termination notice Incident reports Investigation notes.
12.0	Changes made	None.

ABC Company Limited	Procedures Manual	Flowchart SP 018.1 Page 1 of 2	
	Disciplinary Procedure	Date Released dd/mm/yyyy	Date Reviewed dd/mm/yyyy
Link SP 018	Approved:	Issue No: 01 Prepared by:	Revision No: 00

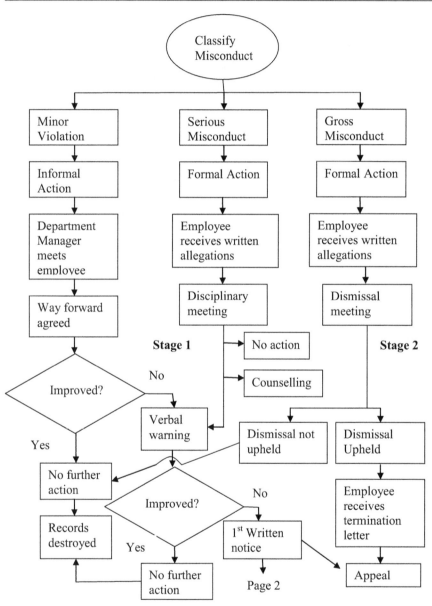

ABC Company Limited	Procedures Manual	Flowchart SP 018.1 Page 2 of 2	
	Disciplinary Procedure	Date Released dd/mm/yyyy	Date Reviewed dd/mm/yyyy
Link SP 018	Approved:	Issue No: 01 Prepared by:	Revision No: 00

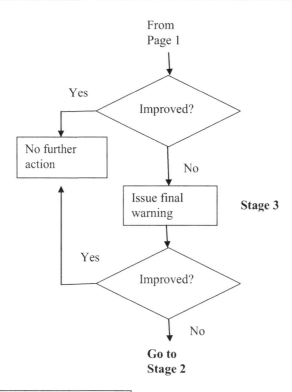

Note 1: When there is no
further action, the employee
is advised and matter
concluded
Note 2: If the appeal is
successful there is no further
action and the employee is
advised and matter concluded

SP 019 Grievance Procedure

ABC Company Limited	Procedures Manual		Reference SP 019 Page 1 of 2	
	Grievance Procedure		Date Released dd/mm/yyyy	Date Reviewed dd/mm/yyyy
Support Processes	Approved:		Issue No: 01 Prepared by:	Revision No: 00

Process Owner		Human Resource (HR) Manager
	Process Headings	**Process Details**
1.0	Purpose	To describe the procedure for handling employee grievances.
2.0	Scope	This procedure shall apply to all grievances.
3.0	Input	Grievance, company handbook, employment contract and employment regulations.
4.0	Output	Resolution of grievance.
5.0	Competency requirements	Problem resolution skills, human resolution skills, communication skills and investigation skills.
6.0	Responsibility	Supervisor shall: • Investigate the cause of grievance • Provide counselling support to employees who need support • Resolve conflicts among the staff in the unit. HR department shall: • Train supervisors and managers in handling grievances • Communicate with trade union representative or a third-party mediator, when required • Keep records of all grievances. Department Manager shall: • Investigate grievances if they have been escalated or the person involved is the supervisor.
7.0	Associated documents	Grievance form 1(Form 117) Grievance form 2 (Form 118) Grievance form 3 (Form 119).
8.0	Resources	Third-party mediator, if needed.
9.0	Measures/Controls	Rate of resolution of grievances Number of grievances.
10.0	System description	

ABC Company Limited	Procedures Manual		Reference SP 019 Page 2 of 2	
	Grievance Procedure		Date Released dd/mm/yyyy	Date Reviewed dd/mm/yyyy
Support Processes	Approved:		Issue No: 01 Prepared by:	Revision No: 00

	Process Headings	**Process Details**
10.1	Stage one	1. An employee who has a grievance shall at first raise the matter with the Supervisor immediately either verbally or in writing. If the matter concerns the Supervisor, the matter shall be raised with the Department Manager. 2. If the Supervisor is unable to resolve the grievance, the employee shall submit a formal written grievance form to the Supervisor who shall respond within two working days giving his or her explanation of the Supervisor's decision and who to appeal to if still aggrieved. The time period for response may be extended with the consent of both parties.
10.2	Stage two	The employee shall make the appeal in writing to the Department Manager within 10 working days of the original response to the employee's grievance. The Department Manager shall investigate and resolve the grievance. His or her response shall be sent to the employee within seven working days of receipt of the grievance form. The Department Manager shall inform the manager that the employee has the right to appeal to the General Manager.
10.3	Stage three	1. The appeal to the General Manager shall be made in writing within 10 working days of receipt of stage two response. The General Manager shall hear the appeal with another management representative not previously involved with the grievance resolution and respond within 20 working days of receiving the appeal. 2. If the grievance is against the General Manager, the employee shall submit the grievance to the CEO who shall then hear the appeal or the grievance with HR Manager.
10.4	Mediation	If the employee is still grieved, and if both parties agree that it could be resolved by a third party, the HR Manager shall make arrangements for mediation by a mutually acceptable third party. The mediator is in charge of the process of seeking to resolve the problem.
11.0	Records	Grievance forms Notes of discussions All records related to the incident shall be filed in the employee's personal file.
12.0	Changes made	None.

SP 020 Performance Review

ABC Company Limited	Procedures Manual	Reference SP 020 Page 1 of 2	
	Performance Review	Date Released dd/mm/yyyy	Date Reviewed dd/mm/yyyy
Support Process	Approved:	Issue No: 01 Prepared by:	Revision No: 00

Process Owner		Department Manager
	Process Headings	**Process Details**
1.0	Purpose	To describe the procedure for conducting performance reviews.
2.0	Scope	This procedure shall apply to all grades of staff.
3.0	Input	Previous performance review record, job descriptions, records of incidents affecting performance (both positive and negative) and appraisal form.
4.0	Output	Employee's comments on the review and agreed action plan.
5.0	Competency requirements	Performance evaluation skills, empathy and communication skills.
6.0	Responsibility	Defined in Flowchart SP 020.1. Additional responsibilities are: Supervisor shall: • Make a recommendation after the appraisal • Arrange further training or coaching as necessary • Keep records of performance reviews. HR department shall: • Keep records of performance reviews • Train Supervisors and Managers to conduct performance appraisals • Resolve disputes following the appraisals. Department Manager shall: • Review the performance of Supervisors.
7.0	Associated documents	Self-evaluation form (Form 120) Performance review form (Form 121) Core competencies evaluation (Form 122) Action plan (Form 123).
8.0	Resources	No new resources are required.
9.0	Measures/Controls	Feedback from the person whose performance has been appraised.
10.0	System description	Flowchart SP 020.1 shows the process for performance review.
10.1	Performance review is carried out in two parts	(a) Monitoring work performance and (b) Evaluation of management and leadership skills.
10.1.1	Monitoring work performance (Form 121)	This is measured at intervals stipulated in the job description. When the performance does not meet the standard, the employee is instructed to determine the causes of failure and submit an action plan for improvement.

ABC Company Limited	**Procedures Manual**		**Reference SP 020** Page 2 of 2	
	Performance Review	Date Released dd/mm/yyyy	Date Reviewed dd/mm/yyyy	
Support Process	Approved:	Issue No: 01 Prepared by:	Revision No: 00	

	Process Headings	Process Details
10.1.2	Evaluation of managerial and leadership roles	This step may be omitted when the performance of non-supervisory staff is evaluated. 1. The definition of each core competency is clarified to the employee with detailed comments and supporting examples about how the competency can be demonstrated. Each competency is ranked as exceeds expectation, meets expectations and needs improvement. 2. The employee is given advance notice of the meeting and documents relating to the review. The meeting shall be held in a non-threatening manner. The Supervisor shall open the meeting with specific examples of good performance. If there is a disagreement on the rankings, the Supervisor shall justify his or her ranking with specific examples of non-performance.
10.2	Action plan	The employee has to develop an action plan to improve his or her performance and should be approved by the Supervisor.
10.3	Feedback	After the performance review, HR function shall request feedback from the employee whose performance had been appraised. HR Manager shall discuss the findings with the Supervisor and take whatever action is necessary.
11.0	Records	Management skills records and work performance record.
12.0	Changes made	None.

ABC Company Limited	Procedures Manual	Flowchart SP 020.1 Page 1 of 1	
	Performance Review	Date Released dd/mm/yyyy	Date Reviewed dd/mm/yyyy
Link SP 020	Approved:	Issue No: 01 Prepared by:	Revision No: 00

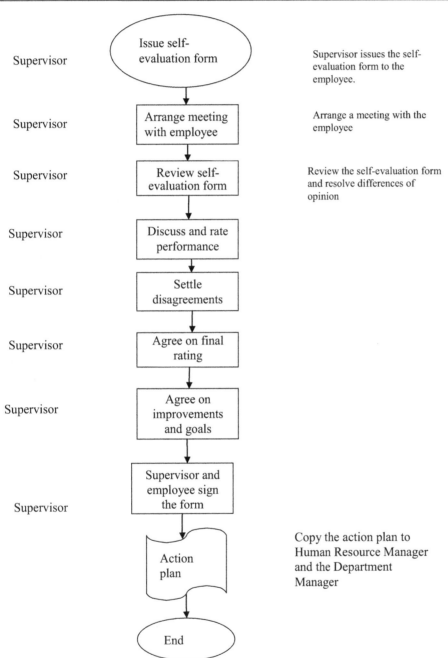

Supervisor — Issue self-evaluation form — Supervisor issues the self-evaluation form to the employee.

Supervisor — Arrange meeting with employee — Arrange a meeting with the employee

Supervisor — Review self-evaluation form — Review the self-evaluation form and resolve differences of opinion

Supervisor — Discuss and rate performance

Supervisor — Settle disagreements

Supervisor — Agree on final rating

Supervisor — Agree on improvements and goals

Supervisor — Supervisor and employee sign the form

Action plan — Copy the action plan to Human Resource Manager and the Department Manager

End

SP 021 IT Resources, Usage and Security

ABC Company Limited	Procedures Manual	Reference SP 021 Page 1 of 3	
	IT Resources, Usage and Security	Date Released dd/mm/yyyy	Date Reviewed dd/mm/yyyy
Support Process	Approved:	Issue No: 01 Prepared by:	Revision No: 00

Process Owner		Manager Information Systems
	Process Headings	**Process Details**
1.0	Purpose	To define ABCCL's information technology (IT) resources, its usage and security.
2.0	Scope	This procedure shall apply to all IT resources including files and data and all users.
3.0	Input	IT resources.
4.0	Output	Usage and security of IT resources.
5.0	Competency requirements	IT skills.
6.0	Responsibility	Manager Information Systems shall: • Purchase hardware and software necessary for business activities • Manage, secure and control access to ABCCL's IT resources including electronic files and data • Develop security awareness among all employees, which includes descriptions of security breaches intended to overcome programme security management • Define the policy for usage of resources • Train the users and provide support • Ensure the efficient use of resources. IT staff shall: • Address IT usage issues • Respond to users' requests • Locate servers, networking equipment and other essential computer devices in an environment that protects them from unauthorised physical access. Users shall: • Use ABCCL's IT resources in a cooperative and responsible manner to make the maximum use of the resources • Promptly inform IT staff of problems or faults in any IT systems.
7.0	Associated documents	Privacy and the use of resources Employee handbook Workplace practices Information use and security manual Usage reports.
8.0	Resources	IT equipment (software and hardware).
9.0	Measures/Controls	Usage reports

ABC Company Limited	Procedures Manual	Reference SP 021 Page 2 of 3	
	IT Resources, Usage and Security	Date Released dd/mm/yyyy	Date Reviewed dd/mm/yyyy
Support Process	Approved:	Issue No: 01 Prepared by:	Revision No: 00

	Process Headings	Process Details
		Breakdown log.
10.0	Definitions	**Record**: Any information kept, held, filed, produced and reproduced by, with or for a programme in any form or media including, but not limited to, reports, statements, memos, folders, publications, files, manuals, forms, papers, maps, images, letters, computer disks. **Property**: All records, software and hardware that are part of a programme's information system.
11.0	System description	
11.1	Property rights	ABCCL shall consider all records, software and hardware that are part of a programme's information system as ABCCL's property. This property, as defined earlier, shall only be used for business purposes.
11.2	Disclosure of information	1. Access to ABCCL's IT resources shall be restricted for business purposes. 2. Employees shall not disclose ABCCL information and data to any person or any organisation that is not related to any business activity. 3. ABCCL's information and data shall not be transmitted over the internet or via email to unauthorised personnel except for business purposes. 4. Confidential employee information shall not be communicated to anyone unauthorised to receive it.
11.3	Suspicious activities	Suspicious activities such as unauthorised equipment usage, phone requests from unidentifiable callers for access to secure information, unidentifiable files in network servers and abnormal activity recorded in log files shall all be reported promptly to the Manager Information Systems.
11.4	Access security	1. Employees shall log off computers when unattended or not in use. 2. Computer hard drives shall not be shared with any other computer or person unless authorised by the IT Manager. 3. Employees shall not leave unattended portable computer devices unless the devices have been physically secured. 4. When travelling devices such as laptops should be packed in a personal bag.

ABC Company Limited	Procedures Manual	Reference SP 021 Page 3 of 3	
	IT Resources, Usage and Security	Date Released dd/mm/yyyy	Date Reviewed dd/mm/yyyy
Support Process	Approved:	Issue No: 01 Prepared by:	Revision No: 00

	Process Headings	Process Details
11.5	ABCCL owned or administered IT resources	IT resources of ABCCL include computer system hardware and software, network equipment, servers, software and services, email and instant messaging systems, voicemail and telephone equipment and services, video equipment, printers, scanners and other imaging systems, fax machines, copiers and other electronic equipment and all electronic files and storage media.
11.6	Resource usage	1. Access to and usage of ABCCL's IT resources is made available to employees at the discretion of the department head and only for the purpose of conducting business activities. 2. All employees are prohibited from using ABCCL's IT resources to engage in behaviour that would violate ABCCL's policies, regulatory requirements or the integrity of contents. 3. Email, voicemail, electronic files and the internet should not be used for personal purposes. 4. Users who require access to ABCCL's IT resources should obtain prior approval from the Manager Information Systems.
12.0	Records	Inventory of IT resources Access rights.
13.0	Changes made	None.

SP 022 Email, Internet Use & Security

ABC Company Limited	Procedures Manual		Reference SP 022 Page 1 of 5	
	Email, Internet Use & Security	Date Released dd/mm/yyyy		Date Reviewed dd/mm/yyyy
Support Process	Approved:	Issue No: 01 Prepared by:		Revision No: 00

Process Owner	**Manager Information Services**
Process Headings	**Process Details**

1.0	Purpose	To describe the procedure for email and the internet use, promotion of performance and the stability of the ABCCL's email management system, and safe and effective use of ABCCL email and internet resources.
2.0	Scope	This procedure shall apply to all emails sent and received by users of the internet.
3.0	Input	Email and internet services.
4.0	Output	Secure communication, stability of the information system and protection of data and information.
5.0	Competency requirements	IT skills.
6.0	Responsibility	Manager Information Systems shall:

Manager Information Systems shall:
- Create email accounts, as appropriate
- Offer internet access to employees to facilitate communication, information sharing, research, resource development, design and development and training
- Approve a reliable internet provider and provide technology for internet access
- Install firewalls to block inappropriate or objectionable websites.

Information Technology staff shall:
- Conduct a monthly purge of email accounts
- Prevent archiving of email messages
- Monitor employees' internet activity to block inappropriate sites and content and limit access to employees at its discretion
- Unblock any sites that are business-related
- Block inappropriate sites that have not been blocked by content filtering method
- Implement various measures to control spam, phishing, spyware and adware which can disrupt and damage email and internet services
- Use anti-spyware and intrusion detection software on the main ABCCL firewall
- Install anti-spyware software to clean up infected computer or prevent infection.

ABC Company Limited	Procedures Manual	Reference SP 022 Page 2 of 5	
	Email, Internet Use & Security	Date Released dd/mm/yyyy	Date Reviewed dd/mm/yyyy
Support Process	Approved:	Issue No: 01 Prepared by:	Revision No: 00

	Process Headings	Process Details
		Employees shall: • Be responsible for any access to inappropriate sites that are not blocked • Inform the IT department of any sites that are blocked but are business-related • Surf the web safely and not click on any link that says "I agree" or on responses to any pop-up advertisements or messages • Help prevent spam and manage any spam that reaches their group mailbox • Ignore all spam messages and never click on any link within a spam • Use the trash or spam folder to get rid of spam emails.
7.0	Associated documents	Policies and procedures manualPrivacy and the use of ABCCL resources Employee handbook Workplace practices.
8.0	Resources	Email and collaboration software and internet technology Virus and anti-spyware protection software.
9.0	Measures/Controls	Audits of email accounts and websites accessed by employees Virus logs.
10.0	Definitions	**Spam**: Electronic junk mail or email advertisements. **Phishing**: Fraudulent email that appear to be from a genuine email address. **Spyware**: Software that is installed in the computer without the knowledge of the user. Spyware promotes advertisements, tracks the online behaviour of the computer or modifies the computer settings. They can also gather email addresses, passwords or credit card details. **Adware**: Form of spyware that tracks user's browsing information in order to display advertisements in the web. **Malware**: Malicious software consisting of programming code that disrupts or causes programming code to disrupt or cause computer

ABC Company Limited	Procedures Manual	Reference SP 022 Page 3 of 5	
	Email, Internet Use & Security	Date Released dd/mm/yyyy	Date Reviewed dd/mm/yyyy
Support Process	Approved:	Issue No: 01 Prepared by:	Revision No: 00

Process Headings	Process Details
	malfunction, gather confidential information in the computer, gain unauthorised access to computer resources and other damaging behaviour. It can include Trojan horses, spyware and adware.
11.0 System description	
11.1 Email standard	1. Employees shall only use email accounts approved by the IT department. Other email systems or clients including personal email accounts or webmail accounts shall be deleted by the IT department without prior notice. 2. All email accounts shall follow the format firstname.lastname@ABCCL.org 3. Employees shall receive email messages at the discretion of the Manager Information Systems.
11.2 Using email accounts	1. Employees shall use email accounts for business activities only. Any other use is prohibited.
11.3 Blocking of email messages	IT department shall block incoming email attachments larger than eight megabytes. Email messages with such attachments shall be delivered with a note from the IT department that an attachment larger than eight megabytes was detected and blocked.
11.4 Email retention and maintenance	1. IT department shall run a monthly purge of group email messages from the mailbox and messages in other locations including sent items, trash, work-in-progress and user-created folders. Calendar items are not purged. 2. Any exceptions to this rule shall be approved by the Manager Information Services. 3. Email messages purged can be retrieved using back-up tapes within 15 days. 4. Employees are advised to save email attachments and messages outside the system to an appropriate storage device.
11.5 Method of internet access	IT department shall implement various methods of internet access depending on the availability and the cost of the type of connection and the number of employees at each location.
11.6 Permitted usage	ABCCL shall provide access to the internet for

ABC Company Limited	Procedures Manual	Reference SP 022 Page 4 of 5	
	Email, Internet Use & Security	Date Released dd/mm/yyyy	Date Reviewed dd/mm/yyyy
Support Process	Approved:	Issue No: 01 Prepared by:	Revision No: 00

	Process Headings	Process Details
		the sole purpose of conducting business and related activities in compliance with internal and regulatory requirements.
11.7	Prohibited activities	• Charitable contributions, support for political or organisational activities • Viewing, storing, soliciting or forwarding pornographic material or other perceived obscene, offensive, racist or harassing messages or material • Non-business-related material • Soliciting, distributing or forwarding electronic games, videos, music or other non-business-related material such as request for signatures or donations • Bidding or purchasing of merchandise or services • Promotion of non-business-related material or services • Forwarding chain letters • Hacking and attempting to gain access to restricted sites • Gambling • Other activities not in keeping with ABCCL policies and procedures • Inserting email addresses into a public webpage • Disclosing personal information or account details to anyone • Disclosing the email address to any unauthorised person.
11.8	Controlling spam, phishing, spyware, adware and malware	1. Delete all fraudulent emails. 2. Understand the symptoms of abnormal behaviour of the computer due to spam, phishing, spyware, adware and malware.
11.9	Downloads that should be avoided	1. Games, music, movies or other file sharing programmes 2. Desktop themes, screen savers and cursors 3. Toolbars and pop-up blockers 4. Free downloaded software.
12.0	Records	Inventory of equipment and users Access rights.

ABC Company Limited	Procedures Manual	Reference SP 022 Page 5 of 5	
	Email, Internet Use & Security	Date Released dd/mm/yyyy	Date Reviewed dd/mm/yyyy
Support Process	Approved:	Issue No: 01 Prepared by:	Revision No: 00

Process Headings	Process Details
13.0 Changes made	None.

SP 023 Computer Hardware & Software Installation

ABC Company Limited	**Procedures Manual**		**Reference SP 023** Page 1 of 2	
	Computer Hardware & Software Installation	Date Released dd/mm/yyyy		Date Reviewed dd/mm/yyyy
Support Process	Approved:	Issue No: 01 Prepared by:		Revision No: 00

Process Owner	**Manager Information Technology (IT)**
Process Headings	**Process Details**
1.0 Purpose	The purpose of this document is to describe the procedure for efficient and rapid hardware and software installation, maintenance and promote stability and longevity of hardware.
2.0 Scope	This procedure shall apply to all computer hardware, standard software applications and programme-specific software.
3.0 Input	Hardware, software and user manuals.
4.0 Output	IT hardware and software in good working order and trained staff.
5.0 Competency requirements	IT skills.
6.0 Responsibility	IT Manager shall: • Purchase hardware and necessary software • Authorise software maintenance agreements • Be responsible for licensing arrangements. IT staff shall: • Install and maintain hardware and software • Identify all hardware with a number or name • Keep records of installed hardware, software and location • Replace hardware every three years or in case of breakdown • Monitor and prevent the installation of unauthorised software • Provide technical support. Department Manger shall: • Pay for any repairs outside the warranty period. Employees shall: • Not move hardware from the original location • Notify about computer equipment located in unsafe places • Take care of computer equipment assigned to the employee • Download or install only authorised software.

ABC Company Limited	Procedures Manual	Reference SP 023 Page 2 of 2	
	Computer Hardware & Software Installation	Date Released dd/mm/yyyy	Date Reviewed dd/mm/yyyy
Support Process	Approved:	Issue No: 01 Prepared by:	Revision No: 00

	Process Headings	Process Details
7.0	Associated documents	Hardware and software.
8.0	Resources	User manuals.
9.0	Measures/controls	Service log Breakdown log Hardware and software inventory.
10.0	System description	
10.1	Request for hardware and software	1. All requests for hardware and software shall be included in the annual department budget. 2. Programme-specific software shall be installed only after the approval by the Department Manager.
10.2	Licensing agreements and copyright laws	All users shall adhere to all licensing agreements and software copyright laws.
11.0	Records	IT equipment and software inventory Training programmes.
12.0	Change made	None.

SP 024 Phone, Voicemail, Fax

ABC Company Limited	Procedures Manual		Reference SP 024 Page 1 of 2	
	Phone, Voicemail, Fax	Date Released dd/mm/yyyy	Date Reviewed dd/mm/yyyy	
Support Process	Approved:	Issue No: 01 Prepared by:	Revision No: 00	

Process Owner	Manager Information Systems
Process Headings	**Process Details**
1.0 Purpose	To describe information technology (IT) office and employee procedure and responsibilities for the use and support of ABCCL's phone systems, voicemail and fax devices.
2.0 Scope	This procedure shall apply to all employees using the above devices.
3.0 Input	Communication method and communication messages.
4.0 Output	Communicated message.
5.0 Competency requirements	Skills for using communication media.
6.0 Responsibility	Manager Information Systems shall: <ul><li>Purchase, organise the installation and support of ABCCL's phone systems, voicemail systems and fax devices</li><li>Authorise the use of third-party telecommunication providers, if necessary.</li></ul> IT staff shall: <ul><li>Provide the necessary support for employees and arrange for repairs, if necessary</li><li>Provide training for the staff to use the devices.</li></ul> Employees shall: Add their mailbox into the voicemail address book and record an appropriate greeting Update the greeting when out of office Regularly check their voicemail.
7.0 Associated documents	Policies and procedures manual Privacy and the sue of ABCCL resources Employee handbook Workplace practices Usage of ABCCL IT resources.
8.0 Resources	Phone, voicemail and fax devices.
9.0 Measures/controls	Usage logs.
10.0 System description	1. IT Manager and the Department Manager shall determine which employees may have direct lines to their offices for business use. 2. Except in the case of employees provided with direct lines all outgoing calls shall be directed via the switchboard.

ABC Company Limited	**Procedures Manual**	**Reference SP 024** Page 2 of 2	
	Phone, Voicemail, Fax	Date Released dd/mm/yyyy	Date Reviewed dd/mm/yyyy
Support Process	Approved:	Issue No: 01 Prepared by:	Revision No: 00

	Process Headings	Process Details
		3. Except in the case of employees provided with direct lines all outgoing calls shall be directed via the switchboard. 4. Employees are discouraged from taking private phone calls except in an emergency. 5. No employee shall make a call on behalf of, or allow, an unauthorised person to make a private call from either a direct line or through the switchboard. 6. International calls shall only be taken with the approval of the Department Manager.
10.1	Cellphones	1. Cellphones, hands on/hands off or other devices shall not be used while driving, whether the business conducted is personal or company-related. 2. Employees shall restrict personal calls during work time and shall use personal cellphones during breaks except in an emergency. 3. Cellphones shall not be used while at any work site at which its operation would be a distraction to the user and/or could create an unsafe work environment. 4. Loss of cellphones provided by the company shall be promptly reported to the Manager Information Systems.
10.2	Prohibited activities	1. Employees shall not use phones, voicemail or fax devices to engage in behaviour that would violate ABCCL policies and procedures, including but not limited to, communications containing racist content or any other inappropriate and objectionable content.
11.0	Records	Usage logs.
12.0	Changes made	None.

SP 025 Password Management

ABC Company Limited	Procedures Manual	Reference SP 025 Page 1 of 2	
	Password Management	Date Released dd/mm/yyyy	Date Reviewed dd/mm/yyyy
Support Process	Approved:	Issue No: 01 Prepared by:	Revision No: 00

Process Owner	Manager Information Systems
Process Headings	**Process Details**
1.0 Purpose	To describe the procedure for using passwords to gain access to ABCCL's information technology (IT) resources.
2.0 Scope	This procedure shall apply to all employees who need access to ABCCL's IT resources.
3.0 Input	Password log.
4.0 Output	Secure IT use.
5.0 Competency requirements	IT skills.
6.0 Responsibility	IT Manager may: • Request for the password or direct the IT staff to change or clear employee passwords in order to access or protect ABCCL IT resources. IT staff shall: • Provide employees with a log-in ID or username and default password to gain access to resources • Advise employees to change password every 90 days or more frequently if it has been compromised • Not be responsible for password protection issues of individual files • Implement the boot-up password process and maintain a record of the password. Employees shall: • Take steps to protect the confidentiality of their passwords • Create a password that could not be easily guessed • Not use computer-based passwords.
7.0 Associated documents	Activity log Password log.
8.0 Resources	None.
9.0 Measures/controls	Monitoring password usage.
10.0 System description	
10.1 Password usage	1. Passwords are required to access to computer, network and telecommunication resources including network log-in accounts, email, finance, human resources, voicemail and other confidential information.

ABC Company Limited	Procedures Manual	Reference SP 025 Page 2 of 2	
	Password Management	Date Released dd/mm/yyyy	Date Reviewed dd/mm/yyyy
Support Process	Approved:	Issue No: 01 Prepared by:	Revision No: 00

	Process Headings	Process Details
		2. Password shall be at least six characters long and shall include a combination of numbers, letters (upper and lower case) and symbols.
		3. Passwords shall not be used for protecting individual files such as Microsoft documents without the Department Manager's approval. Such passwords shall be communicated to the Department Manager.
		4. Forgotten passwords on Microsoft documents cannot be recovered and the files will not be accessible.
11.0	Records	Activity log.
12.0	Changes made	None.

SP 026 Virus Protection

ABC Company Limited	Procedures Manual	Reference SP 026 Page 1 of 2	
	Virus Protection	Date Released dd/mm/yyyy	Date Reviewed dd/mm/yyyy
Support Process	Approved:	Issue No: 01 Prepared by:	Revision No: 00

Process owner	Manager Information Systems
Process Headings	**Process Details**
1.0 Purpose	To describe the procedure for protecting ABCCL's information technology (IT) resources against viruses.
2.0 Scope	This procedure shall apply to all programmes that require virus protection such as servers, computers and selected network hardware.
3.0 Input	Antivirus software.
4.0 Output	Secure IT environment.
5.0 Competency requirements	IT skills.
6.0 Responsibility	IT staff shall: • Install or implement well-tested virus protection software on all ABCCL servers, computers, main ABCCL firewall and email gateways where all incoming email is scanned for viruses • Create awareness among employees of the dangers of viruses and how they can help prevent virus contamination • Apply security patches and updates to servers and computers, as necessary, to prevent security breaches and potential virus intrusion. Employees shall: • Delete all emails from unrecognised and doubtful sources • Not open attachments that cannot be recognised, are not expected or appear to be non-work-related, even if the sender is known to the employee • Not change virus protection settings • Not download or install software from the internet or email • Report to the IT department any abnormal behaviour on the computer.
7.0 Associated documents	Information resources usage manual.
8.0 Resources	Virus protection software.
9.0 Measures/controls	Virus logs.
10.0 System description	
10.1 Virus software	1. IT Manager shall select appropriate virus protection software. This software shall be capable of daily updating automatically to protect against most current viruses, configuring for real-time protection and cleaning and notifying, if a virus is detected.

ABC Company Limited	Procedures Manual	Reference SP 026 Page 2 of 2	
	Virus Protection	Date Released dd/mm/yyyy	Date Reviewed dd/mm/yyyy
Support Process	Approved:	Issue No: 01 Prepared by:	Revision No: 00

	Process Headings	Process Details
		2. Measures for protection: ABCCL shall employ a combination of technology measures and develop an awareness and action to help protect network, computers and data and all programmes from virus contamination.
10.2	Cleaning after infection	1. In case of virus contamination the IT department shall take immediate technology steps to remove the virus and archive infected programmes and files. 2. The IT department shall ensure that affected programmes and files are not used by the users until the programmes and files have been made virus-free.
11.0	Records	Virus logs.
12.0	Changes made	None.

SP 027 System Access

ABC Company Limited	Procedures Manual		Reference SP 027 Page 1 of 2	
	System Access		Date Released dd/mm/yyyy	Date Reviewed dd/mm/yyyy
Support Process	Approved:		Issue No: 01 Prepared by:	Revision No: 00

Process Owner	**Manager Information System**
Process Headings	**Process Details**

	Process Headings	Process Details
1.0	Purpose	To establish security controls for approving access to ABCCL's network, system applications, phone and voicemail.
2.0	Scope	This procedure shall apply to network, system applications, phone and voicemail.
3.0	Input	Organisation chart and access rights.
4.0	Output	Access rights information.
5.0	Competency requirements	Information technology (IT) skills.
6.0	Responsibility	IT staff shall: • Create network account or group account, as necessary, assign a phone number and create a voicemail account • Install applicable software on the employee's computer, establish proper network access rights and create user names and password, as necessary • Delete all accounts and log-in information on termination of employment. Department Manager shall: • Inform the details of appointment of all new employees who need system access • Inform access requirements for the new employee • Inform changes to employment status which may affect access rights • Inform the termination of employment of an employee.
7.0	Associated documents	Access rights Employee information.
8.0	Resources	None.
9.0	Measures/controls	Access log.
10.0	System description	
10.1	Creating an account	The Department Manager shall inform the IT office of details of the employment of a new employee. The details shall include the name of the employee, job title, the department and access requirements.
10.2	Change in employment status	The Department Manager shall inform the IT department of the termination of employment of an employee so that all accounts and log-in and password details can be deleted.

ABC Company Limited	Procedures Manual	Reference SP 027 Page 2 of 2	
	System Access	Date Released dd/mm/yyyy	Date Reviewed dd/mm/yyyy
Support Process	Approved:	Issue No: 01 Prepared by:	Revision No: 00

	Process Headings	Process details
11.0	Records	Access rights log.
12.0	Changes made	None.

SP 028 Back-up and Recovery

ABC Company Limited	Procedures Manual	Reference SP 028 Page 1 of 3	
	Back-up and Recovery	Date Released dd/mm/yyyy	Date Reviewed dd/mm/yyyy
Support Process	Approved:	Issue No: 01 Prepared by:	Revision No: 00

Process Owner		Manager Information Systems
	Process Headings	**Process Details**
1.0	Purpose	To describe the procedure for back-up and recovery of ABCCL data.
2.0	Scope	This procedure shall apply to servers located in the facility.
3.0	Input	Back-up programme and recovery programme.
4.0	Output	Recovered system and files.
5.0	Competency requirements	Information technology (IT) skills.
6.0	Responsibility	Manager Information Systems shall: • Select suitable back-up media and software (backup-media may include cloud computing technology). IT staff shall: • Schedule, carry out back-ups as scheduled and complete the back-up log book • Secure back-up media • Monitor, label, supply and replace back-up media • Store back-up media offsite • Perform file/data restores from back-up media • Validate the accuracy, completeness and integrity of the back-ups • Notify back-up errors to the Manager Information Systems. Employees shall: Back-up data and file in the hard drive of employee's computer Request restore when necessary.
7.0	Associated documents	Back-up and restore procedure Offsite storage log.
8.0	Resources	Back-up media.
9.0	Measures/controls	Back-up log Restore log Downtime due to network or computer failure.
10.0	System description	
10.1	Back-up schedule	1. Incremental daily back-up: Daily incremental back-ups are run on Monday to Friday at 5pm each day onto recovery media. The back-up media are labelled Monday, Tuesday, Wednesday, Thursday and Friday. The media shall be used on the day stated on the label of the media. Back-up on Monday will be

ABC Company Limited	Procedures Manual	Reference SP 028 Page 2 of 3	
	Back-up and Recovery	Date Released dd/mm/yyyy	Date Reviewed dd/mm/yyyy
Support Process	Approved:	Issue No: 01 Prepared by:	Revision No: 00

Process Headings	Process Details
	removed offsite on Tuesday and returned on Thursday. This method will ensure that one media is always stored offsite. IT staff shall complete the offsite media log. 2. Weekly full back-up: Weekly back-ups are performed at the end of the regular business day every Thursday of the week. The media are labelled as "Month xxx, Week xx". Thursday's media shall be taken offsite on Monday and returned on Wednesday. 3. Monthly full back-up: Monthly full back-ups will be performed on the last business day of the month at the end of the regular business day. Four media will be used and reused every three months and labelled as such. Friday following the back-up, the media shall be taken to the offsite location.
10.2 Recovery of data	The Manager Information Systems shall establish a disaster recovery plan for business continuity. The data is recovered in this way: 1. Back-up the system onto an unused media. Copy the "bad" data into a subdirectory where it is out of the way. 2. Locate the most recent back-up data media with the data that is needed. 3. Activate the write protect mechanism of the media to prevent accidental erasure. 4. Insert the back-up media. 5. Set up restore with the back-up software. 6. Use the software to restore the files to a location different from the original location. 7. Perform restore. 8. Copy the data from the temporary location to the actual location where the data should reside. 9. Eject the media, remove write protection and return it to the proper location. 10. Test the restored data.
10.3 Deploying cloud computing	Cloud computing technology can be conveniently employed to store, back-up and restore files and data. A storage medium is not required which saves time and cost. Since the data is stored in the "cloud" the process of recovery is easy.

ABC Company Limited	**Procedures Manual**	**Reference SP 028** Page 3 of 3	
	Back-up and Recovery	Date Released dd/mm/yyyy	Date Reviewed dd/mm/yyyy
Support Process	Approved:	Issue No: 01 Prepared by:	Revision No: 00

	Process Headings	**Process Details**
11.0	Records	Back-up and recovery log.
12.0	Changes made	None.

SP 029 Service and Support

ABC Company Limited	Procedures Manual		Reference SP 029 Page 1 of 1	
	Service and Support		Date Released dd/mm/yyyy	Date Reviewed dd/mm/yyyy
Support Process	Approved:		Issue No: 01 Prepared by:	Revision No: 00

Process Owner		Manager Information Systems
	Process Headings	**Process Details**
1.0	Purpose	To describe the procedure for request for service and support and for information technology (IT) response.
2.0	Scope	This procedure shall apply to all requests for service and support from users of IT equipment.
3.0	Input	Request for service and support.
4.0	Output	Completion of support and service and system in good working order.
5.0	Competency requirements	IT skills.
6.0	Responsibility	IT staff shall: • Provide service and support in a timely manner based on priority and availability of resources. Department Manager shall: • Prepare guidelines for requesting IT office support, which employees have to follow.
7.0	Associated documents	Work order for service or support request.
8.0	Resources	Equipment for service and support.
9.0	Measures/controls	Stoppages due to IT failure Effectiveness of service support.
10.0	System description	Procedure for managing request is shown in Flowchart SP 029.1.
10.1	Requests from employees	Employees can request these services from the IT office: • Problems with computer applications • Network and email problems • Printing and printer problems • Problems with operations related to hardware.
10.2	Requests from Department Managers	The Department Manager shall make requests for these services: • Access permissions • Replacing, moving or configuring equipment • Creating new accounts • Software installation.
11.0	Records	Service log.
12.0	Changes made	None.

ABC Company Limited	Procedures Manual	Flowchart SP 029.1 Page 1 of 1	
	Service and Support	Date Released dd/mm/yyyy	Date Reviewed dd/mm/yyyy
Link SP 029	Approved:	Issue No: 01 Prepared by:	Revision No: 00

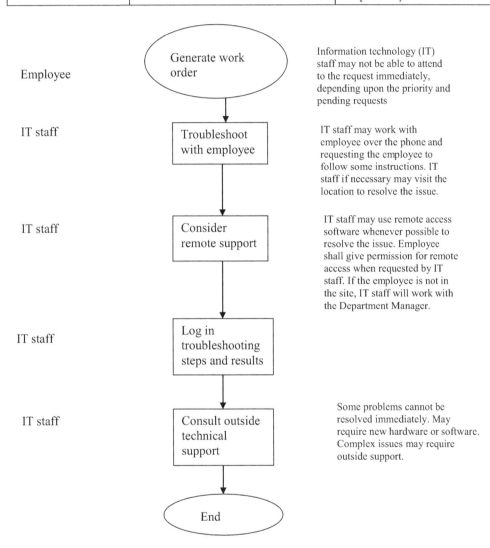

Employee — Generate work order

Information technology (IT) staff may not be able to attend to the request immediately, depending upon the priority and pending requests

IT staff — Troubleshoot with employee

IT staff may work with employee over the phone and requesting the employee to follow some instructions. IT staff if necessary may visit the location to resolve the issue.

IT staff — Consider remote support

IT staff may use remote access software whenever possible to resolve the issue. Employee shall give permission for remote access when requested by IT staff. If the employee is not in the site, IT staff will work with the Department Manager.

IT staff — Log in troubleshooting steps and results

IT staff — Consult outside technical support

Some problems cannot be resolved immediately. May require new hardware or software. Complex issues may require outside support.

End

SP 030 Electronic File Storage

ABC Company Limited	Procedures Manual		Reference SP 030 Page 1 of 2	
	Electronic File Storage	Date Released dd/mm/yyyy		Date Reviewed dd/mm/yyyy
Support Process	Approved:	Issue No: 01 Prepared by:		Revision No: 00

Process Owner		Manager Information Systems
	Process Headings	**Process Details**
1.0	Purpose	To describe the procedure for storage of electronic files to meet business needs and maintain the resources in a secure manner.
2.0	Scope	This procedure shall apply to all files containing data and information generated by users in their daily business activities.
3.0	Input	Electronic file storage system and electronic files.
4.0	Output	Files stored for easy access and retrieval.
5.0	Competency requirements	IT skills and database management skills.
6.0	Responsibility	Information technology (IT) staff may: • Request users to delete their unneeded files • Delete inappropriate files that jeopardise network or server functionality and integrity.
7.0	Associated documents	User manual.
8.0	Resources	IT equipment.
9.0	Measures/controls	Audits.
10.0	System description	
10.1	Types of files	Employees may store files related to business activities with some restrictions and limitations such as word processing documents, spreadsheets, presentations, databases, newsletters, flyers, low quality digital images, video instructional files and other types of business documents in the assigned location.
10.2	Locations for file storage	1. IT department shall create two folders for each user: Individual folder that can be used to store the user's files; and a group folder that can be used to store the files to be shared by other network users. 2. Files in the group folder can be accessed by a user from any network connected computer that has been granted access rights. 3. Employees are not encouraged to save files in the hard drive and the IT department shall not be responsible for backing up files in the user's hard drive. 4. Employees who do not log onto a network file server shall store the files in the computer. They may request an external hard drive, flash drive or a DropBox

ABC Company Limited	Procedures Manual	Reference SP 030 Page 2 of 2	
	Electronic File Storage	Date Released dd/mm/yyyy	Date Reviewed dd/mm/yyyy
Support Process	Approved:	Issue No: 01 Prepared by:	Revision No: 00

	Process Headings	Process details
		account for online storage for back up of such files. The purchase and the use of these devices must comply with ABCCL's personnel policies and procedures. 5. High-resolution digital images shall not be stored in the network for extended periods. They should be transferred to external devices such as CD/DVD, flash drives, etc.
10.3	File deletion	1. Users shall regularly monitor file storage and delete unnecessary files from the network or the computer. Such files may be moved to external storage devices with approval from the IT department. 2. IT department from time to time may request the users to delete unneeded files from storage. Inappropriate files that can harm the network or the computer will be deleted by the IT department without prior notice. 3. Shared files shall not be deleted by users without the approval of the Manager Information Systems. A user shall make a request to the IT department for deletion of a shared file. 4. The IT department shall consult the Department Managers who are users for necessary advice.
11.0	Records	Inventory of users and files Access rights.
12.0	Changes made	None.

SP 031 Use of IT to Ensure Food Safety

ABC Company Limited	Procedures Manual	Reference SP 031 Page 1 of 2	
	Use of IT to Ensure Food Safety	Date Released dd/mm/yyyy	Date Reviewed dd/mm/yyyy
Support Process	Approved:	Issue No: 01 Prepared by:	Revision No: 00

Process Owner		Manager Information Systems
	Process Headings	**Process Details**
1.0	Purpose	To describe the use of information technology (IT) to ensure safety of food products.
2.0	Scope	This procedure shall apply to the production of food products.
3.0	Input	IT equipment.
4.0	Output	Application of IT equipment.
5.0	Competency requirements	Knowledge of IT equipment and food safety.
6.0	Responsibility	All staff involved in food processing shall: • Be aware of food safety practices. Manager Information Systems shall: • Procure IT equipment • Train staff to use IT equipment.
7.0	Associated documents	Food safety programme Purchasing IT equipment (CP 006).
8.0	Resources	Monitoring equipment.
9.0	Measures/controls	Process control records.
10.0	System description	
10.1	Software	• Manager Information Systems shall install real value-adding and time-saving enhancements, which are user-friendly, intuitive, and satisfy the needs of consumers, retailers, consultants, inspectors and auditors • They are fully integrated and meet the global food safety standards using best practices • They enable quick updating in keeping up with changes in global food standards and regulations • They provide real-time data on food safety issues such as recalls, outbreaks and changing legislation • They enable real-time monitoring of multiple sites in a large corporate structure • They allow remote access to the user on their food safety system • They are capable of generating quick reports.
10.2	Process control	Use IT equipment to test raw materials and monitor processes.

ABC Company Limited	Procedures Manual	Reference SP 031 Page 2 of 2	
	Use of IT to Ensure Food Safety	Date Released dd/mm/yyyy	Date Reviewed dd/mm/yyyy
Support Process	Approved:	Issue No: 01 Prepared by:	Revision No: 00

	Process Headings	Process Details
10.3	Product tracking	1. The source of products used in processing, processing steps and the distribution of the final product can be monitored using tracking systems. 2. IT can identify products, capture information associated with them and share it with others, if necessary.
11.0	Records	Inventory of IT equipment.
12.0	Changes made	None.

SP 032 Brand Management

ABC Company Limited	Procedures Manual	Reference SP 032 Page 1 of 2	
	Brand Management	Date Released dd/mm/yyyy	Date Reviewed dd/mm/yyyy
Support Process	Approved:	Issue No: 01 Prepared by:	Revision No: 00

Process Owner	Marketing Manager
Process Headings	**Process Details**
1.0 Purpose	To describe the procedure for designing and implementing a marketing programme to build and maintain brand equity.
2.0 Scope	This procedure shall apply to all products offered to the market by us.
3.0 Input	Most important customers, motivating factors, marketing mix, marketing plan, advantages and disadvantages over competitors' products, social media and intended brand position.
4.0 Output	Improved brand position, expanding customer base and improved market share.
5.0 Competency requirements	Marketing qualifications and brand management skills.
6.0 Responsibility	Brand Manager shall: • Prepare the marketing plan • Develop programmes and campaigns • Stimulate sales and distribution • Gather market intelligence • Initiate product improvements. Marketing Manager shall: • Approve the marketing plan • Approve promotional programmes and campaigns.
7.0 Associated documents	Company logo Marketing and sales manual.
8.0 Resources	Brand management software.
9.0 Measures/Controls	Brand audit Brand values Brand equity measurement system.
10.0 System description	
10.1 Identification and establishing brand position	Identify and establish brand position through: (a) Differences that demonstrate advantages and differences over competitors; (b) Core brand association that describe benefits and attributes which characterise the brand; and (c) Brand essence, which is a core brand promise.
10.2 Plan and implement brand management programme	Plan and implement brand management programme using logos, images, packaging, symbols, slogans, etc. and integrate the brand with marketing activity associating the brand with country, sports, culture, etc.

ABC Company Limited	Procedures Manual	Reference SP 032 Page 2 of 2	
	Brand Management	Date Released dd/mm/yyyy	Date Reviewed dd/mm/yyyy
Support Process	Approved:	Issue No: 01 Prepared by:	Revision No: 00

	Process Headings	**Process Details**
10.3	Measure brand performance	Measure brand performance using brand audit, brand value chain and brand equity measurement system, and determine ways to take tactical decisions.
10.4	Growing and sustaining brand equity	Adopt tools such as brand-product matrix, brand hierarchy and brand portfolios. Consider long-term and short-term view of future marketing plans.
11.0	Records	Marketing plan Brand development strategy.
12.0	Changes made	None.

SP 033 Promoting and Advertising

ABC Company Limited	Procedures Manual	Reference SP 033 Page 1 of 2	
	Promoting and Advertising	Date Released dd/mm/yyyy	Date Reviewed dd/mm/yyyy
Support Process	Approved:	Issue No: 01 Prepared by:	Revision No: 00

Process Owner		Marketing Manager and Sales Manager
	Process Headings	**Process Details**
1.0	Purpose	To describe the procedure for promoting and advertising the products.
2.0	Scope	This procedure shall apply to all products offered to the market by us.
3.0	Input	Customer database, promotion and advertising material, samples, promotion and advertising campaign, and promotion and advertising media.
4.0	Output	Product and brand awareness among customers, increased sales and enhanced market position.
5.0	Competency requirements	Marketing qualifications and advertising and promotion skills.
6.0	Responsibility	Marketing Manager in consultation with the Sales Manager shall: • Decide which products should be advertised and promoted • Decide the channels for advertising and promotion • Decide on the duration of the campaign(s) • Decide whether the campaign should be handled by a third party • Approve the advertisement and promotional material. Brand Manager shall: • Gather market intelligence • Prepare the brief for the campaign • Organise and implement advertising and promotional activities • Communicate internally and externally.
7.0	Associated documents	Advertisements Promotional materials.
8.0	Resources	Artwork and design software.
9.0	Measures/controls	Consumer response.
10.0	Definitions	**Promotion:** Includes all disciplines of advertising, public relations and sales activities designed to generate sales for the product and it is used in conjunction with a promotional plan. **Advertising:** In contrast to other disciplines of promotion is a paid form of mass communication through TV, radio, print (magazines, newspapers, flyers), outdoor bill boards and internal placements.

ABC Company Limited	Procedures Manual	Reference SP 033 Page 2 of 2	
	Promoting and Advertising	Date Released dd/mm/yyyy	Date Reviewed dd/mm/yyyy
Support Process	Approved:	Issue No: 01 Prepared by:	Revision No: 00

	Process Headings	Process details
11.0	System description	1. Evaluate the products and services offered by assessing the competitors' products and their business and marketing techniques. 2. Identify the target market: Assess the demographics, disposal income and customers' preferences. Generate a profile of an ideal customer. 3. Determine the allocated marketing budget. 4. Evaluate marketing options: Newspaper, radio, websites, social media, direct mail, email, TV, etc. 5. Prepare the promotional material and the advertisement. 6. Create a marketing campaign: Identify the specific goals of the campaign. Select a medium for the campaign. Determine the timeframe for the campaign. Test market the campaign. 7. Evaluate the test marketing results.
12.0	Records	Promotion and advertisement plan Promotion and advertising campaign.
13.0	Changes made	None.

SP 034 Marketing Forecast

ABC Company Limited	Procedures Manual		Reference SP 034 Page 1 of 2	
	Marketing Forecast		Date Released dd/mm/yyyy	Date Reviewed dd/mm/yyyy
Support Process	Approved:		Issue No: 01 Prepared by:	Revision No: 00

Process Owner		Marketing Manager
	Process Headings	**Process Details**
1.0	Purpose	To describe the procedure for preparing a marketing forecast for our products.
2.0	Scope	This procedure shall apply to all products marketed by us.
3.0	Input	Previous forecast, historical data, market potential and sales potential.
4.0	Output	Market forecast.
5.0	Competency requirements	Marketing qualifications and forecasting skills.
6.0	Responsibility	Marketing Manager shall: • Analyse and project marketing and production folio information • Prepare the marketing forecast • Evaluate and assign priorities • Control planning and implementation of action plan. Brand Manager shall: • Collect marketing and production information • Determine individual product strategies and tactical plans • Monitor the progress of the product development programme • Control progress of the plans.
7.0	Associated documents	Demographics Previous forecast Historical data.
8.0	Resources	Marketing tool for evaluating and projecting market information.
9.0	Measures/controls	Accuracy of the forecast Checks against published data.
10.0	Definitions	**Market forecast:** Prediction of how much of all brands in a product category will be sold in a given time. **Sales forecast:** Prediction of sales of a single brand in a given time.
11.0	System description	The procedure for creating a marketing forecast is shown in Flowchart SP 034.1.
11.1	Forecasting methods	Any one of the following methods may be used for generating the market forecast: (1) Qualitative methods: Subjective methods based on the judgement and opinion

ABC Company Limited	**Procedures Manual**		**Reference SP 034** Page 2 of 2	
	Marketing Forecast		Date Released dd/mm/yyyy	Date Reviewed dd/mm/yyyy
Support Process	Approved:		Issue No: 01 Prepared by:	Revision No: 00

Process Headings	Process Details
	of experts or consumers when no historical data is available. These methods are useful for making medium to long-term decisions:
	(a) Expert opinion: Forecast based on the opinion and judgement of a group of experts. Marketing Manager shall invite the experts as necessary;
	(b) Delphi method: Forecast based on the opinion and judgement of a group of experts using a set questionnaire. Individual forecasts are reviewed by a team and returned to the individuals for revision. The process continues until a consensus is reached;
	(c) Sales force methods: Forecast based on the opinion of individual sales people; and
	(d) Consumer surveys: Marketing Team shall obtain the views of consumers to prepare the forecast.
	(2) Quantitative methods: Forecast based on historical data and employed to make short- to medium-term decisions. It is assumed that sales patterns are likely to continue in the future:
	(a) Naïve method: Forecast based on historical quantitative data assuming that previous trade patterns are likely to continue in the future;
	(b) Moving averages method: Forecast based on the average of a previous period;
	(c) Exponential method: Forecast based on a weighted average of a previous period; and
	(d) Consumer surveys: Forecast based on consumer feedback.
12.0 Records	Market surveys Forecast.
13.0 Changes made	None.

ABC Company Limited	Procedures Manual	Flowchart SP 034.1 Page 1 of 1	
	Marketing Forecast	Date Released dd/mm/yyyy	Date Reviewed dd/mm/yyyy
Link SP 034	Approved:	Issue No: 01 Prepared by:	Revision No: 00

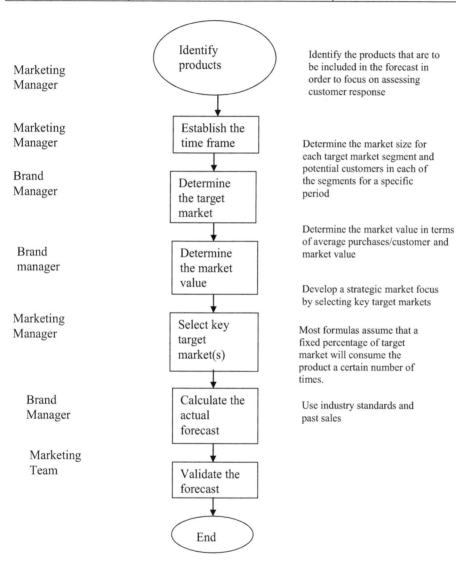

Marketing Manager

Identify products

Identify the products that are to be included in the forecast in order to focus on assessing customer response

Marketing Manager

Establish the time frame

Brand Manager

Determine the target market

Determine the market size for each target market segment and potential customers in each of the segments for a specific period

Brand manager

Determine the market value

Determine the market value in terms of average purchases/customer and market value

Marketing Manager

Select key target market(s)

Develop a strategic market focus by selecting key target markets

Most formulas assume that a fixed percentage of target market will consume the product a certain number of times.

Brand Manager

Calculate the actual forecast

Use industry standards and past sales

Marketing Team

Validate the forecast

End

SP 035 Market Research

ABC Company Limited	Procedures Manual	Reference SP 035 Page 1 of 2	
	Market Research	Date Released dd/mm/yyyy	Date Reviewed dd/mm/yyyy
Support Process	Approved:	Issue No: 01 Prepared by:	Revision No: 00

Process Owner	Marketing Manager
Process Headings	**Process Details**
1.0 Purpose	To describe the procedure for conducting market research.
2.0 Scope	This procedure shall apply to all products marketed by us.
3.0 Input	Research objective, research methods and historical data.
4.0 Output	Research results.
5.0 Competency requirements	Marketing qualifications, data collection and analysis skills, knowledge of statistical techniques and problem-solving skills.
6.0 Responsibility	Marketing Manager shall: • Identify the products for research • Set a timeframe • Determine how the findings will be applied • Provide resources to conduct research. Brand Manager shall: • Identify the sources for research • Collect data • Validate data.
7.0 Associated documents	Trade association journals Market surveys prepared by independent organisations Reviewing results of recent market research on similar or identical requirements Reviewing catalogues and literature published by service providers.
8.0 Resources	Knowledge management tool for coding and using the information.
9.0 Measures/controls	Relevance of research findings Checks against published data.
10.0 System description	An overview market research process is presented in Flowchart SP 035.1.
10.1 Who is going to do research?	Marketing Manager shall decide whether to outsource the research project or nominate a research team.
10.2 Research stages	**Stage 1: Formulate the research problem** The management problem is translated to a research question. For example: Management problem: Sales are declining.

ABC Company Limited	Procedures Manual	Reference SP 035 Page 2 of 2	
	Market Research	Date Released dd/mm/yyyy	Date Reviewed dd/mm/yyyy
Support Process	Approved:	Issue No: 01 Prepared by:	Revision No: 00

Process Headings	Process Details
	Research questions: Determine whether declining sales are due to (a) poor expectations that lead to a lack of desire to purchase; or (b) poor performance of the product leading to a lack of desire to repurchase. **Stage 2: Method of enquiry** Follow the stages in the research process: Formulating the problem, developing a hypothesis, making predictions based on the hypothesis, devising test methods, conducting tests and analysing the results. **Stage 3: Research method** Research methods include experimental or non-experimental methods. **Stage 4: Research design** Devise specific methods and procedures to collect the required information. **Stage 5: Selection of data collection techniques** Interviews and observations are the two main methods of collecting the data. They may be based on a properly designed questionnaire. **Stage 6: Sample design** Design a sampling plan for data collection. **Stage 7: Data collection** This stage requires the deployment of a considerable number of employees and consumes a major portion of the research budget. A marketing research collection agency may have to be employed for personal (face-to-face) and telephone interviews. Internet surveys require fewer personnel, are lower cost and can be completed in days rather than weeks or months. **Stage 8: Analysis and evaluation** Analytical techniques to be used depend on the type of data and measurements collected. **Stage 9: Research report** This report will include all of the information, including an accurate description of your research process, the results, conclusions and recommended courses of action.
11.0 Records	Market research report.
12.0 Changes made	None.

ABC Company Limited	Procedures Manual	Flowchart SP 035.1 Page 2 of 2	
	Market Research	Date Released dd/mm/yyyy	Date Reviewed dd/mm/yyyy
Support Process	Approved:	Issue No: 01 Prepared by:	Revision No: 00

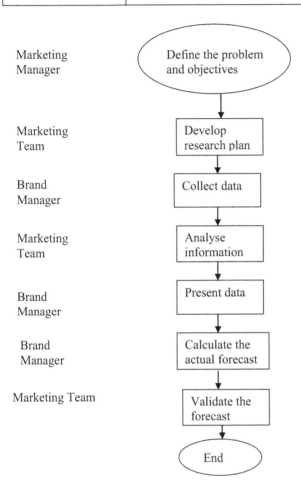

Marketing Manager — Define the problem and objectives

Marketing Team — Develop research plan

Brand Manager — Collect data

Marketing Team — Analyse information

Brand Manager — Present data

Brand Manager — Calculate the actual forecast

Marketing Team — Validate the forecast

End

Research can be exploratory or descriptive. Exploratory study briefly describes the marketing situation. Descriptive study is an in-depth investigation. Can also be used to find cause and effect relationships

Plan includes decisions on data sources, research approaches, research instruments, sampling plans and contact methods.

The information is tabulated and measured to find answers to the questions.

SP 036 Budgeting

ABC Company Limited	Procedures Manual	Reference SP 036 Page 1 of 2	
	Budgeting	Date Released dd/mm/yyyy	Date Reviewed dd/mm/yyyy
Support Process	Approved:	Issue No: 01 Prepared by:	Revision No: 00

Process Owner	Financial Manager
Process Headings	**Process Details**
1.0 Purpose	To describe the procedure for preparing the annual budget.
2.0 Scope	This procedure shall apply to all cost centres of ABCCL.
3.0 Input	Cost management plan, scope, cost estimates of each activity, basis of estimates, costs assigned for the calendar period and resource cost allocation.
4.0 Output	Budget provisions.
5.0 Competency requirements	Financial qualifications and experience.
6.0 Responsibility	Financial Manager shall: • Prepare budget proposals for consideration by the Board • Explain the current fiscal conditions, fiscal prospects and budget proposals to the Board • Implement the budget proposals and monitor to ensure that fiscal policies are followed. Chief Accountant shall: • Coordinate the budgeting process • Perform a significant policy guidance function and become involved in all financial issues relating to the budget • Directly supervise the budget implementation • Issue budget preparation forms and instructions to Department Managers with cost centre responsibility • Consolidate the budget proposals and prepare the final budget. Department Managers shall: • Prepare budget proposals for each department • Review the proposals when requested to do so by the Financial Manager.
7.0 Associated documents	Budget preparation forms Budget proposals.
8.0 Resources	Financial management module.
9.0 Measures/controls	Budget spending versus budget allocation Achievement of financial goal.

ABC Company Limited	Procedures Manual		Reference SP 036 Page 2 of 2	
	Budgeting		Date Released dd/mm/yyyy	Date Reviewed dd/mm/yyyy
Support Process	Approved:		Issue No: 01 Prepared by:	Revision No: 00

	Process Headings	**Process Details**
10.0	System description	The procedure for budget preparation is shown in Flowchart SP 036.1. Budget shall be prepared according to the instructions issued by the Financial Manager. Each department shall prepare its draft budget within the financial framework issued by the Financial Manager.
10.1	Items to be included in the budget	• Expected revenue and expenditure to meet the goals of the department • Employee salaries, bonuses, etc. • Repairs and maintenance • Minor fixtures and fittings • Insurance costs and depreciation • Transport costs • Supplies and services and establishment expenses • Financing costs • Income.
10.2	Capital expenditure	A separate budget shall be prepared for capital expenditure.
10.3	Budget approval	All proposed plans and budgets shall be reviewed and approved by each successive level of supervisory management.
10.4	Budget limits	All spending shall be within the financial limits imposed by the Financial Manager.
10.5	Internal control	Financial Manager shall review the accuracy and completeness of proposals and budgets.
10.6	Budget format	The consolidated budget shall be prepared in the prescribed format and shall include: • Recurrent expenditure • Capital expenditure • Estimates for each cost centre • Statement of proposed tariffs and income from each tariff classification • Estimated cash flow statement • Associated documents to substantiate budget proposals.
11.0	Records	Budget Departments' financial requirements.
12.0	Changes made	None.

ABC Company Limited	Procedures Manual	Flowchart SP 036.1 Page 1 of 2	
	Budgeting	Date Released dd/mm/yyyy	Date Reviewed dd/mm/yyyy
Link SP 036	Approved:	Issue No: 01 Prepared by:	Revision No: 00

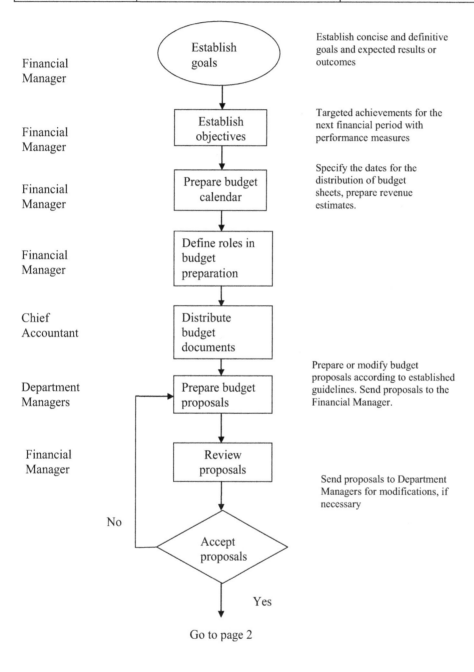

Financial Manager — Establish goals — Establish concise and definitive goals and expected results or outcomes

Financial Manager — Establish objectives — Targeted achievements for the next financial period with performance measures

Financial Manager — Prepare budget calendar — Specify the dates for the distribution of budget sheets, prepare revenue estimates.

Financial Manager — Define roles in budget preparation

Chief Accountant — Distribute budget documents

Department Managers — Prepare budget proposals — Prepare or modify budget proposals according to established guidelines. Send proposals to the Financial Manager.

Financial Manager — Review proposals

Send proposals to Department Managers for modifications, if necessary

No — Accept proposals — Yes

Go to page 2

ABC Company Limited	Procedures Manual	Flowchart SP 036.1 Page 2 of 2	
	Budgeting	Date Released dd/mm/yyyy	Date Reviewed dd/mm/yyyy
Link SP 036	Approved:	Issue No: 01 Prepared by:	Revision No: 00

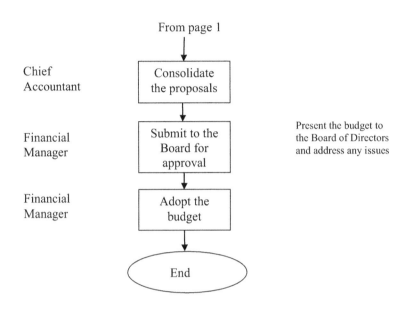

From page 1

Chief Accountant — Consolidate the proposals

Financial Manager — Submit to the Board for approval

Financial Manager — Adopt the budget

End

Present the budget to the Board of Directors and address any issues

SP 037 Accounts Payable

ABC Company Limited	Procedures Manual	Reference SP 037 Page 1 of 3	
	Accounts Payable	Date Released dd/mm/yyyy	Date Reviewed dd/mm/yyyy
Support Process	Approved:	Issue No: 01 Prepared by:	Revision No: 00

Process Owner		Chief Accountant
	Process Headings	**Process Details**
1.0	Purpose	To describe the procedure for the payment of money owed by ABCCL.
2.0	Scope	This procedure shall apply to all payments to suppliers, customers and others for money owed to them.
3.0	Input	Invoices for payment, supporting documents, cost centre and mode of payment.
4.0	Output	Fulfilled payment.
5.0	Competency requirements	Financial qualifications and experience.
6.0	Responsibility	Defined in Flowchart SP 037.1.
7.0	Associated documents	Invoices Voucher package Expense report form.
8.0	Resources	Financial management module (Accounting software).
9.0	Measures/Controls	Reconciliation of payments with invoices and supporting documents Cheque reconciliation.
10.0	System description	Flowchart SP 037.1 shows the account payable process.
10.1	Receiving invoices	Only original invoices are considered for processing for payment unless duplicate copies have been verified as unpaid. Vendors are instructed to submit invoices direct to the Accounting Department. All invoices shall be received by the Administration staff and date stamped. Any invoice out of control of accounting staff shall be kept in the Accounts Payable file for further action.
10.2	Processing invoices	1. Invoices are processed weekly. On receipt of the vendor invoice by the Accounts Payable staff, the accuracy of the invoices shall be verified. Compare the nature, quantity and prices of all items in the invoice against the purchase order or request and packing slip. 2. Information from approved invoices and expense vouchers shall be recorded in the accounting system. 3. All invoices received and approved with supporting documents by the 10th of each month shall be processed at the end of the month.

ABC Company Limited	Procedures Manual	Reference SP 037 Page 2 of 3	
	Accounts Payable	Date Released dd/mm/yyyy	Date Reviewed dd/mm/yyyy
Support Process	Approved:	Issue No: 01 Prepared by:	Revision No: 00

	Process Headings	Process Details
		4. At the end of the financial year, Accounts Payable cut-off may be extended to permit all information to be recorded in the accounting system in that year.
10.3	Preparation of payment pack	Before any invoice is processed for payment, Accounts Payable staff shall check invoices and supporting documents for payment and prepare a payment package consisting of vendor invoice, packing slip (if applicable), and other appropriate supporting documents.
10.4	Processing payment pack	Invoices shall be stamped "Invoices held for payment".
10.5	Preparation of cheques	1. The payment package shall be checked by the Chief Accountant and signed off for payment. Any discrepancy shall be investigated by the Accounts Payable staff. 2. Accountant Accounts Payable shall prepare cheque requirements weekly using pre-numbered cheques. 3. All cheques with supporting documents (voucher package) are forwarded to the Accountant Accounts Payable for review and approval by signing off the cheques. If a second signature is required as stated in the financial manual, the Accountant Accounts Payable shall obtain the second signature. 4. After the cheques have been signed, the Accounts Payable staff shall stamp the cheque request and all supporting documents as "Paid". 5. Accounts Payable staff shall make all necessary entries in the accounting system according to the financial manual.
10.6	Staff expenses	1. Reimbursement of expenses related to business shall only be made on receipt of properly approved and completed reimbursement form. 2. The approval shall be made by the immediate Supervisor. 3. All required receipts shall be attached and a brief description of the business purpose must be noted on the form. Complete expense reports shall be processed for payment in the next vendor payment cycle.

ABC Company Limited	Procedures Manual	Reference SP 037 Page 3 of 3	
	Accounts Payable	Date Released dd/mm/yyyy	Date Reviewed dd/mm/yyyy
Support Process	Approved:	Issue No: 01 Prepared by:	Revision No: 00

	Process Headings	Process Details
10.7	Internal controls	1. At the end of each month, the Chief Accountant shall reconcile the payments made with the General Ledger. All differences are investigated and adjustments made as necessary. The reconciliation and any results of investigations are reviewed by the Financial Manager. 2. The Chief Accountant shall periodically check expense reports against time-sheets to ensure agreement of dates and activities.
11.0	Records	Invoices Supporting documents.
12.0	Changes made	None.

ABC Company Limited	**Procedures Manual**		**Flowchart SP 037.1** Page 1 of 1	
	Accounts Payable		Date Released dd/mm/yyyy	Date Reviewed dd/mm/yyyy
Link SP 037	Approved:		Issue No: 01 Prepared by:	Revision No: 00

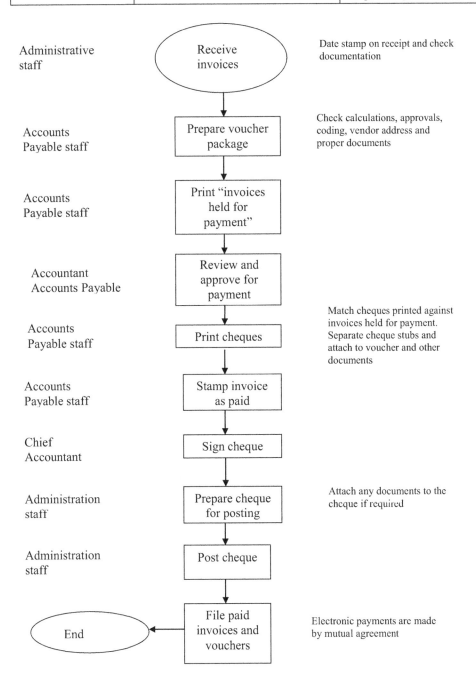

Administrative staff	*Receive invoices*	Date stamp on receipt and check documentation
Accounts Payable staff	Prepare voucher package	Check calculations, approvals, coding, vendor address and proper documents
Accounts Payable staff	Print "invoices held for payment"	
Accountant Accounts Payable	Review and approve for payment	
Accounts Payable staff	Print cheques	Match cheques printed against invoices held for payment. Separate cheque stubs and attach to voucher and other documents
Accounts Payable staff	Stamp invoice as paid	
Chief Accountant	Sign cheque	
Administration staff	Prepare cheque for posting	Attach any documents to the cheque if required
Administration staff	Post cheque	
End	File paid invoices and vouchers	Electronic payments are made by mutual agreement

SP 038 Accounts Receivable

ABC Company Limited	Procedures Manual	Reference SP 038 Page 1 of 2	
	Accounts Receivable	Date Released dd/mm/yyyy	Date Reviewed dd/mm/yyyy
Support Process	Approved:	Issue No: 01 Prepared by:	Revision No: 00

Process Owner	Chief Accountant
Process Headings	**Process Details**
1.0 Purpose	To describe the procedure for accounts receivable.
2.0 Scope	This procedure shall apply to all income received by ABCCL.
3.0 Input	Copy of invoice, credit reports and monthly statements.
4.0 Output	Received funds.
5.0 Competency requirements	Financial qualifications and experience.
6.0 Responsibility	Chief Accountant shall: • Check and process all creditor and debtor accounts • Reconcile accounts • Resolve disputes arising from financial transactions. Administrative staff shall: • Sent out invoices • Keep records of all invoices and related communications • Notify the Chief Accountant of bad debtors. Revenue collections staff shall: • Process receipts • Update accounting software package • Prepare bank deposit documentation. Financial Manager shall: • Approve writing off bad debts.
7.0 Associated documents	Invoice Receipt forms New account creation form Financial manual.
8.0 Resources	Financial management module (Accounting software).
9.0 Measures/controls	Reconciliation of accounts Revenue collected.
10.0 System description	Accounts receivable process is shown in Flowchart SP 038.1.
10.1 Posting invoices	1. All invoices are sent weekly or monthly. Reminder letters for payment are also sent monthly. 2. All invoices must contain a notification "Payable within 15 days. Late payments unless agreed with the Chief Accountant shall incur a set percentage monthly penalty".

ABC Company Limited	Procedures Manual	Reference SP 038 Page 2 of 2	
	Accounts Receivable	Date Released dd/mm/yyyy	Date Reviewed dd/mm/yyyy
Support Process	Approved:	Issue No: 01 Prepared by:	Revision No: 00

	Process Headings	Process Details
		3. Wherever possible the purchase order should be noted on the invoice to avoid disputes and delays in receiving payment. 4. If an invoice is cancelled prior to being sent to the customer, the customer copy and the accounts copy should be forwarded to the Chief Accountant clearly marked "Cancelled". If an invoice is cancelled after it has been issued, the Chief Accountant shall issue a credit note.
10.2	Receiving payments	1. Payments can be received in cash, cheque or by credit card. On receipt of funds, a banking slip is created detailing the amount received and the source funds. 2. Whenever possible, banking should be done daily. If it is not done daily, all cash, cheques and documents relating to payments shall be kept in the safe. 3. All amounts received shall be banked in full. Payment of expenses shall not be taken from funds received. 4. Any remittance advices or other communications accompanying the payment shall be retained and files in the sales invoice file. 5. The amount received shall be posted in the accounting software regularly.
10.3	Bad debts	1. Special provision shall be made for all bad debts. Bad debts shall be written off when all reasonable steps to recover them have been taken. 2. Bad debt policy should state the percentage of outstanding debt at the financial year end to be provided as bad debts. This may vary with different categories of customers and the age of debt. 3. When no transactions have been received from a debtor in the previous 13 months, the Chief Accountant shall remove the account from the debtors' list and invoke write-off procedure.
11.0	Records	All documents associated with the invoice.
12.0	Changes made	None.

ABC Company Limited	Procedures Manual	Flowchart SP 038.1 Page 1 of 1	
	Accounts Receivable	Date Released dd/mm/yyyy	Date Reviewed dd/mm/yyyy
Link SP 038	Approved:	Issue No: 01 Prepared by:	Revision No: 00

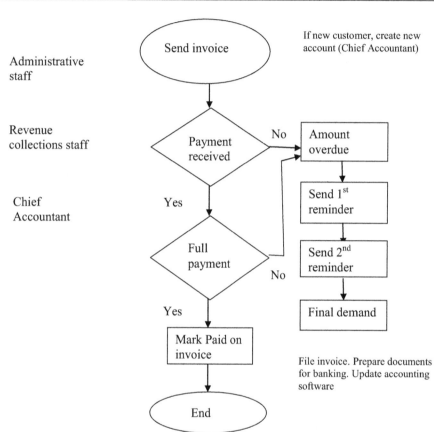

Administrative staff

Revenue collections staff

Chief Accountant

If new customer, create new account (Chief Accountant)

File invoice. Prepare documents for banking. Update accounting software

SP 039 Internal Control

ABC Company Limited	Procedures Manual	Reference SP 039 Page 1 of 3	
	Internal Control	Date Released dd/mm/yyyy	Date Reviewed dd/mm/yyyy
Support Process	Approved:	Issue No: 01 Prepared by:	Revision No: 00

Process Owner	Financial Manager	
	Process Headings	**Process Details**
1.0	Purpose	To describe the procedure for internal controls applied to the financial management system.
2.0	Scope	This procedure shall apply to the activities of the financial department.
3.0	Input	Financial manual, financial transactions and reports.
4.0	Output	Regulatory compliance and effective financial procedures.
5.0	Competency requirements	Financial qualifications and internal financial control skills.
6.0	Responsibility	Financial Manager shall: • Appoint an internal control team which shall include the Chief Accountant • Review the internal control report and initiate actions to resolve • Instruct further investigation, if necessary • Bring fraudulent activities to the attention of the CEO. Chief Accountant shall: • Plan internal control activities • Act as the head of the internal control team • Prepare and submit the internal control report.
7.0	Associated documents	Internal control report Financial manual.
8.0	Resources	Financial management module (Accounting software).
9.0	Measures/controls	Completion of internal control activities.
10.0	System description	
10.1	General considerations	Internal control includes all controls exercised over the policies and procedures adopted by ABCCL to assist in achieving management's objectives of orderly, efficient and effective and ethical conduct of business, adhering to management policies, safeguarding assets, prevention and detection of fraud and errors, accuracy and completeness of accounting records, and the timely preparation of financial information.

ABC Company Limited	Procedures Manual	Reference SP 039 Page 2 of 3	
	Internal Controls	Date Released dd/mm/yyyy	Date Reviewed dd/mm/yyyy
Support Process	Approved:	Issue No: 01 Prepared by:	Revision No: 00

	Process Headings	Process Details
10.2	Purpose of internal controls	Internal controls are established to manage risks and to ensure that ABCCL's resources are used efficiently and effectively. ABCCL's Financial Manager shall continuously assess risks and introduce controls to prevent or mitigate risks to an acceptable level.
10.3	Control methods	1. Training and supervision of staff and clearly defining their roles and responsibilities. Authorities and responsibilities of the staff shall be clearly defined. The training programme shall ensure that they can perform their tasks efficiently and effectively. 2. Adequate separation of duties: The staffing levels and circumstances of each cost centre shall be considered when segregation of duties is contemplated. These guidelines are recommended: <ul><li>Separation of financial functions</li><li>Separation of the authorisation of transactions from the custody of related assets. For example, the person processing invoices in the financial department shall not process cheques</li><li>Separation of operating duties from financial record-keeping</li><li>Separation of custody of assets from maintenance of associated accounting records</li><li>Existence of adequate and complete documentation and records. Compliance with policies and procedures for the procurement of various value-added items and payment of accounts.</li></ul>
10.4	Internal audits	Internal audits shall be performed on these activities: 1. Receipts and payments: All funds shall be receipted and the receipt numbers recorded on the banking summary document submitted to the bank. Cash boxes shall be securely locked with access restricted to designated staff. Banking shall be performed as soon as cash is received or at the earliest opportunity.

ABC Company Limited	Procedures Manual	Reference SP 039 Page 3 of 3	
	Internal Controls	Date Released dd/mm/yyyy	Date Reviewed dd/mm/yyyy
Support Process	Approved:	Issue No: 01 Prepared by:	Revision No: 00

	Process Headings	Process Details
		All payments shall be recorded according to the instructions in the financial manual.
		2. Orders and invoices: Orders shall be completed for all purchases, both internally and externally, and they shall be approved and signed by the Purchasing Manager. Invoices shall be authorised for payment only after being traced to the original purchase order and on fulfilment of the order.
		Department Managers shall review order authorisation and invoice authorisation to ensure that the roles are segregated.
		3. Fixed assets: Those items whose lifespan exceeds one year. Management shall ensure that they are listed in the assets register with an adequate description and a serial number.
		A physical check of fixed assets shall be done regularly against the asset register. All attractive assets such as trophies shall be protected from deterioration, fire and theft.
11.0	Records	Audit reports.
12.0	Changes made	None.

SP 040 Payment of Salaries and Wages

ABC Company Limited	Procedures Manual	Reference SP 040 Page 1 of 3	
	Payment of Salaries and Wages	Date Released dd/mm/yyyy	Date Reviewed dd/mm/yyyy
Support Process	Approved:	Issue No: 01 Prepared by:	Revision No: 00

Process Owner		Chief Accountant
	Process Headings	**Process Details**
1.0	Purpose	To describe the procedure for the payment of salaries and wages to ABCCL's employees.
2.0	Scope	This procedure shall apply to all employees, both permanent and temporary.
3.0	Input	Time-sheets, employment contract documents, payslips and employment letters.
4.0	Output	Pay-sheets, bank deposits, cash.
5.0	Competency requirements	Payroll administration skills.
6.0	Responsibility	Chief Accountant shall: • Check the payroll • Reconcile payments with the payroll • Approve advance payments. Payroll Clerk shall: • Check time cards • Prepare the payroll • File documents. Treasurer's staff shall: • Obtain and prepare pay packets • Record all receipts.
7.0	Associated documents	Time-sheets Payroll Direct debit deposits Financial manual.
8.0	Resources	Financial management module (Accounting software).
9.0	Measures/Controls	Reconciliation of payments with payroll information Direct deposit records.
10.0	Definitions	**Wage:** Financial compensation based on the number of hours worked multiplied by the total number of hours worked. **Salary:** Financial compensation based on the annual rate quoted in the employment contract.
11.0	System description	
11.1	Payday	Salaries are paid monthly via direct debit on the 20th of each month. If the 20th falls on a weekend, payments shall be made on the working day immediately prior to the 20th. Wages are a paid fortnightly on the first and third Thursday of each month.

ABC Company Limited	Procedures Manual	Reference SP 040 Page 2 of 3	
	Payment of Salaries and Wages	Date Released dd/mm/yyyy	Date Reviewed dd/mm/yyyy
Support Process	Approved:	Issue No: 01 Prepared by:	Revision No: 00

	Process Headings	**Process Details**
11.2	Payment rates	All personnel salaries and wage rates and changes in payroll data shall be authorised by the CEO or Executive Director as per letters of appointment or trade union agreements.
11.3	Preparation of time-sheets for payment of wages	1. Each Supervisor shall submit to the Accounting department a signed and approved time-sheet for two weeks ending on a Tuesday. 2. Where facilities are available, time-sheets shall be prepared electronically. In all other instances, manually prepared time-sheets are acceptable. 3. Each time-sheet shall reflect all hours worked during the pay period. 4. Allowable absences shall be recorded on time-sheets. 5. Any alterations shall be signed by the employee and approved by the Supervisor, who shall ensure that all time-sheets are duly signed by the employee before his or her approval. 6. The accuracy of the information shall be checked by the immediate Supervisor before submitting them to the Accounting department.
11.4	Preparation of salary sheets	Salary sheets are prepared by the Payroll Clerk with the information on personal files.
11.5	Processing time-sheets and salaries	1. The Payroll Clerk shall process all time-sheets and salaries by checking them for accuracy and entering the information in the payroll system. The Payroll Clerk shall not alter time-sheets or salary information. 2. The Cashier shall collect the funds and make preparations for payment of wages. 3. The Chief Accountant shall authorise direct deposit of salaries to all employees. 4. The Payroll Clerk shall prepare direct deposit slips to be given to all employees after the funds have been transferred to employees' accounts. He or she shall also prepare payslips to be handed over to employees on wages.
11.6	Payment of wages	On the payday, the Cashier, Payroll Clerk and the immediate Supervisor shall summon each employee and hand over the pay packet. The employee shall sign the pay-sheet and check the accuracy of payment against the payslip. Any discrepancy shall be immediately brought to the attention of the Payroll Clerk.

ABC Company Limited	Procedures Manual	Reference SP 040 Page 3 of 3	
	Payment of Salaries and Wages	Date Released dd/mm/yyyy	Date Reviewed dd/mm/yyyy
Support Process	Approved:	Issue No: 01 Prepared by:	Revision No: 00

	Process Headings	**Process Details**
11.7	Payment of salaries	Salaries are paid by direct debit, and the first working day following the payday direct deposit slips shall be distributed to the salaried staff via internal mail. The direct deposit slip shall also contain the salary amount, any deductions and extra payments.
11.8	Non-scheduled payments	Non-scheduled payments include partial or full advance payment of the salary or payment for an employee who is travelling out of the area on company business. Such employees may request a non-scheduled payment. All non-scheduled payments shall be approved by the Chief Accountant.
11.9	Internal controls	The Chief Accountant shall conduct an annual internal audit of certain payroll data. The purpose of this internal audit is to determine the integrity of the payroll record. The Chief Accountant shall: • Trace a sample of salaries, withholdings, deductions and direct deposit information to supporting documents in each selected employee's payroll and/or personal file • Trace a sample of new recruits and departures to their personal files including verification of first and last pay dates • Cross-check the payroll master file for employees with identical addresses, social security data or direct deposit information.
12.0	Records	Pay-sheets Time-sheets Bank deposits.
13.0	Changes made	None.

SP 041 Management of Fixed Assets

ABC Company Limited	Procedures Manual		Reference SP 041 Page 1 of 2	
	Management of Fixed Assets		Date Released dd/mm/yyyy	Date Reviewed dd/mm/yyyy
Support Process	Approved:		Issue No: 01 Prepared by:	Revision No: 00

Process Owner		**Managing Director**
	Process Headings	**Process Details**
1.0	Purpose	To describe the procedure managing ABCCL's fixed assets.
2.0	Scope	This procedure shall apply to plant, buildings and equipment that can be used for a period longer than one financial year and exceed *[state the dollar value here]*.
3.0	Input	Fixed asset register.
4.0	Output	Update for depreciation, maintenance, repair, improvement and disposal.
5.0	Competency requirements	Skills in managing fixed assets.
6.0	Responsibility	Accounting staff shall: • Prepare and maintain the fixed asset register. Accounting audit staff shall: • Carry out fixed asset audits.
7.0	Associated documents	Fixed asset register.
8.0	Resources	Financial management module (Accounting software).
9.0	Measures/controls	Audit of fixed assets.
10.0	System description	ABCCL's assets are widely distributed and the responsibility for their safeguarding them rests with the manager of the department, unit or division. All assets should be securely marked and should not be removed from its location without permission from the Financial Manager.
10.1	Registration of assets	1. A registration form shall be sent to the appropriate department/unit/division where the asset is located. The manager of the department/unit/division shall document any fixed asset under their control. 2. Management accounts are prepared and presented to the Board of Directors as specified in the financial manual. However, monthly, the CEO and the Financial Manager shall review the monthly management accounts and when necessary make any necessary suggestions, amendment and deductions.
10.2	Asset register	Nominated accounting staff member shall keep an accurate record of the asset owned by ABCCL, description of the asset, its location, purchase date and its written down value. Copies of invoices for the purchase of assets shall be filed in the fixed asset register file.

ABC Company Limited	Procedures Manual	Reference SP 041 Page 2 of 2	
	Management of Fixed Assets	Date Released dd/mm/yyyy	Date Reviewed dd/mm/yyyy
Support Process	Approved:	Issue No: 01 Prepared by:	Revision No: 00

	Process Headings	Process Details
10.3	Depreciation	1. Additions will be depreciated from the month of their purchase. Any disposable items will be accounted for in the month of disposal. 2. At the end of each year, the fixed asset register will be reconciled with the fixed asset control account in the ledger. 3. Depreciations shall be calculated as specified in the financial manual.
10.4	Audits	1. Accounting staff shall carry our audits at intervals specified in the financial manual to ensure that the accuracy and completeness of the register is maintained. 2. The audits will take the form of a cyclical check to ensure that asset is still in the location specified in the register, that all new assets have been correctly entered in it, and that the other information included in the entry is accurate.
11.0	Records	Updated record of fixed assets.
12.0	Changes made	None.

SP 042 Preparation of Management Accounts

ABC Company Limited	Procedures Manual		Reference SP 042 Page 1 of 2	
	Preparation of Management Accounts		Date Released dd/mm/yyyy	Date Reviewed dd/mm/yyyy
Support Process	Approved:		Issue No: 01 Prepared by:	Revision No: 00

Process Owner		Financial Manager
	Process Headings	**Process Details**
1.0	Purpose	To describe the procedure for the preparation of management accounts.
2.0	Scope	This procedure shall apply to the activities of the Financial department.
3.0	Input	ABCCL's accounts.
4.0	Output	Accounts statements.
5.0	Competency requirements	Financial qualifications and skills in managing accounts.
6.0	Responsibility	Financial Manager shall: • Prepare the management accounts • Submit to the CEO for review and approval. CEO shall: • Review and approve management accounts • Submit the accounts to Board members • Act on their recommendations.
7.0	Associated documents	Financial statements.
8.0	Resources	Financial management module (Accounting software).
9.0	Measures/controls	Accuracy of the statement Timely preparation of the statements.
10.0	System description	
10.1	Review of monthly management accounts	Management accounts are prepared and presented to the Board of Directors as specified in the financial manual. However, monthly, the CEO and the Chief Accountant shall review the monthly management accounts and when necessary make any necessary suggestions, amendment and deductions.
10.2	Management accounts pack	Management accounts pack shall include these documents: • Profit and loss • Balance sheet • Forecast to the end of the financial year • Debtor and creditor statements • Cash flow statement • Comments on variances and assumptions • Other supporting documents.

ABC Company Limited	Procedures Manual	Reference SP 042 Page 2 of 2	
	Preparation of Management Accounts	Date Released dd/mm/yyyy	Date Reviewed dd/mm/yyyy
Support Process	Approved:	Issue No: 01 Prepared by:	Revision No: 00

	Process Headings	Process Details
10.3	Report	Financial Manager shall prepare a report after the Board meeting detailing any suggestions, discussions, amendments and decisions that arise from it. This report shall be filed with a copy of the management accounts pack.
11.0	Records	Accounts statements.
12.0	Changes made	None.

SP 043 Management of Bank Accounts

ABC Company Limited	Procedures Manual		Reference SP 043 Page 1 of 2	
	Management of Bank Accounts		Date Released dd/mm/yyyy	Date Reviewed dd/mm/yyyy
Support Process	Approved:		Issue No: 01 Prepared by:	Revision No: 00

Process Owner		**Chief Accountant**
	Process Headings	**Process Details**
1.0	Purpose	To describe the procedure managing ABCCL's bank accounts.
2.0	Scope	This procedure shall apply to all bank accounts held by ABCCL.
3.0	Input	Bank deposits, withdrawals, direct debit statements and other financial transactions.
4.0	Output	Reconciled bank statements.
5.0	Competency requirements	Financial qualifications and skills in managing bank accounts.
6.0	Responsibility	Banking Officer shall: • Access bank statements from the bank(s) • Check bank entries • Post direct entries in the ledger • Prepare reconciliation statement. Accounting Administrative Officer shall: • Check and sign off reconciliations statement • Investigate any fraudulent activities.
7.0	Associated documents	Bank statements Reconciliation statement.
8.0	Resources	Financial management module (Accounting software).
9.0	Measures/controls	Reconciliation of bank accounts with ledger.
10.0	System description	
10.1	Bank statements	Banking Officer shall obtain bank statement from the bank every week (or download from the bank site) and check for direct entries not in the General Ledger. Direct entries normally include bank charges, ledger fees and interest earned. They should be posted to the correct account.
10.2	Reconciliation	(a) At the end of each month, a reconciliation statement shall be prepared by the Banking Officer from the monthly bank statement obtained from the bank. The statement shall be scrutinised for direct entries and posted in the ledger. (b) A copy of the reconciliation statement shall be submitted to the Accounting Administration Officer for review and signature. (c) Any cheques outstanding for a period longer than six months shall be reviewed and written back when necessary. (d) Any differences between the nominal ledger and the bank account shall not be written off without careful investigation and explanation of the difference to the Accounting Administration Officer.

ABC Company Limited	Procedures Manual		Reference SP 043 Page 2 of 2	
	Management of Bank Accounts		Date Released dd/mm/yyyy	Date Reviewed dd/mm/yyyy
Support Process	Approved:		Issue No: 01 Prepared by:	Revision No: 00

	Process Headings	Process Details
11.0	Records	Reconciled bank statements.
12.0	Changes made	None.

SP 044 Management of Credit Cards

ABC Company Limited	Procedures Manual		Reference SP 044 Page 1 of 4	
	Management of Credit Cards		Date Released dd/mm/yyyy	Date Reviewed dd/mm/yyyy
Support Process	Approved:		Issue No: 01 Prepared by:	Revision No: 00

Process Owner		Chief Accountant
	Process Headings	Process Details
1.0	Purpose	To describe the procedure managing credit card accounts of ABCCL.
2.0	Scope	This procedure shall apply to all credit issued by ABCCL to its staff.
3.0	Input	Employee's position, business-related expenses and expense limit.
4.0	Output	Availability of a credit card for business-related expenses within allocated limits.
5.0	Competency requirements	Financial qualifications and experience in managing credit cards.
6.0	Responsibility	Accounting Administration Officer shall: • Authorise the issue of credit cards • Review credit card transactions and approve payment • Post direct entries in the ledger • Prepare reconciliation statement. Credit Card Officer shall: • Check all credit card statements against purchases • Prepare a monthly credit card statement.
7.0	Associated documents	Credit card statements Reconciliation statement Credit card request form.
8.0	Resources	Financial management module (Accounting software).
9.0	Measures/controls	Reconciliation of credit card accounts with purchases.
10.0	System description	
10.1	Issue of credit cards	1. Credit cards are issued for the purpose of enabling online and business purchases that are not easily handled through normal disbursement processing. Credit card holders shall sign a statement acknowledging that the card will be used exclusively for legitimate ABCCL business purposes and to take reasonable precautions to protect the card from loss or theft. 2. Credit cards are only issued to those specified in the financial manual. Any departure from this has to be approved by the Financial Manager. Upon approval from the credit card company, a card will be issued bearing both the name of the holder and ABCCL.

ABC Company Limited	Procedures Manual	Reference SP 044 Page 2 of 4	
	Management of Credit Cards	Date Released dd/mm/yyyy	Date Reviewed dd/mm/yyyy
Support Process	Approved:	Issue No: 01 Prepared by:	Revision No: 00

	Process Headings	Process Details
10.2	Card holder's responsibilities	1. Credit shall only be used for ABCCL-related business transactions. A receipt shall be obtained for every transaction. All receipts shall be submitted to the Accounting department at the end of each month. 2. The credit card holder shall immediately report the loss of the credit card issued to the holder to the Chief Accountant.
10.3	Credit card statements	• Each month, the credit card company provides a master credit card statement along with individual statements for each credit card • The Credit Card Officer shall check the statements against the purchases for compliance with ABCCL credit card policy. If discrepancies are found the statement is forwarded to the card holder for comments • The card holder shall check the statement within three days for any allowable changes or inadvertent personal or unauthorised use of the card • The card holder shall reimburse ABCCL for any inadvertent personal charges within the same three-day period • The card holder shall investigate the origin of any unauthorised charges and resolve the problem. All communication related to the issue shall be documented. The card holder may seek the help of the Accounting department for resolving the issue • Any fraudulent activity detected by the Credit Card Officer or the individual shall be brought to the attention of the Financial Manager immediately • The use of the credit card for personal use is strictly forbidden. The company has the authority to take disciplinary action in such instances as stated in the financial manual • The credit card holder shall immediately report the loss of the credit card issued to them to the Chief Accountant.

ABC Company Limited	Procedures Manual	Reference SP 044 Page 3 of 4	
	Management of Credit Cards	Date Released dd/mm/yyyy	Date Reviewed dd/mm/yyyy
Support Process	Approved:	Issue No: 01 Prepared by:	Revision No: 00

	Process Headings	Process Details
10.4	Cancellation of credit cards	1. Abuse of the credit card shall result in the revocation of credit card privileges. The Financial Manager and the Accounting Administration Officer shall jointly determine whether the credit card should be revoked and, if so, the Supervisor of the credit card holder shall be notified of credit card misuse and proposed disciplinary action. 2. Upon termination of employment or separation from ABCCL, the card holder shall return the card to the Accounting department. The credit card then will be cancelled. The card holder remains responsible for unbilled transactions up through to the day the card is cancelled.
10.5	Gasoline credit cards	Some employees may be issued with a gasoline credit card for purchasing gasoline and oil for ABCCL vehicles used by the staff on business travel. When making a gasoline purchase using the gasoline credit card, the driver shall attach a receipt and enter the details in the vehicle log book.
10.6	Review of credit card statements	1. The Accounting Administration Officer shall review the summary schedule accompanying the credit card statements issued by the credit card company and make necessary adjustments. Original copies of receipts shall be attached to the schedule. 2. The Credit Card Officer shall record all credit card accounts in the accounting software package monthly. He or she shall prepare a spreadsheet showing for whom the purchases were made. The spreadsheet shall be signed off by the Accounting Administration Officer.

ABC Company Limited	Procedures Manual		Reference SP 044 Page 4 of 4	
	Management of Credit Cards		Date Released dd/mm/yyyy	Date Reviewed dd/mm/yyyy
Support Process	Approved:		Issue No: 01 Prepared by:	Revision No: 00

	Process Headings	**Process Details**
10.7	Credit card payments	All payments of credit cards are by direct payment.
11.0	Records	Credit card statements Credit card holders register Purchase receipts.
12.0	Changes made	None.

SP 045 Control of External Provision

ABC Company Limited	Procedures Manual	Reference SP 045 Page 1 of 6	
	Control of External Provision	Date Released dd/mm/yyyy	Date Reviewed dd/mm/yyyy
Support Process	Approved:	Issue No: 01 Prepared by:	Revision No: 00

Process Owner	Purchasing Manager

	Process Headings	Process Details
1.0	Purpose	To describe the procedure for controlling the provision of processes, products and services by an external party.
2.0	Scope	This procedure applies to processes, products and services outsourced by our company.
3.0	Input	Decision to outsource, requirements for outsourced products, processes and services, information on supplier market, applicable procedures and specifications.
4.0	Output	Information on outsourced products, processes and services, contract or agreement, information about documents of external origin, and products, processes and services.
5.0	Competency requirements	Knowledge of outsourced products, processes and services, control mechanisms, approval of supplier procedure, audits and inspection skills.
6.0	Responsibility	Management Team shall: • Identify the requirements for outsourcing processes, products and services • Identify resource needs. Plant Manager shall: • Obtain the necessary resources for outsourcing • Negotiate contracts with suppliers. Purchasing Manager shall: • Identify external providers for the provision of necessary processes, products and services • Communicate with external providers • Maintain a list of approved suppliers. QA Manager shall: • Specify controls for outsourced processes, products and services • Carry out necessary inspections and audits • Measure the performance of external providers.
7.0	Associated documents	Approved Supplier List (ASL) (Form 039) Specifications for processes, products and services Specifications for processes, products and services Contract Establishing controls (Form 124).

ABC Company Limited	Procedures Manual	Reference SP 045 Page 2 of 6	
	Control of External Provision	Date Released dd/mm/yyyy	Date Reviewed dd/mm/yyyy
Support Process	Approved:	Issue No: 01 Prepared by:	Revision No: 00

	Process Headings	**Process Details**
8.0	Resources	Financial resources
9.0	Measures/controls	Percentage of on-time deliveries Extent of non-conforming processes, products and services Withdrawals and recalls.
10.0	Definitions	**Outsourced processes:** All processes that the organisation has identified as being necessary for its operations and IQFSE management system, and carried out by an external provider outside the managerial control of the organisation. **External provider:** An outside organisation selected to provide processes, products and services to our organisation.
11.0	System description	
11.1	External provision controls within the Integrated Quality, Food Safety and Environmental Management System (IQFSE) management system	Activities of external providers that are related to ABCCL's business activities are included in the IQFSE management system. The procedures include: CP 001 Approval of suppliers CP 003 Purchasing information CP 004 Purchasing CP 006 Purchasing IT CP 005 Purchasing engineering items CP 002 Offering contracts CP 007 Inward goods receipt CP 008 Inward goods inspection.
11.2	Need for external providers	(a) The Management Team shall identify the processes, products and/or services required to be provided by an external provider. A request is made to the Plant Manager for approval; and (b) The organisation considers the provision of these categories of outsourcing: • Products and processes intended to be incorporated into our own products and services. For example, packaging material (product), cleaning the facility (service) • Process or part of a process intended to be carried out. For example, filling wine in 200 ml bottles • Products and services intended to be provided directly to our customers. For example, promotional material (product), shelf display at customer's facility (service).

ABC Company Limited	Procedures Manual		Reference SP 045 Page 3 of 6	
	Control of External Provision		Date Released dd/mm/yyyy	Date Reviewed dd/mm/yyyy
Support Process	Approved:		Issue No: 01 Prepared by:	Revision No: 00

	Process Headings	**Process Details**
11.3	Controls applied to external providers and resulting output	Controls can be engineering controls and/or procedures based on (a) elimination; (b) substitution; or (c) administration. When controls are established (Form 124), the QA Manager shall: (a) Consider the impact of externally provided products, processes and services on the ability to meet quality, service and delivery requirements demanded by our organisation to meet customer needs; (b) Consider maintenance activities, management of on-site contractors and relationship with external providers because they may affect the environmental performance; (c) Consider environmental aspects and associated impacts, risks and opportunities associated with production and service provision and our compliance obligations; and (d) Exercise controls through a wide range of activities such as: • Indicating the requirements on the purchase order • Qualifying external providers • Inspecting outsourcing work • Auditing the external provider • Requesting inspection records from the external provider • Ensuring that the external provider's management system is certified to ISO standards • Establishing clear goals for the external provider • Meeting providers regularly • Measuring the performance.

ABC Company Limited	Procedures Manual	Reference SP 045 Page 4 of 6	
	Control of External Provision	Date Released dd/mm/yyyy	Date Reviewed dd/mm/yyyy
Support Process	Approved:	Issue No: 01 Prepared by:	Revision No: 00

	Process Headings	Process Details
11.4	Control of externally provided processes, products and services	
11.4.1	Levels of controls exercised	(a) Outsourcing a process that has been carried out in our plant: Apply existing process details, applicable specifications and controls about supplier requirements for compliance. The QA Manager shall obtain evidence of compliance from the supplier; and (b) Outsourcing a process that cannot be carried out in the organisation: QA Manager shall ensure that the process details, applicable specifications and controls proposed by the supplier are clearly defined, adequate and ensure the organisation's requirements are met.
11.4.2	Supply chain management	For products and services supplied directly to the customer by the external provider, the QA Manager shall carry out inspections at the supplier's premises before delivery to the customer.
11.4.3	Purchasing management	All purchased products which are incorporated into the organisation's products and services are evaluated on receipt according to the organisation's requirements.
11.5	General considerations of effects on customers and regulatory requirements	The QA Manager shall ensure that externally provided products, processes and services do not adversely affect the quality, service and delivery requirements demanded by the organisation to meet customer requirements. This is achieved through the process of selection of suppliers (CP 001), exercising controls over the external provider and over the products, processes and services delivered by the external provider.
11.6	Effectiveness of controls over external provider	1. The selection of suppliers in the process ensures that the external provider has met the requirements for controls within the external provider's facility to realise the needs of ABCCL. Verification activities include quarterly meetings with supplier, audits of the external provider's management system, performance ratings according to procedure CP 001 and the ability to meet goals jointly established between the organisation and the external provider. 2. Their output is verified by procedures CP 007 Inward goods receipt and CP 008 Inward goods inspection. Services, if any, are also verified on delivery.

ABC Company Limited	Procedures Manual	Reference SP 045 Page 5 of 6	
	Control of External Provision	Date Released dd/mm/yyyy	Date Reviewed dd/mm/yyyy
Support Process	Approved:	Issue No: 01 Prepared by:	Revision No: 00

	Process Headings	Process Details
11.7	Information submitted to external provider	The information communicated to the external provider includes: 1. Products and services to be provided and processes to be outsourced. This information shall be included in the agreement or the contract with the external provider. 2. Methods of approval or release of products, services, processes, specifications and equipment. These requirements are defined clearly by the QA Manager and incorporated into the agreement or contract. 3. Competence and qualification requirements of personnel and the need to have a clear understanding of requirements. The external provider shall maintain a system ensuring the understanding of requirements by personnel. 4. The interaction with the external provider's management system. The external provider becomes a part of the IQFSE management system through the approval supplier process, contracts or agreements, audits and inspections. 5. Performance measurement. A clear process of monitoring and control shall be established and communicated to the external provider. This may include the controls defined through specifications, inspection and audit schedule, performance measurements, evaluation of risk to products and services and quarterly meetings with suppliers. 6. Verification activities. The QA Manager shall communicate the verification and validation activities that the organisation intends to carry out at the external provider's premises. 7. Confidentiality and disclosure statement. 8. Expectations of risk-based thinking. This includes the ability of the external provider to apply risk-based thinking to outsourced products and services and take appropriate action to eliminate or minimise risks. 9. Agreement on delivery requirements. 10. Agreement on process changes by the external provider. 11. Means of managing non-conforming products and services. 12. Product liability expectations.

ABC Company Limited	Procedures Manual	Reference SP 045 Page 6 of 6	
	Control of External Provision	Date Released dd/mm/yyyy	Date Reviewed dd/mm/yyyy
Support Process	Approved:	Issue No: 01 Prepared by:	Revision No: 00

	Process Headings	Process Details
12.0	Records	Purchasing Manager shall maintain contract agreements and records and documents relating to purchases. QA Manager shall maintain procedures, specifications, inspection and audit records and records of performance measurement.
13.0	Changes made	None.

SP 046 Customer Satisfaction

ABC Company Limited	Procedures Manual		Reference SP 046 Page 1 of 3	
	Customer Satisfaction		Date Released dd/mm/yyyy	Date Reviewed dd/mm/yyyy
Support Process	Approved:		Issue No: 01 Prepared by:	Revision No: 00

Process Owner	**Customer Relations Manager**
Process Headings	**Process Details**
1.0 Purpose	To describe the procedure for measuring and customer satisfaction.
2.0 Scope	This procedure shall apply to all our customers.
3.0 Input	See section 10.1.
4.0 Output	Ability to deliver customer needs and expectations, satisfied customers, continual improvement and meeting sales targets.
5.0 Competency requirements	Customer relations skills and communication skills.
6.0 Responsibility	Marketing Manager shall: • Review customer satisfaction and implement procedures to improve customer satisfaction. Sales Manager shall: • Identify and measure customer satisfaction using the procedures described here. QA Manager shall: • Address issues and take corrective actions.
7.0 Associated documents	Customer survey (Form 133) Customer complaint reports (Form 134) Customer feedback Customer focus (MP 016).
8.0 Resources	Customer relations database.
9.0 Measures/controls	Customer satisfaction rating.
10.0 System description	
10.1 Information and data collection	Customer satisfaction information is collected from customer feedback and by analysing their responses to: • Customer satisfaction surveys • Customer complaints • Recognition and awards from customers, associations, community groups and consumer groups • Product returns • Warranty claims • Repeat customers • Market share • Delivery performance • Corrective action reports.

ABC Company Limited	Procedures Manual		Reference SP 046 Page 2 of 3	
	Customer Satisfaction		Date Released dd/mm/yyyy	Date Reviewed dd/mm/yyyy
Support Process	Approved:		Issue No: 01 Prepared by:	Revision No: 00

	Process Headings	Process Details
10.2	Unsolicited feedback	1. Customer complaints and unsolicited spontaneous feedback from customers are collected and processed by the Marketing and Sales Teams. 2. Customer complaints are statistically analysed by grouping them into selected categories for evaluating customer satisfaction. 3. Customer satisfaction data is compiled and analysed by the Marketing and Sales Managers and reviewed at the management review meeting and monthly sales and marketing meetings.
10.3	Product returns and warranty claims	Sales Team is responsible for coordinating product return requests and warranty claims. The return for each claim is recorded, categorised and reviewed at the management review meeting. QA Manager is responsible for determining the validity of the claim.
10.4	Recognition and rewards	1. ABCCL encourages feedback from customers and seeks to participate in recognition and award programmes. 2. All customer ratings, awards and recognitions are analysed and used in the same way as customer feedback. Sales and Marketing Managers shall identify the products and aspects of service responsible for awards and recognition. The results are presented at the management review meeting and monthly sales and marketing meetings.
10.5	Repeat customers, referrals and market share	1. Sales and Marketing Teams shall analyse sales data to monitor repeat customers and referral to identify their purchasing behaviour. 2. Marketing Team shall collect and analyse data on competition, competitive products in the market and market share. The results are presented at the management review meeting and monthly sales and marketing meetings.
10.6	Customer satisfaction surveys	1. Customer satisfaction surveys are administered by the Sales Team. The survey template is reviewed by the Marketing Managers as and when required. 2. Customer satisfaction survey may also include information on customer report cards and user opinion surveys. 3. If a response is not received by the customer within four weeks, a follow-up telephone call is made to conduct the survey verbally. 4. Sales and Marketing Teams shall compile customer satisfactions surveys and combine the data with other customer satisfaction data to determine the performance of ABCCL's products and services. The results are presented and discussed at the management review meeting and monthly sales and marketing meeting.

ABC Company Limited	Procedures Manual	Reference SP 046 Page 3 of 3	
	Customer Satisfaction	Date Released dd/mm/yyyy	Date Reviewed dd/mm/yyyy
Support Process	Approved:	Issue No: 01 Prepared by:	Revision No: 00

	Process Headings	**Process Details**
10.7	Monitoring needs and expectations	Through customer complaints, customer satisfaction surveys, warranty claims, informal meetings with customers regularly by the Sales Team and internal audits, we are able to monitor the degree to which customer needs and expectations are fulfilled.
10.8	Using the information	QA Manager attends both management review meetings and monthly sales and marketing meetings. Results presented by the Sales and the Marketing teams are evaluated by the QA Manager and action taken to address issues relating to products and services through the corrective action procedure. This may involve changes to procedures, developing new procedures and redesigning products and services.
11.0	Records	Results of customer satisfaction surveys Complaint reports Warranty claims Corrective actions.
12.0	Changes made	None.

SP 047 Customer Complaints

ABC Company Limited	Procedures Manual		Reference SP 047 Page 1 of 3	
	Customer Complaints		Date Released dd/mm/yyyy	Date Reviewed dd/mm/yyyy
Support Process	Approved:		Issue No: 01 Prepared by:	Revision No: 00

Process Owner		Customer Relations Manager
	Process Headings	**Process Details**
1.0	Purpose	To describe the procedure for handling customer complaints.
2.0	Scope	This procedure shall apply to all product and service complaints from customers.
3.0	Input	Customer's concern or customer's compliment.
4.0	Output	Resolved complaint, customer satisfaction, staff satisfaction and continual improvement of products and services.
5.0	Competency requirements	Communication skills, problem-solving skills, customer relations management skills.
6.0	Responsibility	Customer Relations Manager shall: • Receive and document all complaints • Respond to all complaints • Direct complaints to appropriate Department Managers for investigation. Department Managers shall: • Investigate all complaints • Submit report to the Customer Relations Manager • Resolve issues and take corrective and preventive action.
7.0	Associated documents	Complaints log (Form 135) Complaints report (Form 134).
8.0	Resources	Customer relationship module.
9.0	Measures/controls	Number of complaints received Number of compliments received Turnaround time for resolving complaints.
10.0	Definitions	**Complaint:** An expression of dissatisfaction by a customer(s) about ABCCL's action or lack of action or about the quality of products and/or services provided by the company or on behalf of ABCCL. **Compliment:** An expression of satisfaction by a customer or customers about ABCCL's action or lack of action or about the quality of products and/or services provided by the company or on behalf of ABCCL.
11.0	System description	The procedure for handling customer complaints is shown in Flowchart SP 047.1.

ABC Company Limited	Procedures Manual	Reference SP 047 Page 2 of 3	
	Customer Complaints	Date Released dd/mm/yyyy	Date Reviewed dd/mm/yyyy
Support Process	Approved:	Issue No: 01 Prepared by:	Revision No: 00

	Process Headings	**Process Details**
11.1	Frontline resolution	Issues that are straightforward and easily resolved with little or no investigation shall be dealt by the Customer Relations Manager or alternatively referred to the appropriate manager for frontline resolution. The resolution may involve a quick apology explanation or any other action within two working days. Details of the issuer, outcome and resolution are recorded for continual improvement.
11.2	Response to customer complaints which require further investigation	1. If (a) the customer refuses to agree to a frontline resolution; or (b) the customer is dissatisfied with the frontline resolution offered; or (c) issue is complex and requires further investigation; or (d) issue is serious, the Customer Relations Manager shall escalate the complaint for investigation. 2. On receipt of a complaint, the Customer Relations Manager shall send a response in the form of an apology to the customer within two working days. Customer Relations Manager shall inform the customer that the matter will be investigated and a report will follow. 3. Within seven working days, the Customer Services Manager shall inform the customer of the action taken to resolve the issue. If the matter has not been resolved, he or she shall inform the customer of intended action. 4. On resolution of the issues, the Customer Services Manager shall offer compensation in accordance with ABCCL policies.
11.3	Serious complaint	For a serious complaint such as death, serious illness, repeated failures to provide a satisfactory resolution or it poses a serious risk to the organisation's operations, it shall be referred to the General Manager who shall consult the Legal Officers, the CEO and the Senior Executive Managers for appropriate action.
11.4	Handling compliments	All compliments are received by the Customer Relations Manager who shall direct them to the relevant Department Manager. The compliment may be posted in the Bulletin Board for the information of all staff.

ABC Company Limited	Procedures Manual	Reference SP 047 Page 3 of 3	
	Customer Complaints	Date Released dd/mm/yyyy	Date Reviewed dd/mm/yyyy
Support Process	Approved:	Issue No: 01 Prepared by:	Revision No: 00

	Process Headings	Process Details
11.5	Customer relations database	Customer relations database shall include this information in relation to the complaint: • Customer's details • Date of complaint • Details of the complaint and how it was received • Frontline resolution, if applicable • Date of closure of frontline investigation, if applicable • Date of escalation to investigation stage, if applicable • Cause of the problem • Corrective action taken • Date of closure of the complaint.
12.0	Records	Customer relations database.
13.0	Changes made	None.

ABC Company Limited	Procedures Manual	Flowchart SP 047.1 Page 1 of 1	
	Customer Complaints	Date Released dd/mm/yyyy	Date Reviewed dd/mm/yyyy
Link SP 047	Approved:	Issue No: 01 Prepared by:	Revision No: 00

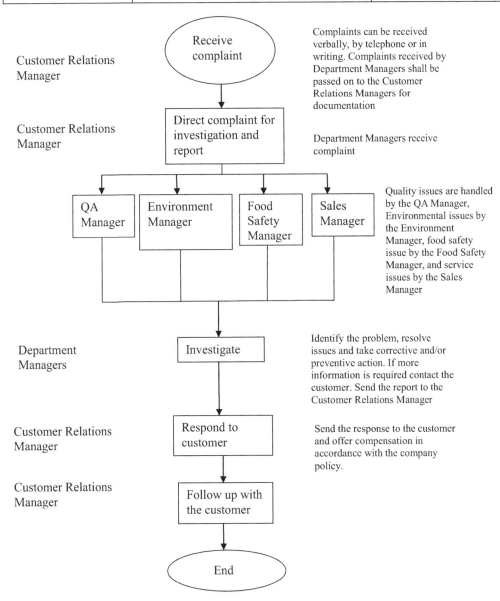

Customer Relations Manager

Receive complaint

Complaints can be received verbally, by telephone or in writing. Complaints received by Department Managers shall be passed on to the Customer Relations Managers for documentation

Customer Relations Manager

Direct complaint for investigation and report

Department Managers receive complaint

QA Manager Environment Manager Food Safety Manager Sales Manager

Quality issues are handled by the QA Manager, Environmental issues by the Environment Manager, food safety issue by the Food Safety Manager, and service issues by the Sales Manager

Department Managers

Investigate

Identify the problem, resolve issues and take corrective and/or preventive action. If more information is required contact the customer. Send the report to the Customer Relations Manager

Customer Relations Manager

Respond to customer

Send the response to the customer and offer compensation in accordance with the company policy.

Customer Relations Manager

Follow up with the customer

End

SP 048 Employee Participation

ABC Company Limited	Procedures Manual		Reference SP 048 Page 1 of 3	
	Employee Participation		Date Released dd/mm/yyyy	Date Reviewed dd/mm/yyyy
Support Process	Approved:		Issue No: 01 Prepared by:	Revision No: 00

Process Owner		Plant Manager
	Process Headings	**Process Details**
1.0	Purpose	To describe the manner in which ABCCL's employees, contractors and other interested parties participate in decision-making process.
2.0	Scope	This procedure applies to all employees, contractors and other interested parties associated with ABCCL.
3.0	Input	Subject matter, changes to products and processes, solutions to problems that require input from employees, ideas for continual improvement and for safety and welfare of employees.
4.0	Output	Staff satisfaction, staff empowerment and enhanced staff motivation.
5.0	Competency requirements	Team work skills, problem-solving skills and communication skills.
6.0	Responsibility	All Managers and Supervisors shall: • Encourage participation of employees, contractors and other interested parties in decision-making.
7.0	Associated documents	Minutes of meetings/briefings.
8.0	Resources	None.
9.0	Measures/controls	Feedback from employees, contractors and other interested parties.
10.0	System description	
10.1	Meetings	Major form of participation is through meetings: • Senior Managers meet monthly to discuss financial matters, objectives, targets • Compliance issues, business performance and other matters that impact on strategy • Management Team meet monthly to discuss performance issues • Production Team together with marketing, sales and logistics functions meet weekly to discuss production planning • Department Managers hold meetings weekly with their reporting personnel to discuss issues that affect performance • Supervisors meet with their reporting personnel to discuss matters that affect daily operations. These meetings are brief and generally held at shut-down

ABC Company Limited	Procedures Manual	Reference SP 048 Page 2 of 3	
	Employee Participation	Date Released dd/mm/yyyy	Date Reviewed dd/mm/yyyy
Support Process	Approved:	Issue No: 01 Prepared by:	Revision No: 00

	Process Headings	Process Details
		• QA Manager, Purchasing Manager and Plant Manager meet suppliers and contractors and other interested parties at least quarterly to discuss matters that affect the delivery of products and services • At these meetings, participants are encouraged to provide ideas and suggestions for improvement, which are then considered by the Management Team for continual improvement.
10.2	Meetings as needed	• QA Manager, Environment Manager and the Food Safety Manager may solicit employee involvement in resolving problems, investigating complaints and non-conformities, providing suggestions for continual improvement projects, hygiene and sanitation issues and other matters which employees feel are significant • All employees are encouraged to participate in identifying risks and opportunities, food safety hazards and controls and environmental aspects and impacts • Changes that affect the Integrated Quality, Food Safety and Environmental (IQFSE) management system are notified to employees via meetings, emails, Bulletin Board postings, newsletters and other methods of communications • Employees participate in the development of processes through informal discussions • ABCCL has an open door policy where an employee may directly contact top management with their concern if the issue has not been addressed by the immediate Supervisor.
10.3	Contractors and suppliers	Apart from regular meetings with suppliers and contractors, when changes are made to the IQFSE management system that could affect the performance of suppliers and contractors, ABCCL shall review such changes with individuals or their management.

ABC Company Limited	Procedures Manual	Reference SP 048 Page 3 of 3	
	Employee Participation	Date Released dd/mm/yyyy	Date Reviewed dd/mm/yyyy
Support Process	Approved:	Issue No: 01 Prepared by:	Revision No: 00

	Process Headings	Process Details
10.4	Other interested parties	As appropriate, ABCCL shall consult relevant interested parties about pertinent IQFSE management system matters.
11.0	Records	Records of meetings.
12.0	Changes made	None.

ASSURANCE PROCEDURES

AP 001 Control of Specifications

ABC Company Limited	Procedures Manual		Reference AP 001 Page 1 of 3	
	Control of Specifications		Date Released dd/mm/yyyy	Date Reviewed dd/mm/yyyy
Assurance Process	Approved:		Issue No: 01 Prepared by:	Revision No: 00

Process Owner		**QA Manager**
	Process Headings	**Process Details**
1.0	Purpose	To describe the procedure for controlling specifications for raw materials, engineering items, finished goods and monitoring devices.
2.0	Scope	This procedure applies to inward goods, engineering items, finished goods and monitoring devices used in production.
3.0	Input	ABCCL standards, codes of practice, user manuals, published material relevant to the product, applicable statutory and regulatory requirements.
4.0	Output	Completed specification sheet, test methods and acceptance criteria.
5.0	Competency requirements	Knowledge of products and relevant technology skills.
6.0	Responsibility	Food Safety Manager shall: <ul><li>Define specifications for all ingredients used in food productions and for all finished food products</li><li>Review the specifications (as and when necessary).</li></ul> Environment Manager shall: <ul><li>Define specifications for items required for managing environmental aspects</li><li>Review the specifications (as and when necessary).</li></ul> QA Team shall: <ul><li>Define specifications for all other raw materials and products</li><li>Review the specifications (as and when necessary).</li></ul>
7.0	Associated documents	Specifications manual Testing methods.
8.0	Resources	Applicable drawings Reference samples.
9.0	Measures/controls	Accuracy of specification.
10.0	System description	
10.1	Generating specifications	Specifications may be generated by one or more of these methods: <ul><li>Specifications may refer to recognised external standards such as British Pharmacopoeia (BP), United States Pharmacopoeia (USP), Analar, etc.</li><li>Specifications may be generated in consultation with the suppliers, which is the most common method for developing specifications for packaging materials</li><li>ABCCL may accept the specifications used by the supplier, e.g. specifications for glass bottle.</li></ul>

ABC Company Limited	Procedures Manual	Reference AP 001 Page 2 of 3	
	Control of Specifications	Date Released dd/mm/yyyy	Date Reviewed dd/mm/yyyy
Assurance Process	Approved:	Issue No: 01 Prepared by:	Revision No: 00

	Process Headings	Process Details
10.2	Generating specifications in-house	ABCCL may generate specifications in-house: 1. When specifications are generated in-house, ABCCL shall define the qualifications and skills of personnel responsible for generating them. 2. Qualifications shall be established for engineering personnel responsible for generating specifications for engineering items. 3. Specifications for food items and devices for controlling environmental aspects shall be devised by a person or a panel qualified in food production and environmental management. 4. Specifications for wine shall be defined by a Winemaker qualified in Wine Technology.
10.3	Generating specifications for food items and wine during design and development	The Food Safety Manager (for food items) or the Winemaker (for wine) shall establish a tasting panel and establish sampling and tasting methods for the wine and food products considered during design and development.
10.4	Generating specifications for raw materials, ingredients and food contact material	Consider items listed in Form 163
10.5	Generating specifications for end product	Consider items listed in Form 163
10.6	Essential qualifications	1. The Food Safety Manager shall be a graduate in food technology and undergo training for one year under the incumbent Food Safety Manager. The first person appointed to the position of Food Safety Manager shall have the qualifications specified above with at least one year of experience in the food industry. 2. The Winemaker shall be a graduate in wine technology and undergo training for one year under the incumbent Winemaker. The first person appointed to the position of Winemaker shall have the qualifications specified above with at least one year of experience in the wine industry.

ABC Company Limited	**Procedures Manual**	**Reference AP 001** Page 3 of 3	
	Control of Specifications	Date Released dd/mm/yyyy	Date Reviewed dd/mm/yyyy
Assurance Process	Approved:	Issue No: 01 Prepared by:	Revision No: 00

	Process Headings	**Process Details**
10.7	Changes to specifications	1. If changes to specifications are needed, the person or the panel responsible for generating the specifications shall make the necessary changes in consultation with those affected by the change(s). 2. The changes must follow the Document Control Procedure (SP 001).
11.0	Records	Specification sheet Reference material.
12.0	Changes made	None.

AP 002 Control of Monitoring and Measuring Devices

ABC Company Limited	Procedures Manual		Reference AP 002 Page 1 of 6	
	Control of Monitoring and Measuring Devices		Date Released dd/mm/yyyy	Date Reviewed dd/mm/yyyy
Assurance Process	Approved:		Issue No: 01 Prepared by:	Revision No: 00

Process Owner		Engineering Manager
	Process Headings	**Process Details**
1.0	Purpose	To describe the procedure for controlling monitoring and measuring (MM) devices needed to provide evidence of conformity of product, processes, materials and environmental activities to specified standards.
2.0	Scope	This procedure applies to MM devices used to monitor and measure ABCCL's products and activities.
3.0	Input	Statutory requirements, work instructions, MM devices, relevant standards, user manuals and performance metrics.
4.0	Output	Calibrated equipment and instruments, accurate information and data, calibration programme and skilled staff.
5.0	Competency requirements	Knowledge of calibration requirements, calibration principles, uncertainty, tolerance and statistical tools, MM devices and operating skills.
6.0	Responsibility	Defined in Flowchart AP 002.1. Additional responsibilities are set out below. Quality Assurance Manager shall: • Establish a calibration programme which shall include calibration methods, acceptance criteria and standards to be used • Determine (if required) that devices are in the inventory • Order, fabricate and authorise the use of employee-owned or customer required devices. Supervisors shall: • Ensure that the equipment and instruments used for calibration and MM are within their calibration period • Ensure that the equipment and instruments are capable of measuring to the required accuracy and tolerances • Train the staff to use the equipment and instruments.
7.0	Associated documents	Calibration methods and procedure Calibration database (Form 126) Equipment inventory (Form 125).

ABC Company Limited	Procedures Manual	Reference AP 002 Page 2 of 6	
	Control of Monitoring and Measuring Devices	Date Released dd/mm/yyyy	Date Reviewed dd/mm/yyyy
Assurance Process	Approved:	Issue No: 01 Prepared by:	Revision No: 00

	Process Headings	Process Details
8.0	Resources	Devices for calibration including traceable reference standards User manuals Statistical methods.
9.0	Measures/controls	Monthly trends in the number of out-of-calibration MM devices Number of measurement devices whose calibration period has expired Calibration errors Number of errors due to wrong measurement Number of MM devices used and not controlled Reduction of the number of untrained personnel found using the devices.
10.0	Definitions	**Monitoring and measurement (MM) devices:** Devices used to gather data and measure, gauge, test, inspect or otherwise check items to determine their compliance to specified requirements. **Calibration:** Detecting, correlating, reporting or eliminating by adjusting any variation in the accuracy of a measurement when compared with a measurement standard of known accuracy. **Verification:** Confirming that the device is meeting or performing to acceptable national measurement standards and does not require any correction and adjustment. **Calibration period:** The period within which the calibration is valid. **Critical Control Point (CCP):** A stage at which a control is applied in order to prevent or eliminate or reduce a food safety hazard to an acceptable level. **Control Point (CP):** A step that monitors the process to keep the process within acceptable limits. **Reference standard:** A standard of known accuracy in a calibration system for establishing the accuracy of the system. **Working standard:** A designated measuring item used in calibration whose accuracy is known and is traceable to a reference standard. **Traceability:** The ability to trace a measurement to an external national standard.

ABC Company Limited	Procedures Manual		Reference AP 002 Page 3 of 6	
	Control of Monitoring and Measuring Devices	Date Released dd/mm/yyyy		Date Reviewed dd/mm/yyyy
Assurance Process	Approved:	Issue No: 01 Prepared by:		Revision No: 00

	Process Headings	Process Details
11.0	System description	Flowchart AP 002.1 shows the procedure for controlling MM devices.
11.1	Suitability and fitness for purpose	1. MM devices shall be capable of making the measurements required with sufficient resolution to detect the expected increments. Fitness for purpose is achieved through calibration, verification, preventive and reactive maintenance, repairs, visual inspection for damage and deterioration, automatic replacement at the end of lifespan, repeatability and reproducibility studies, and statistical analysis of measurement deviation. 2. QA Manager, Engineering Manager and the Laboratory Manager shall jointly determine the suitability and fitness for purpose of MM devices. 3. MM devices are used to monitor product and process conformity, process performance, environment and MM devices themselves.
11.2	Request for calibration	The request for calibration may originate from our company itself or from the customer, regulatory authorities or the industry sector.
11.3	Calibration system	1. QA Manager shall maintain a calibration master file which identifies the products and processes to be monitored and measured, the criteria for acceptance, the equipment and/or instruments that need to be calibrated, the location of such devices, calibration status and frequency of calibration, and range of accuracy and calibration history. Calibration master file also identifies working standards that are used in the calibration system. 2. QA manager shall communicate the need for calibration to the Supervisor who is responsible for the maintenance of equipment or instruments at least a week in advance. 3. All equipment and/or instruments listed in the calibration master file shall bear a tag stating the equipment and/or instrument, calibration status and calibration date, calibration due date and the person performing the calibration. 4. Gauges which do not require calibration shall bear the label "No calibration required". All gauges that do not bear calibration tags shall be returned to the QA Department for calibration. 5. The frequency of calibration and verification between calibrations shall be established by the QA Manager, Engineering Manager and the Laboratory Manager on the basis of the type of measurements to be made, the frequency of use, the manufacturer's specifications and the calibration history of the device. 6. QA Manager shall maintain records relating to calibration, repeatability and reproducibility. 7. The Engineering Manager shall make the necessary corrections or adjustments after calibration.

ABC Company Limited	Procedures Manual	Reference AP 002 Page 4 of 6	
	Control of Monitoring and Measuring Devices	Date Released dd/mm/yyyy	Date Reviewed dd/mm/yyyy
Assurance Process	Approved:	Issue No: 01 Prepared by:	Revision No: 00

	Process Headings	Process Details
11.4	Using monitoring and measuring devices	1. All personnel using MM devices shall ensure that all devices that need calibration bear the calibration tag. 2. The Supervisor shall provide the necessary training to the personnel operating the devices to ensure that they are competent in using them in terms of function, range, precision, reliability, use and maintenance. 3. In the event of damage, the QA Department shall be immediately alerted.
11.5	Calibration procedures (Flowchart AP 002.1)	QA Manager shall establish documented procedures for calibrating each type of equipment or instrument and shall include these requirements (as applicable): 1. Calibration shall be performed by comparison to working standards traceable to a national standard with an accuracy of 4 to 10 times greater than that of the measuring device to be calibrated. The precision depends on the industry requirements and the criticality of the end use of the product. 2. Comparison shall be done at several points within the range of use to assure linearity working order under a preventive maintenance programme. When not in use such devices shall be kept protected. 3. Calibrations shall be performed in a suitable environment with due consideration to temperature, humidity, vibration, cleanliness and other controlling factors that affect the precision of measurement. 4. All MM devices shall be handled, stored and maintained in a manner that does not adversely affect the calibration or condition of the equipment.

ABC Company Limited	Procedures Manual		Reference AP 002 Page 5 of 6	
	Control of Monitoring and Measuring Devices	Date Released dd/mm/yyyy		Date Reviewed dd/mm/yyyy
Assurance Process	Approved:	Issue No: 01 Prepared by:		Revision No: 00

	Process Headings	Process Details
11.6	Out of tolerance	1. If a device is found to be out of tolerance, the QA Manager shall immediately inform the Supervisor who is responsible for the measurement. 2. The Supervisor and the QA Manager shall assess the effects of invalid measurements and take immediate remedial action for the disposal of affected in-process and finished products.
11.7	Use of software for calibration	When software is used for calibration, the QA Manager shall ensure that the software is capable of meeting the requirements and is re-checked at predetermined intervals. The calibration status must be established before initial use and reconfigured and verified at defined intervals.
11.8	Review of the calibration programme	1. The calibration programme shall be reviewed at least annually and the QA Manager shall report the findings to the Management Committee. 2. QA Manager shall review the calibration process to determine whether it has been effectively implemented. Suitable corrective action shall be taken if the process is not followed correctly or has been inadequate. 3. Customer or internal engineering changes may result in a change in MM requirements and the devices used for MM. In such cases, the MM programme shall be reviewed.
11.9	Absence of national or international standards	In the absence of national or an international standards industry standard, the manufacturer's standard or ABCCL's own standard may be used to validate accuracy and reliability. If contractual requirements demand, the customer shall be consulted.

ABC Company Limited	Procedures Manual	Reference AP 002 Page 6 of 6	
	Control of Monitoring and Measuring Devices	Date Released dd/mm/yyyy	Date Reviewed dd/mm/yyyy
Assurance Process	Approved:	Issue No: 01 Prepared by:	Revision No: 00

	Process Headings	Process Details
12.0	Records	At a minimum, the calibration record shall contain this information: • Equipment name and identification number • Date of purchase/use • Calibration due date • Last calibrated • Method and standards used • Person performing the calibration • Adjustment/repairs needed.
13.0	Changes made	None.

ABC Company Limited	Procedures Manual	Flowchart AP 002.1 Page 1 of 1	
	Control of Monitoring and Measuring Devices	Date Released dd/mm/yyyy	Date Reviewed dd/mm/yyyy
Link AP 002	Approved:	Issue No: 01 Prepared by:	Revision No: 00

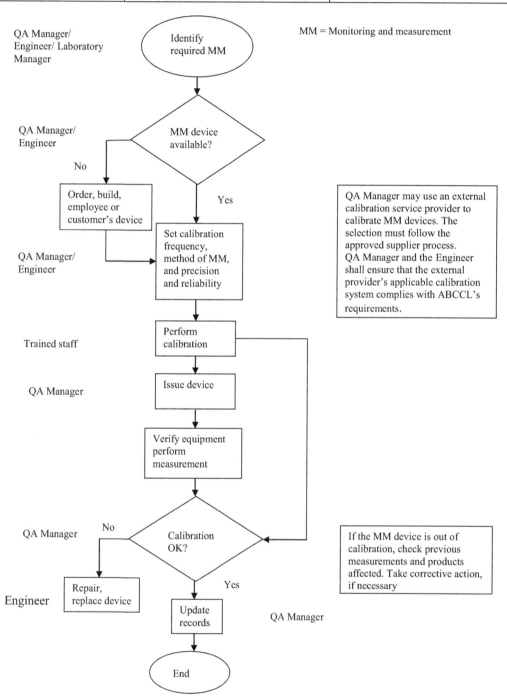

QA Manager/ Engineer/ Laboratory Manager

Identify required MM

MM = Monitoring and measurement

QA Manager/ Engineer

MM device available?

No

Order, build, employee or customer's device

Yes

QA Manager/ Engineer

Set calibration frequency, method of MM, and precision and reliability

QA Manager may use an external calibration service provider to calibrate MM devices. The selection must follow the approved supplier process. QA Manager and the Engineer shall ensure that the external provider's applicable calibration system complies with ABCCL's requirements.

Trained staff

Perform calibration

QA Manager

Issue device

Verify equipment perform measurement

QA Manager

No

Calibration OK?

If the MM device is out of calibration, check previous measurements and products affected. Take corrective action, if necessary

Engineer

Repair, replace device

Yes

Update records

QA Manager

End

AP 003 Monitoring, Measurement, Analysis and Evaluation

ABC Company Limited	Procedures Manual	Reference AP 003 Page 1 of 5	
	Monitoring, Measurement, Analysis and Evaluation	Date Released dd/mm/yyyy	Date Reviewed dd/mm/yyyy
Assurance Process	Approved:	Issue No: 01 Prepared by:	Revision No: 00

Process Owner	**Department Managers**
Process Headings	**Process Details**
1.0 Purpose	To describe the procedure for monitoring, measuring, analysis and evaluating the IQFSE Management System and associated processes.
2.0 Scope	This procedure applies to all the activities within the IQFSE Management System to assure that ABCCL's products and services conform to specified requirements.
3.0 Input	Critical process monitoring and measuring (MM) equipment and devices, process and service requirements, and legal requirements.
4.0 Output	Data on parameters selected for MM, maintained equipment and calibrated devices, and input for improvement of overall performance.
5.0 Competency requirements	Skilled and qualified employees, knowledge of equipment and measuring devices and of calibration needs and MM skills.
6.0 Responsibility	Quality Assurance Manager, Food Safety Manager and Environment Manager shall:

Quality Assurance Manager, Food Safety Manager and Environment Manager shall:
- Define the measurements required
- Define the methods of measurement
- Analyse and evaluate the data
- Take appropriate actions
- Communicate the requirements to appropriate personnel.

QA Manager shall:
- Determine the MM skill requirements and ensure that personnel who perform MM activities have appropriate skills.

Department Managers shall:
- Monitor the processes
- Provide resources for MM
- Identify and maintain calibration of equipment and devices necessary for MM.

Employees who are closest to the process shall:
- Measure as specified in the work instructions
- Report deviations to the Line Supervisor.

ABC Company Limited	Procedures Manual		Reference AP 003 Page 2 of 5	
	Monitoring, Measurement, Analysis and Evaluation	Date Released dd/mm/yyyy	Date Reviewed dd/mm/yyyy	
Assurance Process	Approved:	Issue No: 01 Prepared by:	Revision No: 00	

	Process Headings	**Process Details**
7.0	Associated documents	Control of Monitoring and Measurement Devices Procedure (AP 002) Validation and Verification Procedure (AP 009, AP 010, AP 011) Resource management (SP 009) Non-conformance reports Corrective actions Audit reports Inspection reports Monitoring and measurement framework (Form 127).
8.0	Resources	Statistical tools.
9.0	Measures/controls	Number and the measurements which are obsolete Uncalibrated equipment and devices Number of measurements that fail to capture key performances.
10.0	Definitions	**Measurement:** Assign a value to a defined characteristic of a product or process, e.g. measure unplanned down time. **Monitoring:** Observation of a defined characteristic of a product or process to ensure compliance to specified requirements, e.g. monitor the effectiveness of inspections that detect a non-conforming product.
11.0	System description	
11.1	General	1. ABCCL regularly monitors and measures the key characteristics of the operation that can have a significant impact on the performance of ABCCL's IQFSE Management System. This includes the documentation of information to analyse trends and monitor and/or measure the effectiveness of (a) its process; (b) products; (c) customer satisfaction; and (d) IQFSE Management System. 2. Appropriate statistical tools for each process shall be determined during planning and are included in the control plan. Results of MM shall be recorded in specifically designed control charts or data sheets. 3. Those who are responsible for MM shall understand variation, control or stability, process capability, statistical control limits and over-adjustment. 4. ABCCL's MM plans include inward goods, in-process inspections, final production inspections and external providers.

ABC Company Limited	Procedures Manual	Reference AP 003 Page 3 of 5	
	Monitoring, Measurement, Analysis and Evaluation	Date Released dd/mm/yyyy	Date Reviewed dd/mm/yyyy
Assurance Process	Approved:	Issue No: 01 Prepared by:	Revision No: 00

	Process Headings	**Process Details**
11.2	Determining monitoring and measuring items (Form 128)	1. QA Manager, Food Safety Manager and Environment Manager shall identify, establish and maintain methods and procedures to regularly monitor and measure the key characteristics of operations and activities having a significant quality, or environmental and food safety impact (through a risk analysis process), and to evaluate compliance with relevant statutory regulations. 2. If external providers are required to conduct MM, the Purchasing Manager shall select suitable external providers from the approved supplier list.
11.3	Monitoring and measurement of processes	1. Recorded information is provided to monitor performance, relevant operational controls and conformance with the ABCCL policies, objectives and associated targets. 2. Emergency preparedness and response plans shall be reviewed and revised, where necessary, and in particular after the occurrence of incidents and emergency situations. These procedures are regularly tested. 3. When planned results are not achieved, Department Managers shall take appropriate corrective action to (a) correct the deficiency; (b) evaluate whether the process non-conformity has resulted in product non-conformity; (c) determine if the process non-conformity is limited to a specific case or whether it could have affected other processes or products; and (d) control the non-conforming process and product. 4. Engineering Manager and the QA Manager shall calibrate and maintain all measuring equipment and instruments in good working order. 5. Special processes when identified shall be controlled and monitored in accordance with established procedures.
11.4	Monitoring and measuring of product	1. ABCCL shall monitor and measure the characteristics of the product to verify that product requirements have been realised. This is achieved by (a) carrying out tests and product verification activities at various stages of product realisation process and (b) recording and authorising the release of product for delivery to the customer. 2. Product specification sheet shall specify (a) the criteria for acceptance and rejection; (b) the test methods and points at which they are carried out; (c) the limits of acceptance or rejection; and (d) the equipment or instruments to be used. 3. Final inspection: Finished goods shall be tested according to CP 014 Release of Finished Goods Procedure. They shall not be picked for delivery until records resulting from verification and test points have been reviewed and conformed as acceptable. Records shall identify the personnel responsible for authorising product release of product for delivery to the customer.

ABC Company Limited	Procedures Manual	Reference AP 003 Page 4 of 5	
	Monitoring, Measurement, Analysis and Evaluation	Date Released dd/mm/yyyy	Date Reviewed dd/mm/yyyy
Assurance Process	Approved:	Issue No: 01 Prepared by:	Revision No: 00

	Process Headings	**Process Details**
11.5	Customer satisfaction	Customer satisfaction shall be carried out according to SP 046 customer satisfaction.
11.6	Monitoring and measuring the effectiveness of the IQFSE Management System	The effectiveness of the IQFSE Management System is determined through internal and external audit finding, management reviews, corrective and preventive actions and analysis of process and product performance data.
11.7	Updating testing and inspection methods and techniques	Testing and inspection methods shall be validated and verified. Discrepancies shall be investigated and resolved by the QA Manager and the Laboratory Manager. When new testing and inspection methods are available, the feasibility of introducing them and updating testing and inspection methods shall be carried out by the QA Manager and the Laboratory Manager.
11.8	Controlled conditions for monitoring and measuring	MM shall be conducted under controlled conditions that include: • Selection of suitable sampling and data collection techniques • Calibration and verification of MM devices using measurement standards traceable to an international standard (AP 002) • Use of skilled personnel • Use of suitable Quality Control (QC) methods that include data interpretation and trending.

ABC Company Limited	Procedures Manual	Reference AP 003 Page 5 of 5	
	Monitoring, Measurement, Analysis and Evaluation	Date Released dd/mm/yyyy	Date Reviewed dd/mm/yyyy
Assurance Process	Approved:	Issue No: 01 Prepared by:	Revision No: 00

	Process Headings	**Process Details**
11.9	Analysis and evaluation	See AP 004.
12.0	Records	Data collection and analysis reports.
13.0	Changes made	None.

AP 004 Analysis and Evaluation of Data

ABC Company Limited	Procedures Manual		Reference AP 004 Page 1 of 3	
	Analysis and Evaluation of Data		Date Released dd/mm/yyyy	Date Reviewed dd/mm/yyyy
Assurance Process	Approved:		Issue No: 01 Prepared by:	Revision No: 00

Process Owner		QA Manager
	Process Headings	**Process Details**
1.0	Purpose	To describe the procedure for analysing and evaluating data collected through monitoring and measurement (MM).
2.0	Scope	This procedure applies to data collected from MM.
3.0	Input	Results from MM activities.
4.0	Output	Improvement of products, processes and services, reduced level of non-conformities, trained and skilled staff and continual improvement.
5.0	Competency requirements	Data analysing skills, knowledge of statistical tools used for analysing data and presentation skills.
6.0	Responsibility	QA Manager, Food Safety Manager and Environment Manager shall: • Analyse and evaluate data • Recommend improvements. QA Manager shall: • Address non-conformities • Plan for improvements. Department Managers shall • Implement improvement plans.
7.0	Associated documents	Measurement and Analysis Procedure (AP 003) Form 127 Framework for analysis and evaluation of data and information Form 128 Monitoring and measurement items Form 129 Analysis and evaluation of data Form 130 Waste and recycling data Form 131 Solid waste generation Form 132 Water and power consumption Records of MM.
8.0	Resources	Statistical tools for analysis.
9.0	Measures/Controls	Verification of measurements Corrective actions.
10.0	System description	
10.1	Tools for analysis and evaluation	Appropriate statistical tools shall be used for analysing and evaluating data. The output of analysis and evaluation may be presented graphically, statistically or by any other suitable method.

ABC Company Limited	Procedures Manual	Reference AP 004 Page 2 of 3	
	Analysis and Evaluation of Data	Date Released dd/mm/yyyy	Date Reviewed dd/mm/yyyy
Assurance Process	Approved:	Issue No: 01 Prepared by:	Revision No: 00

	Process Headings	**Process Details**
10.2	Conformity of products, services and processes	This data can yield the information needed to determine conformity of products and services to specified requirements: Inspection and warranty • Inspection rates and trends • In-process and final inspection rates • Trends in return and warranty trends Performance • Process capability against specifications • Performance against project plans • Products and processes with highest and lowest rates of non-compliance • Delivery failure rates • Service failure rates • Number of jobs completed on time Audits • Product audit • Test data Statutory and regulatory compliance • Number of incidents of statutory and regulatory non-compliance.
10.3	Enhancing customer satisfaction	These categories of data can provide useful information to evaluate the level of customer satisfaction: Complaints • Timely response rates for customer complaints • Customer complaint trends • Highest complaints categories • Response rate from customer feedback tool Product • Most important product attributes and features • Most significant product strengths • Number of products that do not move because of competitors' products or higher prices Strengths and suggestions for improvement • Positive comments and praise • Suggestions for improving the feedback tool.

ABC Company Limited	Procedures Manual	Reference AP 004 Page 3 of 3	
	Analysis and Evaluation of Data	Date Released dd/mm/yyyy	Date Reviewed dd/mm/yyyy
Assurance Process	Approved:	Issue No: 01 Prepared by:	Revision No: 00

	Process Headings	Process Details
10.4	Effectiveness of the IQFSE Management System	The effectiveness of the IQFSE Management System is assessed by analysing data from internal audits and management reviews. The effectiveness of corrective actions resulting from non-conformances is used as the indicator of the effectiveness of the IQFSE Management System.
10.5	Effectiveness of planning	The effectiveness of planning is assessed in terms of the effectiveness of (a) actions taken to address risks and opportunities; (b) planning to achieve objectives; and (c) change management actions.
10.6	Evaluation of supplier performance	The performance of suppliers is evaluated according to the Approval of Suppliers Procedure (CP 001).
10.7	Performance of processes	The performance of processes is evaluated by analysing the corrective actions taken in response to non-compliances.
10.8	Determining the need for improvement of the IQFSE Management System	Several categories of data can be used to determine the need for improvement within the IQFSE Management System: • Trends in non-conformities realised in internal and external audits • Failure to achieve objectives • Failure to address risks and opportunities • Customer complaints relating to the same product category or cause • Customer feedback • Poor performance of suppliers • Market share • Unsuccessful change management actions • Employee suggestions • Investigations into company activities by internal or external investigators • Knowledge management gaps.
11.0	Records	Monitoring and measurement records Data analysis records.
12.0	Changes made	None.

AP 005 Management Review

ABC Company Limited	Procedures Manual	Reference AP 005 Page 1 of 3	
	Management Review	Date Released dd/mm/yyyy	Date Reviewed dd/mm/yyyy
Assurance Process	Approved:	Issue No: 01 Prepared by:	Revision No: 00

Process Owner	QA Manager
Process Headings	**Process Details**
1.0 Purpose	To describe the procedure for conducting management reviews of the IQFSE Management System at planned intervals as a basis for continual improvement and ensuring the continuing suitability, adequacy and effectiveness of associated policies and objectives.
2.0 Scope	The management review includes all departments and applies to all activities comprising the management systems.
3.0 Input	Company's activities and products as defined in section 10.2.
4.0 Output	Improvements of the adequacy and effectiveness of the IQFSE Management System, improvements of products and services related to customer requirements, revision of ABCCL's policies and objectives, resource needs, need for changes to the IQFSE Management System, risks identified, assurance of food safety, environmental initiatives and improvement of environmental performance.
5.0 Competency requirements	Knowledge of the company's quality, environment and food safety management programmes, objectives and targets, strategic direction and initiative.
6.0 Responsibility	Defined in Flowchart AP 005.1.
7.0 Associated documents	Management review meeting agenda (Form 158) Management review record Input data.
8.0 Resources	ISO 9001, ISO 14000 and ISO 22000 standards Input data (Form 159).
9.0 Measures/controls	Validation of management review procedure Timely completion of actions arising from the meeting Number of successful improvements Performance of the IQFSE Management System Attendance.
10.0 System description	Management Review Procedure is shown in Flowchart AP 005.1.
10.1 Management Review Team	Management Review Team (MRT) consists of the Plant Manager, QA Manager, Food Safety Manager, Environment Manager and other Department Managers.

ABC Company Limited	Procedures Manual	Reference AP 005 Page 2 of 3	
	Management Review	Date Released dd/mm/yyyy	Date Reviewed dd/mm/yyyy
Assurance Process	Approved:	Issue No: 01 Prepared by:	Revision No: 00

	Process Headings	Process Details
10.2	Input reports (Form 159)	**Performance measures:** Product/process performance, product safety and conformity, supplier performance, external provision performance, corrective actions, audit reports. **Safety:** Environment and safety risk issues, emergency situation incidents, recalls or withdrawals. **Customer feedback:** Customer feedback reports complaints, market feedback and trends. **Human and other resources:** People and competence issues, infrastructure issues. **Compliant issues:** Legal, regulatory and voluntary codes compliant issues. **Change and improvement opportunities:** Changes that could affect quality, environment and food safety of products, improvement opportunities, IQFSE management system changes, and changes to internal and external issues. **Audit results and verification results:** Positive and negative findings, improvement opportunities, non-compliances and review of verification results. **Actions to address risks and opportunities:** Effectiveness of action plans. **Opportunities for improvements:** Suggestions from various units and employees and other interested parties, and improvements to product safety related to customer requirements. **Objectives and policies:** Progress against major company objectives and policies.
10.3	Agenda	See Form 158.
10.4	Conduct of meeting	All Department Managers shall attend the meeting. If a person is unable to attend, he or she shall nominate a person from the same business unit to attend the meeting. That person is responsible for producing the required documents. The meeting shall be chaired by the QA Manager.
10.5	Outcome of the meeting	Management review meeting shall generate: • Corrective and/or preventive action requests • Any other recorded action as a result of review topics with a view to continual improvement • Objectives and policy updates • Projects for improvement of products, processes and reviews • New ideas for follow-up • Reports on review activities and making them accessible to relevant staff.

ABC Company Limited	Procedures Manual	Reference AP 005 Page 3 of 3	
	Management Review	Date Released dd/mm/yyyy	Date Reviewed dd/mm/yyyy
Assurance Process	Approved:	Issue No: 01 Prepared by:	Revision No: 00

	Process Headings	Process Details
10.6	Frequency of meetings	Meetings shall be held quarterly.
10.7	Other informal management review activities	1. Updating (as necessary) on objectives, data on trends, product non-conformities, corrective actions, customer complaints, audit results with intranet access. 2. Weekly meetings to discuss issues and problems and to ensure compliance with IQFSE Management System requirements. 3. Daily production meetings to discuss production and delivery issues.
11.0	Records	Minutes of meetings together with reviewed data and information.
12.0	Changes made	None.

ABC Company Limited	Procedures Manual	Flowchart AP 005.1 Page 1 of 1	
	Management Review	Date Released dd/mm/yyyy	Date Reviewed dd/mm/yyyy
Link AP 005	Approved:	Issue No: 01 Prepared by:	Revision No: 00

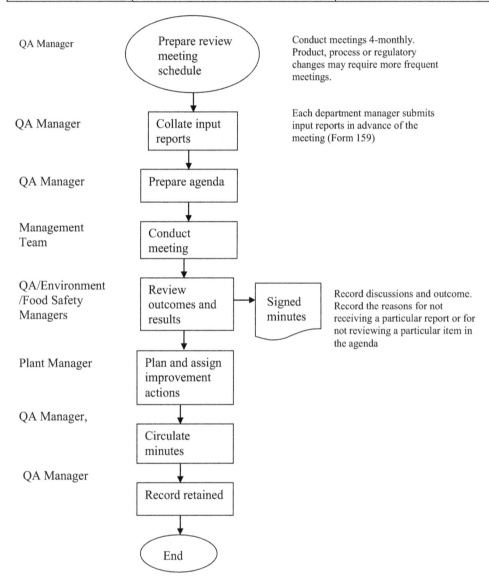

QA Manager — Prepare review meeting schedule

Conduct meetings 4-monthly. Product, process or regulatory changes may require more frequent meetings.

QA Manager — Collate input reports

Each department manager submits input reports in advance of the meeting (Form 159)

QA Manager — Prepare agenda

Management Team — Conduct meeting

QA/Environment /Food Safety Managers — Review outcomes and results → Signed minutes

Record discussions and outcome. Record the reasons for not receiving a particular report or for not reviewing a particular item in the agenda

Plant Manager — Plan and assign improvement actions

QA Manager, — Circulate minutes

QA Manager — Record retained

End

AP 006 Continual Improvement

ABC Company Limited	Procedures Manual		Reference AP 006 Page 1 of 3	
	Continual Improvement		Date Released dd/mm/yyyy	Date Reviewed dd/mm/yyyy
Assurance Process	Approved:		Issue No: 01 Prepared by:	Revision No: 00

Process Owner		Plant Manager
	Process Headings	**Process Details**
1.0	Purpose	To describe the procedure continual improvement of ABCCL's management systems through the use of policies, objectives, analysis of data, corrective and preventive action, management review and updating the management systems.
2.0	Scope	It applies to all activities and departments included in ABCCL's management systems.
3.0	Input	See section 11.1.
4.0	Output	Improvements, customer satisfaction, financial improvement and staff satisfaction.
5.0	Competency requirements	Data analysis skills, project management skills, problem-solving skills and knowledge of products, processes and services.
6.0	Responsibility	Defined in Flowchart AP 006.1. Additional responsibilities are set out below. Management Team shall: • Determine risk, cost vs benefit and importance of improvements • Prioritise improvements. QA Manager, Food Safety Manager and Environment Manager shall: • Recommend actions to resolve these problems. Department Managers shall: • Implement plans. QA Manager shall: • Keep records of continual improvement.
7.0	Associated documents	Project reports Date analysis reports Process control data Management Team meeting minutes.
8.0	Resources	ISO 9001, ISO 14000 and ISO 22000 standards Project management tools.
9.0	Measures/controls	Process variability Quality, food safety and environmental issues Process performance Number of recalls Deviation from critical food safety limits Financial performance.

ABC Company Limited	Procedures Manual	Reference AP 006 Page 2 of 3	
	Continual Improvement	Date Released dd/mm/yyyy	Date Reviewed dd/mm/yyyy
Assurance Process	Approved:	Issue No: 01 Prepared by:	Revision No: 00

	Process Headings	Process Details
10.0	Definitions	**Continuous improvement:** Single, uninterrupted non-stop event. **Continual improvement:** A series of infinite changes or breakthrough projects that bring improvement. **Management Team:** Department Managers and at least one representative from top management.
11.0	System description	Continual improvement process is shown in Flowchart AP 006.1.
11.1	Data sources and collection	Opportunities for improvement and deficiencies are identified through such sources as: • Product and process characteristics and their trends • Records of product and process non-conformities • Customer feedback including complaints and surveys • Market research analysis of competitors' products • Feedback from employees, suppliers and other interested parties (SP 048) • Internal and external audits • Management reviews • Compliance audits • Environmental performance • Verification activities • Validation activities of food safety control • Results of measurement and monitoring activities. • Request for change (Form 109) • Request for comments (Form 136) Other opportunities for improvement may arise from such sources as: • Effective utilisation of floor space • Unnecessary levels of inspections and testing • Excessive handling and storage • Rising failure costs • Unplanned down time.
	Data analysis	The Management Team shall analyse the data using appropriate statistical tools (AP 004 Analysis and Evaluation Procedure). The data is presented in a form to highlight performance trends, effects of process improvement projects and process problems.

ABC Company Limited	Procedures Manual	Reference AP 006 Page 3 of 3	
	Continual Improvement	Date Released dd/mm/yyyy	Date Reviewed dd/mm/yyyy
Assurance Process	Approved:	Issue No: 01 Prepared by:	Revision No: 00

	Process Headings	**Process Details**
		Using problem-solving techniques, root causes of the problem are identified, and appropriate solutions are generated for improvement. The recommendations together with data are presented to the Management Review Team (MRT).
11.3	Review of recommendations	1. The Management Team shall prioritise improvement opportunities for their relevance for achieving objectives. When opportunities for improvements are not supported by current policies and objectives, the Management Team shall establish new policies and objectives through the management review process. 2. For improvement projects, the Management Team may nominate members to plan and implement the improvement. 3. The recommendations are either approved or declined. If the recommendations are declined, the Management Team shall review their findings and solutions.
11.4	Planning for improvement	The MRT shall develop plans for implementation of recommendations. The plans include, but are not limited to, assigning responsibilities, developing action plans, establishing timeframes, provision of resources and training requirements.
11.5	Implementation of improvement plans	Action plans are implemented as scheduled with the support of employees in the department.
11.6	Measure effectiveness	The QA Manager shall measure the effectiveness of improvement activities according to the metrics in this procedure. The criteria for evaluating the suitability, adequacy and effectiveness of the IQFSE Management System are presented in Form 137. The continual improvement cycle is shown in Figure AP 006.1.
12.0	Records	Improvement plans Records shall be maintained by the QA Manager.
13.0	Changes made	None.

ABC Company Limited	Procedures Manual	Flowchart AP 006.1 Page 1 of 2	
	Continual Improvement	Date Released dd/mm/yyyy	Date Reviewed dd/mm/yyyy
Link AP 006	Approved:	Issue No: 01 Prepared by:	Revision No: 00

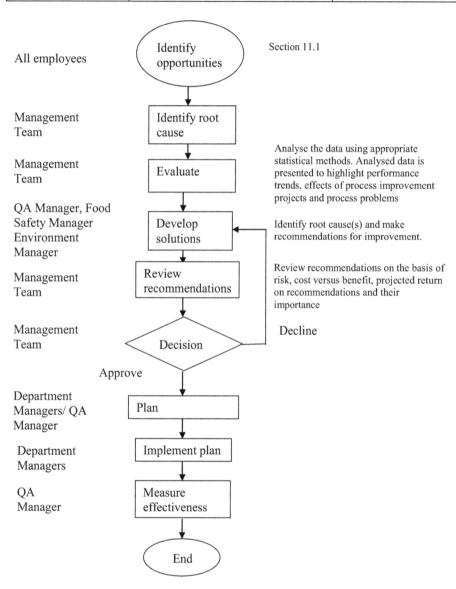

All employees — Identify opportunities — Section 11.1

Management Team — Identify root cause

Management Team — Evaluate — Analyse the data using appropriate statistical methods. Analysed data is presented to highlight performance trends, effects of process improvement projects and process problems

QA Manager, Food Safety Manager Environment Manager — Develop solutions — Identify root cause(s) and make recommendations for improvement.

Management Team — Review recommendations — Review recommendations on the basis of risk, cost versus benefit, projected return on recommendations and their importance

Management Team — Decision — Decline

Approve

Department Managers/ QA Manager — Plan

Department Managers — Implement plan

QA Manager — Measure effectiveness

End

ABC Company Limited	Procedures Manual	Flowchart AP 006.1 Page 2 of 2	
	Continual Improvement	Date Released dd/mm/yyyy	Date Reviewed dd/mm/yyyy
Link AP 006	Approved:	Issue No: 01 Prepared by:	Revision No: 00

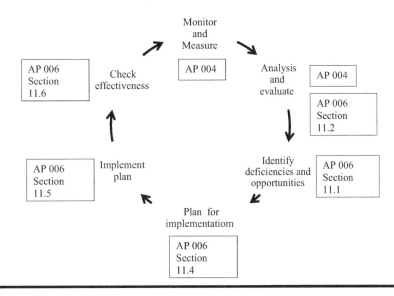

Figure AP 006.1   Continual improvement cycle (Link AP 006).

AP 007 Identification and Traceability

ABC Company Limited	Procedures Manual	Reference AP 007 Page 1 of 4	
	Identification and Traceability	Date Released dd/mm/yyyy	Date Reviewed dd/mm/yyyy
Assurance Process	Approved:	Issue No: 01 Prepared by:	Revision No: 00

Process Owner	QA Manager
Process Headings	**Process Details**

1.0	Purpose	To describe the procedure for controlling, documenting and performing product identification and traceability through all stages of production and service operations.
2.0	Scope	This procedure applies to the identification of all incoming materials on receipt and throughout all stages of production, delivery and installation to provide traceability of individual components and/or batches.
3.0	Input	Raw materials, ingredients, packaging materials, processing aids, measurement tools, documents relating to incoming materials and processing operations, warehousing, re-worked materials and statutory and legal requirements.
4.0	Output	Properly identified materials that aid traceability throughout the supply chain.
5.0	Competency requirements	Knowledge of items receiving processes, processes and finished products, inventory management skills, warehouse management skills.
6.0	Responsibility	Inward Goods Officer shall:

6.0 Responsibility — Inward Goods Officer shall:
- Identify all incoming materials using the documents provided by the supplier and compare the product details against the documents such as packing slip, pallet label and/or test results
- Assign a unique identification number to each delivery and record the details in the inward goods log book. These details shall include the supplier's batch number, manufacturing date and expiry date/best before date as appropriate.

Quality Control Officer shall:
- Assign and record a unique laboratory test number when samples are taken for testing
- Apply appropriate status labels to applicable records and products following testing.

Engineering Manager shall:
- Assign a part number or serial number to all engineering items and parts which are used
- Maintain all applicable documents and records.

Stock Room Personnel shall:
- Ensure proper labels and markings are applied when required for associated records and products
- Store the products in a suitable environment and prevent mix-ups.

Line Supervisor shall:
- Ensure the batch code is applied to all items during production
- Follow-up processing steps.

ABC Company Limited	Procedures Manual	Reference AP 007 Page 2 of 4	
	Identification and Traceability	Date Released dd/mm/yyyy	Date Reviewed dd/mm/yyyy
Assurance Process	Approved:	Issue No: 01 Prepared by:	Revision No: 00

	Process Headings	Process Details
7.0	Associated documents	Product and packaging specifications (Form 050, Form 138) Recipe or the process (Flowchart CP 012.3, Flowchart CP 012.4) Skill chart In-process test methods (Form 051).
8.0	Resources	Reference samples.
9.0	Measures/controls	Accuracy of the batch code or assigned number Records of distribution.
10.0	Definitions	**Product:** Includes any part, assembly or item ordered by the customer, deliverable reports or documents, finished product or work-in-progress product. **Raw material:** Includes any material or item used in processing, incorporated into the finished product and/or becomes a part of the finished product. **Measuring device:** Includes equipment used for measuring and monitoring and set-up. **Traceability:** Ability to trace history, application or location of an item using recorded information. **Internal traceability:** Ability to trace production history using recorded information. **External traceability:** Refers to the methods, elements and procedures necessary to obtain traceable data between the organisations that constitute the supply chain.
11.0	System description	The process for identification and traceability is shown in Flowchart AP 007.1

ABC Company Limited	Procedures Manual	Reference AP 007 Page 3 of 4	
	Identification and Traceability	Date Released dd/mm/yyyy	Date Reviewed dd/mm/yyyy
Assurance Process	Approved:	Issue No: 01 Prepared by:	Revision No: 00

	Process Headings	Process Details
11.1	Identification and traceability of raw materials	Raw materials are identified with the unique inventory control number assigned to each consignment on receipt and marked on the product. This number is carried through to production on the specification sheet when the item is issued to the production unit.
11.2	Identification and traceability of finished products	1. All finished products carry a product code and a batch code which identifies the product, production date, line number and other information related to the product. 2. All finished products shall bear this information on a label on immediate packaging, i.e. bottle, carton, can etc.: • Brand name and/or generic name • Ingredients list complying with legal requirements • Allergen information • Handling and storage conditions • Method of reconstitution (if applicable) • Batch number • Expiry date or best before date • Quantity in the final container • Packed date and time.
11.3	Identification and traceability of work-in-progress items	All work-in-progress products shall bear a label indicating the status (work in progress), product, production date, line number and the reason for classifying as work in progress.
11.4	Verification status	1. Verification status of finished products: Verification activities relating to finished products are defined in Release of Finished Goods Procedure (CP 014) and Inspection and Test Status Procedure (CP 010). 2. Verification status of inward goods: Verification activities relating to inward goods are defined in Receipt of Inward Goods Procedure (CP 007) and Inspection of Inward Goods Procedure (CP 008). 3. Verification status when shipping: Verification activities during shipping are defined in Delivery Procedure (CP 021).

ABC Company Limited	Procedures Manual	Reference AP 007 Page 4 of 4	
	Identification and Traceability	Date Released dd/mm/yyyy	Date Reviewed dd/mm/yyyy
Assurance Process	Approved:	Issue No: 01 Prepared by:	Revision No: 00

	Process Headings	Process Details
11.5	Internal traceability	1. When the production process involves several steps, Form 139 shall be used to enable internal traceability. Each step of the process is assigned a process number as shown in Form 139. The document is tagged into the product in-process by the operator responsible for the step.
		2. If tests have not been completed or indicate errors, the Line Supervisor shall be summoned to resolve the issue. The Line Supervisor may request QA staff to check and make a decision.
		3. An operator or a Supervisor shall be responsible for each process step.
		4. Assembly line processes such as filling, corking, capsuling, labelling and packing into cases do not require Form 139. In-process check sheets provided at each station provide sufficient information for traceability.
11.6	Service traceability	Service traceability is achieved through (a) the date of service; (b) details of the client; (c) the person who performed the service; and (d) the documentation related to the service.
11.7	Review of traceability	1. QA Manager shall review the traceability system and audit at least quarterly to determine if it is being properly implemented and continues to conform to company requirements and legal requirements. A third-party body should be assigned to conduct an audit of the traceability system at least annually.
11.8	Traceability summary	Form 140 shows an example of traceability summary.
12.0	Records	Production records Inward goods records Inventory of inward, work-in-progress and finished goods records.
13.0	Changes made	None.

ABC Company Limited	Procedures Manual	Flowchart AP 007.1 Page 1 of 1	
	Identification and Traceability	Date Released dd/mm/yyyy	Date Reviewed dd/mm/yyyy
Link AP 007	Approved:	Issue No: 01 Prepared by:	

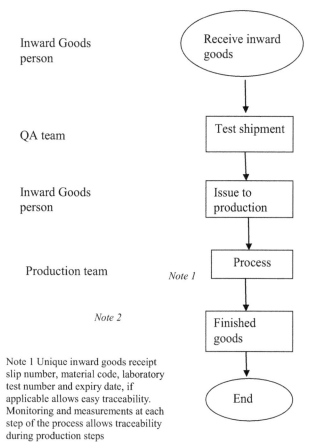

Inward Goods person

Check consignment against packing slip and description on each pallet. Assign a unique number to each shipment and record in the log book

QA team

QA team assigns a test number and maintains a full list of component codes, description and approved suppliers

Inward Goods person

Vendor's batch number and expiry date of the product, if applicable are maintained throughout the production process steps using the product specification form.

Production team   *Note 1*

Note 2

Note 1 Unique inward goods receipt slip number, material code, laboratory test number and expiry date, if applicable allows easy traceability. Monitoring and measurements at each step of the process allows traceability during production steps

Note 2 All finished goods are assigned two numbers: a unique product code and a batch code for each batch of product. The batch code identifies the line number, production shift and the date of manufacture.
For food products, an expiry date or a best before date is assigned.
Work order number is assigned by the Production Planner.
The product code, batch code, inward goods receipt slip number and the expiry date or best before date (if applicable) in combination produces a system which enables traceability through production and distribution.

AP 008 Handling Non-Conformities

ABC Company Limited	Procedures Manual	Reference AP 008 Page 1 of 8	
	Handling Non-Conformities	Date Released dd/mm/yyyy	Date Reviewed dd/mm/yyyy
Assurance Process	Approved:	Issue No: 01 Prepared by:	Revision No: 00

Process Owner	QA Manager

	Process Headings	Process Details
1.0	Purpose	To describe the procedure for handling non-conforming products and services of ABCCL.
2.0	Scope	Applies to all activities, products, processes and services under the management of the quality, environment and food safety system of ABCCL.
3.0	Input	Specifications, service contract, non-conforming product or service, legal requirements, performance criteria and communication from customers.
4.0	Output	Segregated non-conforming product, corrective action, continual improvement, compensation and customer satisfaction.
5.0	Competency requirements	Knowledge of processes, specifications and performance criteria, communication skills and problem-solving skills.
6.0	Responsibility	All staff shall:

6.0 Responsibility (Process Details continued):

All staff shall:
- Report non-conformities immediately to the supervisor.
- Supervisor shall:
- Bring the non-conformity to the attention of QA Manager.

QA Manager shall:
- Initiate non-conforming reports (NCRs)
- Identify non-conforming products
- Maintain records of handling non-conforming products, processes, activities and services
- Identify, label and make arrangements to segregate non-conforming products
- Verify that repaired or reworked items conform to customer or ABCCL requirements
- Implement disposition decisions
- Analyse non-conformance patterns and trends and identify improvement opportunities.

Department Manager shall:
- Ensure that non-conforming product under his or her custody is segregated to prevent dispatch to customers.

ABC Company Limited	Procedures Manual	Reference AP 008 Page 2 of 8	
	Handling Non-Conformities	Date Released dd/mm/yyyy	Date Reviewed dd/mm/yyyy
Assurance Process	Approved:	Issue No: 01 Prepared by:	Revision No: 00

	Process Headings	Process Details
		Plant Manager shall:
		• Evaluate non-conforming products and services for functionality, safety, cost, schedule and other aspects
		• Authorise the manner of disposition of non-conforming products. For rejecting or accepting under a waiver, ABCCL Plant Manager shall also be a party to the authorisation
		• Authorise and define criteria for rework, repair and re-inspection criteria
		• Initiate waivers.
		Environment Manager shall:
		• Initiate and implement action in case of environmental incidents identified as critical non-conformances.
		Food Safety Management Systems Manager shall:
		• Initiate and implement action in case of food safety issues identified as critical non-conformances.
		Customer Relations Manager shall:
		• Communicate with all external parties, including regulatory authorities and media, on critical non-conformances
		• Communicate with affected groups and (if required) notify customers of non-conformances and obtain their approval for rework or repair.
		Warehouse Manager shall:
		• Segregate identified non-conforming products and ensure that picking is prevented from such stock
		• Make the stock unallocable in the warehouse computer system.
7.0	Associated documents	Disposal of non-conforming product (Form 141) REJECT, PASSED, HOLD, QUARANTINE labels Non-conforming products log (Form 142) Non-conformance report (Form 143).
8.0	Resources	ISO 9001, ISO 14000 and ISO 22000 standards Management system Regulatory requirements.

ABC Company Limited	**Procedures Manual**	**Reference AP 008** Page 3 of 8	
	Handling Non-Conformities	Date Released dd/mm/yyyy	Date Reviewed dd/mm/yyyy
Assurance Process	Approved:	Issue No: 01 Prepared by:	Revision No: 00

	Process Headings	**Process Details**
9.0	Measures/controls	Number of non-conformances Timeliness of response to non-conforming situations Numbers rejects, repaired and reworked.
10.0	Definitions	
10.1	Generic definitions	**Non-conformance:** Failure to adhere to management system requirements, standards, policies and procedures. **Critical non-conformance:** A situation which causes or has the potential to cause serious harm to the consumer, complete breakdown of a product or process, and/or complete interruption of a business activity. **Major non-conformance:** A high-risk or a potential high-risk situation where the potential impact is likely to compromise quality, food safety and environmental standards, and/or a temporary breakdown of a business activity. **Minor non-conformance:** A low-risk or a potential low-risk situation where the standards and requirements have been violated but the impact is not likely to be serious or imminent to the product, its performance, business activity or public health. **Deviation:** A customer request issued before manufacture allowing a deviation from specified requirements. **Repair:** Action to make the item conform to specified requirements which can affect or change parts of the non-conforming item. **Rework:** Reprocessing through the use of original or other equivalent processing in a manner that assures compliance with specified requirements. **Regrade:** Use in another application which has less significant requirements. **Waiver:** Approval to accept a non-conforming item after manufacture/test and is considered acceptable as is or after repair. **Reject:** A non-conforming product that is not usable and cannot be economically reworked, repaired or regraded. **Unallocable:** Means to prevent the stock being picked for delivery to customers. **Hold:** A label to indicate that the non-conforming product is under investigation. **Quarantine:** A label to indicate that a finished product or a raw material is undergoing tests. **Passed:** A label to indicate that the product or raw material has passed the tests and is ready for use. (All stocks in the warehouse not bearing a HOLD, QUARANTINE or REJECT sticker are deemed passed.)

ABC Company Limited	Procedures Manual		Reference AP 008 Page 4 of 8	
	Handling Non-Conformities	Date Released dd/mm/yyyy		Date Reviewed dd/mm/yyyy
Assurance Process	Approved:	Issue No: 01 Prepared by:		Revision No: 00

	Process Headings	Process Details
10.2	Definitions relating to the food safety management system	**Potentially unsafe product:** Any ingredient, additive or end product that does not meet food safety specifications and/or regulatory requirements. **Acceptable level:** Level of a food safety hazard considered acceptable to the consumer. The acceptable level of the end product is designated as the target level which shall be set below the statutory/regulatory limits. It may be set at a higher level in an intermediate step in production to achieve an acceptable level in the end product. **Critical Control Point (CCP):** A step in a process at which control can be exercised and is essential to prevent or eliminate a food safety hazard or reduce it to an acceptable level. **Recall:** Removal of a product from the market because of a possibility of harm to the consumer and may be based on internal or external findings.
11.0	System description	
11.1	Types of non-conformities	Non-conformities shall include, but are not limited to: • Deviations from the documented procedure/instructions not followed • Unsafe practices/unsafe conditions, accidental emissions/discharges, spillages, leakages, emissions, accidents, result of unsafe handling, any accident or impact having a significant impact on the environment, health and safety of individuals, and/or the quality of product or delivery • Violations of legal requirements • Unsafe handling of hazardous materials waste • Potentially unsafe product • Product whose safety level has exceeded the acceptable level • Product performance failure.

ABC Company Limited	Procedures Manual	Reference AP 008 Page 5 of 8	
	Handling Non-Conformities	Date Released dd/mm/yyyy	Date Reviewed dd/mm/yyyy
Assurance Process	Approved:	Issue No: 01 Prepared by:	Revision No: 00

	Process Headings	Process Details
11.2	Identification and segregation of non-conforming product	1. QA Manager on identification of non-conforming material shall tag such products with a REJECT sticker. On a pallet, labels shall be applied on all four sides on the bottom layer of the pallet. Also, this information shall be displayed on the rejected product: <ul><li>Name of product and identification number (if applicable)</li><li>Quantity rejected</li><li>Date and time of rejection</li><li>Reason for rejection</li><li>Signature of the person who is authorised to reject.</li></ul> 2. QA Manager shall instruct the Warehouse Manager to segregate the stock relating to the non-conforming product and make the stock "unallocable" in the computer. 3. QA Manager shall keep a log of non-conforming products.
11.3	Identification of non-conforming service	Service failure is identified and then (a) details of failure are attached to the work order and (b) note is attached to customer receipt.
11.4	Non-conforming product detected after delivery or use	1. Customer Relations Manager shall issue a reference number to the customer who is requested to return the item quoting the reference. On receipt of the item, the procedure described on this document shall be followed. 2. Non-conforming products returned from a customer shall be reviewed by the Review Team. Any stock remaining in the warehouse with the same production details shall be put on hold and reviewed by the Review Team.
11.5	Review Team	1. The Plant Manager may appoint a Review Team to evaluate non-conformances. Individuals appointed to the Review Team shall have the necessary skills to evaluate non-conforming products and services for functionality, safety, cost, schedule and other aspects. 2. Critical non-conforming products: Evaluation of critical non-conforming products shall take precedence over other activities. The product in storage should be segregated immediately. The Recall Procedure shall be implemented in case of unsafe products and those that can harm the consumer. The Emergency Procedure shall be invoked in case of environmental incidents such as spillages, toxic fumes, etc. 3. Customer Services Manager shall handle all communication issues including communication with customers and consumers, regulatory bodies, media and/or other interested parties.

ABC Company Limited	Procedures Manual	Reference AP 008 Page 6 of 8	
	Handling Non-Conformities	Date Released dd/mm/yyyy	Date Reviewed dd/mm/yyyy
Assurance Process	Approved:	Issue No: 01 Prepared by:	Revision No: 00

	Process Headings	Process Details
11.6	Control of non-conforming product	Controls exercised over non-conforming product include, but are not limited to: • Proper identification and segregation to prevent inadvertent delivery to customers • Product stored in a protected area • Defining responsibilities for identification, segregation (QA Manager) and disposal of non-conforming product (Plant Manager) • Communicating with customers (Customer Relations Manager) • Taking corrective action (QA Manager) • Implementing corrective actions (Department Managers) • Originating documents related to non-conformance: • Non-conforming product log and disposal of non-conforming product form (QA Manager).
11.7	Remedial action	These options are available to deal with a non-conforming product or service: (a) Corrective action: See Corrective Actions Procedure AP 013; (b) Replacement of stock – the stock is replaced at ABCCL's expense. After evaluating the non-conformance, the Review Team shall make recommendations for its disposal. The product may be disposed of by one of these methods: • Rework • Repair • Regrade • Reject • Accept with a concession.

ABC Company Limited	Procedures Manual	Reference AP 008 Page 7 of 8	
	Handling Non-Conformities	Date Released dd/mm/yyyy	Date Reviewed dd/mm/yyyy
Assurance Process	Approved:	Issue No: 01 Prepared by:	Revision No: 00

	Process Headings	Process Details
11.7.1	Rework or repair	Rework shall be carried out according to the criteria established by the Review Team If the rework method involves a method not applied for manufacturing, the QA Manager shall seek customer approval. After manufacture, the product is held in quarantine identified with a quarantine sticker until it has been re-inspected and passed according to ABCCL procedures. The Production Manager shall ensure that any scrap produced is disposed of and any other material is reworked.
11.7.2	Reject	All reject items identified by the Review Team shall bear a REJECT sticker and shall be disposed of or recycled according to regulatory requirements. QA Manager shall keep records of rejects.
11.7.3	Return to supplier	Goods received from a supplier identified as non-conforming goods shall be returned to the supplier. Purchasing Manager shall communicate with the supplier for a replacement or credit.
11.7.4	Waiver	(a) The Review Team may recommend a waiver when a product fails to meet ABCCL specifications but meets customer requirements and can be used without reworking. QA Manager shall communicate with the customer about the identified defect and obtain approval for supplying the product. Label on the product shall clearly bear all the details and that it has been accepted under a waiver. (b) If a supplier wants to offer a product under a waiver, the Review Team shall review the request. If the request is approved, the QA Manager shall communicate with the supplier and the Purchasing Manager and advise the supplier on extra labelling requirements.

ABC Company Limited	Procedures Manual	Reference AP 008 Page 8 of 8	
	Handling Non-Conformities	Date Released dd/mm/yyyy	Date Reviewed dd/mm/yyyy
Assurance Process	Approved:	Issue No: 01 Prepared by:	Revision No: 00

	Process Headings	Process Details
11.8	Evaluation for release	All reworked or repaired products shall be inspected by the QA Staff according to ABCCL inspection procedures prior to release. The product shall be released under these conditions: • Control measures put in place have been effective • Results of sampling, tests and/or other verification activities show that the repaired/reworked product meets food safety, quality and environmental management system requirements.
12.0	Records	Non-conformance report Non-conformance log Records of disposal.
13.0	Changes made	None.

AP 009 Validation of Products, Processes and Equipment

ABC Company Limited	Procedures Manual		Reference AP 009 Page 1 of 3	
	Validation of Products, Processes and Equipment		Date Released dd/mm/yyyy	Date Reviewed dd/mm/yyyy
Assurance Process	Approved:		Issue No: 01 Prepared by:	Revision No: 00

Process Owner	QA Manager
Process Headings	**Process Details**
1.0 Purpose	To describe the procedure for validating products, processes and equipment.
2.0 Scope	This procedure applies to products, processes and equipment which require validation.
3.0 Input	Products, processes and equipment which require validation, calibration schedule, validation check list, verification schedule, previous reports, control schedule, standards and codes of practice.
4.0 Output	Validation report, verification report, reliable control measures and accurate data.
5.0 Competency requirements	Knowledge of products, processes and equipment, data analysis skills, knowledge of statistical techniques and validation principles.
6.0 Responsibility	Defined in Flowchart AP 009.1. Additional responsibilities are set out below. Validation Team shall: • Prepare validation/verification schedule • Review validation/verification findings • Appoint an external expert when required. Engineering Manager shall: • Organise resources and define methods for validating equipment. QA Manager shall: • Lead validation activities.
7.0 Associated documents	Validation form (Form 144) Validating elements (Form 145) Validation protocol (Form 146) Validation report (Form 147).
8.0 Resources	External consultant.
9.0 Measures/controls	Audits of the validation schedule Audits of the verification schedule Deviations.

ABC Company Limited	Procedures Manual		Reference AP 009 Page 2 of 3	
	Validation of Products, Processes and Equipment		Date Released dd/mm/yyyy	Date Reviewed dd/mm/yyyy
Assurance Process	Approved:		Issue No: 01 Prepared by:	Revision No: 00

	Process Headings	Process Details
10.0	Definitions	**Monitoring:** The act of conducting a planned sequence of observations or measurements of control parameter to determine whether the control measure is effective. **Qualification:** Action of providing that any premises and equipment work correctly, and actually perform as expected. **Validation:** Process of establishing by objective evidence that the product, process, equipment or design meets its predetermined requirements. **Verification:** Confirmation by examination and demonstration of objective evidence that the specified requirements have been met.
11.0	System description	Flowchart AP 009.1 shows the validation process.
11.1	Validation Team	Plant Manager shall appoint the Validation Team, which shall include the QA Manager, Food Safety Manager, Environment Manager, Engineering Manager, Laboratory Manager and others (as appropriate).
11.2	Selection for validation or verification	The decision tree for selecting the option is shown in Flowchart AP 009.2. QA Manager, Engineering Manager and the Laboratory Manager shall jointly determine the products, processes and equipment to be validated or verified. For example, processes such as sterilisation, aseptic filling processes and heat treatment processes require validation. Verification can be applied to processes such as manual cutting processes, testing for colour pH and turbidity, and visual inspection of packaging.
11.3	Approaches to validation	1. Reference to scientific or technical literature, previous validation studies, historical data of the performance of the element. 2. Scientifically valid experimental studies that demonstrate the adequacy of control measures/performance. 3. Review of data during operating conditions on the whole operation. 4. Use of mathematical models. 5. Surveys. 6. Expert opinion. 7. Internal scientific studies. 8. Industry standards/codes of practice.
11.4	Validation process	Validation process is shown in Flowchart AP 009.1 Validation checklist is shown in Form 148.
11.5	Validating elements	Form 145 shows some examples of validating elements.

ABC Company Limited	Procedures Manual		Reference AP 009 Page 3 of 3	
	Validation of Products, Processes and Equipment		Date Released dd/mm/yyyy	Date Reviewed dd/mm/yyyy
Assurance Process	Approved:		Issue No: 01 Prepared by:	Revision No: 00

	Process Headings	**Process Details**
11.6	Validation Plan	The key elements of the Validation Plan (VP) are: (a) scope which defines both the system and its elements to be validated and the required documentation; (b) roles and responsibilities of those responsible for validating the system; and (c) the strategy for validating the system within the operating environment. The approach covers the standards, procedures and methodologies of the implementing organisation.
11.7	Validation protocol	Validation protocols shall include the elements shown in Form 146
11.8	Validation of equipment	1. Installation qualification (IQ): Evaluation of correct installation. 2. Operational qualification (OQ): Checks on process parameters to ensure that they will result in a product that meets specified requirements under expected conditions of operation. 3. Performance qualification (PQ): Checks to ensure that the process will consistently yield acceptable product under normal operating conditions. During all three phases, the Validation Team shall decide: • What to verify or measure • How to verify or measure • Quantity to be verified or measures • When to measure • Acceptance criteria and rejection criteria • Required documentation.
11.9	Maintaining a state of validation	This is achieved by monitoring and controlling the process continuously and appropriate revalidation. Revalidation is necessary in case of: • System failure • Product, process or equipment changes • Regulatory requirement changes • Scheduled revalidation.
11.10	Validation report	Validation report template is shown in Form 148.
12.0	Records	Test results and documentation relating to validation and verification.
13.0	Changes made	None.

ABC Company Limited	Procedures Manual	Flowchart AP 009.1 Page 1 of 1	
	Validation Process	Date Released dd/mm/yyyy	Date Reviewed dd/mm/yyyy
Link AP 009/010	Approved:	Issue No: 01 Prepared by:	Revision No: 00

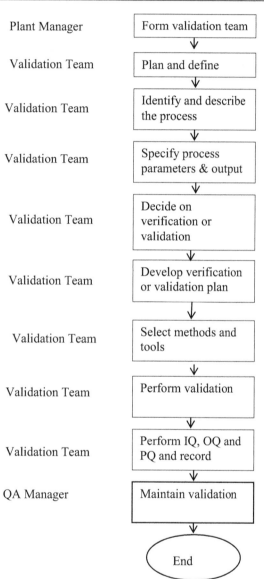

Plant Manager	Form validation team
Validation Team	Plan and define
Validation Team	Identify and describe the process
Validation Team	Specify process parameters & output
Validation Team	Decide on verification or validation
Validation Team	Develop verification or validation plan
Validation Team	Select methods and tools
Validation Team	Perform validation
Validation Team	Perform IQ, OQ and PQ and record
QA Manager	Maintain validation
	End

ABC Company Limited	**Procedures Manual**	**Flowchart AP 009.2** Page 1 of 1	
	Validation Decision Tree	Date Released dd/mm/yyyy	Date Reviewed dd/mm/yyyy
Link AP 009/010	Approved:	Issue No: 01 Prepared by:	Revision No: 00

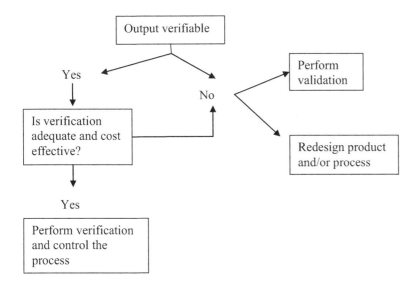

AP 010 Validation of Food Safety Programme

ABC Company Limited	Procedures Manual		Reference AP 010 Page 1 of 4	
	Validation of Food Safety Programme		Date Released dd/mm/yyyy	Date Reviewed dd/mm/yyyy
Assurance Process	Approved:		Issue No: 01 Prepared by:	Revision No: 00

Process Owner		Food Safety Manager and QA Manager
	Process Headings	**Process Details**
1.0	Purpose	To describe the procedure for the validation of the food safety control system.
2.0	Scope	This procedure applies to the food safety control system. This procedure is a subset of procedure AP 009.
3.0	Input	Hazard Analysis and Critical Control Point (HACCP) plan, calibration schedule, validation checklist, verification schedule, previous reports, control schedule, standards and codes of practice.
4.0	Output	Validation report, verification report, reliable control measures and accurate data.
5.0	Competency requirements	Knowledge of HACCP principles, biological, physical and chemical hazards, risk analysis and management, company's food products and recipes, food microbiology, Pre-requisite Programmes (PRPs), Operational Pre-requisite Programmes (oPRPs) and critical limits.
6.0	Responsibility	Defined in Flowchart AP 009.1. Additional responsibilities are set out below. Food Safety Manager and QA Manager shall: • Prepare validation/verification schedule • Review validation/verification findings • Appoint an external expert when required. Food Safety Manager shall: • Appoint a Food Safety Team (FST) (CP 024 Preparation for hazard analysis).
7.0	Associated documents	Validation checklist (Form 148) Validation form (Form 144) Validation elements (Form 149) Validation report (Form 147) Summary of validation and verification activities (Form 150).
8.0	Resources	External consultant.
9.0	Measures/controls	Audits of the validation schedule Audits of the verification schedule Deviations.
10.0	Definitions	See procedure AP 009.
11.0	System description	
11.1	Selection for validation or verification	The decision tree for selecting the option is shown in Flowchart AP 009.2.

ABC Company Limited	Procedures Manual	Reference AP 010 Page 2 of 4	
	Validation of Food Safety Programme	Date Released dd/mm/yyyy	Date Reviewed dd/mm/yyyy
Assurance Process	Approved:	Issue No: 01 Prepared by:	Revision No: 00

	Process Headings	Process Details
11.2	Pre-validation activities	1. Identify the hazards associated with the product and/or environment that need to be controlled. 2. Identify the food safety outcome required. This may be derived from existing outcomes or industry targets, applicable to the intended use of the product established by a competent authority or industry. 3. Identify measures to be validated. 4. If the control measure has already been validated ensure that the conditions of operation are similar to those at the time of validation. 5. Prioritise validation on the basis of (a) adverse health effects in case of failure of the control measure; (b) historical evidence; (c) ability to monitor and verify control measures; and (d) scientific and technical feasibility of validation.
11.3	Validation process	1. Establish outcome. 2. Decide on the approach or combination of approaches. 3. Establish parameters and decision criteria that will demonstrate the effectiveness of control measures that are in place for controlling the hazards. 4. Assemble the required validation information and conduct studies (if needed). 5. Analyse the results. 6. Record and review the validation. 7. If a control measure or a combination of control measures is not capable of achieving the outcome, the FST shall re-evaluate product formulation, process parameters and other appropriate decisions or actions.
11.4	Validation Plan	The key elements of the Validation Plan (VP) are (a) scope which defines both the system and its elements to be validated and the required documentation; (b) roles and responsibilities of those responsible for validating the system; and (c) the strategy for validating the system within the operating environment. The approach covers the standards, procedures and methodologies of the implementing organisation.

ABC Company Limited	Procedures Manual	Reference AP 010 Page 3 of 4	
	Validation of Food Safety Programme	Date Released dd/mm/yyyy	Date Reviewed dd/mm/yyyy
Assurance Process	Approved:	Issue No: 01 Prepared by:	Revision No: 00

	Process Headings	Process Details
11.5	Validation of control measures combination	The FST shall review the effectiveness of supporting evidence in the HACCP programme, i.e. control measures, monitoring system for PRPs, oPRPs, Critical Control Points (CCPs), as well as corrective actions taken for any deviations. Form 149 may be used for guidance.
11.6	Initial validation	1. The FST shall validate the HACCP plan for adequacy and completeness on the basis of quantifiable and objective results derived from in-process quality control monitoring, end product testing and customer feedback by demonstrating the items listed in Form 148.
		2. At the initial validation the FST shall evaluate whether the HACCP plan is valid for controlling the food safety hazards associated with the ingredients, process and product, and ensure that the plan can be implemented as written.
11.7	Ongoing validation and re-validation	1. Before implementing the plan the FST shall determine whether it can be implemented as planned.
		2. Re-validation shall be performed at least annually or in these instances: • System failure • Product, process or equipment changes • Regulatory requirement changes • Scheduled re-validation.
		3. For new HACCP plans or brand new product categories, the Food Safety Manager shall decide whether a HACCP plan implementation validation is warranted.
11.8	Process/equipment validation	A process/equipment validation shall be carried out (a) before the equipment is first used in production; (b) when changes to the equipment/product occur which could impact on food safety; (c) if the food safety risk is higher than originally encountered; and/or (d) if evidence suggests that the hazard is not adequately controlled (see AP 009).
11.9	Maintaining a state of validation	This is achieved by monitoring and controlling the process continuously and appropriate re-validation.

ABC Company Limited	Procedures Manual	Reference AP 010 Page 4 of 4	
	Validation of Food Safety Programme	Date Released dd/mm/yyyy	Date Reviewed dd/mm/yyyy
Assurance Process	Approved:	Issue No: 01 Prepared by:	Revision No: 00

	Process Headings	Process Details
11.10	Validation report	Validation report template is shown in Form 147.
12.0	Records	Test results and documentation relating to validation and verification Form 150 presents a summary of validation and verification activities.
13.0	Changes made	None.

AP 011 Verification of Products, Processes and Equipment

ABC Company Limited	Procedures Manual	Reference AP 011 Page 1 of 3	
	Verification of Products, Processes and Equipment	Date Released dd/mm/yyyy	Date Reviewed dd/mm/yyyy
Assurance Process	Approved:	Issue No: 01 Prepared by:	Revision No: 00

Process Owner		Food Safety Manager, QA Manager
	Process Headings	**Process Details**
1.0	Purpose	To describe the procedure for the verification of products, processes and equipment.
2.0	Scope	This procedure applies to ABCCL products, processes/equipment and externally provided products and processes.
3.0	Input	Design and development processes, purchased products, in-process activities, monitoring procedures and equipment, Hazard Analysis and Critical Control Point (HACCP) plan, calibration schedule, validation checklist, verification schedule, previous reports, control schedule, standards and codes of practice.
4.0	Output	Verified products, processes and equipment, verification report, reliable control measures and accurate data.
5.0	Competency requirements	Knowledge of ABCCL products, processes and equipment, food safety principles and HACCP programme.
6.0	Responsibility	Food Safety Manager and QA Manager shall: • Prepare validation/verification schedule • Appoint a Verification Team • Review validation/verification findings • Appoint an external expert when required.
7.0	Associated documents	Verification schedule (Form 151) Verification form (Form 152).
8.0	Resources	External consultant.
9.0	Measures/controls	Audits of the verification activities Deviations and non-conformances.
10.0	System description	
10.1	Verification activities	Verification activities include the verification of (a) purchased product; (b) in-process activities; (c) calibration; (d) finished products; (e) external provision; and (f) during design and development activities.
10.2	Verification methods	(a) A periodic review of written procedures to ensure programmes are operating as planned; (b) checks to ensure documents are being done at specified intervals; (c) direct observation of procedures; (d) direct observation and/or testing of equipment and facilities; and (e) ensuring that operators are trained and competent to perform the tasks assigned to them.

ABC Company Limited	Procedures Manual	Reference AP 011 Page 2 of 3	
	Verification of Products, Processes and Equipment	Date Released dd/mm/yyyy	Date Reviewed dd/mm/yyyy
Assurance Process	Approved:	Issue No: 01 Prepared by:	Revision No: 00

	Process Headings	Process Details
10.3	Critical Control Points (CCPs) and other verification activities	• Calibration of monitoring devices (AP 002) • Calibration record review (AP 002) • Review of monitoring records and corrective action reports • Independent check on the adequacy of CCPs to control the hazard • Targeted sampling and testing to ensure the equipment settings are accurate for product safety • Supplier compliance may be checked by targeted sampling when receipt of material is a CCP and product specifications are relied on as critical limits • CCP and monitoring records review.
10.4	HACCP system verification	The verification shall focus on the: • Flow diagram and product description accuracy • Evidence of CCP monitoring according to HACCP plan • Operation of processes within critical limits • Completion of records accurately according to the control schedule and reviewed • Resolving consumer complaints and taking appropriate corrective actions • Performance of monitoring activities at the locations and at frequencies specified in the plan • Addressing deviations appropriately • Completion of calibration according to the calibration schedule • Verification of Pre-Requisite Programmes (PRPs) • Analytically testing or auditing monitoring procedures • Microbiological testing of end product.

ABC Company Limited	Procedures Manual		Reference AP 011 Page 3 of 3	
	Verification of Products, Processes and Equipment	Date Released dd/mm/yyyy		Date Reviewed dd/mm/yyyy
Assurance Process	Approved:	Issue No: 01 Prepared by:		Revision No: 00

	Process Headings	Process Details
10.5	External verification	Performed by a regulatory body, a customer, private consultant or a certifying body and may include: • Reviews of the hazard analysis, HACCP plan and any modifications, CCP monitoring records, corrective actions, verification records • Observation of operations to check whether the HACCP is being followed and • (if required) that records are maintained • Collection and testing of random samples
10.6	Other verification activities	• Verification of purchased product (CP 008) • Verification during design and development (CP 013) • Verification of finished product (CP 014) • Verification during processing (CP 012) • Calibration of measuring devices (AP 002) • External provision (SP 045).
10.7	Observation of operations at CCPs	Verification person shall observe the operation being performed and confirm the operator's knowledge of the process, CCPs, control limits, monitoring and recording activities of the HACCP plan and actions to be taken in case of deviation.
10.8	Verification process	1. Determine the element to be verified. 2. Collect required reference material and previous findings. 3. Conduct verification activity and record findings.
10.9	Verification schedule	Food Safety Manager and QA Manager shall establish the verification schedule (see Form 152).
11.0	Records	Test results and documentation relating to validation and verification Form 150 presents a summary of validation and verification activities.
12.0	Changes made	None.

AP 012 Internal Audit

ABC Company Limited	Procedures Manual	Reference AP 012 Page 1 of 4	
	Internal Audit	Date Released dd/mm/yyyy	Date Reviewed dd/mm/yyyy
Assurance Process	Approved:	Issue No: 01 Prepared by:	Revision No: 00

Process Owner	QA Manager	
	Process Headings	**Process Details**
1.0	Purpose	To describe the procedure for assessing the effectiveness of the IQFSE Management System.
2.0	Scope	This procedure applies to the IQFSE Management System.
3.0	Input	Regulatory requirements, previous audit reports, corrective action reports, relevant ISO standards, management reviews, audit schedule and IQFSE Management System Manual and changes therein.
4.0	Output	Audit report describing the performance of the IQFSE Management System, continual improvement and enhanced performance.
5.0	Competency requirements	Knowledge of relevant ISO standard and, competency as a Lead Auditor. Other members must have completed audit skills training and three supervised audits with the Lead Auditor.
6.0	Responsibility	Defined in Flowchart AP 012.1.
7.0	Associated documents	Internal audit checklist (Form 154) Audit schedule (Form 153) Audit plan (Form 155) Internal audit report (Form 156) Non-conformance report (Form 143).
8.0	Resources	Skilled auditors ISO 9001, ISO 14000 and ISO 22000 standards.
9.0	Measures/controls	Internal audits completed as planned Number, frequency and degree of non-conformances Average time to correct non-conformances Corrective actions closed out.

ABC Company Limited	Procedures Manual	Reference AP 012 Page 2 of 4	
	Internal Audit	Date Released dd/mm/yyyy	Date Reviewed dd/mm/yyyy
Assurance Process	Approved:	Issue No: 01 Prepared by:	Revision No: 00

	Process Headings	Process Details
10.0	Definitions	**Audit criteria:** Set of policies, procedures and requirements. **Audit scope:** Extent and boundaries of the audit. **Audit plan:** Detailed outline of the purpose, scope, objectives and activities for an audit. **Audit programme:** Annual summary of the areas to be audited, the schedule for each audit and the auditors. **Audit frequency:** The entire IQFSE Management System shall be audited annually and can be broken into categories or sections depending on the type of activity, time availability or the season in which the activity takes place. **Planned arrangements:** Schedule of activities planned in advance to ensure that the outcome meets expectations.
11.0	System description	The procedure for internal audit is shown in Flowchart AP 012.1.
11.1	Criteria, schedule and plan	Audit criteria: Requirements of the Integrated Quality, Food Safety and Environmentaal (IQFSE) Management System, ISO 9001:2015, ISO 14000:2015 and ISO 22000:2017. Audit schedule (Form 153): Consideration shall be given to the following when developing the audit schedule: (a) Importance of processes: For example, management reviews, corrective actions, auditing, actions to address risks and opportunities, operational planning and control, quality, food safety and environmental objectives and policies, environmental aspects and impacts, food safety hazard analysis, critical control points (CCPs) are some important processes; (b) Suppler performance; (c) Changes affecting the organisation: Changes are influenced by internal and external factors, the needs of interested parties, regulatory changes, etc.; (d) Results of previous audits: Previous audit results indicate how well the processed have been managed. Audit resources shall be directed to where they are most needed; and (e) Audit Plan (Form 155).
11.2	Audit Team	Select the Audit Team on the basis of competency and skill requirements. Audit Team members shall not audit activities for which they are responsible.
11.3	Conducting the audit	1. Observe the activities being performed, check relevant documents and records, and interview personnel. Check non-conformance product list and ascertain the effectiveness of controls implemented to prevent intentional or unintentional sale or delivery to customers. 2. Assess the findings against the relevant clauses of ISO 9001:2015, ISO 22000:2017 and ISO 14001:2015 standards. 3. Professionalism: All auditors shall set aside biases and prejudices and develop a good relationship with the auditee. Auditors shall not audit the activities for which they are responsible.

ABC Company Limited	Procedures Manual		Reference AP 012 Page 3 of 4	
	Internal Audit	Date Released dd/mm/yyyy		Date Reviewed dd/mm/yyyy
Assurance Process	Approved:	Issue No: 01 Prepared by:		Revision No: 00

	Process Headings	**Process Details**
11.4	Effectiveness of implementation of the system	Determine whether the objectives, customer satisfaction and continual improvement have been achieved.
11.5	Audit report	Audit report shall include at least: • The purpose, scope, criteria and objectives of the audit • Strengths and weaknesses • Overall conclusionRecommendations (if any) • Follow-up activities and timeframe. Initially, the findings are communicated to applicable managers verbally at the exit meetings. Final version of the report is submitted by the Lead Auditor within two working days.
11.6	Corrective actions	The timeframe for corrective actions shall be mutually agreed between the auditor and the auditee. Follow-up visits are necessary to check on corrective actions related to critical and major non-compliances. Corrective actions for minor non-compliances may be followed up at the next scheduled audit.
11.7	Legislation audit	At least annually the QA Manager shall conduct a legislation audit to determine continued compliance with applicable legislation in the legal register. The auditor shall select the most significant legislation applicable to ABCCL based on current risks and verify by objective evidence that they are current and complied with. Samples of legislation are noted and updated as necessary. The whole register is audited at least once every three years.
12.0	Records	Non-conformance reports Corrective actions Checklists and audit notes Auditor training records Audit reports Audit schedule Audit plan.

ABC Company Limited	Procedures Manual	Reference AP 012 Page 4 of 4	
	Internal Audit	Date Released dd/mm/yyyy	Date Reviewed dd/mm/yyyy
Assurance Process	Approved:	Issue No: 01 Prepared by:	Revision No: 00

	Process Headings	Process Details
13.0	Changes made	None.

ABC Company Limited	Procedures Manual	Flowchart AP 012.1 Page 1 of 1	
	Internal Audit	Date Released dd/mm/yyyy	Date Reviewed dd/mm/yyyy
Link AP 012	Approved:	Issue No: 01 Prepared by:	Revision No: 00

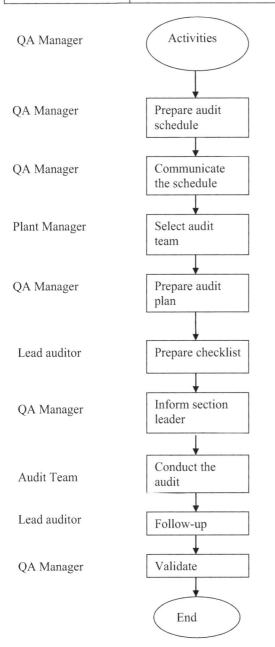

QA Manager — Activities

In consultation with the Environment Manager and the Food Safety Manager, QA Manager shall specify the activities to be audited based on the significance of impact on quality, environment and food safety

QA Manager — Prepare audit schedule

Activities shall be audited at least annually. If deviations are found or new products or processes are introduced, audits may be scheduled more frequently. Form 153

QA Manager — Communicate the schedule

Communicate at least one month prior to schedules date.

Plant Manager — Select audit team

Select members based on competency and skill requirements. The team shall appoint a Lead Auditor. Team members shall not audit activities for which they are responsible.

QA Manager — Prepare audit plan

Plan shall include the purpose, scope, criteria, objectives, audit team members, activities to be audited and documents to be checked. In preparation the QA Manager shall review the results of previous audit reports, corrective actions, customer surveys and other documents deemed relevant. Forms 154, 155

Lead auditor — Prepare checklist

QA Manager — Inform section leader

Inform the Section Leader/Supervisor about the audit and the details.

Audit Team — Conduct the audit

Entry meeting: Lead Auditor shall explain the purpose, scope, criteria, objectives, activities to be audited and documents to be checked. Introduce team members. Respond to queries.
Conduct the audit through observation, checking records and documents and speaking to operators/

Lead auditor — Follow-up

Agree on non-conformances. Review the nature of non-conformances with the team after the audit.

QA Manager — Validate

Prepare the report and conduct the exit meeting.

End

AP 013 Corrective and Preventive Action

ABC Company Limited	Procedures Manual	Reference AP 013 Page 1 of 3	
	Corrective and Preventive Action	Date Released dd/mm/yyyy	Date Reviewed dd/mm/yyyy
Assurance Process	Approved:	Issue No: 01 Prepared by:	Revision No: 00

Process Owner	QA Manager
Process Headings	**Process Details**
1.0 Purpose	To establish and describe the procedure for identifying, documenting, analysing and implementing corrective and preventive actions.
2.0 Scope	This procedure applies to all operations which may eventually affect the quality, food safety of ABCCL products and services and the environment.
3.0 Input	Activity, product, process or service that does not meet requirements and corrective action request.
4.0 Output	Conforming activity, product, process or service, continual improvement, reduction of non-conforming products/services, non-conforming data and customer satisfaction.
5.0 Competency requirements	Problem-solving skills, communication skills, and knowledge of specifications and requirements.
6.0 Responsibility	Defined in Flowchart AP 013.1. Additional responsibilities are set out below. Plant Manager shall: • Appoint a Review Team (AP 008). • Environment Manager shall: • Monitor progress of corrective and preventive actions for environmental issues. Food Safety Manager shall: • Maintain records of corrective and preventive actions • Monitor progress of corrective and preventive actions for food safety issues. All employees shall: • Identify non-conforming conditions and reporting the findings to the QA Manager (quality issues), Environment Manager (environmental issues) or the Food Safety Manager (food safety issues) • Use the corrective action request form to report a non-conformance.
7.0 Associated documents	Non-conformance report (NCR) Form 143 Corrective action request (CAR) Form 157 Corrective action report (CAR) Form 160 Non-conforming product/service log (Form 142).

ABC Company Limited	**Procedures Manual**		**Reference AP 013** Page 2 of 3	
	Corrective and Preventive Action		Date Released dd/mm/yyyy	Date Reviewed dd/mm/yyyy
Assurance Process	Approved:		Issue No: 01 Prepared by:	Revision No: 00

	Process Headings	**Process Details**
8.0	Resources	ISO 9001, ISO 14000 and ISO 22000 standards IQFSE Management System Management review meeting report Audit reports.
9.0	Measures/controls	Timeliness of corrective action. Number of corrective actions/preventive actions Non-conformance rate Non-conformance type.
10.0	Definitions	**Non-conformance:** Failure to meet specific standard, criteria or requirements. **Correction:** Any action taken to eliminate a non-conformity. It can be a rework or a regrade and can be done in conjunction with corrective action. **Minor non-conformance:** A deficiency that will not affect the system or certification requirements and if not addressed may lead to a risk to food safety, quality or the environment. **Major non-conformance:** Actual or potential deficiency that will seriously affect ABCCL's quality, environment or food safety programme. **Critical non-conformance:** Includes, but is not limited to, (a) failure of controls at Critical Control Points (CCPs), Pre-Requisite Programmes (PRPs) or other process steps in a food safety programme or environmental management programme that has the potential to harm the consumer and is likely to result in a recall or harm the public due to a catastrophic environmental disaster; and (b) falsification of records relating to food safety controls.
11.0	System description	The corrective action process is shown in Flowchart AP 013.1.
11.1	Issues requiring corrective action	Some of the issues that require corrective action are: • Customer returns and complaints • Product or process failure • Health and safety incidents • Environmental incidents • Unsafe product or process • Service delay or failure • Supplier failure • Ideas from employees • Poor performance.

ABC Company Limited	Procedures Manual	Reference AP 013 Page 3 of 3	
	Corrective and Preventive Action	Date Released dd/mm/yyyy	Date Reviewed dd/mm/yyyy
Assurance Process	Approved:	Issue No: 01 Prepared by:	Revision No: 00

	Process Headings	Process Details
11.2	Dealing with non-conformities	The Review Team appointed by the Plant Manager shall recommend action to control and correct and deal with consequences of non-conformance.
11.3	Review and analysis of non-conformances	The Review Team shall consider the issues shown in Form 161. The team shall also consider whether similar non-conformances exist in the organisation.
11.4	Plan for corrective action	The plan for corrective action is recorded in Form 162. The verification process shall determine whether the implemented action resolves the root cause of the problem, the proposed action has been implemented, and if the implementation has been effective.
11.5	Identifying risks and opportunities	After implementing corrective action, the Review Team shall carry out a risk assessment to determine the necessity to reduce the risk rating or add to existing risks.
11.6	Preventive action	The Review Team shall also (a) identify potential non-conformities and root causes using processes and operations performance which impact on the IQFSE Management System, product, waivers, audit reports, customer complaints, etc. to detect, analyse and eliminate potential sources of non-conformance; (b) evaluate the need to address potential non-conformances; (c) implement such action with adequate controls; (d) record actions taken; and (e) review the effectiveness of preventive action.
11.7	Changes to the IQFSE Management System	QA Manager shall review the need to make appropriate changes to the IQFSE Management System and make relevant changes according to the Change Management Procedure MP 020.
12.0	Records	Non-conformance report (NCR) Form 143 Corrective action request (CARQ) Form 157 Corrective action report (CAR) Form 160 Non-conforming product/service log (Form 142).
13.0	Changes made	None

ABC Company Limited	Procedures Manual	Flowchart AP 013.1 Page 1 of 1	
	Corrective and Preventive Action	Date Released dd/mm/yyyy	Date Reviewed dd/mm/yyyy
Link AP 013	Approved:	Issue No: 01 Prepared by:	Revision No: 00

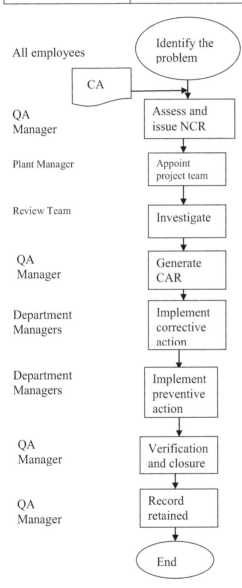

Any employee may initiate corrective action. All employees are obliged to initiate corrective action when it appears to them that the quality and safety of ABCCL's products and services are compromised and/ or that the activities(s) may have an adverse impact on the environment. The completed CAR form shall be submitted to the respective management representative for evaluation

The Review Team is appointed on the basis of skills required to analyse and identify the root cause(s) of the problem

Depending on the problem more personnel may be appointed. Apparent cause is rarely the root cause. Identify the apparent cause and the contributory cause(s). Further analysis can lead to the root cause(s). The findings are recorded in the CAR form

Take action prevent a recurrence or similar problems that may occur in other areas.

Verify the corrective and preventive actions taken and determine appropriate follow up or verification required. Long-term solutions require more time and corrective action remains open until completion. If actions have been effective corrective action is closed. If it had not been effective a new NCR is generated according to this procedure.

Appendix 1: Gap Analysis

Reference	Title	Applicable Clauses		
		ISO 9001:2015	ISO 14001: 2015	ISO 22000: 2018
MP 000	Our Company	4.1	4.1	4.1
MP 001	Internal and External Issues	4.1	4.1	4.1
MP 002	Interested Parties	4.2	4.2	4,2
MP 003	Statutory and Regulatory Requirements	8.2.2, 8.2.3	6.1.3, 9.1.2	4.2, 5.2.1, 6.2.1, 8.2.3
MP 004	Scope	4.3	4.3	4.3
MP 005	Planning IQFSE Management System	4.4	4.4	4.4
MP 006	IQFSE Management System and its Processes	4.4	4.4	4.4
MP 007	Risk Management	6.1	6.1	6.1.2
MP 008	Objectives	6.2	6.2	6.2
MP 009	Integrated Quality, Food Safety and Environment Policy	5.2	5.2	5.2
MP 010	Our Commitment	5.1	5.1	5.1
MP 011	Roles, Responsibilities and Authorities	5.3	5.3	5.3
MP 012	IQFSE Management System Planning Processes	6.1.1, 6.2.2, 9.1.3d	6.2.1, 6.2.2	6.2.2
MP 013	Operational Planning and Control	8.1	8.1	8.1
MP 014	Strategic Planning	4.1	4.1	4.1
MP 015	Production Planning	8.1	8.1	8.1
MP 016	Looking after Our Customers	5.1.2		
MP 017	Management of Emergencies	8.2.1e	8.2	8.4
MP 018	Emergency Response Planning	8.2.1e	8.2	8.4
MP 019	Actions to Address Risks and Opportunities	6.1	6.1	6.1
MP 020	Change Management	6.3	8.1	6.3
MP 021	Control of Product and Service Changes	8.5.6		6.3, 8.2.4f

(Continued)

Reference	Title	Applicable Clauses		
		ISO 9001:2015	**ISO 14001: 2015**	**ISO 22000: 2018**
CP 001	Approval of Suppliers	8.4.1	8.1	7.1.6
CP 002	Offering Contracts	82.2, 8.2.3	8.1	7.1.6
CP 003	Purchasing Information	8.4.3	8.1	7.1.6
CP 004	Purchasing	8.4	8.1	7.1.5, 7.1.6
CP 005	Purchasing Engineering Items	8.4.2	8.1	7.1.5, 7.1.6
CP 006	Purchasing Technology Resources	8.4.2	8.1	7.1.5, 7.1.6
CP 007	Inward Goods Receipt	8.4.2, 8.5.3	8.1	7.1.6, 8.2.4g
CP 008	Inward Goods Inspection	8.4.2, 8.6	8.1	7.1.6
CP 009	Issue of Inward Goods	8.5.1		8.1
CP 010	Inspection and Test Status	8.5.1	8.1	8.9.1
CP 011	Management of Customers' and Suppliers' Property	8.5.3		
CP 012	Production Process Control	8.5.1	8.1	8.1, 8.5.4.5
CP 013	Design and Development	8.3	8.1	
CP 014	Release of FG	8.6		8.9.4.2
CP 015	Handling and Storage of Goods	8.5.4		8.2.4g
CP 016	Customer Requirements	8.2.2 8.2.3	4.2	4.2, 7.4.2, 8.5.1.5.3
CP 017	Take Order	8.2.2	4.2	7.4.2
CP 018	Processing Orders	8.5.1	8.1	8.1
CP 019	Picking Orders	8.5.1		
CP 020	New Product Development	8.3	8.1	
CP 021	Delivery	8.5.1		8.1
CP 022	Post-delivery Activities	8.5.5	8.1	8.1
CP 023	Business Continuity	8.2, 6.1.2	8.2	8.4.2
CP 024	Preparation for Hazard Analysis			8.5.1
CP 025	Hazard Analysis: Assessment of Hazards			8.5.2
CP 026	Hazard Analysis: CCPs and Control Measures			8.5.4
CP 027	Management of HACCP Plan			8.5.4
CP 028	Pre-requisite Programmes			8.2
CP 029	Recall Procedure			8.9.5
CP 030	Initial Environmental Review (IER)		6.1.4	
CP 031	Identification of Environmental Aspects and Impacts		6.1.2	

(Continued)

Reference	Title	Applicable Clauses		
		ISO 9001:2015	ISO 14001: 2015	ISO 22000: 2018
CP 032	Assessment of the Significance of Environmental Aspects and Impacts		6.1.2	
CP 033	Managing Environmental Impact of Sales and Marketing		6.1.2	
CP 034	Managing Food Safety Issues in Sales and Marketing			8.5.1, 8.5.2.2
CP 035	Managing Environmental Impact of IT		6.1.2	
CP 036	Sales Process	8.2, 4.4		7.4.2
CP 037	Visit Planning	8.2.1, 5.1.2		7.4.2
CP 038	In-store Procedure	8.2.1, 5.1.2		7.4.2
CP 039	Offer of Samples	8.2.1		
CP 040	Sales Meetings	7.4		
CP 041	Receiving and Storing Food Items			8.5.4
SP 001	Document Control	7.5	7.5	7.5
SP 002	Record Control	7.5	7.5	7.5, 8.5.4
SP 003	Maintenance Management	7.1.3	9.1	7.1.3
SP 004	Set-up Procedure	7.1.3		7.1.3
SP 005	Internal Communication	7.4	7.4.2	7.4.3
SP 005	External Communication	7.4	7.4,3	7.4.2
SP 007	Communication with Customers	8.2.1, 7.4	7.4.3	7.4.2
SP 008	Organisational Knowledge	7.1.6	7.2	7.2
SP 009	Resource Management	7.1	7.1	7.1.3
SP 010	Managing the Infrastructure and Work Environment	7.1.3	7.1	7.1.3
SP 011	Planning for Human Resources	7.1.2		7.1.2
SP 012	Recruitment	7.1.2 7.1.3	7.2	7.1.2
SP 013	Induction	7.1.3	7.2	7.1.2
SP 014	Training and Development	7.2, 7.3	7.2, 7.3	7.2, 7.3
SP 015	Leave	7.1.2		
SP 016	Safety and Wellbeing	7.1.4		7.1.4
SP 017	Promotions and Transfers	7.1.2, 7.2, 7.3		
SP 018	Disciplinary Procedure	7.1.2		
SP 019	Grievance Procedure	7.1.2		
SP 020	Performance Review	7.2	7.2	7.2

(Continued)

Reference	Title	Applicable Clauses		
		ISO 9001:2015	**ISO 14001: 2015**	**ISO 22000: 2018**
SP 021	IT Resources, Usage and Security	7.1.3, 7.2	7.1	7.1.3
SP 022	Email, Internet Use and Security	7.1,3, 7.4	7.1	7.1.3
SP 023	Computer Hardware and Software Installation	7.1.3	7.1	7.1.3
SP 024	Phone, voice mail, fax	7.4	7.4	7.4
SP 025	Password Management	7.5, 7.4	7.5, 7.4	7.5, 7.4
SP 026	Virus Protection	7.1.5	9.1.1	7.1.4
SP 027	System Access	7.5.3.2	7.5.3	7.5.3.2
SP 028	Backup and Recovery	7.5.3.2	7.5.3	7.5.3.2
SP 029	Service and Support	7.1.3, 7.2		7.4.2
SP 030	Electronic File Storage	7.5		7.5
SP 031	Use of IT to Ensure Food Safety			6.1.3, 7.1.3
SP 032	Brand Management	8.1.2, 4.4		
SP 033	Promoting and Advertising	8.2.2, 4.4		
SP 034	Marketing Forecast	4.4, 8.1, 7.1.6		
SP 035	Market Research	4.4, 7.1.6, 9.1.3		
SP 036	Budgeting	7.1	7.1	7.1
SP 037	Accounts Payable	7.1, 4.4	7.1, 4.4	
SP 038	Accounts Receivable	7.1, 4.4	7.1, 4.4	
SP 039	Internal Control	4.4c, 9.1	4.4, 9.1	
SP 040	Payment of Salaries and Wages	7.1.2		
SP 041	Managing Fixed Assets	7.1.3		
SP 042	Preparation of Management Accounts	9.1.3		
SP 043	Management of Bank Accounts	9.1.3, 8.4		
SP 044	Management of Credit Cards	9.1.3, 8.4		
SP 045	Control of External Provision	8.4	8.1	7.1.6
SP 046	Customer Satisfaction	9.1.2		7.4.2
SP 047	Customer Complaints	8.2.1, 9.1.2, 9.3	7.4.2, 9.3	7.4.2, 8.9.2, 9.3
SP 048	Employee Participation	4.2, 7.4	4.2, 7.4	4.2, 7.4
AP 001	Control of Specifications	8.5.1, 8.1, 7.5	8.1	8.5.1.2
AP 002	Control of Monitoring and Measuring Devices	7.1.5, 8.5.1	8.1	8.7
AP 003	Monitoring, Measurement, Analysis and Evaluation	7.1.5, 9.1.3	9.1.1	9.1
AP 004	Analysis and Evaluation of Data	9.1.3	9.1.2	9.1.2

(Continued)

Reference	Title	Applicable Clauses		
		ISO 9001:2015	**ISO 14001: 2015**	**ISO 22000: 2018**
AP 005	Management Review	9.3	9.3	9.3
AP 006	Continual Improvement	10.1, 10.3	10.1, 10.3	10.2
AP 007	Identification and Traceability	8.5.2		8.3, 8.5.1.2
AP 008	Handling Non-conformities	8.7, 10.2.1	10.2	8.9.4
AP 009	Validation of Products, Processes and Equipment	8.5.1	8.1	8.5.1.3
AP 010	Validation of Food Safety Programme			8.5.3
AP 011	Verification of Product, Processes and Equipment	8.4.2, 8.6	9.1.1	8.8.1, 8.8.2
AP 012	Internal Audit	9.2	9.2	9.2
AP 013	Corrective and Preventive Action	10.2, 6.1	10.2	8.9.3

Appendix 2: Abbreviations and Acronyms

AP	Assurance process
ASL	Approved supplier list
BCP	Business continuity plan
BCPC	Business continuity plan coordinator
BP	British Pharmacopoeia
CA	Corrective action
CAR	Corrective action report
CARQ	Corrective action request
CCP	Critical control point
CEO	Chief executive officer
CFT	Cross functional team
CP	Core process
CRT	Chemical response team
DPP	Design and development plan
eMail	Electronic mail
EMS	Environmental management system
EPA	Environmental Protection Agency
ERP	Enterprise resource planning
ERT	Emergency response team
FIFO	First in first out
FMEA	Failure mode and effects analysis
FSMS	Food safety management system
FST	Food safety team
FSTL	Food safety team leader
FTA	Fault tree analysis
GHP	Good hygiene practices
GMP	Good manufacturing practices
HACCP	Hazard analysis and critical control point
HR	Human resources
IER	Initial environmental review
IQ	Installation qualification
IQFSE	Integrated quality, food safety and environmental management system

ISO	International Organization for Standardization
IT	Information technology
LCA	Life cycle assessment
MAO	Maximum acceptable outage
MID	Material identification label
MP	Management process
MSD	Material safety data sheets
ODS	Ozone-depleting substance
oPRP	Operational prerequisite programme
OQ	Operational qualification
PA	Preventive action
PDCA	Plan-Do-Check-Act
PEST	Political, economic, social and technological
PO	Purchase order
PRP	Prerequisite programme
PQ	Performance qualification
QA	Quality assurance
QC	Quality control
QS-9000	Quality system requirements (U.S. Automative)
QSE	Quality, environment and safety management system
R&D	Research and development
SD	Standard deviation
SOP	Standard operating procedure
SP	Support process
SPC	Statistical process control
SWOT	Strengths, weaknesses, opportunities and threats
TQM	Total quality management
UNCED	United Nations Conference on Environment and Development
USP	United States Pharmacopoeia

Appendix 3: Bibliography

A & S Integrated Services limited. (2016). *Quality Manual: ISO 9001:2015 Quality Management System. Issue 1.* Watford: A &S Integrated Services Limited.

AFC. (2011). *Management of pest control OPRP verification.* OPRP 2. Retrieved June 20, https://www.scribd.com/document/370035363/OPRP-2-Management-of-Pest-Control-Verification-Record

Biswas, P. (n.d). *ISO 14001;2015 Clause 7.5 Documented information.* Retrieved June 20, 2019 from http://isoconsultantpune.com/iso-140012015-clause-7-5-documented-information/

Bizmanualz Inc. (2008). *ISO 22000 Standard Procedures for Food Safety Management System.* Missouri: Bizmanuals Inc.

BSI. (2018). *BS EN ISO 22000:2018: Food Safety Management Systems Requirements for Any Organization in the Food Chain.* UK: British Standards Limited.

Cochran, C. (2015). ISO 9001:2015 in Plain English. Chico: Paton Professional.

Compasspoint. (2012). *Non-profit fiscal policies and procedures: A template and guide.* Retrieved June 20, 2019 from https://www.compasspoint.org/sites/default/files/documents/Guide%20to%20Fiscal%20Policies%20and%20%20Procedures.pdf.

Dellinger. (2017). *Integrated Management Manual. Revision 4.0.* Dillingen: Dellinger.

eFresh. (n.d.). *Sample ISO 22000 manual.* Retrieved June 20, 2019 from https://www.scribd.com/document/294410112/Sample-Iso-22000-Manual

Environmental Protection Agency. (2001). *Environmental Management Systems: An Implementation Guide for Small and Medium-Sized Organisations* (2nd ed.). Michigan: NSF International.

Environmental Protection Department. (n.d.). *Environmental management system manual. Revision 1.* Retrieved June 20, 2019 from https://www.epd.gov.hk/epd/misc/env_management_sme/eng/pdf/E_E/EM01.pdf

Hafele. (2017). *Integrated Management System Manual.* Rugby: Hafele UK Ltd.

Hong Kong Civil Service. (1995). *Human resource management.* Retrieved June 19, 2019 from https://www.csb.gov.hk/english/publication/files/e-hrmguide.pdf.

Hoyle, D. (2018). *ISO 9000 Quality System Handbook: Updated for the ISO 9001:2015 Standard.* Abinghdon: Routledge.

ISO. (2019). *ISO 9001 Checklist.* Retrieved June 20, 2019 from https://www.iso-9001-checklist.co.uk/free-iso-downloads.htm.

JSM. (2012). *Integrated Management System Manual: Safety, Quality and Environmental.* Potters Bar: JSM Construction Ltd.

Mango. (2017). *Integrated Management System (IMS) Manual.* Christchurch: Mango Ltd.

MAS Solutions LLC. (2017). *Free ISO 9001: 2015 documents.* Retrieved June 20, 2019 from https://www.masquality.com/free-iso-9001-2015-documents.html.

Mo-Sci. (2018). *Mo-Sci quality manual, Issue 3, Revision 5.* Retrieved June 19, 2019 from https://mo-sci.com/uploads/documents/QM%203.5.pdf.

Nestle. (2003). *Sales Representative Manual.* Vevey: Nestle.

NQA. (n.d.). *ISO 14001: 2015 Environmental management system implementation guide.* Retrieved June 20, 2019 from https://www.nqa.com/medialibraries/NQA/NQA-Media-Library/PDFs/NQA-ISO-14001-Implementation-Guide.pdf.

Oxbridge. (n.d.). *Oxbridge totally free ISO 9001:2015 QMS documentation template.* Retrieved June 20, 2019 from https://www.oxebridge.com/emma/template-kit-individual-file-downloads/?drawer=procedures.

Safer Pack Limited. (2011). *Management of cleaning validation.* OPRP 4. Retrieved June 20, 2019 from https://www.ifsqn.com/pdf/OPRP%204%20Management%20of%20Cleaning%20Validation.pdf.

Safer Pack Limited. (2011). *Maintenance verification record.* OPRP 6. Retrieved June 20, 2019 from https://www.ifsqn.com/pdf/OPRP%206%20Maintenance%20Verification%20Record.pdf.

Shah Promoters and Developers. (2016). *Quality Management System for ISO 9001:2015, Issue No. 2.* Pune: Shah Promoters and Developers.

Sunnyridge. (2014). *Quality Management System Manual, Version F.* Florida: Dole Berry Company.

The State of Victoria. (2015). *Model financial policies and procedures.* Retrieved June 20, 2019 from https://www2.delwp.vic.gov.au/__data/assets/pdf_file/0026/46727/Model-Financial-Policies-and-Procedures-e-alert-01-attachment.pdf.

Toshiba International Corporation. (2019). *Quality, environment, health and safety manual.* Retrieved June 20, 2019 from https://www.toshiba.com/tic/cms_files/QEHS_Manual.pdf.

Wasim, S. (2018). *Internal audit checklist ISO 9001:2015.* Retrieved June 20, 2019 from https://www.researchgate.net/publication/326175688_Internal_Audit_Checklist_QMS_ISO_90012015.

Widget Works Company Inc. (2018). *Quality system manual.* Retrieved June 20, 2019 from https://www.scribd.com/document/192656885/Sample-Iso-9001-08-Qsm#.

Appendix 4: Forms

Form 001 Factors to Be Considered for Identifying Internal and External Issues

Internal	External
Goals and objectives	Environment
Organisation structure, functions and key processes	Business, social, regulatory, cultural, competitive, financial and political situation, Physical SWOT
Physical and technological infrastructure and maintenance programme	Organisation's SWOT
Business location sites and other operations	Stakeholders
Internal stakeholders	Objective and expectations of individuals, groups and organisations with a significant interest in the business
Organisation's culture and workforce morale	Other issues
Resource capabilities such as people, systems processes and capital	Economic shifts
Regulatory requirements	Our competitors
Relationships with staff, labour unions	Events that may affect the reputation
Products and services	Changes in technology
Standards, guidelines, best practices	Food fraud
	Intentional contamination of food
	Cybersecurity

Form 002 Examples of Internal and External Issues

Internal (I) External (E)	Issue	How It Affects
I	Failure to meet deadlines	Loss of reputation; loss of customers
I	Failure to manage environmental issues	Financial penalties by regulatory authorities Damage image of the company Poor utilisation of resources
I	High inventory levels	Inefficient use of financial resources Obsolescence
I	Low profits	Poor financial performance Viability of the company
E	Competitors have a similar product	Possible loss of sales in this category
E	Single supplier policy	Unavailability of item(s) for production Cannot meet deadlines Production schedule has to be changed Customer dissatisfaction

Form 003 External and Internal Issues Assessment

Internal (I) External (E)	Type	Issue	How It Affects	Bias
I	Learning and growth	Availability of skilled staff	Effective and efficient operations	+
I	Processes	Successful marketing strategies	Increased sales	+
I	Processes	Reputation for innovation	Positive company image	+
I	Customer	Fails to meet deadlines	Loss of sales, lower profit	−
I	Processes	Environmental issues	Possible litigation, poor company image	−
I	Financial	High inventory levels	Utilisation of financial resources	−
I	Financial	Low profits	Financial viability	−
E	Processes	New winemaking technology	Better quality products	+
I	Customer	Use of screw caps for lower category wines	Reduced production costs	+
I	Customer	Inability to meet demand	Loss of sales, customers	−
E	Customer	Competitors have similar products	Loss of sales in these categories	−
E	Customer	New shop in the neighbourhood	Possible loss of customers	−
I	Learning and growth	Encourage professional skills development	Efficient and effective operations	+
E	Financial	Export incentives	Increase sales Enhance company image	+

Form 004 PEST Analysis

Political	Economical
Extension of bars opening hours	Increase in the prices of consumer goods
Wine regulations	Less disposable income
Trade agreements with other countries	Tax on imported wines
More stringent regulations on emissions	Tax incentives for wine exports
Trade unions and lobbying groups	Increase sale of low price wines
Bioterrorism	Overall economic performance of the country
Standards and certification industry sector	More competitive environment
	Trade agreements between countries
	Climate changes affecting production

Social	Technological
Higher perception of quality	Advances in technology
Preference of beer over wine among the young generation	Hand picking versus use of machines for grape picking
Environmental concerns	Advances in packaging technology
Dietary factors that promote obesity	Increasing use of screw caps instead of corks for lower wine categories
Changing patterns of food selection, preparation and consumption	New technologies for identifying food hazards
Customer demographics	
Community concerns over environmental issues	

Form 005 SWOT Analysis

Internal Environment	
Strengths	Weaknesses
Excellent sales staff with strong knowledge of existing products Stability of workforce Low staff turnover Good relationship with customers and the community Good internal communications Professional development activities Successful marketing strategies Reputation for innovation Flexible payment terms for customers	More often fail to meet deadlines too much work? High rental costs Market research data may be out of date and inadequate Low profits High inventory levels Inadequate monitoring of non-renewable resources Inability to meet increase in demand Controlling environmental issues Inflexible organisation structure
External Environment	
Opportunities	Threats
Similar products on the market are not as reliable or are more expensive Loyal customer base Satisfy all market segments New winemaking technology Develop skill base Use of crew caps instead of corks Opening a new supermarket in the neighbourhood	Competitors have a similar product Competitors have launched a new promotion campaign Competitor opening a shop in the neighbourhood Downturn in economy may mean less disposal income Upcoming regulatory changes Environmental regulations Single supplier policy Demand for environmental friendly green products Labour unions Evolution of new pathogens Insolvency of customer

Form 006 External Parties and Their Needs

Interested Party	Reason for the Interest	Management System Processes
Government authorities	Payment of taxes, compliance with laws Compliance with regulatory authorities	Financial processes Human resource processes
Emergency services	Risk management, emergency procedures in place, emergency drills	Risk management process Emergency processes
Shareholders	Good financial return, compliance with laws, regulations and by-laws, ethical behaviour, social responsibility	Financial processes
Local community	Local employment, good reputation, concern for the environment	Communication process
Law enforcement agencies and regulators	Awareness and understanding of laws and regulations applicable to our organisation and our products and services that we offer, compliance with laws and prompt response to investigations and enquiries	Legal and other requirements Human resource processes
Customers/ consumers	Delivery on time, value for money, high quality at lower cost, safe and environmentally friendly products, quick response to service and installation issues at reasonable cost, quick response to complaints	Sales processes Warehousing processes Quality assurance processes
Suppliers	Prompt payment, clear work instructions	Purchasing process Financial processes
Financial institutions	Payment of dues on time, good return on investment and good cash flow	Financial processes
Employee dependants	Maintenance of income, company reputation	Human resource processes
Insurers	Implementation of risk management, regular monitoring of risks, no claims, payments on time	Financial processes
External providers	Clear unambiguous contracts, honouring the contracts, good relationships, payments on time	Approval of supplies Contracts process
Labour unions	Good working relationship with management, compliance with laws, safe working environment for employees, prompt resolution of conflicts	Human resource processes
Contractors	Prompt payment, clear work instructions, good working conditions	Financial processes
Consumer	Safe food for consumption	Hazard analysis process
Environmental pressure groups	Good risk management, efficient use of natural resources, active regeneration projects	Initial environment review process Environmental aspects and impacts process
Utility firms	Prompt payment, efficient use of utilities	Financial processes
Media	Response to requests for information	Customer relations processes

Form 007 Internal Parties and Their Needs

Interested Party	Reason for the Interest	Management System Processes
Working directors	Good risk management, continued growth	Financial processes
Business partners	Good risk management, continued growth, good reputation	Financial processes
Union representatives	Good working conditions, training and development opportunities, maintenance of company reputation, stable employment	Human resource processes
Employees	Good working conditions, training and development opportunities, maintenance of company reputation, stable employment	Human resource processes
Managers	Current information for decision-making	Management review process IQFSE management system performance

Form 008 Impact of Needs

Stakeholders	Need	Finance Gain/Loss	Environment	Legal	Quality/ Safety/Service	Reputation	Business as Usual
Government	Pay tax			✓			
	Comply with regulations			✓			
Authorities	Comply with regulations			✓			
Emergency services	Risk management				✓		
	Procedures in place			✓	✓		
	Emergency drill			✓			
Shareholders	Good financial return	✓					
	Compliance with laws			✓		✓	
	Ethical behaviour					✓	
	Social responsibility					✓	
Local community	Concern for the environment		✓			✓	
Regulators				✓			
Customers consumers					✓		
Suppliers	Prompt payment	✓					
	Clear work instructions						✓
Financial institutions	Payment of dues	✓					
	Good financial return	✓					
Authorities	Comply with regulations			✓			
Employee dependants	Maintenance of income	✓					
	Maintain reputation					✓	
Insurers	Prompt payment	✓					
	Risk management		✓				
	No claims	✓					
External providers	Clear contract			✓			
	Payment on time	✓					

(*Continued*)

Stakeholders	Need	Finance Gain/Loss	Environment	Legal	Quality/ Safety/Service	Reputation	Business as Usual
Environment pressure groups	Risk management					✓	
	Protecting natural resources						✓
	Regeneration projects				✓		
Utility usage	Prompt payment	✓					
	Efficient use of utilities						✓

Form 009 Items Required for Identifying Legal Requirements

Category	Item
Documents	Existing legislation applicable to the operation of the organisation
	Permits and licences issued by regulatory and compliance authorities
	Solid and liquid waste treatment procedure
	Complaints from the community
	Labelling schemes and containment procedures for control of specific substances such as hazardous materials
	Criteria for keeping food safe
	Needs of interested parties
	Organisational context.
Records	Penalties imposed
	Data and records relating to the use of specific substances, emissions and discharges
	Records of communication with regulatory and compliance authorities
	Pest entry records
	Records of fire drill
	Employees' health monitoring records
	Workplace accidents and incidents
	Food recall notices
	Environmental aspects and impacts
	Risk analysis.
Equipment and devices	Emissions and discharge monitoring devices
	Waste treatment equipment
	Sensor alarms and other warning devices
	Equipment and devices used to control, prevent or limit the impact of releases, spills, etc.
	Special containers and storage of hazardous substances
	Devices used to control emission
	Devices used to prevent food spoilage
	Fire extinguishers.

Form 010 Determining the Relevance of Legislations

Product/Process/Substance/Service	Legislation	How It Applies

Form 011 Plan for Identifying Legal Requirements

1. Current process for identifying legal requirements	Prepare a list
2. Person(s) or team responsible for identifying legal requirements	Plant Manager, QA Manager, Environment Manager and Food Safety Manager
3. Sources of information currently available	Prepare a list of currently held documents
4. Sources of information required	Commercial databases Trade associations Industry sector Communication with federal, regional, state and local environmental regulatory authorities Conferences and workshops Certifying bodies
5. Methods and tools used to access relevant information	List methods used such as World Wide Web, commercial services and consultants
6. List of persons who need the information and the method of communication	Prepare a distribution list
7. Person(s) responsible for analysing and acquiring new information	QA Manager in consultation with the Environment Manager and Food Safety Manager
8. Method of documentation	Database
9. Payment of subscriptions, obtaining required licences and permits	Plant Manager

Form 012 Evaluation of Compliance

Item	Legal Requirement	Evaluation Frequency	Evaluation Method	Responsibility	Compliance Yes/No

Form 013 Register of Legal Requirements Applicable to the IQFSE Management System

Reference	Title	Effective Date	Expiry Date	Impacts on	Supersedes	Distribution	Comments

Form 014 Identification of Core Processes

Customer's Needs	Preceding Activity	Core Processes
Goods	Customer receives goods	Storage and distribution (integrity)
	Deliver goods to the customer	Selling (reliability)
	Receive order	Orders fulfilment (reliability)
	Process order	Warehousing (reliability)
	Pick order	Warehousing (reliability)
	Store goods	Production, design (transformation)
	Produce goods	Purchasing (assembly)
	Purchase components	
Statutory bodies: Compliance	Identify legislative requirements	Legal and other requirements
Safe food	Maintain hygiene and Critical Control Point (CCP) control schedule	HACCP plan

Form 015 Identification of Support Processes

Core Process	Activities that Support the Core Process	Support Processes
Storage and distribution	Human resources (HR), information technology, management systems	HR Information technology Management of Quality, Environment and Food Safety Systems
Sales	Marketing, accounting, HR, customer services, management systems	Marketing Financial management HR Customer relations Management of Quality, Environment and Food Safety Systems
Order fulfilment	Accounting (financial management), HR, information technology, customer services, management systems	Financial management HR Information technology Customer relations Management of Quality, Environment and Food Safety Systems
Production, design	HR, information technology, marketing, accounting, management systems	HR Information technology Marketing Financial management Management of Quality, Environment and Food Safety Systems
Purchasing	HR, information technology, marketing, accounting, management systems	HR Information technology Marketing Financial management Management of Quality, Environment and Food Safety Systems

Form 016 Assurance Processes

Control Measures	Verification Activities
In-process controls	Audits, non-conformance work reviews' corrective and preventive action,
Efficiency reports	equipment calibration, monitoring and data analysis management reviews
Production figures	Sales performance, audits
Sales	Audits
Price	Audits, supplier performance
Timeliness of delivery	Customer services
Feedback	Financial audits
Accuracy of payment	Performance reviews
Evaluation of training	

Form 017 Identification of Sub-processes

Process	Entry Criteria	Exit Criteria	Activities
Purchasing	Select suppliers	Receive goods	Evaluate suppliers Generate specifications Purchasing data process Verification of purchased product
Production	Plan production	Send finished goods to the warehouse	Production planning Process control Manage resources Validate processes Controls, specifications Control identification and traceability of products, review non-conforming products
Design	Design Requirements	Design Output	All Design Activities
Storage and distribution	Receive finished goods	Deliver goods to customer	Store goods Assemble orders Package, deliver Stock management Manage non-conforming goods
Order fulfilment	Take order	Generate pick list	Determine customer requirements Customer communication, order process
Information technology	Request for information services support	Completeness of service	Control of documents, back-up Knowledge management Help desk Software and hardware management
Sales and marketing	Request for sales marketing information and support	Provision of information and support to customers	Product development, promotions Sales visits Customer communication
HR	Request for HR support	Provision of HR services	Training Recruitment Induction Dismissal Promotion Performance review Leave Internal communication
Financial management	Receipt of invoices, orders and request for financial support	Payments and financial reports	Payroll Accounts payable Accounts receivable Taxes GST Budget preparation reports
Management of quality, environment and food safety systems	Goals and objectives	Systems and procedures to meet objectives and goals	Planning and management Provision of resources Continual improvement

Form 018 Quality, Environment and Food Safety Requirements Associated with Some Processes

Process	Quality Requirements	Environment Requirements	Food Safety Requirements
Planning (**P**)	Achieve product quality, customer satisfaction and continuous improvement	Planning to achieve undesirable impact on the environment, customer satisfaction and continual improvement	Planning to control food safety hazards, customer satisfaction and continual improvement
Approval of suppliers (**D**)	Ability to meet quality, cost and delivery requirements	Ability to meet environmental requirements, possess necessary environmental permits, cost and delivery requirements	Ability to meet food safety requirements, cost and delivery requirements
Customer satisfaction (**C**)	Customer views and perception of the organisation, its processes and its goods and services	Customer views and perception of the organisation on environmental issues, evaluate compliance with legal requirements and voluntary obligations	Customer views and perception of the organisation, its processes and its goods and services, particularly with regard to food safety
Managing non-conformances (**A**)	Detail structure of how to deal with non-conformity	Detail structure of how to deal with non-conformity	Detail structure of how to deal with non-conformity and disposal of unsafe product

Form 019 Procedure Template

ABC Company Limited	Procedures Manual	Reference QP Page 1 of	
	[Insert Title]	Date Released dd/mm/yyyy	Date Reviewed dd/mm/yyyy
Process	Approved:	Issue No: 01 Prepared by:	Revision 00

1.0 Purpose
2.0 Scope
3.0 Process owner
4.0 Input
5.0 Output
6.0 Competency requirements
7.0 Responsibility
8.0 Associated documents
9.0 Resources
10.0 Measures/controls
11.0 Definitions
12.0 System description
13.0 records
14.0 Changes made

Form 020 Risk Identification Form Example

Process	Item	Risk	Consequences	Identified by	Date
Purchasing	Specification	Wrong specification	Affects production schedule Production delay	Purchasing Manager	dd/mm/yyyy
	Ordered item	Delivery of wrong item	Affects production schedule Production delay	Purchasing Manager	dd/mm/yyyy
	Delivery	Late delivery	Affects production schedule Production delay	Purchasing Manager	dd/mm/yyyy
	Cost	Cost increase	Production cost increase Production delay	Purchasing Manager	dd/mm/yyyy
Filling	Glass bottles	Blowing up in filler	Injury to operator	Production Manager	dd/mm/yyyy
	Supplier capability	Inability to deliver	Production delay Need to seek alternate sources	Purchasing Manager	dd/mm/yyyy
Marketing	Export	Opportunity to increase export	Increased sales Enhance profit	Marketing Manager	dd/mm/yyyy
Document control	Obsolete forms	Obsolete forms in use	Production mistakes Process control failures	QA Manager	dd/mm/yyyy
Hazard Analysis and Critical Control Point (HACCP) plan	Critical Control Points (CCPs)	Not correctly identified	Affects food safety	Food Safety Manager	dd/mm/yyyy
Sales	Sales outlets	New supermarket	Opportunity to increase sales	Sales Manager	dd/mm/yyyy
Utilities usage	Water and energy use	Increase use	Affects profit	Environment Manager	dd/mm/yyyy
Waste management	Disposal	Ineffective	Opportunity to better disposal	Environment Manager	dd/mm/yyyy
Design and Development	Plant extension	Operating with-out a permit	Legal action	Plant Manager	dd/mm/yyyy
Customer satisfaction	Product	Obsolescence	Loss of market	Sales Team	dd/mm/yyyy

Form 021 Risk Register [Examples]

1. Identify Risk	2. Prioritise Risk				3. Manage Risk/Opportunity			4. Report
Risk/ Opportunity Description	Probability	Impact	Risk Level	Treatment	Current Controls	Further Controls	Responsibility Timeframe	Status
Quality Management System								
1 Purchasing wrong specification	Low	High	Medium	Mitigate	Purchase order merely specifies specifications	Check accuracy of specifica- tions	Originator Immediate	Closed
2 Late delivery	Medium	Medium	Medium	Mitigate	Delivery date speci- fied in the purchase order	Obtain confirma- tion of delivery date	Purchasing Manager Next order	Closed
4 Export incentives				Opportunity		Explore new overseas markets Increase export quantities	Marketing Manager by dd/mm/yy	Open
Food Safety Management System								
1 CCPs not defined correctly	Low	High	Medium	Mitigate	CCPs devel- oped by the Food Safety Manager	Food Safety Team to review all CCPs	Food Safety Team Immediate	Open
Environmental Management System								
1 Consumption of water, power	High	High	Extreme	Eliminate	Monitor	Monitor and review usage	Plant Manager by dd/ mm/yy	Open
2 Waste removal					Opportunity	Negotiate with con- tractor to remove	Plant Manager by dd/mm/yy	Open
Legal Non-compliance								
1 Plant extension Operating with- out a permit Violating xxxxx statute	Medium	Medium	Medium	Eliminate	None	Obtain permit	Plant Manager by dd/mm/yy	Open

Form 022 Organisational Risk Matrix

IMPACT			
Extremely High	Tsunami Catastrophic		
High	Medium	High	Power failure Extreme
Medium	Theft Low	Information Technology risk Medium	High
Low	Telephone disruption Insignificant	Low	Technical solution failure Medium
LIKELIHOOD ⇨	Low	Medium	High

	Business Continuity Plan "Black Swan Event"
	Eliminate
	Mitigate
	Transfer
	No action

Form 022-1 Legal Non-compliance Risk Matrix

IMPACT			
Extremely High	Catastrophic		
High	High	High	Extreme
Medium	Low	Medium	High
Low	Insignificant	Low	Medium
LIKELIHOOD ⟹	Low	Medium	High

	Business Continuity Plan "Black Swan Event"
	Immediate action is required to address this risk in addition to inclusion in training and education and outside monitoring plans. Senior management review and approval
	Address this risk. Proactively monitor in addition to inclusion in training and education. Middle management review and approval
	Periodic evaluation Team Leader/ team management review and approval
	No action required

Form 023 Risk Descriptors

	Quality	Environment	Food Safety
Catastrophic	Complete production shutdown due to regulatory non-compliance, major product or service failure or other causes.	Major disaster – tsunami, earthquake, major flood, huge fire, nuclear accident, explosion	Fatality, bad reputation reported in social media
High	Immediate and significant risk to product quality, user safety, data integrity or a combination/repetition of major deficiencies, customers dissatisfied with product quality and service, encourage others to keep away. Production delay more than 30 minutes.	Major financial loss, fatalities or permanent illnesses, significant risk to an ecosystem, major reputational damage, major spillage	Serious illness, bad reputation in the market and/or stakeholders
Medium	Customers dissatisfied with product quality and service and do not want to return. Production delay less than 30 minutes. Unavailability of materials/equipment/employees. Can still operate with other materials/equipment/employees.	Moderate financial loss, single death or multiple injuries, leaking of contaminants from a site, pollution of non-sensitive waters, contamination exceeds generic or site-specific criteria, significant change in the ecosystem, significant damage to buildings making it unsafe to occupy	Product recall, bad reputation in fixed subscribers and suppliers
Low	Customers dissatisfied with product quality and service. Unavailability of materials/equipment/employees. Can still operate with current inventory.	Minor or no personal injury, loss of plants in a land site, temporary adverse health effects, easily repairable damage to buildings	Customer complaint, bad publicity within the company

Form 024 Legal Risk Impact and Likelihood Descriptors

Severity	Event	Impact
Extremely high	Serious legal non-compliance e.g. fraud, destroying financial documents	Prosecution Operations shutdown
High	Major legal non-compliance	Major reputational damage High impact on business strategy Temporary suspension of operations
Medium	Moderate financial loss due to legal non-compliance Operating without a permit	Moderate reputational damage Outside monitoring or enforcement
Low	Minimum financial loss Minor legal non-compliance Failure to inform legal authorities	Insignificant reputational damage Failure to achieve objectives

Likelihood		
Estimation	Description	Indicators
High (Probable)	Likely to occur each year or more than 25% chance of occurrence	Strong possibility that it will occur Has occurred in the past
Medium (Possible)	Likely to occur or less than 25% chance of occurrence within the next 12 months	May occur at some point No previous history of occurrence
Low (Remote)	Not likely to occur or less than 2% chance of occurrence	Has not occurred Not likely to occur

Form 025 Process Risk Evaluation [Example]

Process	What Can Go Wrong? or Opportunity	Risk Evaluation			Current Controls	Risk Evaluation			Reason
		Probability (P)	Impact (I)	Risk Category		Probability (P)	Impact (I)	Risk Category	
Quality Management System									
Purchasing	Wrong specification Wrong item delivered Delivered late Cost increases Supplier incapability	Low Low Medium Low Low Low	High Medium Medium Medium High High	Medium Low Medium Low Medium Medium					Mitigate No action Mitigate No action Mitigate Mitigate
Marketing	Increase exports				Opportunity				
Document control	Continue to use obsolete process, document or record Obsolete items not retrieved IT problem	Low Low Low	High Medium Low	Medium Low Low					Mitigate No action No action
Food Safety Management System									
HACCP	CCPs not defined correctly	Low	High	Medium					Mitigate
Environmental Management System									
Non-renewable resources	High water and power consumption	High	High	Extreme	Eliminate				
Product Risk									
Filling glass bottles	Blowing up in filler	Medium	High	High	Eliminate				
Legal Non-compliance									
Operation	Operating without a license	Medium	High	High	Eliminate				

Form 026 Opportunity Register

Process	Opportunity	Probability			Benefit Potential (1–5)							
		Likelihood	Previous Occurrence	Probability Score (P) 1–5	New Business	Business Expansion	Improving Regulatory Compliance	Improving Management Systems	Improving Image Reputation	Cost of Implementing	Benefit Score (B)	Opportunity Factor Decision P × B
Sales	New supermarket	High	-	5	5	5			5	Nil	5	25
Waste management	Better disposal	High	-	5	-	-	5	4	5	Low	5	25

Form 027 Action Plan [Examples]

Category	Item	Performance Indicator Target	Action Plan Method of Control[a]	By Whom	Checking Dates dd/mm/yyyy
Organisational risk	Purchasing process 1.Check accuracy of specifications 2. Late delivery	Order mistakes No errors Deliveries on time All	Check the accuracy of specifications before the order is placed. Indicate the urgency of delivery when the order is placed. P – CP 003 Purchasing information	Purchasing Manager	dd/mm/yy
	Market research Opportunity to increase exports	Number of export orders Five	Evaluate possible export markets P – SP 035 Market research	Marketing Manager	dd/mm/yy
	Document control Obsolete documents in use	Number of obsolete documents in use None	Shall retrieve obsolete documents when replaced with new documents or when the document is not required P – SP 001 Document control P – SP 002 Record control	QA Manager	dd/mm/yy
	HACCP Plan CCPs not correctly defined	Review CCPs Correct and complete CCPs	Establish CCPs according to P – CP 026 CCPs and control schedule	Food Safety. Manager	dd/mm/yy
	Market research New supermarket in the vicinity	X orders from the supermarket per month	Meet management team of the new supermarket and promote our products and services P – CP 036 Sales process	Sales Manager	dd/mm/yy
Environmental risk	Waste disposal in effective	Amount of waste disposed	Negotiate a contract S – Form 130 Waste and recycling data	Plant Manager	dd/mm/yy
Legal Risk	Permit to operate plant extension	Necessary permit	Obtain the necessary permit to extend the operation P – CP 013 Design and development	Engineering Manager	dd/mm/yy

[a]P –Procedurally controlled through procedures and operating instructions
O- Organisationally controlled through training, consultation and skill enhancement
S – Supervision through inspections, checks, measuring, etc.
T –Technically controlled through the provision of technical and technological material and measurement devices.

Form 028 Management Plan to Achieve Objectives

Objective #   Objective: Responsible:
Current performance: Key performance indicator:

Target	Key Tasks	Responsibility	Resources	Start Date	Target Date for Completion	Actual Completion Date	Monitoring Frequency	Signature	Comments

Form 029 Examples of Identified Objectives

Reduce new glass bottle use by 10%
Action: Use recycled glass bottles for non-premium products
Resources: Recycled glass
Responsibility: Purchasing Manager
Timeframe: Achieve 10% reduction in 6 months
Measures/controls: Quantity of used recycled glass replacing new glass bottles.

Increase the sale of sparkling wines by 5% during the next 6 months
Action: Promotion campaign, new sales leads
Resources: Cost of promotions and advertisements
Responsibility: Sales Manager
Timeframe: 6 months
Measures/controls: Sales volume

Form 030 High-Level Responsibilities and Authorities of Top Management

Position	Responsibility	Authority
CEO	Profitability Ethical business practices	Approves resources for developing the company
Financial Manager	Effective financial operations	Allocates finance for operations
Managing Director	Efficient and effective operation of the organisation	Approves resources for operations
HR Manager	Management of HRs	Approves HR requirements
Marketing Manager	Promote the organisation and its products and services	Provides resources for marketing activities
Sales Manager	Increase sales	Provides resources for sales activities
Plant Manager	Efficient and effective running of the plant	Provides resources for plant operations
Chief Risk Officer	Analyse and treat risks	Provides expertise and resources for managing risks
Health and Safety Officer	Health, safety and wellbeing of employees	Provides safety equipment, organise training, make improvement to health and safety of employees
QA Manager	Overall responsibility for the quality and coordinates food safety and environmental aspects and reports on the effectiveness of the IQFSE management	Takes appropriate steps to prevent the production of sub-standard goods and delivery of poor service
Food Safety Manager	Overall responsibility for food safety training and producing safe food	Select training methods, organise training and take appropriate action to ensure food safety
Environment Manager	Overall responsibility for environmental training and ensure environment-friendly operations	Select training methods, organise training and take appropriate action to ensure the effectiveness of the environmental programme
Customer Relations Manager	Overall responsibility for customer related activities	Communicates with customers Initiate action to resolve customer dissatisfaction

Form 031 Specific Responsibilities and Authorities

Specific Responsibilities and Authorities	Assigned Person	How It Is Done
Ensure IQFSE management system conforms to relevant ISO standards	QA Manager	Establish procedures needed to meet all requirements Conduct internal audits and management reviews Receive training on practical application of relevant ISO standards Train others who are expected to perform activities Keep staff informed on the IQFSE management system and how it is related to ISO standards Gain certification to ISO 9001: 2015, ISO 14001:2015 and ISO 22000:2017 standards
Ensure processes deliver expected outcomes	QA Manager, Food Safety Manager and Environment Manager	Define processes, measures and controls to meet objectives Measure and report on process controls
Report on the IQFSE management system and improvement opportunities to top management	QA Manager	Analyse the results of measurements and controls Identify improvement opportunities Drive specific projects Conduct management reviews
Promote of customer focus	QA Manager Customer Relations Manager	Collect and analyse customer feedback Communicate results Improve customer-related processes Create an awareness of satisfying internal customers Promote product and service innovation
Maintain the effectiveness of the IQFSE management system when changes occur	QA Manager	Design new processes or revising existing ones Provide the necessary training Plan for changes Communicate changes Monitor the impact of changes

Form 032 Strategic Plan Template

Section 1: Executive Summary This section is completed last, and it summarises the other sections of the plan. It helps other stakeholders such as employees, advisors, investors and clients quickly understand and support the plan.
Section 2: Business Description This is also known as elevator pitch, and it enables employees to understand the business so that it could be articulated to others.
Section 3: Company Mission Statement The mission statement guides employees to make right decisions to achieve their goals. It inspires external parties such as investors, partners and customers to action expected by the organisation.
Section 4: SWOT Analysis SWOT analysis helps organisation determine the best opportunities for growth, strengths to be developed in the near future, weaknesses to be addressed and take counter measures to overcome the threats.
Section 5: Goals Identify the goals for the next 3–5 years, followed by goals for the next year. Quarterly and monthly goals should also be established. It is necessary to review quarterly and monthly goals regularly.
Section 6: Key Performance Indicators (KPIs) KPIs are essential for measuring the performance of the organisation.
Section 7: Target Customers Wants and needs of each customer group are essential for the marketing campaign to get higher returns on advertising expenditure.
Section 8: Industry Analysis Industry analysis is conducted to ensure that the market size is expanding and to identify opportunities for growth.
Section 9: Competitive Analysis and Advantage Identify who the competitors are and their strengths and weaknesses. Determine the competitive advantage and how it can be developed further.
Section 10: Marketing Plan A comprehensive marketing plan describes ways to attract potential customers, transform them to paying customers and maximise lifetime customer value.
Section 11: Human Resources Include the current team members and determine extra human resources needed to achieve the goals.
Section 12: Operation Plan The operation plan helps organisation transform goals to an action plan. The roles and responsibilities for achieving the goals are defined.
Section13: Financial Projections Financial projections not only measure the financial outputs of the goals but also enable the organisation to map out or change the goals for the next quarter or next month.

Reference

Lavinsky, D. (2013). Strategic Plan Template: What to include in yours. *Forbes*. Retrieved July 8, 2015 from http://www.forbes.com/sites/davelavinsky/2013/10/18/strategic-plan-template-what-to-include/#d7cfa667e2f4

Form 033 Some Potential Emergencies

Location	Potential Emergency	Impact	Prevention
Warehouse (raw materials, finished goods, packaging)	Electrical fire Cigarette fire	Adverse health effects Air pollution Land pollution	Preventive maintenance "No Smoking" signs Fire extinguishers
Electrical panel	Electrical fire Short-circuiting Overloading Water spillage	Adverse health effects Air pollution	Secure electrical connections Load distribution "No Smoking" signs Dry areas
Manufacturing area	Fire Chemical spillage Hot spray of cleaning in place (CIP) solution Steam escape	Water pollution Air pollution Adverse health effects Product damage	Safety gear Maintenance of pipes and fittings "No Smoking" signs
Food preparation area	Fire Gas leak Electrical fire Cigarette fire	Fire and explosion Air pollution Product damage Facility damage Adverse health effects	Preventive maintenance of gas pipe fittings "No Smoking" signs Fire extinguishers Safety gear Monitoring LPG
Building and construction work	Slip or fall	Adverse health effects	Safety gear Proper ladder Proper scaffoldings
Cleaning glass windows	Glass breakage Slip or fall	Adverse health effects	Safety gear Proper ladder Proper scaffoldings
Production/food preparation area	Bioterrorism Sabotage Infections	Adverse health effects	Restriction of entry Security arrangements Raw materials checked on arrival Finished goods released prior to storing and dispatch Disposal of culture media after autoclaving
Administration	Power failure	Product and document losses Deliveries not on time	Emergency power source Back-up

Form 034 Emergency Response Plan Template

Part one
1. Contact details (External and Internal)
2. Description and location of warning devices
3. Evacuation plans, assembly points and persons assigned to assembly points
4. Responsibility to evacuate all personnel in the site
5. Location of fire extinguishers, emergency exits, gas and water shut-off valves, power shut-down devices, first aid kits, first aiders and instruction for operation of devices
6. Location of containment facilities and method of identifying contaminated product
7. Emergency protocols and procedures
9. List of critical data and records
10. List of internal and external contacts
11. Records of emergency drills
12. Records of emergency procedures training
13. Other issues

Part two: Action plans
1. Notification
2. Levels of threat
3. Responding to emergency situations

Part three: Review

Approved: Plant Manager   **Date:**

Form 035 Emergency Response Internal Contacts

Contact Details

---

1. Emergency Response Team
Emergency Coordinator:
Phone Numbers (mobile, land, home):
Office Location:
Back-up:
Phone Numbers (mobile, land, home):
Office Location:
Responsibilities: Implement emergency response plan

2. Chemical Response Team:
Phone Numbers (mobile, land, home):
Office Location:
Back-up:
Phone Numbers (mobile, land, home):
Office Location:
Responsibilities: Implement chemical response plan

3. Administrative Head:
Phone Numbers (mobile, land, home):
Office Location:
Back-up:
Phone Numbers (mobile, land, home):
Office Location:
Responsibilities: Media relations, stakeholder relations, personnel, financial, data protection and other administrative functions

4. Emergency Coordinator:
Phone Numbers (mobile, land, home):
Office Location:
Back-up:
Phone Numbers (mobile, land, home):
Office Location:
Responsibilities: Coordinate operation, security, telecommunication, business continuity

5. Environment Manager:
Phone Numbers (mobile, land, home):
Office Location:
Back-up:
Phone Numbers (mobile, land, home):
Office Location:
Responsibilities: Environmental impact assessment, spill management and clean-up, regulatory affairs compliance issues

6. Food Safety Manager:
Phone Numbers (mobile, land, home):
Office Location:
Back-up:
Phone Numbers (mobile, land, home):
Office Location:
Responsibilities: Product safety, managing unsafe damaged product

6. **Plant Engineer:**
Phone Numbers (mobile, land, home):
Office Location:
Back-up:
Phone Numbers (mobile, land, home):
Office Location:
Responsibilities: Equipment, facilities

Form 036 Emergency Response External Contacts

Contact Details

External Agency	Contact Details
Local fire department Environmental authority Food safety authority Local police Plant healthcare worker Hospital Medical practitioner Others	

Form 037 Emergency Response Activity Record

Date: Commenced: End:

Location: ....

Description of the emergency:..

....

....

Team Leader:...

Response to the emergency:..

Estimated losses:

Injuries:

Effectiveness of the response:

Recommendations:

Team Leader

Emergency Response Team   Date:

Form 038 Supplier Evaluation Form

SUPPLIER DETAILS \

Name of supplier	
Address	
Contact	
Phone	
Fax	
Email	
Web address	
Year of establishment	
Facility size	
Category	

1. Financial stability	Score (1–5)
Financial performance	
Accounting procedures	
Financial sustainability	
2. Manufacturing	
Availability of machinery & equipment to supply ABCCL needs	
Preventive maintenance	
Knowledge of manufacturing processes	
Tools, jigs, dies reconfirmed for compliance with manufacturing specifications after the prescribed period	
3. Raw materials	
Testing/inspection of raw material and ingredients	
Records of raw materials and inspection reports	
4. Production area	
Process flow in working area and work stations	
Adequacy of space at work stations, lighting, ventilation, cleanliness, arrangement of tools	
Pest control programme	
Cross contamination possibility	

Availability of relevant documents and records at work stations	
Aseptic control (if applicable)	
Adequacy of temperature control, chemical hazard control, electricity hazard control	
Protective equipment use, if appropriate	
Provision of safeguards for machinery and workers	
Written procedures for disposal of chemicals	
5. Quality and food safety	
Availability and accessibility of the supplier to resolve quality and food safety issues	
Hazard analysis programme and pre-requisite programmes (for food manufacturers)	
In-process controls and inspections	
Laboratory facilities, test methods, calibrations	
Traceability of products	
Complaints management system	
Rejects/recalls	
Certification status of the quality and food safety management system	
6. Logistics	
Availability and accessibility of the supplier to resolve logistics issues	
Accuracy of logistics data	
Hitrate[a] quantity	
Hitrate time	
Efforts to reduce lead time	
Short-term flexibility to order volume	
Information technology maturity	
7. Product development	
Product development process	
R&D support	
Availability and accessibility of the supplier to resolve quality and food safety issues	
Technical support	
Innovation capability	
Level of details of drawings and specifications and availability of MSD sheets at locations	
8. Purchasing	
Availability and accessibility of the supplier to resolve purchasing issues	
Cost reduction efforts	

Supply chain risk assessment	
Capacity for increased demand	
Knowledge about second tier supplier	
Transparency in supplier's cost drivers	
9. Environment	
Evaluation of environmental management system of supplier's second tier supplier	
Location–distance	
Certification status of the environmental management system	
Compliance to regulatory requirements	
Penalties for violating environmental regulations	
Energy and water usage	
Waste disposal	
Public disclosure of environmental record	
Social responsibility	
Efforts to reduce non-recyclable packaging	
Use of environmental-friendly packaging	
10. Training	
Availability of job descriptions	
Clearly defined roles and responsibilities	
Training programmes	
Knowledge of operating procedures by operating staff	
11. Financial strength	
Financial strength of supplier to manage and secure supply chain	
Credit facilities	
Investment plans	
12. Employment	
Recruitment procedure	
Relationship with trade unions	
Employee turnover rate	
Child labour	
Employee hygiene	
Employee training in quality, food safety and environmental management	

13. Food safety risk	
Food safety policy	
Food safety risk assessment	
Sanitation programme	
Pest control programme	
Cross contamination control	
Allergen control programme	
Liability plan	
Other food control plans	
Incidents of recalls	
TOTAL SCORE	

Very good = 5
Good = 4
Average = 3
Poor = 2
Very poor = 1
Negative = 0

1. Score individual blocks

2. Total rating = Total score ÷ number of scored blocks

^aHitrate is an affiliated programme where strategic suppliers' delivery accuracy and delivery security are stored and evaluated monthly.

Form 039 Approved Suppliers' List

Supplier	Contact Details	Products/Services	Approval Date	Performance Rating	Insurance Yes/No

Form 040 Supplier Performance

	Quality/Food Safety/ Environment Concern	Delivery	Price	Service	Cooperation	Total Score
Weightage[a]	30	20	20	10	10	
Measurement[a]	1 = worst 5 = best	1 = worst 5 = best	1 = worst 5 = best	100% = good 70% = fair 40% = poor	100% = good 70% = fair 40% = poor	
Supplier A score	2	4	3	70%	50%	
Supplier A rating	$(2/5) \times 30$	$(4/5) \times (20)$	$(3/5) \times (20)$	$(70/100) \times (10)$	$(50/100) \times (10)$	
Supplier A Weighted score	12	16	12	7	5	**52**
Supplier B score	3	4	4	70%	40%	
Supplier B rating	$(3/5) \times (30)$	$(4/5) \times 20$	$(4/5) \times 20$	$(70/100) \times (10)$	$(40/100) \times (10)$	
Supplier B Weighted score	18	16	16	7	4	**61**

[a]Change as necessary

Form 041 Supplier Risk Analysis

Impact (I)	**Low O & high I** Implement joint procedures with suppliers for improvements Establish emergency plans Subscribe to contingency insurance	**High O & high I** Find new suppliers Commence resourcing efforts on stock control units Redesign production
	Low O & low I Review and improve quality assurance and food safety procedures	**High O & low I** Monitor performance of suppliers
	Frequency of occurrence (O)	

Form 042 Purchase Requisition

ABC Company Limited				PR No. _____	
PURCHASE REQUISITION				Date: _____	
Requesting Department: _____					
Item #	Qty	Ref #	Description	Purpose	Price / Unit
Deliver to: _____				**Required date of delivery** _____	
Additional information, if required					
Preferred Supplier(s): _____ _____ _____				Signature of authorized person Title	
Justification if there is no budget provision					

Form 043 Purchase Order

Billing address   Date: _____

....

....

....

....

....

The following number must appear in all correspondence, delivery documents and invoices

PO No:

Accounts payable contact
Phone
Email

Delivery address

....

....

....

Vendor contact
Phone
Email

Vendor

....

....

....

PO Date	Requested by	Contact Details	Terms

Quantity	Catalogue No: or Supplier's item No:	Description	Unit Price	Total
			Subtotal	
			Tax	
			Other	
TAX ID if not on file			Total	

Approval: Purchasing Manager: Plant Manager:
Date:
Additional requirements:

Form 044 Packing Slip

Customer ID

Date:

....................Company

Address..........................

....

....

....

Billing Address

....

....

....

....

Delivery Address

....

....

....

....

Date Shipped	Purchase Order (PO) #	PO Date	Customer contact

Item #	Description	Pack Size	Quantity Ordered	Quantity Delivered	Number of Cartons
P123	Product 1	750 G	48 x 750 G	36 x 750 G	3

Back orders: Back orders will be delivered by...[insert date]...12 x 750G...............

If you have any queries regarding this packing slip or quantity please contact...

Form 045 Inward Goods Log Book

Received Date	PO #	Material Code	Description	Weight (kg) If Applicable	Lot #	Quantity Received	Suppler	Carrier	Vehicle Inspection[a]

[a]

- Visual   ☐
- Odour   ☐
- Pest/Rodent activity   ☐
- Truck/Trailer No:

Form 046 Generic Inward Goods Inspection Report

QC No: **Date of inspection:**   **Inventory Control No:**

Purchase Order No: **Supplier**   **Condition of goods:**   **Condition of packaging:**

Received Date	Item	Material Code	Description	Visual Inspection	No. of Samples Tested	Test Method	Dimensions	Chemical Tests

- Accepted   ☐
- Rejected   ☐
- Waiver   ☐
- Comments

QC Officer:.................................... **Date:**..................................

Form 047 Material ID Label

Material Identification Label

Date Received:.............................

From:...

Material Code:............................

PO Number:.................................

Location:...................................
Inventory Control No:...................

Comments:.................................
....
....

Received by:...................

Form 048 Invoice

From

....

....

....

....

To

....

....

....

....

Invoice #

Invoice date

Due date

Item #	Description	Unit price	Quantity	Amount

Sub total	
Total	
Amount paid	
Amount due	

For any queries regarding this invoice please contact...

Form 049 Food Items Inspection Report

QC No: **Date of inspection:**   **Inventory Control No:**

Purchase Order No: Supplier: Condition of goods: Condition of packaging:

Date Received	Inspection Date & Time	Transporter	Food Type	Food Temperature °C High Risk Items	Date Code Use by (U) Best before (BB) Expiry (E) Batch No: (B)	Test Method Reference	Accept (A) Reject (R)	QC Person	Remarks

Comments
- Test method describes the sampling plan and the details of test procedure.

Form 050 Packaging Specification for Sparkling Wine

ABC COMPANY LIMITED

Specification no:………………..   Date of Issue:
Product: Sparkling Wine   Pack size: 750 ml
Production volume: 9000 litres   Tank:
Wine release no:
Production location:…………………………………………………Work order No:
………………………………………………………………………………

Product Code	Unit	Description	Inventory Control Number	Batch No.	Quantity Issued	Quantity Used	Cost
SW 001		Sparkling wine			9000 litres		
B 001	1	750 ml sparkling wine glass bottles			12,000		
C 001	1	Plastic corks			12,000		
M 001	1	2-post muselets			12,000		
S 001	1	Sparkling wine shrouds			12,000		
NL 001	1	Neck label			12,000		
BD 001	1	Body label			12,000		
BK 001	1	Back label			12,000		
SC 001	1/12	Sections			1000		
CS 001	1/12	Cases			1000		

Line Supervisor……….

Instructions:
1. Fill level………….
2. Carbonation:…………..
3. Neck label position:………………
4. Body label position…….
5. Back label position……………
6. See test methods for carbonation, cork depth, muselet application, shroud application and label application.
7. See palletising pattern for palletising
8. Write the pallet number on a case at the bottom layer on all 4 sides.
9. Shrink wrap the pallet
10. Write the pallet number on the warehouse docket.
11. Sampling: remove 2 samples from each line every two hours in each shift
12. See laboratory manual for finished goods inspection
……
……

…………………   ……………………..   ………..
Prepared by   Checked by   Date

Form 051 Example of In-Process Controls for Sparkling Wine Production

Test Method No.	Operation	Test Method	Description	Samples	Limits	Frequency of Checks
1	Wine release for bottling	Organoleptic and chemical tests	Check wine from the filler before filling commences	Sample from the filler	Complies with specifications	Before commencing filling
2	Bottle rinsing	Temperature of bottle rinsing water	Measure the temperature with a calibrated gauge	From the rinser	Complies with specified temperature	At start up
3	Filling	Carbonation volume (Use Zahm carbonation tester)	Measure the carbonation	2 from the filler	… – … gas volumes	hourly
4	Filling	Fill volume	Measure the fill height using the gauge	5	750 – … ml	2-hourly
5	Corking	Cork depth	Measure the cork depth using the ruler	5	… – … mm from the top	2-hourly
6	Muselet application	Muselet application (Visual)	Correct application	5	Tucked under all round	hourly
7	Shroud application	Shroud application (Visual)	Correct application	5	See reference sample	2-hourly
8	Labelling	Glue coverage (Remove label and look for glue coverage)	Measures glue coverage of labels	3	Complete coverage with no bubbles	Hourly
9	Labelling	Label height	Measure the label position and application (Absence of wrinkles or bubbles)	3	See reference sample	Hourly
10	Insertion of section	Label damage (Open two cases and examine all bottles in the case)	Evaluate label damage due to wrong insertion of the section	2	No label damage	Hourly
11	Finished products	Microbiological contamination	Microbiological test procedure	2	No growth	At start up and after every break

Form 052 Control Schedule for Bottling Wine

Processing Step	Item to Be Controlled	Control Limit	Control Methods	Frequency	Corrective Action	Responsibility	Record
Filling CCP	P Bottle breakage at filler; possible glass particles contamination B None C None	No glass particles	Bottle breakage procedure	Whenever a bottle breaks	Put current pallet of filled bottles on HOLD	Line Supervisor	Bottle breakage record
Labelling CCP	P None B None C Labels from previous run not cleared; possibility of allergen declaration mistake	No materials from previous job not allowed in the area	1. Line clearance at start up 2. Inspection of the first labelled bottle 3. Inspection of label bundles before loading onto the magazine	At start up and when loading the magazine	Inspect labelled products on track and put on HOLD for relabelling	Line Supervisor	Downtime record

P: Physical contamination B: Microbiological contamination C: Chemical contamination

Form 053 ABCCL Design and Development Plan

Reference.............   Version..........
Product/Process.............

Brief description of the product/Process

Phase 1 Design concept			
		Responsibility	Date Completed
☐	User needs	Marketing/Sales	
☐	Select design team	Project Manager	
☐	Commercial and technical feasibility	Engineering/Production	
☐	Evaluate risk and establish risk management plan	Quality Assurance Manager	
☐	Evaluate environmental impact and establish mitigation steps	Environment Manager	
☐	Develop Hazard Analysis and Critical Control Point (HACCP) plan	Food Safety Management Systems Manager	
☐	Create design history file	Project Manager	
☐	Health and safety report	Human Resources	
☐	Identify stages which require approval and signatories for approval	Project Manager	
☐	Identify verification and validation steps	Design Team	
☐	Establish methods for verification and validation	Engineering/Production/Quality Assurance	
☐	Identify applicable regulations and check compliance	Quality/Environment/Food Safety Management System Managers	

Phase 1 Outputs
Design input
Design stages
Risk management plan
Environmental impact report
HACCP plan
Verification and validation steps and methods
Marketing plan

Phase 1 review

Phase 2 Design development planning

		Responsibility	Date Completed
☐	Check action items from phase 1 review	Project Manager	
☐	Establish duration of the project	Project Manager	
☐	Establish responsibilities	Project Manager	
☐	Identify resource needs	Design Team	
☐	Establish the need to involve customers and users	Design Team	
☐	Define the level of control	Design Team	
☐	Translate design inputs and design stages into detailed requirement specifications including software requirements (Design outputs)	Design Team	
☐	Establish specifications for components, ingredients, packaging, labeling	Quality Assurance/ Design Team	
☐	Complete test protocols for verification and validation activities	Engineering/Production/ Quality Assurance	
☐	Identify contributors and their interfaces	Design Team	
☐	Documentation requirements to establish compliance	Project Manager	

Phase 2 Outputs
Review of phase 2 activities
Product/Process Master file
Specifications
Test protocols for verification and validation activities
Interfaces
Hazard analysis
Ease of cleaning and disinfection
Biocompatibility

Phase 2 review

Phase 3 Verification and validation

		Responsibility	Date Completed
☐	Check action items from phase 2 review	Project Manager	
☐	Complete verification and validation tests	Design Team/Engineering	
☐	Establish essential requirements checklist	Engineering/Design Team	
☐	Risk management activities	Quality Assurance Manager	

Phase 3 Outputs
Review of phase 2 activities
Verification and validation test reports
Risk management report
Regulatory submission
Essential requirements

Phase 3 review

Phase 4 Design transfer

		Responsibility	Date Completed
☐	Transfer of the product from R&D to production	Project Manager	
☐	Establish facility qualifications		
☐	Develop manufacturing processes	Production/Engineering	
☐	Validate manufacturing processes	Design Team/Engineering	
☐	Validate inspection/test methods	Production/Design Team	
☐	Identify overall residual risk for the product and essential outputs	Quality Assurance Manager	
☐	Serviceability report	Engineering	
☐	Conduct final risk analysis	Quality Assurance Manager	
☐	Approve suppliers for components, ingredients	Purchasing	
☐	Final costing	Accounting	

Phase 4 Outputs
Review of phase 3 activities
Manufacturing procedures and controls including food safety
Risk Management report and risk management file
Process validation report
Device master record
Design history file
Service plan and implementation
Technical details
Approved supplier
Cost structure
Final product release

Form 054 Environmental Review for New Products, Processes or Materials

Product/Process Description

Design Stage	Environmental Concern	Impact	Significance Yes/No	Mitigation

Environmental considerations

Consider the following at each stage of design:
Energy usage
Water usage
Materials
Supplies/consumables
Chemicals

Impact
Evaluate the impact on the basis of potential:
Emissions
Waste water discharge
Storm water discharge
Noise/odour/radiation/aesthetic
Land use
Spillage
Potential community concerns

Significance   Yes   No
Statutory requirements
Community concern
Material reduction potential
Pollution prevention potential
Potential impact on the environment

Evaluation Report

Signed (Environment Systems Manager: .... Date..........

Form 055 Design and Development Risk Evaluation

Risk Element	Assessment				
	Critical	Significant	Important	Minor	Negligible
Protecting patent and/or intellectual property rights					
Ability to meet funding deadlines					
Purchasing special components at affordable prices					
Supplier's financial stability					
Supplier changing specifications or manufacturing method					
Cash flow					
Change in premises					
Location change affecting labour					
Labour disputes					
Special engineering requirements					
High initial investment in relation to low initial sales					
Component loss or damage during design					
Retaining competent skilled staff					
Lack of technological support					

Form 056 Topics to Be Considered at the Review

Topics	Description
1. Resources	Identify necessary resources
	Specifications for raw materials and component parts
	Possibility of using standard parts
	User requirements and technical specifications
2. Product / production related	Comparison with competitor's products and services Comparison of similar designs for understanding previous issues and recurrences
	Applicable tolerances
	Ease of manufacture, assembly, installation and service issues
	Packaging, handling, storage, distribution, shelf life and final disposal
	Appearance and acceptance criteria
	Failure Mode and Effects Analysis (FMEA)
	Any special processes
3. Performance	Ability to withstand inspections and tests
	Performance under expected conditions of use and environment
	Safety and potential liability during unintended use and misuse
	Reliability, serviceability and maintainability
4. Statutory and regulatory requirements	Environmental impact on processes, storage, inspections, testing, delivery and in use.
	Compliance with regulatory requirements
5. Design and design plan	Evaluation of progress on the design Comparison of progress against the design plan
	Reach agreement on actions needed to resolve any issues
	Consider revisions to the plan, if necessary
	Ensure the design team stay focused on inputs
	Confirm the design is ready to move to the next stage
	Project acceptance/rejection criteria
	Motivate the design team
6. Risks and warnings	Identify risk and obstacles encountered and decide on a course of action to manage them
	Ability to diagnose, prevent and correct problems
	Identification, warnings, labelling, traceability and user instructions

Form 057 Design Output Checklist

Project name: Project description:
Project Manager:

Design Output Item	Completion			Comments
	Date	Not Completed	Not Applicable	
Engineering drawings, blue prints, sketches, flowcharts				
Installation instructions				
Specifications for components, labelling and packaging, handling and storage, appearance standards, product specifications				
Bills of material				
Hardware and software design description				
Computer code				
Device master record				
Manufacturing instructions and service instructions				
User manuals, trouble shooting				
Operating criteria				
Risk analysis				
Inspection and acceptance instructions including testing standards				
Hazard analysis				
Ease of cleaning and disinfection				
Biocompatibility				
Interfaces				

Checklist completed by: Date:

Form 058 Product Release Authorisation Form

Product name: Product ID:
Product description:

Production date: Batch number: Expiry date:
Production quantity:

Work order number:

Location:

Test method:

Test method reference:

Result:

All test results relating to the above product meet specified requirements.

Signed: Date:
QA Manager

For food products:

Signed
Food Safety Manager

Distribution: Plant Manager, Production Manager, Warehouse Manager, Sales Manager

Form 059 Pallet Docket

Pallet Docket
Product:

Code:

Pallet No:

Form 059

Form 060 Order Form

XXXX Company
Order Form

Customer Information	XXXX Company Limited Address Contact person: Email: Telephone:		PO No:	
Customer Name				

Billing Address:		Instructions for Delivery	Shipping Address:	
Item No:	Description	Quantity	Unit of Measure	Unit Cost

CP 018 Section 7.0

White Copy: Department
Yellow Copy: Supplier

Form 061 Price List

ABC COMPANY LIMITED
PRICE LIST
Valid until:

Code	Description	Unit	Unit Price	Pack Size

Shipping Charges:

Company Information

Form 062 Pick List

ABC COMPANY LIMITED
Address
Pick List No: **Page:**
                                                                     Date:
                                                                     Ref:

Customer Details

Pick SKU	Pick Item	Pick Quantity	Pick from	Unit Price	Total	Order Details

Form 063 Delivery Note

Company Details   Delivery Note
                                                                       Order Date:
                                                                       Order No:
                                                                       Delivery Note No:
                                                                       Customer ID:
                                                                       Dispatch Date:
                                                                       Delivery Method:

Shipping Address   Invoice Address

Product Code   Description   Ordered Delivered   Balance

Conditions

Contact Details

Form 064 Maintenance Report

Item:

Serial No: Manufacturer: Date of Purchase:

Maintenance/Service Frequency:

Service Details	Parts Used	Service Date	Previous Service	Condition after Service Good Working (GW) Order Not Working (NW)	Additional Comments	Service by:
Customer's Comments: Date:						

Form 065 Work Order for Repair

Part 1

Customer:

Work Required:

Materials Used: [Include items purchased/used, purchased date, invoice number, supplier, unit cost]

Work Performed:

Part II

Date(s):   Hours Worked:

Cost of Materials:

Date of Completion:

Service Engineer:

Customer's Comments and Signature:

Form 066 Key Contact Details

Name	Position/Role/Organisation	Mobile	Landline	Email	Address

Form 067 Business Continuity Plan – Section 1

Essential Activities

Priority 1	Activity needs to be resumed within 0–1 hour of disruption
Priority 2	Activity needs to be resumed within 12 hours of disruption
Priority 3	Activity needs to be resumed within 24 hours of disruption
Priority 4	Activity needs to be resumed within 3 working days of disruption
Priority 5	Activity needs to be resumed within 7 working days of disruption
Priority 6	Activity needs to be resumed after 7 working days of disruption

Priority	Description	Responsibility

Form 068 Business Continuity Plan – Section 2

Key Resources

	Key Resources	Number & Type
1	People	
2	Space and location	
3	Furniture	
4	Food and water	
5	Equipment and vehicles	
6	Information technology	
7	Medical	
8	Communication	
9	Special provisions	
10	Others (state)	

Form 069 Business Continuity Plan – Section 3

Requirements for Business Continuity

Priority	Key Staff Skills, Expertise and Training No. of Staff	Premises Building Facilities Equipment Resources Vehicles Power	Processes Hardware Software Systems Documentation Communication	Suppliers Reciprocal Arrangements Contractors Suppliers ABCCL Services	Profile Reputation Legal Issues Vulnerable Groups

Form 070 Response Log

Ref	Date	Time	Interruption	Details	Action Taken	By	Completed

Form 071 Assessment of Raw Materials and Ingredients

Raw Material/ Ingredient	Microbial Contamination	Microbial Growth	Foreign Matter	Chemical Contamination	Transport	Storage	Level of Risk
Potatoes	+++	+	+++	−	−	−	High
Chicken	+++	+++	−	−	++	++	High

Form 072 Assessment of Processes

Process	Microbial Destruction	Microbial Contamination/ Growth	Foreign Matter Removal/ Destruction	Foreign Matter Introduction	Equipment	Level of Risk	Degree of Control
Potatoes							
Washing	−	+	+++	−	−	Medium	Moderate
Chicken							
Cooking	+++	−	−	−	−	High	High

Form 073 Assessment of the Product

Product	Storage	Delivery	Level of Risk	Degree of Control
Chicken and vegetable salad	+++	+++	High	High

Form 074 Assessment of End Use of the Product

Product	Improper Usage	Consumer Abuse	Level of Risk	Degree of Control
Chicken and vegetable salad	–	++	Low	Low

Form 075 Hazard Assessment: Preventive Measures

Product/Process

Process Step	Description of the Hazard	Preventive Measures

Form 076 Assessment of the Significance of Hazards

Severity

		Low	Medium	High
Likelihood	High			
	Medium			
	Low			

☐ Significance: High
Impact: death or chronic disease if control measures fail

▨ Significance: Medium
Impact: hospitalization, if control measures fail

▦ Significance: Low
Impact: Recoverable illnesses such as diarrhoea, abdominal cramps and

≣ No significance
Impact: No health effects but quality of product may deteriorate

	Likelihood		Severity
Negligible	Unlikely	Negligible	No impact on food safety
Low	Possible	Low	Minor impact on food safety or too low to detect
Medium	Likely	Medium	Marginal- only internal company target levels affected
High	Very likely	High	Critical-public health/product recall; major impact on critical limits

Form 077 Hazard Analysis Form

Processing Step/ Ingredient	Hazard Type	Significance (Y/N)	Hazard Description	Control Measure

Form 078 Identification of Critical Control Points (CCPs) Using Decision Tree

Process Step	Significant Hazard	Q1	Q1a	Q2	Q3	Q4	CCP (Yes/No)

PRP1 Specifications
PRP2 Receiving, storage and transport
PRP3 Personal hygiene

Form 079 The Decision Tree

Question (Q) No:	Question	Response		
		Yes	No	
1	Do control measures exist at this step or subsequent steps for the identified hazard?	Go to Q1a	Are control measures necessary?	
			Yes: Modify step, process or product	**No:** Not a CCP
1a	Are control measures covered by preventive actions?[a]	PRP	Go to Q2	
2	Is this step specifically designed to eliminate or reduce the likely occurrence of the identified hazard to an acceptable level?	oPRP with acceptable criteria or **CCP** with clear measurable limits	Go to Q3	
3	Could contamination with the identified hazard occur in excess of acceptable levels or increase to unacceptable levels?	Go to Q4	Not a **CCP**	
4	Will a subsequent step eliminate the identified hazard or reduce likely occurrence to an acceptable level?	Not a CCP	oPRP with acceptable criteria CCP with clear measurable limits	

[a]Examples of preventive actions: Good hygiene practices, personal hygiene, training, pest control, allergen control, preventive maintenance, product specifications, waste disposal, handling hazardous material, inward goods inspection and recall procedure.

Form 080 Severity and Likelihood of a Risk for Identifying CCPs

	Severity		Likelihood
1	Fatality	A	Common (repeating) occurrence
2	Serious illness	B	Known to occur or "it has happened" (own information)
3	Product recall	C	Could occur or "I have heard it happening" (published information)
4	Customer complaint	D	Not expected to occur
5	Insignificant	E	Practically impossible

Form 081 Matrix for the Assessment of Significance of Risk and CCPs

Likelihood →		A	B	C	D	E
Severity ↓	1	1	2	4	7	11
	2	3	5	8	12	16
	3	6	9	13	17	20
	4	10	14	18	21	23
	5	15	19	22	24	25

Shaded areas CCP

Form 082 Examples of Measures Used in Critical Limits

Time
Rate
Temperature
Humidity
Moisture content
Water activity
pH
Salt content
Chlorine
Specific sanitation procedures
Supplier certification
Specifications for ingredients

Form 083 Control Schedule for CCPs

Process Step	Potential Hazard	Critical Limit	Control Method	Responsible Person/ Signature	Corrective Action	Verification	Records

Form 084 HACCP Plan Template

1. Introduction

Company information
Purpose
Commitment
Signatures of Food Safety Manager and the CEO
Date of release

2. HACCP Team members

Food Safety Manager (Leader)
Quality Assurance Manager
Environment Manager
Production Manager
Others:
....

3. Applicable product or product category

....

4. Product description

Product description
Product name
Important product features such as the pH, preservatives and colour.
Intended use of the product
Type of packaging
Shelf life
Distribution outlets
Storage conditions
Special handling requirements
Intended use

5. Input materials

Ingredients
Raw materials
Packaging materials
Processing aids

6. Flow diagram

Attach the flow diagram for the process

7. Identify the hazards

Identify all food safety hazards associated with each step, their significance and control measures

8. Identify CCPs, PRPs and oPRP

Use the decision tree or risk analysis to identify the CCPs, PRPs and oPRP

9. Define critical limits

Define critical limits for each CCP and the rationale for the selection

10. Describe monitoring activities

Describe monitoring methods and frequencies

11. Describe corrective actions

Describe corrective actions to be taken when the process approaches or exceeds critical limits

12. Establish record keeping requirements

Define records to be maintained

13. Describe verification procedure

Describe the procedure for verifying the HACCP plan

14. Identify training needs

Describe the training needs for all employees involved in food processing operations

15. Recall procedure

A recall procedure should be developed in case a product has to be recalled

----

Food Safety Manager

Date of release

Form 085 Product Description Form

Date of issue:
Approved:

1. Name of product:

2. Important product features:

3. Ingredients:

4. Method of preservation:

5. Labelling requirements:

6. Primary packaging:

7. Secondary packaging:

8. Storage conditions

9. Distribution method:

10. Shelf life:

11. Special labelling:

11. Special handling requirements:

12. Method of preparation prior to consumption:

13. Target population:

14. Sensitive population:

15. Allergen declaration:

Form 086 Daily Cleaning and Sanitation Verification (PRP)

Week of: _____ Department: _____

Checks Circle the applicable answer	Mon	Tue	Wed	Thurs	Fri	Sat	Sun
1. Production area is free from waste and chemicals	No/yes	No/yes	No/yes	No/yes	No/yes	No/yes	No/yes
2. Packaging and food have been removed from the area to be cleaned	No/yes	No/yes	No/yes	No/yes	No/yes	No/yes	No/yes
3. All cleaning and sanitising equipment are in good working condition and appropriate	No/yes	No/yes	No/yes	No/yes	No/yes	No/yes	No/yes
4. Garbage bins have been cleaned by the end of the day	No/yes	No/yes	No/yes	No/yes	No/yes	No/yes	No/yes
5. Manner of dismantling food processing equipment is documented and satisfactory	No/yes	No/yes	No/yes	No/yes	No/yes	No/yes	No/yes
6. All chemicals have been stored and mixed in clean, correctly labelled containers and dispensed and handled only by authorised and properly trained personnel	No/yes	No/yes	No/yes	No/yes	No/yes	No/yes	No/yes
7. Water temperature is between 50° and 60°. Record all measurements	No/yes	No/yes	No/yes	No/yes	No/yes	No/yes	No/yes
8. Correct procedures for foaming, cleaning and sanitising have been followed	No/yes	No/yes	No/yes	No/yes	No/yes	No/yes	No/yes
9. Food processing equipment is clean	No/yes	No/yes	No/yes	No/yes	No/yes	No/yes	No/yes
10. Floors are clean and no spillages							
Sanitation Person's Signature:							

Corrective and Preventive Actions:

_____
_____
_____
_____
_____

Verified by Manager:_____ **Date:** _____

Form 087 Pre-requisite Programmes [HACCP User's Manual]

Pre-requisite Programme	Scope
1. Facilities and premises	Suitability of production environment, including buildings, pathways, drainage and waste management Provision of sufficient space for production, storage, cooling and refrigeration Provision of adequate ventilation, water supply and lighting facilities for staff
2. Supplier control	Procedure for the approval of suppliers An effective GMP and food safety programme
3. Specifications	Documented specifications for all ingredients, packaging and processes
4. Equipment	Calibration procedures Preventive maintenance schedule
5. Cleaning and sanitation	Validation of sanitation methods Documented procedures Regular cleaning and sanitation of equipment
6. Personnel hygiene	Establish a personnel hygiene policy Ensure all employees abide by the policy
7. Training	Provision of training and management of training records in personnel hygiene, GMP, cleaning, sanitation, personal safety and their role in the HACCP programme
8. Management of chemicals	Proper and storage of chemicals and segregation of food and non-food items
9. Receiving, storage and transport	Storage of all raw materials and products under safe and sanitary conditions Maintaining appropriate environmental conditions for storage
10. Traceability and recall	Batch coding of all raw materials and products to enable traceability Establish an effective recall procedure
11. Pest control	Establish and maintain an effective pest control programme

Form 088 Food Delivery Monitoring (oPRP) Record

Date of Delivery	Product	Delivery Docket	Temp on Delivery °C	Date Code Check	Packaging Condition	Supplier	Comments	Received by

1. Check deliveries immediately on receipt and record details

2. Chilled food should be below 4°C

3. Frozen food should be below –18°C

Corrective and Preventive Actions:

_____

_____

_____

_____

_____

Verified by Manager:_____   **Date:**   _____

Form 089 Recall Notice

Food Recall Notice

ABC Company Limited 375G Mixed Fruit Jam

ABC Company Limited is recalling 375G jars of mixed fruit jam because of the discovery of glass fragments in two jars of ABC Company Limited mixed fruit jam. The recall applies to the product having the batch code L23A7.

The products bearing the above code should not be consumed.

As a safety measure, we are recalling all supplies of the product with the above identification on the label.

No incidents of injury or illness have been reported. However, any person concerned about their health as a result of consuming this product should seek medical advice.

Please return the product to the point of purchase for a refund or replacement or phone toll-free number. 0800......

The recall does not apply to ABC Company Limited's any other food product or mixed fruit jam bearing a different batch code.

We sincerely apologise for any inconvenience caused by the recall

ABC Company Limited
(Address)
Fax
(Date)

Form 090 Initial Environmental Review (IER)

1. Description of the organisation

Products, Services and Activities	Describe the Products, Services and Main Activities
Number of employees	
Financial information	Turnover
Organisation chart	Attach organisation chart
Responsible manager	Environmental Manager
Site location and site history	The company locations, proximity to buildings, natural resources and the history of the site
Manufacturing facility	The size and design of the facility and modifications made
Management of the site	Responsible authority for managing the site
Limitation of the review	If the review does not include the whole company, state the applicable sites and the reasons for exclusion

2. Legal and other requirements

Requirements and Responsibility	Description	Current Status
1. Authorisations	Municipal authorities Health regulators Environmental officers Certifying bodies	
2. Legal and other requirements applicable to the product/service	State all regulations and requirements applicable to the product/service	
3. Customers	Complaints from customers on environmental issues and identify their demands	
4. Suppliers	Suppliers' input	
5. Community	Community concerns	
6. Employees	Employees feedback	

3. Previous accidents

Date of Occurrence	Location	Cause of Accident	Environmental Damage and Extent (Include Penalties, If Any)	Corrective Actions Taken

4. Raw materials and components usage

Process	Raw Material Component	Amount	Use	Environmental Impact

5. Chemicals and their usage

Type (According to Classification)	Amount (Annual Quantity)	Use (Where Is It Used)	Usage? (During Use and after Use)	Environmental Impact

5. Energy use

Type of Energy	Usage (MWh)	Cost	Used in	Fuel Conservation Measures

6. Waste generation and recycling

Type (Waste Water, Chemicals, Solids)[a]	Origin	Characteristics[a] Quantity[b]	Treatment (Waste Water) Handling (Chemicals) Disposal (Solids)	Recycling (Waste Water, Chemicals) Disposal (Solids)	Discharge (Waste Water) Disposal (Chemicals, Solids)	Permits Approvals Licenses	Records of Discharges (Waste Water) Disposal (Chemicals, Solids)

[a]For solids specify the type e.g. wood, metal and paper.
[b]For waste water, use waste water analysis reports, for chemicals specify the type of chemicals and for solids specify the quantity.

7. Emissions to air and noise levels

Type of Emission (Gas or Noise)	Origin	Mass (tonnes/year)	Control Method	Emissions Monitored (Yes/No)	Annual Cost of Control Methods	Proposed Control Methods

8. Impact on surroundings

Impact on (Land, Water, Plants, Animals etc.)	Source	Effect of the Impact	Remedial Measures	Penalties, If Any

9. Transportation

Number of Vehicles	Monthly Mileage	Fuel Usage	Emissions	Other Effects	Mitigating Efforts

10. Company's products

Product	Annual Usage	Weight per Product	Packaging (Type and Weight)	Recycling or Efforts to Reduce

11. Summary of consumption and emissions

Input	Type and Amount
Raw materials including packaging	
Energy consumption	
Water usage	
Transportation 　　Total mileage 　　Total fuel consumption	
Output and Source	Type and Amount
Emissions to air	
Waste water discharge	
Solid waste discharge	
Soil pollution	

WRAP. (2013). Your Guide to Environmental Management System: *Business Resource Efficiency Guide.* Retrieved May 26, 2017 from http://www.wrap.org.uk/sites/files/wrap/WRAP%20EMS%20guide%20June%202013.pdf.
Zackrisson, M., Bengtsson, G. and Norberg, C. (2004). *Measuring Your Company's Environmental Impact: Templates and Tools for a Complete ISO 14001 Initial Review.* UK: Earthscan

Form 091 Materials Necessary for an Initial Environmental Review (IER)

Material	Description
Documents	Licenses, permits, consents, registrations etc.
	Relevant legislation
	Customer complaints
	Duty of care document
	Drawings of drainage
	Drawings of plant layout
	Product information
Records	Penalties and court actions
	Maintenance schedules and records
	Monitoring data on discharges
	Operation logs
	Environmental incidents
	Purchasing records
	Raw material specifications
	Material safety data sheets
	Training records
	Transport
	Recycling
Procedures and controls	Raw materials
	Effluents
	Emissions
	Waste management
	Emergencies
	Storage
Utilities	Electricity
	Gas
	Water
	Liquid fuel
	Others

Form 092 Qualitative Assessment of Significance of Environmental Impact

Activity	Aspect	Legal Requirement, Voluntary Commitment, Company Policy	Community Concern	Potential Impact on the Environment	Resource Use	Significant (S) Not Significant (NS)	Reason for Significance	Target
Waste management	Disposal	Voluntary commitment	None	Low	None	S	Commitment to keep environment clean	No accumulation of waste Regular disposal

Form 093 Quantitative Assessment Template

Activity	Aspect	Impact	Probability 1–4	Severity 1–4	Scale 1–4	Duration 1–4	TOTAL Added Score	Significant >18

Form 094 Evaluation of Positive Environmental Aspects

Aspect	Benefits		Cost Savings ($)
	Environmental	Organisational	

Form 095 Environmental Aspects Impacts Register

Activity/ Process	Significant Aspect	Impact	Current Controls	Proposed Controls	Target	Action by	Target Date
Waste disposal	Disposal of waste	Increase environmental hazard Potential to attract pests Unpleasant odour	Disposal irregular Bins not completely emptied	Regular disposal of waste	Negotiate new contract with a new contractor	Plant Manager	dd/mm/yy

Issue date:
Completed by:

Form 096 Environmental Impact of Sales Activities

Activity	Impact	How to Minimise
Packaging	Cardboard use Paper use	Redesigning packaging to minimise packaging material Use recyclable material
Promotional material	Paper use	Use recyclable paper
Delivering goods	Fuel for vehicles	Use fuel economy vehicles Clean driving training
Working in the office	Lighting	Use low-energy bulbs
Advising customers on managing waste	Waste accumulation	Advise on waste disposal
Communication with customers	Environmentally friendly products	Promote clean green image of environmentally friendly products and recyclable packaging

Form 097 Impact of IT Equipment on the Environment

Activity	Impact	How to Minimise
Raw materials of microchip fabrication and circuit board fabrication	Use of chemicals	Reduce the use of toxic chemicals
Raw materials for casing	Plastic (polybrominated diphenyl ethers (PBDEs))	Use PBDE-free plastic
Fabrication of microchips, circuit boards, casing	Chemicals, energy, water	Reduce the use of toxic chemicals Lead-free soldering
Packaging	Cardboard, rigifoam	Use recyclable materials Minimise packaging use
Operation	Energy Emission of greenhouse gas Heat	Use products with energy star symbol, eco-labelled products and use power saving mode
Disposal	Landfill Soil contamination Water contamination	Purchase longer lasting equipment Reuse or resell equipment Recycle according to regulated practices Intelligent liberation

Form 098 Sales Activity Log

ABC COMPANY LIMITED
Address

Page:
Date:
Ref:

Sales Activity Log
Name of the Sales Representative

Last Month's Selling Activity	Target	Achieved
Prospecting Cold calls Telemarketing calls		
Customer service calls		
Appointments		
Surveys		
Proposals		
Demonstrations		
Promotions		
Closes		
New customers		
Sales orders		

Form 099 Field Visit Log

ABC COMPANY LIMITED
Address

Page:
Date:
Ref:

Field Visit Log
Name of the Sales Representative
Time

Prospect	
Objectives	
Actions	
Results	
Comments	
Recommendations	

Form 100 Distribution List of Documents

Document Reference	Document Title	Issue No:	Released Date	Department	Document Location

Form 101 Request for Document Change

Originator:........................   Date:.............
Current document No:
Issue No:
Released date:

Description of the required change and impact on IQFSE Management System

Reason for change

Urgency:............................
Approval:
Department Manager
_____

To be completed by the QA Manager
Date:..............   Document Control No:

Following change has been made: [Attach copy if necessary]   *Document Reference:*   *Released Date:* *Issue No:*

Distribution List: Obsolete document removed: Yes/No Approved: QA Manager:

Form 102 Documents of External Origin

Document No:	Document Ref/ Version No:	Title	Description	Effective Date	Expiry Date	Originator	Used by

Form 103 Master List of Documents

Type	Reference	Title	Issue No:	Issue Date	Comments

Form 104 Master List of Changes

Reference	Title	Changes Made	Issue No: Revision No:	Issue Date	Comments

Form 105 Master List of Common Records

Records Common to All Three Systems			
Title	Location	Responsibility	Comments
SWOT and Pest Analysis, objectives	Head office	Managing Director	
Supplier evaluation	Purchasing	Purchasing Manager	
Purchasing	Purchasing	Purchasing Manager	
Inward Goods receipts and related	Purchasing	Purchasing Manager	
Inward Goods assessment	QA Department	QA Manager	
Process control	Production	Production Manager	
Product release	QA Department	QA Manager	
Storage, processing orders, delivery, stock levels	Warehouse	Warehouse Manager	
Sales	Sales	Sales Manager	
Design and Development	Engineering	Engineering Manager	
Calibration	Laboratory	QA Manager	
Traceability	QA Department	QA Manager	
Analytical	Laboratory	QA Manager	
Equipment and machinery maintenance	Engineering	Engineering Manager	
Minutes of meetings	Related department	Chairperson	
Audit results	QA Department	QA Manager	
Management Review results	QA Department	QA Manager	
Document reviews	QA Department	QA Manager	
Corrective actions	QA Department	QA Manager	
Training	Human Resource (HR)	HR Manager	
Performance review	HR	HR Manager	
Production	Production	Plant Manager	
Non-conforming	QA Department	QA Manager	
Customer complaints	QA Department	QA Manager	
Customer service	Customer Services	Customer Relations Manager	
Contracts	Production	Plant Manager	
Human Resources	HR	HR Manager	
Risk assessment	Risk office	Chief Risk Officer	
Financial	Finance	Financial Manager	
Facility Maintenance	Engineering	Engineering	
Communication	Individual departments	Department Manager	
Change control	QA Department	QA Manager	
Other records			

Food safety records			
Title	Location	Responsibility	Comments
Hazard Analysis and Critical Control Point (HACCP) plan inputs	Production	Food Safety Manager	
HACCP plan	Production	Food Safety Manager	
Control schedule	Production	Food Safety Manager	
Hazard analysis inputs	Production	Food Safety Manager	
Hazard analysis	Production	Food Safety Manager	
Traceability	Production	Food Safety Manager	
Calibration	QA Department	QA Manager	
Measuring equipment	QA Department	QA Manager/ Engineering Manager	
QA Manager	QA Department	QA Manager	
Validation	QA Department	QA Manager	
Flow diagrams	Production	Food Safety Manager	
Emergency records	QA Department	Emergency Coordinator	
Recall	QA Department	QA Manager/ Food Safety Manager	
Modifications to PRPs	Production	QA Manager/ Food Safety Manager	
Other records			

Environmental records			
Title	Location	Responsibility	Comments
Hazardous waste	Production	Environment Manager	
Material safety data sheets	Production	Environment Manager	
Test results	Production	Environment Manager	
Waste analysis	Production	Environment Manager	
Emissions	Production	Environment Manager	
Utility usage	Production	Engineering Manager	
Initial environmental review	Production	Environment Manager	
Environmental aspects and impacts	Production	Environment Manager	
Emergency (environmental)	Plant Manager	Emergency Coordinator	
Other records			

Form 106 Internal Communication Matrix

Information Type	Delivery Method	Originator	Intended Audience	When?
1. Policies, objectives, targets, business performance, strategic direction	Business performance review meeting	CEO	Senior Managers	Annual
2. Department objectives, targets, performance measurements, roles and responsibilities	Department meeting	Department Managers	Supervisors under Department Managers	Annual
3. Financial Reports	Financial review meeting	Financial Manager	Senior Executive team	Annual
4. Environmental policy, significant environmental aspects related to the work, environmental objectives and targets, environmental responsibilities and procedures and environmental emergency action plan	Procedures in manuals and/or specific environmental plan using the intranet	Environment Manager	All employees	At least annually
5. Quality policy and objectives, operational procedures, IQFSE management system performance	Procedures in manuals and/or specific quality plans using the intranet	QA Manager	All employees	At least annually
6. Recipe modifications, new recipes, new food safety hazards with new ways of handling and controlling, food safety measures	Procedures in manuals and/or specific food safety plan using the intranet	Food Safety Manager	All employees	At least annually
7. Notification of legal and other requirements and compliance issues, changes in customer, statutory and regulatory requirements	e-mail	Plant Manager	Employees whose work is affected by the regulations	As required
8. Training programmes, performance reviews	e-mail	Human Resource Manager	Managers	Annual
9. Progress towards meeting objectives, targets	Bulletin Board	Plant Manager	Managers and Supervisors	Monthly
10. Test requirements	Intranet	QA Manager	Supervisors	As required
11. Audit findings, corrective and preventive actions	e-mail	QA Manager	Managers and Supervisors	As required

(Continued)

Information Type	Delivery Method	Originator	Intended Audience	When?
12. Changes to management system elements, procedures and new projects	Intranet	QA Manager	Managers and Supervisors	As required
13. Information regarding IQFSE management system	User product manuals, procedures, work instructions, drawings, specifications, quality, environment and food safety records, on-the-job training via intranet	QA Manager, Environment Manager and Food Safety Manager	Managers and Supervisors	As required
14. Changes in raw materials, ingredients, food products, manufacturing methods, equipment, working environment, personal qualification levels and responsibilities, cleaning and sanitation programmes, storage and distribution systems	Intranet	QA Manager, and Food Safety Manager	Managers and Supervisors	As required
15. Risks and opportunities management	Procedures in manuals	QA Manager, Environment Manager and Food Safety Manager	Managers and Supervisors	Managers and Supervisors

Form 107 External Communication Record

Date communication received	
Type of communication	
Sender	
Address/ Tel. No./Email	
Content of communication [attach photocopy]	
Response required Yes/No	
Date of response	
Person responding	
Position	
Response [attach copy]	
Any internal actions if necessary [attach corrective action form]	

Form 108 External Communication Matrix

Interested Party	Subject	Media	Responsibility
Regulatory agencies	Legal matters, penalties and fines, non-compliance with statutory and/or legal requirements Notifications Emergency situations Inspections	Letter, email	Managing Director
Certifying bodies	Certification Inspections	Verbal, letter, E-mail	Plant Manager
Customers	Quality issues, environmental issues and food safety issues and any relevant information as required by the customer	Verbal, letter, E-mail	QA Manager Environment Manager Food Safety Manager
Suppliers	Information relating to purchasing material Request for improving environment, health and safety protection Product failure Significant impacts/risks from their operations	Letter, E-mail	Purchasing Manager
Community groups	Environmental concerns	E-mail, verbal, letter	Environment Manager
Visitors/Contractors	Request for improving environment, health and safety protection Significant impacts/risks from their operations	E-mail, verbal, letter, notice board	
Media	Initiatives taken and subsequent development Other information	Press releases, seminars, media conferences	Managing Director
Banks/ Insurers	Relevant information as required	Letter, E-mail, financial reports	Financial Manager
All other enquiries	As requested	E-mail, verbal, letter	Customer Relations Manager

Form 109 Request for Change

Change control No:	Date of submission:
(Allocated by the QA Manager)	Change classification:†

Requested by:	Title:

1.0 Change Requested

2.0 Reason for change

3.0 Additional information and knowledge gaps

4.0 Effect of change [consider inputs, processing, storage, delivery, environment, food safety, etc.] and how they are addressed

5.0 Costs and required resources involved*

6.0 Risks, priority and environmental concerns

To be completed by the Management Team

Trials needed ☐ Yes ☐ No
    ☐ Approved ☐ Rejected
If rejected reason:

Date of implementation:
Notes on monitoring:

Authorised by: (QA Manager) Date of authorisation:

---

*For changes that involve costs, the request may be referred to the Plant Manager or the CEO, depending on the cost estimate.

Form 110 Request for Resources

ABC Company Limited	Req. No. _____
Resources Request	Date: _____
Requesting Department: _____ Title of originator:_____	
Request for ☐ Equipment ☐ HR ☐ Material ☐ Maintenance Request for financial resources should be submitted to the Chairman of the Board of Directors with full justification.	
Details of request	Required date of delivery _____
Estimate cost:	
Preferred Supplier(s): _____ _____ _____ _____	Signature of authorized person Title
Justification	
Additional information including any drawings, specifications or other information that can assist the decision.	

Form 111 Training Needs Analysis

Date:..............

Name of employee		Title	
Employee No.:		Department	
Employment (Direct/Indirect)		Joining date	
Immediate supervisor and Designation			
Number of employees reporting to this employee			
Nature of the job			

Training Analysis

	Topic(s)	Training Need	Benefits from Training	
			Employee	Company

Signature of employee:...................
Department Manager:..............................   Approved:...........................

Form 112 Employee Training Plan and Record

Year:..............

ABC COMPANY LIMITED

Date	Training Details (Course, Provider, Frequency, Cost, Location, Support Services)	Training Month	Signature

Attended employees

	Name	Feedback	Effectiveness

Department Manager:...............................

Form 113 Training Topics

Date:..............

ABC COMPANY LIMITED

General Topics

IQFSE Management system, its policies, objectives and targets

Department objectives and targets

Information technology skills

Internal auditing

Continual improvement

Team work

Procedures and work instructions

Operation and maintenance of equipment

Process controls and methods

Personal hygiene

Basic fire training

First aid

Handling non-conformances

Accident incident investigation

Risk analysis and treatment of risk

Emergency preparedness

Hazardous waste management

Specific Topics

Quality and environment	Food safety
Design review process	Pre-requisite programmes
Statistical process control	Hazard analysis
Environmental aspects and impacts	Critical control points
Environmental regulations	Products-related processes
Chemical spill response	Handling unsafe product
	Basic food hygiene
	Recall procedure
	Good Manufacturing Practices (GMPs)

Signature of employee:..................

Department Manager:............................ Approved:.........................

Form 114 Skill Chart

ABC COMPANY LIMITED
Address

Year:..............

Skill Acquired	Employee Name								
	B.Jones	*M.Smith*							
Filler operation	1.2.2015	2.4.2016							

Form 115 Disciplinary Notice

ABC Company Limited

Employee Name	**Date of notice**
Supervisor's Name	
Employee's Position	

Type of problem or violation

☐ Tardiness	☐ Quality of work	☐ Safety
☐ Absenteeism	☐ Quantity of work	☐ Alcohol or drug abuse
☐ Insubordination	☐ Neatness	☐ Carelessness
☐ Other	Date of occurrence	

Details of the incident and impact on the company

Corrective action to be taken

Suspension	☐ with pay	☐ without pay	First day
Other			Last day

Expected improvement (Include a clear statement of the consequences of failing to improve)

Employee statement (Attach paper of necessary)

By signing this notice I acknowledge that I have been counselled about my inappropriate conduct and informed of consequences, if improvements are not made.

Employee's signature	Supervisor's signature	Date

Form 116 Dismissal Letter

ABC Company Limited

<u>IN STRICTEST CONFIDENCE</u>

Dear

<u>DISMISSAL</u>

Further to the disciplinary meeting held on (date) at which the panel considered (details). The decision has been taken to terminate your employment with effect from……..for the following reasons:

Since the response to the final warning in your disciplinary record has not been satisfactory we consider dismissal is the appropriate option.
The following arrangements are made in respect of your dismissal:

*   Your employment with……will terminate on……..and your final date of employment is….
*   You will be paid in lieu of your period of notice stipulated in your employment contract, subject to normal deductions
*   You are entitled to pay in lieu of any accrued untaken leave less normal deductions
*   You must return in good condition any property belonging to the company
*   If you are entitled to reimbursements of any genuine expenses incurred prior to the termination date. Please submit your claim by……..
*   You will receive you final payment of your salary on…..

You have the right of appeal against this dismissal. If you wish to do so, you should write to XXXXXX (state address) detailing the grounds of your appeal within 10 working days from the receipt of this letter.

Yours sincerely

General Manager

Human Resource Manager

Date:

Form 117 Grievance Form Stage One

To: The Supervisor
Grievance 1

From:

Dept:

Date:

Dear

I wish to make a formal grievance against:

_____

in line with ABCCL's Grievance Procedure. The details of my grievance are given below

Yours sincerely,

(Manager should respond to this formal written grievance within 2 working days unless an extended period for response is mutually agreed)

Form 118 Grievance Form Stage Two

To The Department Manager
Grievance 2

From

Dept

Date

Copy Supervisor

Dear

On ………..(within 10 days of the response to the initial formal grievance) my grievance against …….was heard by……….I am not satisfied with the outcome of this meeting and would like to appeal to you for a further hearing of my grievance, in line with ABCCL's Grievance Procedure.

I enclose a copy of the original communication regarding this matter, other correspondence and information related to it.

Yours sincerely

(Manager should respond to this formal written grievance within 7 days unless an extended period for response is mutually agreed)

Form 119 Grievance Procedure Stage Three

To The General Manager:
Grievance 3

From:

Dept:

Date:

Copy: Supervisor

Dear

On ………(within 10 days of the response to the second stage of the formal grievance) I appealed to you against the decision made at my initial grievance against

_____

I am still dissatisfied with the outcome of the meetings and would like to appeal to you for a further hearing of my grievance in line with ABCCL's Grievance Procedure.

I enclose a copy of the original letter regarding this matter, other correspondence and information related to it.

Yours sincerely

*(**General Manager should respond to this formal written grievance within 20 working days unless an extended period for response is mutually agreed**)*

Form 120 Self-Evaluation Form

ABC Company Limited

Self-Evaluation Form

Name: Job Title
Department   Supervisor
Appraisal period
Appraisal Date

This is your own evaluation of your job performance. Complete this form and forward this to your supervisor. Your supervisor may comment on your evaluation and may request you to justify your evaluation.

---

1. What were your major achievements in the job during this period?

2. Describe the areas where your performance can be improved.

3. What are the difficulties for improvements?

4. What are your goals for the coming year?

5. Describe the support, resources and training you need to perform your job better.

6. Any other comment

Date   Signature

Form 121 Performance Review

ABC Company Limited

PERSONAL DETAILS

Name of employee:
Date of joining:
Employee No:
Position:
Department:
Immediate Supervisor:
Period under review:

Part One: Record of appraisal

	Performance Factor	Explanation	Rating
1	Attendance	Excellent: Not late for work, no absence record and available at short notice	
		Good: Not late for work and no absence record	
		Satisfactory: Not more than …..days late or absent	
		Needs improvement: More than …….days late or absent	
	Comment		
2	Job knowledge and skills	Excellent: substantially exceeds job requirements	
		Good: Exceeds job requirements	
		Satisfactory: Meets job requirements	
		Needs improvement: Partially meets or does not meet job requirements	
	Comment		

	Performance Factor	Explanation	Rating
3	Quality of work	Excellent: substantially exceeds job requirements	
		Good: Exceeds job requirements	
		Satisfactory: Meets job requirements	
		Needs improvement: Partially meets or does not meet job requirements	
	Comment		
4	Initiative and motivation	Excellent: substantially exceeds job requirements	
		Good: Exceeds job requirements	
		Satisfactory: Meets job requirements	
		Needs improvement: Partially meets or does not meet job requirements	
	Comment		
5	Team work and communication	Excellent: Substantially exceeds job requirements	
		Good: Exceeds job requirements	
		Satisfactory: Meets job requirements	
		Needs improvement: Partially meets or does not meet job requirements	
	Comment		
6	General conduct	Excellent: Substantially exceeds job requirements	
		Good: Exceeds job requirements	
		Satisfactory: Meets job requirements	
		Needs improvement: Partially meets or does not meet job requirements	
	Comment		
	Performance Factor	Explanation	Rating
7	Discipline	Excellent: No disciplinary record, always follows supervisor's ins	
		Good: No disciplinary record	
		Satisfactory: Minor violation resolved informally	
		Needs improvement: Serious misconduct; action plan agreed	
8	Special achievements and commendation received		
9	Career development opportunities		
Part 2			
	Overall performance		

Date: Employee:………………………..   Supervisor/Manager:…………………..

Form 122 Management Skills Evaluation

	Core competency	Ranking
1	Leadership skills – Ability to lead staff to accomplish their tasks Ensures policies, objectives and goals are understood by employees Supports staff to establish individual goals Maintains a clean and safe work environment Builds trust among employees and create opportunities for their development	
2	Planning, organising and time management – Organises activities in a timely manner to accomplish goals. Supports employees to manage competing tasks Evaluates the amount of supervision required	
3	Communication – Expresses ideas clearly and professionally Conducts open, honest communication Conveys information in a timely manner Listens to others and receive feedback in a positive manner	
4	Problem solving and decision making – Demonstrates effective problem solving skills Makes sound and timely decisions and involve others in decision making Considers all options and selects the best one	
5	Financial performance awareness – Aware of financial constraints and monitor expenses. Expenditure does not exceed the budget Manages resources effectively by providing the necessary resources and support	
6	Delivery of services – The services required are identified and provided efficiently and effectively Ensures staff are competent enough to deliver the services	
7	Customers[a] service – Listen, understands and responds to customers' needs in a pleasant manner Relevant information is provided and reacts to their queries in a problem-solving manner	
8	Skills – Demonstration of skills required for the job	

[a]Internal and external customers

Form 123 Performance Action Plan

ABC Company Limited

Action Plan General

Objective Category	Item	Performance Indicator	Action Plan	By Whom	Checking Dates dd/mm/yyyy
Process objectives	Preventive maintenance process	Percentage of preventive maintenance completed according to schedule	Shall monitor the schedule regularly for completeness and effectiveness Resources required: Engineering manuals, spare parts, skilled technical staff Skills: Operation and maintenance of machinery and equipment	Engineer	dd/mm/yy
Performance objective	Response to customer complaints	Time taken to respond	Respond to customer complaints according to customer complaints procedure	Production Manager	dd/mm/yy

Form 124 Establishing Controls for Externally Provided Products, Processes and Services

Product/ Service/Process : ....
....
External provider:...
Estimated cost:..
Urgency:...

Quality requirements	
Food Safety requirements	
Delivery requirements	
Environmental aspects and associated impacts	
Risks and opportunities associated with production and service provision	
Compliance obligations	
Recommended control(s)	
Justification	
Comments	
QA Manager	Date

Form 125 Equipment Inventory

ABCCL EQUIPMENT INVENTORY

1. Item:

2. Item description:

3. Use of the item:

4. Equipment ID:

5. Serial No.:

6. Manufacturer:

7. Contact details:

8. Location:

9. Software used?   Yes/ No

10. Current status
    ☐ In use   ☐ Repair   ☐ Out of service

11. Calibration requirements:

12. Associated documents:

User Manual
Certificate of conformance:
Documentation of damage, malfunction, modification or repair
Other

Form 126 Calibration Database

CALIBRATION DATABASE

Equipment				Calibration					Condition			
ID	Description	Manufacturer	Purchase Date	Method	Date calibrated	Previous Calibration	Feature Measured	Acceptance Criteria	As received	Modified	Repair	Person Calibrating

Form 127 Monitoring and Measurement Framework

Process	Item to Be Monitored or Measured	Method	Person Responsible	Frequency of Data Collection	Frequency of Analysis
Purchasing	Non-conforming items Accuracy of orders Delivery of items Supplier evaluation Raw material usage	Inward Goods checks Audits Audits Review of supplier performance	QA officer QA Manager QA Manager Purchasing Manager Purchasing Manager	Every delivery Monthly Monthly Annually Annually	Quarterly Management Review meetings
Production Planning	Unscheduled changes to the plan	Monitor the changes	Production Planner	Monthly	Monthly production planning meeting
Production	Process controls	Form 051	Form 051	During production	Daily production meeting
Sales	Accuracy of customer orders Sales opportunities gained Sales opportunities lost	Count of errors Customer interaction Customer interaction	Sales staff	Sales visits	Monthly sales meeting
Warehousing	Picking accuracy Late deliveries Storage temperature	Checking the consignment Customer complaints Monitor	Warehouse staff QA officer	When orders are assembled and checked Weekly	Monthly department meeting Warehouse meeting
Food safety	Control steps and critical control steps Pre-requisite programmes Operational pre-requisite programmes	Hazard Analysis and Critical Control Point (HACCP) plan	Food Safety Manager	During production and assembly	Quarterly Management Review meetings
Environmental safety	Air emissions Liquid and solid waste Noise Power, water and natural gas utilisation Recycling	External provider Hazard manifest Noise survey Utility bills Recycling reports	Environmental Manager	Monthly Monthly Monthly Monthly	Quarterly Management Review meetings

(Continued)

Process	Item to Be Monitored or Measured	Method	Person Responsible	Frequency of Data Collection	Frequency of Analysis
Safety and hygiene	Investigation of accidents	Accident reports	Human Resource Manager	Monthly	Monthly Department Managers Meetings
Objectives	Percentage of objectives achieved	Objective status report	Quality Assurance Manager	Quarterly	Quarterly Management Review meetings
Non-conformances	Corrective actions issued by subject/ topic	Corrective action report (CAR) log	Quality Assurance Manager	Monthly	Quarterly Management Review meetings
Customer relations	Customer satisfaction	Customer surveys	Customer Relations Manager	Monthly	Monthly sales meeting
Product	Conformity of product	Final release check	Quality Assurance Manager	During production	Daily production meeting
Risks and opportunities	Effectiveness of actions taken	Monitor processes	Quality Assurance Manager	Quarterly	Quarterly Management Review meetings
IQFSE Management System	Performance and effectiveness	Audits Management reviews	Quality Assurance Manager	Quarterly	Quarterly Management Review meetings
Continual improvement	Effectives of action plan	Recalls Deviation from critical food safety limits Quality, food safety and environmental issues	Quality Assurance Manager	Quarterly	Quarterly Management Review meetings
Financial Management	Financial performance	Financial reports Budget reports	Financial Manager	Monthly	Quarterly Board meeting
Internal and external audits	Completion of audit schedule	Audit reports	Quality Assurance Manager	Quarterly	Quarterly Management Review meetings
Certifications and licenses	Validity	Review of Certifications and licenses	Plant Manager	Annually	Annually at Quarterly Management Review meetings

(Continued)

Process	Item to Be Monitored or Measured	Method	Person Responsible	Frequency of Data Collection	Frequency of Analysis
Qualification/validation	Qualification/validation of processes, products, machines/facilities, personnel	Validation reports Training records	Quality Assurance Manager	Quarterly	Quarterly Management Review meetings
Design and development	Design changes due to errors	Corrective action reports	Quality Assurance Manager	Quarterly	Quarterly Management Review meetings
Statutory and regulatory requirements Knowledge Management	Compliance with statutory and regulatory requirements Knowledge gaps	Compliance audit Development opportunities	Quality Assurance Manager	Quarterly	Quarterly Management Review meetings
Marketing	Market share	Competitor analysis	Marketing Manager	Quarterly	Monthly Sales and Marketing meeting
Warehousing	Transport	Fuel consumption	Warehouse Manager	Monthly	Monthly warehouse meeting

Form 128 Monitoring and Measurement Items

Management System	What Is to Be Measured and Monitored
IQFSE Management System	Information about external and internal issues (context)
	Information about interested parties and their needs
	IQFSE Management System processes
	Quality, food safety and environmental objectives
	Conform it with products and services offered
	External providers' performance
	Items supplied by external providers
	Customer satisfaction
	Legal compliance
Food Safety specific	Critical Control Points (CCPs)
	Pre-requisite Programmes (PRPs)
	Operational pre-requisite Programmes (oPRPs)
	Control points
Environment Specific	Air emissions
	Liquid and solid waste
	Noise
	Power, water and natural gas utilisation
	Investigation of accidents
	Recycling
	Raw material usage
	Transportation

Form 129 Analysis and Evaluation of Data and Information

Data	Metrics
Characteristics of products and processes	Process performance variation Cycle time Unscheduled down time
Compliance with product specifications and customer requirements	Product and process non-conformances Extent of rework, repair and scrap On-time delivery performance Customer complaints
Suppliers	Supplier performance rating Late deliveries Rejection rates of incoming goods
Environmental impact	Air Waste water Solid waste Noise Hazardous waste Utilities consumption Recycling
Customer evaluation	Customer satisfaction Customer complaints
Management system	Internal audit findings Effectiveness of training
Sales	Market share New customers Customers lost
Financial	Financial performance

Form 130 Waste Recycling Data

Month	Paper	Corrugated Board and Cardboard	Plastic Items	Metal Items	Glass Bottles	Newspaper	Office Paper	Total Recycled A	Solid Waste	Hazardous Waste	Air Emissions	Total Waste B	Net Impact B–A
January													
February													
March													
April													
May													
June													
July													
August													
September													
October													
November													
December													

Form 131 Solid Waste Generation

Month	Quantity Kg A	Cumulative Sum B	Total Cost $X/kg	Production M	Cumulative Sum C	Monthly Rate A/M	Annual Rate B/C
January							
February							
March							
April							
May							
June							
July							
August							
September							
October							
November							
December							

Form 132 Water and Power Consumption

Month	Production M	Cumulative Production N	Water Usage Litres A	Cumulative Usage Litres B	Monthly Rate A/M	Cumulative Rate B/N	Power Consumption KWH C	Cumulative Power Consumption KWH D	Monthly Rate C/M	Annual Rate D/N
January										
February										
March										
April										
May										
June										
July										
August										
September										
October										
November										
December										

Form 133 Customer Satisfaction Survey

ABC COMPANY LIMITED
Address

Time:
Date:
Ref:

Dear Customer
As part of our work towards ensuring our customer's complete satisfaction, we kindly invite you to participate in our brief Customer Satisfaction Survey. We thank you for using our products/services.

Sales Manager

1. For how long have your been using our products/services?

2. How often do you use our products/services?

3. How satisfied/dissatisfied are you with our products and services?

4. What impressed you most about our products and services?

5. What aspects of our products and services disappoint you most?

6. What do you like about our products/services?

7. What do you dislike about our products/services?

8. How do you rate our products when compared to similar products in the market?

9. Would you use our products/services in the future?

10. Would you recommend our products/services to other people?

11. If our products and services did not meet your expectations, please state your reasons

Form 134 Customer Complaint Report

ABC COMPANY LIMITED
Address

Time:
Date:
Ref:

Customer-related information

Company:.. Location:..
Person reporting the complaint:...
Contact details:...
....
....
....
....

Product/service information
Product/service:..
Purchase details:..
....
....
Date of purchase:...

What is the complaint or dissatisfaction?
....
....
....
....
....
....
Complaint taken by:.. Title:..
Date:..
Has the customer returned the product?   Yes/No
If yes, state the extent of damage or the problem

Internal Investigation
Is the complaint justified Yes/No?
Cause of the problem:...
....
....
....
Corrective action taken:...
....
....
....

Follow up by:...Title:... Date:..............

Customer satisfied? Yes/No: If not satisfied actin proposed:...
Management representative:... Date:................................
Person taking the complaint...

Form 135 Complaints Log

ABC COMPANY LIMITED
Address

Reference	Date/ Location	Date of Contact	Complaint Details	Corrective Action	Closed Out Date	Closed Out by

Form 136 Request for Comments

Document Reference:
To:
Date:
_____

Brief description of the document:
_____

Return by:
_____

Please review the attached document and return this form with your comments by the date shown above. You may continue on a separate sheet and please make sure that you sign and date all the pages.
_____

COMMENTS AND REASONS

Signature: Title: Date:
_____

QA Manager

*For changes that involve costs, the request may be referred to the Plant Manager or the CEO, depending on the cost estimate.

Form 137 Criteria for Evaluating the Suitability, Adequacy and Effectiveness of the IQFSE Management System

IQFSE Management System Feature	Criteria for Evaluation
Suitability Capability or fitness of the system to meet defined purpose	Levels of customer satisfaction and loyalty Extent of employee satisfaction Number of improvement of innovative projects Level of customer value Sales income from new or innovative products related to total turnover Number of legal compliance violations Percentage fulfilment of environmental targets
Adequacy Ability of the system to meet regulatory standards, company requirements and ISO standards	Results of audits Extent of non-conforming products in relation to total output Process capability Input yield Results of benchmarking Regulatory non-compliances and penalties Number of licenses and permits with expired validity Average time to respond to interested parties queries
Effectiveness Extent to which planned activities are realised and expected outcome is achieved	Level of realisation of IQFSE Management System objectives Number of returned products and warranty claims Percentage of unfulfilled corrective actions within the specified timeframe Number of non-conformities in relation to the number of products sold Number of product recalls Index of risk level changes Unfulfilled handed contracts to sales ratio

Form 138 Sample Specification Sheet for a Wine

Attribute	Description
Composition	Variety
	Region
	Vintage
	Available volume
Chemical analysis	pH
	Alcohol
	Reducing sugar
	Preservatives
	Total acidity
Certification	Export
	SWNZ
Physical properties	Cold stability
	Protein stability
	Racked
	Filtered
	Malolactic fermentation
	Oak

SWNZ Sustainable Winegrowing New Zealand

Form 139 Internal Traceability Log

Date of Issue:
Product:
Production quantity
Work order No: *[05]*

Pack size:
Location:
Batch code:

	Processing Step Processing Step Number	Description of Step Input/Output	Tests	Completed (Y/N) Time Operator	QA Verification	Comments
1	Step 1: *05-1*		Test 1			
			Test 2			
			Test 2			
2	Step 2: *05-2*		Test 1			
			Test 2			
3	Step 3: *05-3*		Test 2			
			Test 2			
			Test 2			

Form 140 Traceability Summary

Operation Process	Responsible Person	Recorded Information	Traceability Information
1. Receiving goods Receipt of inward goods from suppliers including inspections	Inward goods person	For each lot received at least the following information is recorded: (a) Supplier details – name, address, purchase details (b) Product details – product name, quantity, date and time received, expiry date, if applicable (c) Allocated Inventory Control Number (ICN)	Each lot of goods received is identified by a unique ICN.
2. Storage Individual lots received are stored separately and identified by the ICN. If material is mixed as a bulk of different received lots, a new ICN is allocated for the mix and a record made of the constituent ICNs.	Inward goods person	Inventory level is updated and the following information is recorded: (a) Product details (b) The store contents – ICN, type, quantity (c) In and of materials (ICN, date, quantity and type)	ICN is retained for stored materials
3. Issue to production Components are assembled according to the specification sheet and transferred to production	Inward goods person	Following information is recorded in the specification sheet: (a) Work order number (production schedule) (b) Issue date (c) Product name and product code (d) Description (e) Unit (f) ICN of each item (g) Batch number (h) Quantity	Work Order Number in the specification sheet provides the ICNs of components used in the production run
4. Received by production Information is checked and confirmed	Line Supervisor	The information above is checked and confirmed	Specification sheet containing Work Order Number and the ICNs are retained with other production documents
5. Processing A process run is a batch operation comprising components from one or more lots, and includes several steps	Line Supervisor	For each process run, the following data is recorded (process run record): (a) Process run date and time, personnel responsible (b) Input ICN/Process Step Number (PSN), quantity, type (c) Output quantity, type, allocated batch code for the finished product	Batch code gives the details of the production run and access to all production documents

(Continued)

Operation Process	Responsible Person	Recorded Information	Traceability Information
6. Finished product storage Finished product is stored by the product code. Individual process runs are kept separate.	Warehouse Manager	Inventory level is updated and the following information is recorded: (a) The store contents (Batch code, quantity and type) (b) The materials in and out (Batch code, quantity and type) (c) Expiry date, if applicable The stock remain in unallocated status until released	Product code Received date
7. Dispatch Packed product is assembled into a consignment lot. Loading of transport/containers for onward delivery to customer destination	Warehouse Manager	For each consignment lot for the following details are recorded (product consignment record): (a) Product details (b) Delivery note number (c) Dispatch details – purchase order, customer destination, transport (company, vehicle or container number), date	Each consignment lot is identified by a delivery note number and the date

Form 141 Disposal of Non-conforming Product

Date:
Car No: Page of

Classification: ☐ Critical   ☐ Major   ☐ Minor   ☐ Observation

Management System Reference:
Non-conformance:

Details of non-conforming product/ service	
Concerns (safety, health, cost of rework, repair, regrade, reject, etc.)	
Department/Location:	
Stock in the warehouse	
HOLD sticker applied Yes/ No	
Recommended method of disposal Review Team:	
Reject / waiver approved QA Manager ABCCL Manager	
Disposal completed Yes/No	
Responsible person: Date:	

Form 142 Non-conforming Product/Service Log

Date Identified	Identified by	NCR No:	NCR Category	CAR No:	CA/PA Taken	CA/PA Completion Date	Disposal	Disposal Completion Date	Entered by

CA Corrective action PA Preventive action CAR Corrective action report NCR Non-conformance report

Form 143 Non-conformance Report

Date: Time:
NCR No: Page 1 of 1

Classification: ☐ Critical   ☐ Major   ☐ Minor   ☐ Observation

Auditor (for non-conformances identified during an audit):
Management System Reference:
Activity:
Non-conformance details
Quantity affected
Work order/PO

Issued to:	Issued by:	Issue Date
Requirement (Why it is a non-conformance?) *Does not comply with........* 		
Non-conformance (What is the problem?) 		
Department/Location: Management: Segregated: Yes/No HOLD label Yes/No		
Other details 		
CAR issued? Yes/No If Yes CAR number:.............		
QA Manager.. Date................		

Form 144 Validation Form

Date of Validation	Validation Task	Validation Findings	Frequency of Validation	Outcome and Actions Taken	Validator

Form 145 Examples of Validating Elements

	Element	Validation
1	Document	Contents of the document comply with inputs of the activity that produced the document
2	Customer requirements	Content is relevant and justified to customer expectations, complete and stated in the language of the customer
3	System requirements	Content translate correctly and/or accurately to customer requirements in the language of the customer
4	Design	Demonstrate that it satisfies system requirements
5	Product, service or enterprise	Demonstrate that the product, service or enterprise meets its system requirement and/or customer requirements
6	Activity	Demonstrate that the outputs are compliant with its inputs
7	Process	Demonstrate that outcomes are compliant with its purpose

Form 146 Validation Protocols

	Description
1	Identification and description of processes, products and equipment to be validated
2	Define measureable criteria
3	Define shifts, operators and equipment necessary for validation
4.	Establish qualifications for operators
5	Establish specifications for processes, products and equipment
6	Define special controls to be applied, if necessary during validation
7	Define process parameters to be monitored and establish methods of monitoring and controlling
8	Define product features to be monitored and establish methods of monitoring and controlling
9	Define any subjective criteria to be used for evaluation
10	Criteria for non-conformance
11	Establish statistical techniques for data collection and analysis
12	Consideration of maintenance and repair of equipment
13	Establish criteria for revalidation

Form 147 Validation Report

Validation Team:

1. Title	
2. Product to be covered:	
3. Equipment/process to be validated	
4. Change control number:	
5. Objectives of validation	
6. Reference documents	
7. Validation Plan (attach)	
8. Validation protocol (attach)	
9. Installation qualification	
10. Operational qualification	

11. Performance qualification	
12. Measurement/testing equipment and calibration	
13. Equipment maintenance	
14. Revalidation	
15. Comments	

Date: Signatures of validation team members

Form 148 Validation Checklist

☐ Initial validation
☐ Re-validation
☐ Annual validation
Conducted by:...........................

Initial validation

1. Identified list of potential hazards is based on sound scientific data and includes all hazards

2. Evaluation of the significance of hazards is based on sound scientific and technical knowledge

3. Control measures are adequate for controlling the hazards

4. Deviation of control parameters (process criteria) within the defined critical limits will not affect the safety of the product

5. Parameters and methods applied to measure control measures are appropriate and suitable

6. Corrective actions are appropriate, will prevent the release and dispatch of unsafe product and provide evidence that the problem can be resolved immediately

7. Monitoring activities, record-keeping procedures and verification activities are appropriate and adequate

8. Assurance that the plan is valid for controlling the food safety hazards associated with ingredients, process and products

9. Verify that the plan can be implemented as written

Revalidation

1. Changes related to product, ingredients, process/processing equipment, packaging or storage/distribution conditions

2. Identification of new hazards

3. New scientific information concerning the product, control measures and/or process

4. Unexplained system failures and deviations

5. Consumer complaints, product rejection or recalls

6. Systemic or recurrent product safety issue

7. Adverse review findings

8. Online observations

Form 149 Validation Elements Food Safety

Validating Element	Sources of Evidence	Details
1. Supporting evidence used in the HACCP study	Scientific literature, codes of practice, statutory and regulatory requirements, historical data, professional bodies and company knowledge base	1. Evidence for inclusion and exclusion of all relevant hazards 2. Evidence needed to show established target values and critical limits will adequately control identified hazards 3. Results of testing
2. Control measures including monitoring and corrective actions	Scientific literature, codes of practice, statutory and regulatory requirements, historical data, professional bodies and company knowledge base	1. Cross checking HACCP control schedule and flowcharts 2. Established target values, critical limits and monitoring procedures are adequate 3. Availability of written procedures which include methodology, frequency, acceptable values, action taken in case of deviation 4. Necessary calibrations 5. Disposal of non-conforming product 6. Preventing recurrence
3. CCPs	Scientific literature, codes of practice, statutory and regulatory requirements, historical data, professional bodies and company knowledge base	1. Evidence to demonstrate that CCPs are correctly identified and located 2. Evidence to demonstrate that effective critical limits can be established at each CCP.

Form 150 Summary of Validation and Verification Activities

HACCP Principle	Evidence Required for Validation	Evidence Required for Verification
1. HACCP analysis	Appropriate skills of the FST Flow diagrams are suitable All significant hazards are identified	Validation has been carried out
2. Identification of CCPs for controlling the hazards	All significant hazards are identified during CCP determination CCPs are established to control significant hazards Location of CCPs are appropriate	Validation has been carried out
3. Establishment of critical limits to assure an operation is under control at a particular hazard	Critical limits control the identified hazard	Validation has been carried out
4. Establishment and implementation of system to monitor to control the CCPs	Monitoring system ensures that control measures at CCPs are effective Procedures necessary for calibration of testing equipment are available	Records of monitoring confirming control Statistical Process Control (SPC) techniques are applied Authorised person's review of monitoring Calibration records are available confirming control
5. Establishment of corrective actions (CA) when deviations occur	CAs will prevent non-conforming product from reaching the consumer Authority for CA has been defined	In case of non-conformance CAs are effective CAs are recorded Appropriate action is taken by designated person
6. Establishment of procedures to verify that the HACCP plan is effective	Procedures for information gathering and verification of HACCP system compliance have been developed	All verification procedures have been carried out as planned
7. Available documentation on all procedures and records are appropriate to these principles and their application	Complete documentation has been developed for the entire HACCP system	Documentation and records cover the entire HACCP system Correct format Properly filled out

Form 151 Verification Schedule

Activity	Frequency	Responsibility	Review
Scheduling verification activities	Annual or upon changes	Food Safety Manager	Plant Manager
Initial validation	Prior to and during initial implementation	Expert	Food Safety Manager
Subsequent validation	Upon changes	Expert	Food Safety Manager
Verification of CCP monitoring as described in the plan	According to HACCP plan	Line Supervisor	Food Safety Manager
Review of monitoring corrective actions records	Weekly	QA Manager	Food Safety Manager
Comprehensive HACCP system	Annually	Expert	Food Safety Manager
Verification of purchased product	On receipt	Purchasing Manager	QA Manager
In-process verification	During processing	Line Supervisor	QA Manager
Verification of finished product	On completion	QA Staff	QA Manager
Verification of calibrations	According to the calibration schedule	Engineering Manager	QA Manager
Verification of external provision	When services are provided	QA Staff	QA Manager

Form 152 Verification Form

Date of Verification	Verified Activity (e.g., Hazard Analysis, CCPs, Corrective Actions, Equipment, etc.)	Verification Findings	Frequency of Verification	Outcome and Actions Taken	Verifier

Food Safety Manager:
Date

Form 153 Audit Programme

Management System	Ref	Title	Dept	Frequency	Planned Audit											
					Jan	Feb	Mar	Apr	May	Jun	Jul	Aug	Sep	Oct	Nov	Dec
IQFSE	CP 004	Purchasing	Purchasing	6 monthly	X					X						
IQFSE	CP 002	Offering contracts	Purchasing	Annually						X						

Form 154 Internal Audit Checklist [An Example]

Environmental Management System
Auditor: Date:

C: Critical non-compliance
M: Major non-compliance
N: Minor non-compliance
OK: Complies
O: Observation

ABCCL Internal Audit Checklist

Section	Management System Reference	Activities	Auditor's Comments
7.4 Communication	SP 005	Communicating the environmental aspects and environmental management system internally between various levels and functions	
		Establishing, implementing and maintaining procedures for receiving, documenting and responding to communications from external agencies	
		Decision to communicate externally about its significant environmental aspects?	
		Documentation of the decision	
		Establishing and implementing the method(s) for this communication	
Documents examined:			

Form 155 Audit Plan

Purpose: To evaluate the effectiveness of the IQFSE Management System
Scope: [list the procedures here]
Audit team: [Name of the lead auditor and auditors]
Criteria:
ISO 9001
Quality Management System
Objective:
To determine the state of compliance to the ISO 9001 standard
Date of audit:
ABCCL personnel:
[State the manes of individuals participating in the audit together with their titles]

Agenda

Time	Activity	Auditor	ABCCL Representative
9.00 AM	Entry meeting	Lead Auditor	Management team
[Complete the list]			
4.00 PM	Exit meeting	Audit Team	Management team

Form 156 Section of an Internal Audit Report

Procedure Title:	Auditor:	Audit No:
Procedure No:	Auditee:	Date:

Procedure PRP XX was audited against ISO 22000, section 7.2.3 (i) Pest control			
Item No:	Audited Item	Observation	Rating
0	Corrective actions from previous audit	No corrective actions	
1	Records of pest control visits and treatment	Quarterly visits by the Pest Control Contractor have been recorded. Last visit........ Treatments are also recorded	C
2	Pest control contract	Annual contract dated ......was sighted	C
3	Map of bait stations	All bait stations in the plant were sighted. But there is no map of bait stations	NC
4	Pest sightings	Staff report pest sightings	C
5	Material Safety Data sheets (MSDS)	Up to date MSDs sheets are displayed where chemicals are stored. Sighted MSDs sheets.......	C
6	Action following pest activity	Rodent activity has been recorded in storage area 1 and immediate action has been taken by the contractor. Treatment date.....	C
7	Pest entry points	All pest entry points have been adequately sealed	C

Audit summary: Pest control procedure Pre-requisite Programme (PRP) XX was audited against the ISO 22000 clause 7.2.3 (i) PRP on pest control and the Food Safety Management System.

Strengths: An effective Pest Management Programme is in place. There is no evidence of pests in the facility.

Weaknesses: Since the last visit, the pest control agency has taken over by a new organisation, and it has not been listed an approved supplier. This should be corrected by updating the list of approved suppliers. Bait stations have not been identified.

Obstacles: None

Number of non-compliances: One (minor). The map of bait stations was not available and this non-compliance (minor) should be addressed within one week from today. No follow-up visit is necessary and corrective action will be reviewed at the next audit.

Rating key:	NC Non-compliant	C Compliant	NA Not applicable

Form 157 Corrective action request

To	From:
Request Date	Response due by:
Product/ Service/problem	Non-compliance
Effect of the non-compliance	
Description of condition	
Apparent cause	
Additional comments	
Request Initiator **Date:**	

Form 158 Management Review Agenda

Date:
Time: **Place:**
Attendees:
ABCCL Manager, QA Manager, Environment Manager, Food Safety Manager, Marketing Manager, Sales Manager, Human Resources Manager, Production Manager.......
Chair: QA Manager

Purpose: Evaluate the suitability, adequacy and effectiveness of quality, environment and food safety management systems and make recommendations for continual improvement.

Preparations: Documentation review, audit review and analysis, quality, environmental and food safety management performance, analysis and customer feedback
Document requirements
Minutes of previous meeting
Quality, environmental and food safety system documentation
All audit reports
Performance records
Quality records

Review Agenda	Comments
Status of Manuals, procedures and policies	
Service performance and product performance	
Regulatory non-compliance including recalls and withdrawals	
Internal and external audits	
Corrective and preventive actions	
Customer feedback, complaints, customer satisfaction surveys, reports for external parties	
Training and development	
Improvement projects	
Changes that affect the management systems	
Policies and objectives	
Resources	
Other items: Cost of quality and non-quality Market and customer response to the quality effort	

QA Manager ....

Form 159 Data to Be Considered at the Review

Topics	Description
1. Previous meeting	Review actions from the previous meeting
2. Resources	Identify necessary resources in response to customer feedback, product conformity trends, process performance and audit results. (e.g. tools, equipment, transport, communication, financial, human resources and technology
3. Context	Review of internal and external context, PEST analysis and SWOT analysis
4. Customer feedback	Customer complaints, customer surveys and feedback
5. Progress on quality, food safety and environmental objectives	Review planning to achieve objectives Analyse and evaluate progress on quality, food safety and environmental objectives
6. Performance of the IQFSE management system	Review the results of control and performance measures. E.g. inspection results, product failures, service performance, errors identified and reworks
7. Non-conformances and corrective actions	Analyse categories of corrective action and follow up on current corrective actions. Number of corrective actions overdue.
8. Verifications and validations	Review the results of verification and validation activities
9. Audits	Consider positives, non-conformities and continual improvement opportunities. If there had been no audit since the previous meeting, record this in the report
10. Supplier performance	Review the performance of suppliers. Consider their recommendations and proposals. Review the need for additional suppliers
11. Actions to address risks and opportunities	Analyse the implementation and the results of actions arising from action plans. Include both risks and opportunities
12. Continual improvement	Review the progress on continual improvement projects. Discuss suggestions from employees and other stakeholders for improvement.

Form 160 Corrective Action Report

CAR No:

To	From:
Request date	Response due by:
Product/service/problem	Non-compliance

Actual cause

Recommendations for corrective and preventive actions [Include action to be taken, authorities, resources required and expected completion date, risks and opportunities relating to proposed action]   Project Team:

By whom

Corrective and preventive actions taken   Supervisor/Department Manager

Verification Completed   Yes/No Review Team members: Date:

Form 161 Issues for Consideration to Address Non-conformances

Source	Possible Failures	Causes
Person reporting Person experiencing Details of failure Time/date of failure Location of the failure Frequency of failure	Operator error Failure to follow instructions and procedure Inattention Lethargy Unknown	Missing or wrong information Defective equipment and tools Measurement error Unclear instructions Wrong procedure Misunderstanding requirements and procedures Lack of training Conflicting instructions from multiple authorities Complex procedure Conflicting goals

Form 162 Work Order

Part 1

Customer:
Non-conformance reference

Work required:

Materials used: [Include items purchased/used, purchased date, invoice number, supplier, and unit cost]

Work performed:

Part II

Date(s):   Hours worked:

Cost of materials:

Date of completion:

Service Engineer:

Customer's comments and signature:

Form 163 Generating Specifications for Food Items

Raw Materials, Ingredients and Food Contact Material	End Product
Biological, physical and chemical properties	Product name
Composition of formulated ingredients, additives and processing aids	Composition
Origin of the item	Biological, physical and chemical properties
Method of manufacture, storage, packaging and delivery	Shelf life and storage requirements
Shelf life	Packaging
Method of reconstitution before use	Labelling related to food safety and/or instructions
Acceptance criteria	for handling, reconstitution and intended use
	Methods of deliver and distribution

Index

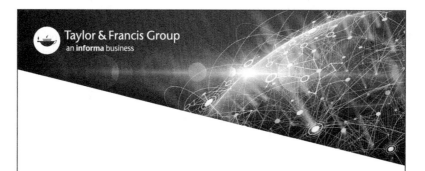

Printed and bound by CPI Group (UK) Ltd, Croydon, CR0 4YY

24/10/2024

01778289-0005